I WALKED THE LINE

My Life with Johnny

VIVIAN CASH

with Ann Sharpsteen

SIMON &
SCHUSTER

London · New York · Sydney · Toronto

A CBS COMPANY

First published in Great Britain in 2007 by Simon & Schuster UK Ltd
A CBS COMPANY

1 3 5 7 9 10 8 6 4 2

Simon & Schuster UK Ltd
Africa House
64–78 Kingsway
London WC2B 6AH

www.simonsays.co.uk

Simon & Schuster Australia
Sydney

A CIP catalogue for this book is available
from the British Library.

ISBN: 978-0-7432-9567-3

Printed and bound in Great Britain by
Mackays of Chatham plc

*For Rosanne, Kathy, Cindy, and Tara
so you may better understand just how much I loved your Daddy*

CONTENTS

I WALKED
THE LINE

"Hope" is the thing with feathers—
That perches in the soul—
And sings the tune without the words—
And never stops—at all—

Emily Dickinson

FOREWORD

In the fall of 2002, I was hired as a freelance writer/producer to produce a television documentary on the life of Johnny Cash for a division of MTV Networks. I remember leaving the production meeting after receiving the job and fielding congratulations, high fives, and pats on the back: "Way to go, Ann!" "Johnny Cash, he's huge!" "Way to bag a big one!"

A big one? Johnny Cash's name didn't exactly register on my personal list of artist "big ones." James Taylor, maybe, or Sting, or Lyle Lovett, or Garth Brooks . . . but Johnny Cash? My exposure to anything Cash was limited at best.

In any event, I had twelve weeks to research Johnny's life, conduct on-camera interviews, write the show's script, approve visual elements, navigate the political minefield that was the approval process, edit the show, and deliver a master tape ready for air. It was during that process that I came to know Vivian.

My first order of business on the Cash project was to create a wish list of people with whom I wanted on-camera interviews: Johnny, June Carter Cash, legendary Sun Records executive Sam Phillips, Johnny's longtime bass player Marshall Grant, Johnny's manager Lou Robin, and so on. Upon learning that Vivian was Johnny's first wife and the mother of his four daughters, I added her name to my list as well. My line producer then began contacting each person, scheduling interviews and arranging for all the necessary travel and camera crews. Much to my surprise, Vivian politely declined my request. Whereas most people scrambled for face time in shows like the one I was producing, I would later learn that Vivian had little or no interest in such things. She was intensely private and wary of the media.

Ordinarily that would have been the end of the story. Given my tight deadline, I had no time to coax an unwilling subject. But something inside me prompted me to stop and call Vivian myself. She would later call it God's hand.

Vivian never did agree to the on-camera interview for the documentary, but she and I became fast friends over the phone as I worked on the project.

1

Before long we were speaking daily on the phone, for hours at a time, as our friendship grew. I found her refreshingly unassuming, warm and funny, and complex in an understated sort of way. On the one hand, she was a quiet, hesitant soul, not wanting to call attention to herself. On the other, she was a fiery Italian whose sense of right and wrong had clear lines of demarcation. She was uncompromising in her integrity, compassionate, and pure of heart. She was regal and elegant yet childlike. I was drawn to her.

But there was a brokenness about Vivian too. There was a sadness and a vulnerability. As time passed and the trust between us increased, she eventually shared with me the true story of what happened to her marriage to Johnny. I was shocked to learn that there exists a vast underlying story that nobody knows about—regrettably a story markedly different from the one I had written and produced in my documentary (and that has been told in countless books and films). Through my friendship with Vivian, I would learn that in the realm of public knowledge and perception, some stories we have long believed to be true are not true at all.

As Vivian explained to me, the truth about many things in Johnny's life had become confused with stories for public consumption, and those stories had become confused with other stories invented to protect the careers and public personas of those closest to him, in the end making for a confusing mess. It's no wonder Kris Kristofferson once wrote of Johnny, "He's a walking contradiction/Partly truth and partly fiction."

I became intrigued, knowing the weight and truth of the story, to learn how Vivian was able to move forward. Just how did she get through it? How did she move on? How did she cope with the injustice? I expected answers, but she had none. She was still seeking reconciliation with the events and emotions of the past, and had been for years.

"Vivian," I said to her one afternoon, "you *need* to share your story—if only to help other women." I spoke not realizing that for years she had longed to do just that. She had longed to tell the world the truth. And she had longed to share her story with their four daughters: Surprisingly, she had never shared with them the full story of what happened. And she hoped that by telling her story she might be able to help other women who similarly suffered lost love. Indeed, Vivian had never stopped loving Johnny.

By Vivian's own choice, the details behind the demise of her marriage to Johnny and the relationship they shared through the years have long remained secret. But after much prayer and consideration—and comfortable with the fact that her children were grown and settled in their lives—Vivian made the decision to finally tell her story. To that end, she and I began working on this book, exploring and discussing her past and setting into motion a yearlong journey that she and I would take together.

Vivian's story is a powerful one of long-kept secrets, lies revealed, prolonged injustice, betrayal, forgiveness, moving on, and the truth at long last being told. It is a story about the decent, God-fearing man that Johnny was. The Johnny that Vivian called her husband was sweet and vulnerable, a warm and loving husband and father, a tender lover. It is also a story about the people, events, and forces that changed him.

It is important to know that this book had the full support of Johnny himself, who insisted it was "time" for this story to be told—though acknowledging that the truths revealed might be difficult for some to hear. And so, with Johnny's encouragement, Vivian brings forward nearly ten thousand pages of private, never-before-seen love letters that Johnny agreed should be shared with the world. They provide a mountain of evidence contradicting many misconceptions the world has about Johnny, reveal startling mistakes Johnny made along his way to becoming a champion for people of all races and stature, and share Johnny's touching confessions and apologies for behavior he later became deeply ashamed of. Moreover, the letters also give astonishing insight into the relationship that he and Vivian shared, and offer undeniable evidence of a great American love story, untold until now.

It was May 2005, one week before Vivian was to undergo surgery for recently diagnosed lung cancer, when I said good-bye to her after a weeklong visit at her home in Ventura, California. We had just completed the manuscript of this book. Eerily, she and I both sensed it would be our last meeting. Two weeks later she died.

It was an extraordinary journey that Vivian and I took in the writing of this book. Together we revisited and relived her times of greatest joy and greatest disappointment. We searched for answers and reconciliation. We made unexpected discoveries, suffered frustrations, celebrated, grieved, and healed. Each step of the way, we felt fate unfolding before us. And in the end, we found forgiveness and a realization that love—true love, in its purest form—never ends. Hers is a sobering and poignant story for those who pause to listen.

Ann Sharpsteen
Brentwood, Tennessee
June 15, 2006

INTRODUCTION

It was September 11, 2003, and although a beautiful day, there was an uneasiness in the air. My daughter Cindy had just arrived in town for a visit along with her husband, Eddie, and she felt it too—an unmistakable sense of something amiss, something dreadful about to happen. So later that night when the phone rang at one thirty a.m., after we had all gone to bed, my heart froze. Phone calls in the middle of the night never bring good news.

And then a bone-chilling scream came from down the hall. Cindy was the first to hear the news: Johnny was dead.

For the rest of the night, none of us slept. Cindy was inconsolable, devastated, virtually drowning in grief after the call. She had spent the last three months with Johnny at his home, caring for him, doting on him, and she had just left for a quick visit to come see me. She was choked in grief now that she wasn't there when he passed. Helpless to do much else, I simply hugged her.

I knew firsthand the pain of losing a parent. I lost both of mine years ago. The coming weeks and months, even years, would be tough, not only for her but also for our other three daughters Johnny and I had together: Rosanne, Kathy, and Tara. Our poor babies would never be the same. I knew that much.

To the world, Johnny was revered as the Man in Black. But to us he was simply Daddy. To the girls, he was their world. And to me he is and will always be my wonderful, caring, protective husband and the father of my children. In disbelief I paced the floor.

Johnny was supposed to have been here in California, recording yet another record. He was to have visited New York for the MTV Music Awards on his way out, where he was excited to have been nominated in six categories. We were all excited. He and the producers of the show secretly planned for him to walk out onto the stage unassisted: Only recently his heath had been improving, and he was walking again. But as fate would have it, what was thought to be a troubling case of heartburn sent him to the hospital instead. That's where he stayed for two weeks before being released. Then this sudden disastrous turn for the worse. And now our lives were spinning out of control.

Within hours, Johnny's death was the top story on all the cable news channels and morning shows. The media frenzy had begun. CNN, Fox News, ABC, CBS, NBC, every channel I turned to, were all talking about our family.

The music world is mourning the death this morning of one of America's most influential performers, Johnny Cash . . .

Johnny Cash, the Man in Black, died this morning in a Nashville hospital at the age of seventy-one . . .

One of the greatest voices in American music is silent today . . .

It was surreal to hear them talking about Johnny in the past tense. Only eight weeks earlier, I had been with him in his home in Hendersonville, just north of Nashville, and we had enjoyed a wonderful visit. We sat and laughed about old times. We reminisced. We hugged and cried. We joked and teased each other. Looking back, that afternoon visit was a precious gift from God. My trip to Nashville had been a very last-minute decision, and I wasn't certain I would even have the chance to see Johnny. But I'm so thankful—very, very thankful—that God let us see each other one last time.

Ironically, it was during that visit that we discussed this book and I told him of my decision to write it. To be honest, I was a little nervous in telling him. I wasn't sure how he would react to me finally deciding to tell my story. Not only have I gone out of my way for years to *not* talk about our years together, but the real truth about our marriage and divorce has never been told. Now that I had decided to tell the truth, I wondered how he would feel about that.

My decision to write this book was a difficult one for me. Early on, I became aware that some of the things I planned on revealing would be upsetting to Johnny's second wife, June. I was also aware that some of her irritation might inevitably be targeted at Johnny. And with all of his medical problems at the time, I cringed at the possibility of imposing any additional misery on him.

Two months earlier, however, something happened that none of us expected: June passed away. It was a devastating blow to Johnny and to our girls, who had known June for many years by that time. However, along with the understandable sadness at her passing, I experienced a sense of liberation that I would be freer to say the things I have to say—and Johnny would be freer to tell the truth too. The full story of our lives, the unvarnished truth, could now be told more easily without hesitancy. Would Johnny agree? I wouldn't know until I spoke with him.

During our visit, I settled in on a sofa by the fireplace in Johnny's bedroom and we chatted. It was so good to see him. He was enjoying improvement in his health in recent weeks. He had gone fishing for the first time in years. He had gone swimming. And he was walking again. On July 11 he took twenty-five steps unassisted. On July 12 he took seventy steps. It made me happy to hear of his continued improvement. And despite the fact that he was still obviously grieving the loss of June, I was thrilled to hear him say, "I'm happy."

One of the household help came into the bedroom with a silver tray carrying coffee and cream and sugar and set it on the coffee table. When she left, we finally had some privacy for me to share my news.

"Johnny," I said. As usual since the divorce, it was hard for me not to call him Honey. Years of habit are hard to break. I concentrated as I chose my words. "Johnny, I have thought long about—and prayed about—writing a book. I want to write a book and tell our story, and the truth of what happened. I spoke with the girls, and they are in support of it. So I've made a decision to do it," I said. "How do you feel about that?" I kept my eyes fixed on Johnny's face, watching for a change in his expression.

"I've been thinking about that for the past couple years," he said without a breath of hesitation. "I think it's a great idea."

"Are you serious?" I asked. It surprised me that he had been thinking about it for a couple years. I was floored.

"Honestly, I have been," he said. "Viv, I've been thinking for years, if anyone on this planet should write a book about me, it should be you. It's time."

As we discussed the book, Johnny became more excited. I could tell his mind was whirling a mile a minute. "If there's anything I can do to help, I'll do it. I'll write the foreword too. All my fans will buy it. I know they will. It's time."

"It's time." Was I really hearing him right? I was overjoyed! Those simple words, "It's time," took on so many dimensions. It was one thing to have his blessing, which I had hoped for. But to have his encouragement and active support was wonderful. I was so glad he thought it was time.

"I hope it will be healing for you too," he added. Ironically, I wished the same for him.

I also explained to Johnny that in telling our story, I might help other women who have gone through troubles such as we had. I so much want for good to come out of those darkest hours.

"Johnny, some of your fans might be upset hearing the details of our divorce and what happened," I said. I do worry deeply about the reaction the public will have.

But Johnny didn't waver in his support. "Like I said, all my fans will read it. They'll love it," he said with confidence. "It's time."

And in that single moment, having Johnny's support and blessing confirmed in my heart that it *was* finally time to tell my story. Too many things were lining up and falling into perfect place, clearing the way for me. I felt God guiding me forward each careful step of the way, assuring me I was on the right path.

The truth is, I have only recently begun to feel the grace and the reconciliation of making sense of what happened to our marriage. And now, with Johnny's blessing, I would finally have what I longed to have for so many years in his shadow: a voice of my own to tell the world the truth.

"Johnny, that makes me so happy I could just *kiss* you!" There was no hiding the tears welling up in my eyes.

I laughed as Johnny stared at me with outstretched arms. "Well, here I am!" We shared one of the sweetest hugs we ever shared.

It hurts my heart to know that afternoon was the last time I would see Johnny. If I had known, I wouldn't have been so quick to leave. I would have spent the rest of the afternoon with him. And I would have savored every minute.

I would have told him all the things I've wanted to tell him over the years but never did. I would have hugged him tighter. I would have told him how special he is, what a good man he is.

I would have held his hands and examined his face and searched for that young Johnny who stole my heart so many years ago. I would have relived so many more of the happy times with him. I would have asked questions that have lingered in my heart. I would have loved to hear him tell me what was in his heart too.

And maybe I would have told him my darkest secret, which I am only now able to admit. I would have told him that I never stopped loving him. Through all of it, despite everything, I never stopped loving him for one second.

Instead I just hugged him happily, said good-bye, and left thinking I would see him again soon. And now he's gone.

While word of Johnny's death spread around the globe, I sat quietly sipping coffee in our den at a window overlooking the Pacific Ocean. A world without Johnny hardly seemed possible.

In the hours that followed the horrible news, I did the only thing I could do, or have learned to do when times are bad: take each hour as it comes. As I managed through the next few days, my mind filled with memories of the life Johnny and I shared—the adventures, the heartache, the success, the failures, the joy, the sadness, the secrets, the lies. And the regret.

~

In the weeks that followed Johnny's passing, it was impossible to escape media coverage of his death. Everywhere I went there was discussion about Johnny, articles about Johnny, and radio programs playing his music. His voice and image were everywhere. Even a simple trip to the dentist, where I hoped for a moment of quiet escape, was in vain. There was Johnny, smiling at me from the cover of *People* magazine sitting atop a stack of newspapers and books on the waiting-room coffee table.

And strangely for me, during this time when I most longed to be left alone to grieve privately, there were repeated mentions and photographs of me amid all the coverage and stories. I felt uncomfortably exposed, thrown into the mix of public examination of Johnny's life.

Curious strangers appeared at our front door. "Is this where Johnny Cash's first wife lives?" they'd ask, peering into our house. And I began noticing the hushed whispers of strangers behind my back as I ran my errands: ". . . that's Johnny's ex-wife, Vivian. . . ." I even received a phone call from a reporter at the *National Enquirer* tabloid, pressing for details of my last meeting with Johnny. A "reliable" source had told them of our meeting, including certain gifts that he gave me. They wanted details.

I have to say I've never been comfortable with the attention I received as Johnny's wife. I've always been a very private person. Even though most people are interested, if they do find out about me having been married to Johnny, they found out on their own. Never from me.

And I have learned over the years that there are two distinct groups of people: people who have a curiosity about me and my past with Johnny, and people of the Nashville mind-set, who prefer that I be written out of Johnny's history altogether.

So on November 10, 2003, when I arrived at the Ryman Auditorium in Nashville—the inner sanctum of the Nashville establishment—to attend a television taping of a memorial tribute to Johnny, I felt something like an unwelcome guest. If it weren't for the girls' insistence that I attend with them, I might have spared myself the anxiety. A public retrospection into Johnny's life would mean retrospection into my life. And that would mean revisiting times and places from my past, whether I was ready or not.

As I stepped closer toward the side entrance of the building, the flashbulbs popped and flashed and the press photographers yelled just like the last time Johnny and I passed through these doors of the historic Grand Ole Opry. Back then I felt like the first lady of country music on Johnny's arm as he shouldered his way through the crush of fans. There was always such commotion wherever Johnny went—women screaming and throwing themselves at him, girls clamoring for autographs. Johnny had a huge following of fans from the very beginning.

But on this November night, there were no screaming women. Outside, fans were quietly gathered in front of the Ryman. They had come from all over the country, some driving eighteen hours or more, just to stand outside in the cold and pay their respects. Many had made makeshift shrines on the sidewalk, candles burning next to framed photos of Johnny. One man stood alone playing his banjo, plucking out "Folsom Prison Blues." Other fans simply stood quietly holding candles. The mood was solemn and reverent.

Johnny's funeral had been a private ceremony, closed to the public. So this evening offered the first chance for fans and fellow artists to publicly honor and remember Johnny, whom they all loved and admired. And everybody, I mean everybody, loved Johnny.

Some of the biggest names in the world of music were on hand on this night, a testament to Johnny's influence: Willie Nelson, Hank Williams Jr., and George Jones. Kid Rock, Sheryl Crow, and John Mellencamp were also slated to perform. It was a Who's Who of celebrities from Al Gore and Whoopi Goldberg to Bono and Tim Robbins, who was acting the role of host.

Rosanne, Kathy, Cindy, Tara, and I, along with our husbands, all took our seats in the wooden pews of the historic church to watch the show. Forty-seven years previous—on Saturday July 7, 1956, to be exact, two months before Johnny's biggest hit, "I Walk the Line," was released—I had sat in these very same pews when Johnny made his first appearance on this very same stage. Johnny was nervous and excited. I was too. I beamed with pride. It was an honor to perform at the Opry. Johnny was sharing billing with the likes of Minnie Pearl and Grandpa Jones and others. I watched from the audience when he took the stage.

"I'd like to dedicate this song to my wife, who is here tonight," Johnny said as he looked over to me with a smile.

It was a smile of pure joy. A smile that said, I'm proud to be here, I'm doing what I love, I'm a blessed man. And with that he started to sing. As always, within minutes he had the audience demanding more. I stopped counting at his fifth encore.

Never did I dream back then that I wouldn't be by his side all these years later. If someone had caught me by the shoulder and told me that Johnny and I wouldn't be married forever, I never would have believed it. Nothing would ever come between Johnny and me. I was the woman he walked the line for.

As I sat and waited for the tribute to begin, I tried to convince myself that Johnny really was gone. Maybe the evening would give me some measure of closure, I hoped. None of it seemed real. In a sense, none of the past forty years have seemed real. Johnny went straight from my arms to God's arms. Anything that happened in between just wasn't supposed to happen.

I wondered what people sitting next to me in the auditorium would think if they only knew the truth about the stories that Johnny insisted it was "time" to finally tell. Could they imagine a truth other than the stories they've been told? They believe what they want to believe—what they've been told to believe. Would they believe the truth?

My thoughts were interrupted as the Fisk Jubilee Singers started the evening off with the rousing gospel hymn "Ain't No Grave Can Hold My Body Down." They sang that song just a few weeks earlier at Johnny's funeral. Then Tommy Cash, Johnny's brother, took the stage to begin the show. As teenagers he and I climbed trees together and chased each other around the yard. We were like brother and sister. It made me proud to see him standing tall during this difficult time.

Next, Rosanne took the stage to perform and speak about Johnny. How she was able to find the composure to sing and speak eloquently amid her grief, I have no idea. But she's just like Johnny, a consummate performer. Once onstage, she's in complete control. She inherited her daddy's genius in that way.

As I watched her perform, I thought of Johnny and me as newlyweds. When I was pregnant with Rosanne, Johnny loved to lay his hands on my stomach, rub my tummy, and sing and play the guitar to her, fascinated by her kicks and rolls. "What are you doing in there?" he'd say. Johnny was amazed by the miracle of his baby growing inside me.

We both adored kids and were anxious for a family of our own. We wanted a large family—eight children as quick as we could have them. After our one-month wedding anniversary passed and I wasn't pregnant, I was so upset that I had disappointed Johnny. I can still hear him, so sweet, telling me, "Don't get discouraged, baby! It's only been one month. We'll get our baby, don't you worry." When we learned that I was pregnant, we literally jumped up and down with joy.

Back then our dreams were so simple, and not even music-related. Johnny sold appliances door-to-door in east Memphis for Mr. Bates at the Home Equipment appliance store, and we scratched by on what he earned. We had no baby crib, no baby clothes, not much of anything. I sewed my maternity clothes from pieces of old bedsheets and leftover costume fabric my sister gave me—blue velvet that she wore as a shepherd in some Christmas pageant.

Our main form of entertainment was Cash family picnics at the park. That's how we had our fun. In the evenings I would roll my hair on our bed while Johnny sat next to me and played his guitar and wrote songs. And we listened endlessly to music on the radio. Hank Snow was always Johnny's favorite. And we both loved George Jones, Ferlin Husky, Ernest Tubb, and the *Grand Ole*

Opry radio program. When I look back, those were the happiest days ever. We didn't have much, but we had each other.

There was nothing back then to suggest a superstar in the making or the material success that would come within a year after we were married. Nothing to suggest that fifty years later, Johnny would be loved by millions of fans and celebrated as the greatest country music artist of all time. Johnny was just my husband back then. A career in music was something we only dreamed about.

I later learned that an astounding ten million viewers tuned in to watch the memorial tribute show on television, and I marvel at the tremendous influence Johnny had in his lifetime. But at the same time I'm not at all surprised.

From the very beginning, even from his very earliest public performance, Johnny had an innate ability to connect with audiences and command their attention. He had a magnetism unlike anyone I have ever met. I don't know if it was his height—he was over six feet tall—or it might have been his distinctive walk. With those long legs of his, you couldn't help but be transfixed by him. I don't know what it was. But he was captivating to watch. You felt the power of his presence when he was in the room. Even as his wife I sensed that. And on that night, just like the enormous black-and-white portrait of Johnny hanging center stage, his presence still loomed large.

While I sat in the church pews of the Opry, watching all those hundreds of people revere Johnny, I was struck by their laughter and comments celebrating Johnny's darker side. They all admire the man who angrily gave the finger in that famous photograph and kicked out the footlights of the Opry. They hail him as "America's favorite bad boy," dangerous and unpredictable. A lot of people think that was all funny. I never did. That wasn't Johnny. That violent, belligerent side wasn't him at all. That was drugs.

The real story, in my mind, that should be told is how one person and so many lives can be unalterably changed because of drugs. Johnny was tortured. Our family was tortured. For years he lived under the control of pills and did things he never would have done if he'd been sober. He fogged his mind so that he lived a double life. And he learned to live and be comfortable in that skin. I know we would still be married today if the drugs hadn't entered our lives.

So as the night unfolded I experienced a whole realm of emotions. Every person taking the stage shared a personal snapshot of memories from the past with Johnny that were vastly different from my own.

I can't remember the lyrics of every song that Johnny ever recorded in his career, or in what order they hit the charts. But I can remember the wonder and silence Johnny and I shared every time we looked at each of our newborn daughters.

I can't remember every city, every venue we visited as we crisscrossed the country on his tours, nor can I remember the names and faces of all of his bookers, label executives, and the like. But I do remember the feel of his hand squeezing mine backstage—his secret assurance to me that I was his.

I can't remember details of each of Johnny's career milestones, but I remember hearing Johnny tell me that he loved me for the first time at our bench along the River Walk in San Antonio.

I remember our wedding day and the pride I felt the first time I wrote my name, Mrs. Johnny Cash.

I remember the soothing sound of Johnny's voice as he gently combed his fingers through my hair and lulled me to sleep with a whisper as he sang "Love Me Tender" at the end of a busy day.

I remember the giggles of our girls—our "babies"—on Christmas morning as Johnny played with them.

I remember the delicious smell of Johnny making biscuits in our kitchen with a recipe only he knew by heart.

I remember all the fun we had at home with our menagerie of animals around the house—horses, dogs, a monkey, and a parrot.

I remember fishing with Johnny alone, just him and me, and how he loved to sit back and watch me cast, then wait and laugh each time I panicked when I caught something.

I remember us dyeing his hair black in the kitchen sink, and one time crying laughing when we tried bleaching it blond—a mistake we quickly fixed before anyone could see.

Those are the slices of life I remember.

Nobody in that auditorium knew Johnny the way I did. Nobody loved him like I loved him. None of the people who tuned in to watch the show on television has any idea about the real man Johnny was. But I do. He was a wonderful, decent man. He was my strong, protective husband, and I knew he loved me.

Johnny was tender, sweet, and vulnerable. A writer of sugary, emotional love poems.

> Here's a box of candy, Viv,
> And if it's good and sweet,
> Say "It's Johnny's love materialized"
> With every bite you eat.
>
> If it isn't tasty, hon,
> Give Shraft the blame for that.
> But if it's like my love for you,
> It's bound to make you fat.

I never did stop loving Johnny, and that made getting on with my life after our divorce very difficult. Of course, he and I both moved on with new marriages and new lives, but I have always believed in my heart that what happened to our marriage should never have happened. I will never believe it was God's will.

Recently our daughter Kathy asked me pointedly, "Mom, you never got over divorcing Daddy, did you?" Leave it to our children to make uncomfortable observations. But she's right. I've never been able to admit that until recently. Years after Johnny and I divorced, I struggled with the pain and grief. I tortured myself with regret and second-guessing. What could I have done differently? Could I have fought harder to save the marriage? I still desperately miss the family we had, just Johnny, the girls, and me.

My daughters have always told me, "Mom, you have to revisit and examine your past in order to heal. You have to walk through it before you can get over it." That might be true, but it's not the easy way out. The easy way out is to stuff your feelings and go on. Pretend it never happened, pretend you don't have all those emotions. That's what I've done up until now.

You would think, wouldn't you, that when Johnny died it would be the end of the story for me. Instead it was just the beginning. It was the beginning of my search for answers and healing and doing all those things that my daughters told me I needed to do in order to heal. Revisiting my past was something I had always avoided. Now I knew I had to. For the first time in my life, my desire for truth was greater than any fear or doubt I had in making the journey. The first step, though, would require me to go back to the very beginning.

PART ONE

I was a seventeen-year-old high school student on summer vacation when I first met Johnny. My life back then generally centered on the three things that interested most girls my age: friends, clothes, and boys. I was a slender girl—skinny as a rail, actually—all legs and elbows, with hazel eyes and chestnut hair, and I was extremely shy.

Mother was a homemaker and Daddy was an insurance salesman and an amateur magician on the side. He performed at private parties and charity events and developed quite a name for himself in Texas as a talented performer and president of the International Brotherhood of Magicians. Mother and I often acted as his onstage assistants, and as such were privy to the closely guarded secrets of the magic world. My starring role in Daddy's show involved crawling inside a dollhouse as he stuck eight swords into the side of the apparatus while I screamed in pretend pain. It was through that association that I had my first taste of show business life. But we were by no means a show business family.

I actually led a very sheltered life. Mother and Daddy were strict with me and my sister, Sylvia, and brother, Ray. During the school year I attended St. Mary's Catholic School for girls, located by the river in downtown San Antonio. In keeping with school tradition, we wore uniforms of dark blue gabardine skirts, white blouses, and navy-and-white saddle oxfords. In most every respect, my life was disciplined and ordered.

I was a good student without a consuming interest in any one subject except maybe typing, my favorite class. Another favorite hour was lunchtime. At noon, the basement auditorium was converted into a cafeteria, and we set a record player up on the stage and danced. Jitterbug, swing, slow dancing, we danced them all. And since there were no boys to be found in an all-girl school, we danced with each other as the nuns looked on, stone-faced. The music was all the favorites of the day—"'Til the End of Time," "P.S. I Love You," anything by Nat King Cole, "I've Got You Under My Skin"—although the nuns banned that one with no explanation, claiming that it plainly "wasn't a good song."

And when not in school, I could most often be found at the local roller-skating rink, listening to music, chattering away with my friends, watching and meeting boys, and generally having the kind of fun young teenage girls have. That's how I spent the summer of '51, the summer I met Johnny.

In fact, the night of July 18, 1951, was typical of hundreds of evenings I spent at the skating rink. On that particular night, I was there with my friend Jeanette. We had arrived early, planning on skating until closing and then heading to her house for a sleepover.

But fifteen minutes before closing, I noticed a handsome boy enter the skating rink. He was a young air force serviceman, tall and distinguished-looking in his uniform. He paid for his skates along with a buddy as they joked and laughed with each other. I watched as he then stood for a bit, looking around the rink. I couldn't take my eyes off him.

The boy exchanged a few words with his friend—a fellow enlisted service-man—and then to my surprise and horror headed straight in my direction. Before I knew it, we were toe-to-toe. He was at least a foot taller than me, and I found myself peering straight up to look into his eyes.

"Would you skate with me?" he asked politely. "I would really like it if you'd skate with me." He flashed a smile and reached out his hand to take mine. "My name is Johnny."

I was struck by how handsome he was. People have always referred to Johnny's look as "rugged," but he wasn't rugged at all back then. He was tall and slender, impeccably dressed in his air force uniform, the creases in his pants razor sharp. His shoes were perfectly polished. He was very, very sexy. The back of my neck began to feel flush as he waited for my response.

"Okay," I said, and took his arm. The butterflies in my stomach kept me from saying any more.

As we circled the rink, Johnny was awkward in his skates. He was not a good skater by any stretch. But he made up for it by entertaining me with singing along to the Rosemary Clooney song playing at the time. *I don't know how it happened, I don't know who's to blame/I don't know how I hurt you, but I hurt you just the same/and even though you say we're through/I still feel the same about youuuu,"* he crooned.

No boy had ever sung to me before. He was playful and talkative, yet I could tell he was a little shy. He was clearly enjoying himself, and I was too. We talked and laughed. We skated and danced. We giggled at his lack of skating prowess. He was clumsy and couldn't make turns without me holding him steady. He told me he was newly enlisted in the air force and only three weeks away from being shipped off to Europe. He was from Arkansas and his parents were cotton farmers. Just as I began to lose track of time, the announcer called, "Last call!" for the last skate before closing.

16

"Can I take you home?" Johnny asked preemptively. He didn't have a car, but he wanted to accompany me home with Jeanette on the bus back to her house.

"Sure," I answered. I wanted to spend more time with him too.

I glanced over to Jeanette and was met with an icy stare. A boy she was interested in had offered to take us home in a car. Needless to say, a car always trumped a bus in our teenage world, but now, because of me, we were stuck taking the bus with Johnny. She was more than a little perturbed all the way home.

When we arrived at her house, Jeanette went inside, leaving Johnny and me alone in the front yard. He took my hand and walked me up to the front porch. "I'd love to see you again," he said. I was struck by his innocence. "Would you consider going out with me? You're the prettiest girl I've seen in Texas since I've been here." If he hadn't been so awkward in his delivery of the compliment, I might not have believed him.

Then he bent his face down close to mine "Can I call you this week?" And before I could answer, he leaned in for a kiss.

"I don't kiss boys on the first date," I said sheepishly, quickly leaning back to avoid his attempt. I then waited for the expected protest. Most boys did, after all, protest. Either that or they'd force a kiss. None of them liked my first-date rule.

But Johnny was silent. He looked surprised, stunned even. There was a long, awkward pause as I wondered what he was thinking.

"I'll call you," he said with a half smile.

Little did I know that at that very moment, my life had just taken a sudden and permanent detour. I stepped inside Jeanette's front door, wondering, *Will he call?* Normally I didn't care at all if the boys called or not. But this time was different. Without question, I wanted this boy named Johnny to call.

~

I didn't know it at the time, but I was exactly the kind of girl Johnny liked: reserved, quiet, and God-fearing. A good girl. He said he liked my smile and my blue eyes. He liked my Italian features, and although he wasn't the first boy to tell me I was pretty, he was the first boy who ever made me believe it.

Johnny did call. He phoned me the next morning at my house, and every day after that. In the coming weeks we became inseparable. The chemistry between us was undeniable. We went to the movies and skating, went for sodas, and took long walks along the River Walk in San Antonio. I had impressed him that first night we met when I wouldn't allow him a kiss on Jeanette's porch. That was the reason he called back and was determined to date me. Boy, was I happy I denied him that first kiss.

Johnny did get that kiss, though (and many more later), late one night

17

while we were sitting atop the hood of a friend's car at the drive-in. We were with a large group of friends, a mix of my girlfriends and Johnny's air force buddies. Four of us climbed atop the hood while the remaining couple sat in the car. Our seats, such as they were, were more suited to stargazing than watching the movie. But after all, no one went to the drive-in to watch movies.

"Hop on up here, angel," Johnny said, patting the top of the hood. I held my skirt down with one hand as he grasped my other to pull me up beside him.

In the dim light of the drive-in, you could make out the faint shadows of other couples similarly sitting on cars. I wondered to myself if parents had any idea what really went on at the outdoor movies.

"Come sit closer," Johnny insisted. He sat with his legs stretched out in front of him, crossed at the ankles. I inched over, happily. It was exciting to be so close, and alone—not on the front porch, feet away from my father's stern and watchful eye. I had spent the last several days daydreaming about the moment we would finally kiss.

"What are you looking at?" Johnny whispered, as he watched me gazing at the stars. I blushed, not wanting to let on what I was really thinking about.

"Oh, nothing. Just staring at the stars."

"Let me give you something else to do," he said, as he bent his face to mine. This time I didn't lean away. He kissed me and I wished it could last forever.

"Vivian," he said finally, "how'd you get to be so wonderful?" He put his arms around me and kissed my forehead. "You're as pretty and perfect as an angel."

"What a line," I giggled, nudging him with my elbow. Johnny just smiled.

And so we spent the next three weeks spending every possible minute together. Never in my life had I felt so alive, so happy. We spent hours holding hands, window-shopping through the streets of San Antonio, taking moonlit walks along the river. We declared one river bench "our bench"—it was more private than the others—where we spent hours sitting and talking, talking and kissing, and dreaming about the future. It was a magical, exhilarating time. For the first time in my life, I was falling in love.

Over the coming weeks, I learned more and more about Johnny: his dreams, his fears, his frustrations, his wonderful sense of humor, his trust in God. And Johnny learned more and more about me: my hopes, my love of children, my dreams. Time was our enemy, though, and we both knew it. As the time for Johnny's departure grew closer, we tried to ignore the inevitable, but before we were ready, it was time for him to leave.

"This is our bench now. You have to promise to keep it up," Johnny said, pointing to the freshly chiseled carving in the seat of the bench: JOHNNY LOVES VIVIAN.

18

"I will," I said, as I admired his handiwork. This was our bench. Our special place. We had spent countless hours sitting at this bench.

"If you don't keep it up, I'm gonna have to come back and hunt you down . . . ," he teased, stealing a kiss.

Tomorrow Johnny would be leaving for Germany, going away for three years. How could I come here without him? Why would I want to come here without him? Three years seemed like a lifetime.

Seeming to read my thoughts, Johnny kissed my hand and pulled away.

"When I'm in Germany—when I get back—" he said, searching for words. Then he wrapped his arms around my shoulders and held me tightly, as if to say exactly what I wanted to hear: that he alone would keep the inevitable from happening. "Everything will be fine," he said.

We took a cab home, affording us added privacy for our final good-bye. As we snuggled in the backseat, holding each other tightly, we laughed as the driver sneaked peeks at us through the rearview mirror to catch us kissing. We were full of tender promises to write to each other, shared more kisses, and then arrived at the final good-bye on my front porch.

"Don't worry, angel. I'll write as soon as I can. And I'll call you too before I leave New York harbor."

Daddy flashed the porch light, signaling the end of our evening. I knew I had better hurry and go inside. Daddy had no patience for missed curfews. It was already late.

"Bye, Viv. I love you," Johnny said.

Johnny's handsome face looked back wistfully as he climbed into the back of the cab. Both of us were helpless to do or say anything more. Daddy flashed the light again. The world has a peculiar way of not stopping for any measure of heartache.

"Good-bye, Johnny," I said to myself.

The driver peered at Johnny through the rearview mirror. "Buddy, if I liked a girl as much as you like that one," he said loudly, "I'd run away and desert the damn air force."

"Mind your own business," Johnny answered flatly. "Brooks Air Base, main entrance." And just like that, the cab pulled away and Johnny was gone.

As I closed the front door, I heard my mother's voice from the living room. "Well, I guess you won't be seeing Johnny again," she said. I knew she and Daddy were glad to see him leave. The intensity of our romance concerned them. Now he was safely heading to the other side of the world.

Logic would tell anybody that our romance was over, that I would never see Johnny again. But my heart told me differently. I knew what we had was more than some silly summer romance. I knew I would see him again. As much as it didn't make sense, I knew I had met the man I was meant to marry.

JOHNNY'S LETTERS

Much thought and prayer has gone into my decision to share Johnny's letters. They are so personal and so intimate. A part of me wants to keep them private. Yet on the other hand, I know that sharing them is the only way to show the world who Johnny really was—and sharing them is the only way to tell our story. I'm reassured by Johnny's words to me during our last meeting, when he expressed his excitement and encouragement at publishing them: "It's time." Those words still ring in my heart.

Our correspondence began, and thrived, immediately after Johnny left San Antonio, on his way to Germany, when he was nineteen years old. He headed first to his family's home in Dyess, Arkansas, for a short visit, and then traveled on to the military post of Camp Kilmer in New Jersey. Throughout those few weeks, he faithfully wrote and called to assure me of his devotion, reinforcing my belief that our romance was indeed real. Our daily letter writing quickly increased in frequency until we were often writing several letters each day.

~

September 4, 1951
Dyess, Ark

Dear Viv,

I suppose you thought that I was the biggest fool in the world this morning when I called, didn't you? And I'll admit that I am. I called because I thought I had a lot of things to talk about, but I forgot them all. I wouldn't blame you if you didn't forgive me for being such a fool.

Honey, please try to forgive me for being such a dumbbell. I think a lot of you, more than I should tell you. A heck of a lot of difference it makes, though.

I want you to send that large picture. You know what I'm going to do with it? Put it over my bed when I get to Germany so I can look at you every night before I go to bed, and every morning when I first get up. But did you ever try to carry on a conversation with a picture? It doesn't work very well. Kind of

21

one-sided. I think I can talk to your picture better than I can you, though. You just sit there with the same sweet smile on your face as if you understand everything I'm saying, even though I am dumb.

Are you still going to keep our bench with the names on it? I hope you do. I can just see the people of SA, walking around with "Johnny Loves Vivian" on the seat of their pants, but I don't care who knows it.

Remember the night we walked on the river? Of course you do. I'll remember that night for a long, long time. It might not mean much to you, but every time I think of you, I think of that night. We couldn't think of a thing to do, remember?

I heard my favorite song last night, "Rose of San Antone." One of my favorites, that is. Honey, I know I'm a drip and a heel, but I wish you would write me. My address in New Jersey will be:

PFC John R. Cash AF18351914
2266th Pers. Proc. Sqdn
1st AF ConAC
Camp Kilmer, New Jersey
Now write, sweetheart, every time you get a chance.

Love always,
Johnny

P.S. I'm sending a picture I had made at Brooks. I thought maybe you might want it, because I don't. Goodbye again, and write, honey.

～

Sept. 11, 1951
Camp Kilmer

Dear Viv,

What have you been doing lately, sweetheart? Going to school? I think you said you didn't like school, didn't you? It seems like it's been a month since I heard from you. I don't suppose it has, but it sure seems like it! I might have a letter from you now, because I didn't get to go to mail call today. You better write, because if you don't, I'm coming back to Texas some moonlit night and wring your sweet little neck. Does the moon still shine in Texas? I don't think it shines up here. I haven't seen it yet. There's no need for a moon up here, anyway. There's no place like Texas. I've sure missed you and Texas.

One of my friends just came in and asked to see your picture. I showed it to him and he said if you had a sister any better looking, you're a liar. Everybody is just crazy over your picture, but I am just crazy over you. Yes, I really am. You don't mind my passing your picture around, do you?

Say, what are you going to do after you finish school? Or do you have any plans? I guess I will be here two weeks or maybe three. It takes about four days to process out, then I have to wait for a ship. I don't think I'll be in Germany but a little over two years. Not very long, is it? I guess it could be longer, but it doesn't seem like it now.

This is not a bad base, it's only about thirty miles from New York City, and they give weekend passes, so I think I'll go this weekend. I was there Sunday night, but didn't get to stay over two hours because I had to catch a train out.

Talk about trouble, honey, I had a little myself. About two hours before I caught a train in Memphis, Tenn, someone stole my Dad's car. I'd just carried my baggage to the train station and parked the car on Main St, and when I came back to get it, someone borrowed it and didn't even have the keys for it. My Mother was with me and she called the police and they started looking for it. I don't know if they found it yet or not, I haven't heard from home. I thought a lot about my not telling you that I was glad that you learned to drive since that happened. Honey, I really am glad you learned to drive, but take it from me, watch it when you park it.

Please write soon. Darling, I am craving a letter from you.

Love you,
Johnny

~

September 12, 1951
Camp Kilmer

Dear Vivian dear,

Darling, I do wish I could be there to help you ruin your lipstick and bobby pins and keep you out late at night again. You know I went for two days and nights without sleeping down there when I was out with you till midnight, then worked from midnight till eight. That was just before I left. I'd like to do it again.

And when your Dad called you in off the porch, I could have shot him that night. Guess he was just taking care of his little girl, though. I wish you could meet my folks. I'm sure you would like them. They've certainly heard enough about you. My mother even said I talked in my sleep when I was home.

I think I'll go to the movies tonight. Want to come along? You're always with me everywhere I go anyway.

I haven't been anywhere since I got here, but I'm planning on that trip to the big city next weekend. I'm going to have as much fun as I can before I have to leave God's Country.

Stay sweet sweetheart, and be thinking of me.

Love you always,
Johnny

~

September 19, 1951
Camp Kilmer

Hi Sweetheart,

I just got your wonderful letter. I should get another one from you tomorrow, but I won't be around, darling. Tomorrow I leave God's Country. I'm shipping out about eight o'clock tomorrow morning from the New York harbor. And do you know what? I'm not looking forward to it so doggone much.

I just found out this morning that I was leaving tomorrow. I take my beautiful cruise across the Atlantic to Florence, Italy. From there I will fly to my base in Germany. Sounds thrilling, huh? Well, it doesn't sound so thrilling to me.

By the way, I saw "Showboat" when I was in Santone. He was away from his wife six years and she still loved him. Hmmm—must be something to it.

Oceans and oceans of love and devotion,
Your Johnny

~

September 27, 1951

Hi Sweetheart,

With nothing to do, and plenty of ink, I thought I'd write you a spell. I had to do something to get my mind off of nothing.

You know, I'm beginning to feel like a salty old sailor now. I even know all the parts of a ship, and I've even learned to stand on my feet when the ship is rocking, like it is now.

We've been listening to English broadcast stations, and we hear the same songs that we heard in the states even Hank Williams. Kind of makes us feel at home.

Are you still taking care of "our bench" honey? All that certainly seems far away now. As a matter of fact, four thousand miles, but maybe it won't be so far some day. I have something to look forward to.

Well darling, my mind is back on nothing and I'm getting sleepy, so I'm going to hit the sack.

Stay sweet sweetheart.

Love always and always,
Your Johnny

~

At Sea
September 22

Darling Vic,
    Well, it's Saturday night Sweetheart. I wonder
what you're doing tonight. Naturally I haven't
been going any place much for the last three
days, because, there's nothing to do but splash
outside the boat. I did go out on deck and
take a walk a few minutes ago, and it was
rather romantic like, the moon shining on
the water, but again, there's no need for it.
You know, there's two women on this boat,
nurses, and two thousand men. I believe
this bunch will go nuts before we get to Ger.
But you know who I'm lonesome for? you! There
must be something to this love business when
someone thinks about someone as much as I
do you.
    We've been having a little intertainment on
the boat every night. You know who's in the
Army? Vic Damone, and he's on this boat. I
sleep in the same compartment with him, and
guess who had to mop the floor this morning.
Vic Damone! He's a nice guy. I thought at
first he would be stuck up, but he's not. He
acts like one of the boys, and he sings for
us every night, and don't let this get out, but
he even shoots craps with us. Why, he's almost human.
    Darling, I'm really sorry I didn't get to
talk to you Tuesday night, but I didn't know
until that morning that I was shipping out
the next day, and I just took a chance

25

on you being at home, but Viv baby was
gone. And I couldn't call you at Jeanette's
cause they wouldn't put a call through on
the base after ten-thirty and I couldn't
get a pass to go to town, so.... something
always happens to us doesn't it darling?
And you know what? I had notes made of
everything I was going to tell you, too.,

Well darling the old sea is showing its teeth
tonight so I'll write more tomorrow. Maybe
it will be calmer— goodnight, Sweetheart.

Hello again, darling. Maybe I can finish
this letter today. This is the 25th. It's
been so rough for the past four days that
it was almost impossible to write. It got
so rough last night that I had to tie
myself to the bunk to keep from falling
off. And I'm sore all over from things
falling against me. The last four days
have been the most horrible that I've been
through in my life. It's calmer now, but
still hard to stand up.

I hope I have some mail from you when
I get there. Seems like it's been a month
since I heard from you. I have all the
letters with me that you've written and
I bet I've read them all a dozen times,
and they're getting a little old by now.

Pardon these crooked lines, but the old sea
doesn't know I'm trying to write to you.

3

You can't imagine how desolate you can feel, way out here in the middle of nowhere. This morning some of the boys were playing with a portable radio, and picked up an English station. Doris Day was singing "Shanghai." Everybody nearly went crazy. We're suppose to see jolly old England sometime tomorrow, but I wont get off there, I have to go on to northern Germany, probably be Friday before I get off.

They had quite a send off for us in New York. They had a big band there and all of Vic Damone's female fans, but what made me want to jump overboard was the band started off playing "Dixie" then "Swanee River," but that wasn't enough, they had to make me bitter by playing "Deep in the Heart of Texas" I could have deliberately and without mercy killed them all.

I'm going to try to make the best of it over here, and try to take things with a smile. It would be a heck of a long time to have the blues. Viv honey, I'm gonna need those prayers.

Well sweetheart, it's time for chow, so I'll try to finish this tonight.

I'm back and better than ever before, and I do mean better. They're only feeding us two meals a day for the last

27

three days, and we have to stand in line one to three hours to get that so I feel like I've accomplished something every time I eat. I don't go hungry, though when I can sleep a lot, but who can sleep when they're nearly upside down half the time. Baby, I'm going to feel like kissing that ground when we get there. We must be pretty close, because I saw a few birds late this afternoon.

We sing a lot to help pass the time away. Vic boy has organized a choir, and we sing our sad songs every night. How do you like that? Pretty big time, huh? Me singing with Vic Damone. He's just another "doggie" to us "fly boys", and we tell him about it too. He won't do anything but sing overseas, but he tries to act like he's protecting his country.

Vivian, darling I've run out of news, (not that there was any in the first place) so I'd better stop. I'll write you again as soon as I get a chance.

Stay sweet, and remember me honey, Always thinking of you.

Love to you Always
your Johnny

P.S. no P.S.

28

October 1, 1951
Sonthofen, Ger.

Hello darling,

Pardon the pencil and the flashy stationery, but that's all I could steal tonight, honey. I received two letters from you tonight, the first mail I've had since leaving the States. I think you're wonderful!

And wow! Have I been doing some galavanting. I came all the way across Germany today on a train. All the way from the North Sea to five miles from the Switzerland border. Just got here a couple of hours ago. Just where it is, I don't know, and if you can pronounce the name of the town, you can beat me. It's the most beautiful place I have ever seen in my life, it's in the Alps mountains and this place here is just like a castle up on top of a mountain, overlooking the town of Sonthofen. The master Hitler had it built for his officers, but they don't live here anymore.

Darling, I want you to keep writing to me, and I agree with everything you said. If I ever decide to quit writing you, I will tell you so, and I don't think I ever will. I believe in two people being honest with each other, no matter how much it hurts. That doesn't sound much like me, does it? Honey, I've seen guys go half crazy over a girl just quit writing without giving any reason, especially when they think a lot of them, and I am no exception when it comes to you. So I think we understand each other, darling.

Yes, honey, I miss those movies we went to together, and it's okay that we do it again some day, not only the movies, but everything else we did together, too. I'm always thinking about those times, and I am looking forward to it, darling. I'm glad you're getting your class ring, honey. I like for my gal to have plenty of book learning. Congratulations!

Goodnight, my sweetheart,
I Love You,
Your Johnny

~

October 8, 1951
Landsberg

Hi darling,

I still remember the last night I was there, and we played "These Things I Offer You" in the Alps café, and the cheese sandwich with the paper on it. I went to the "Alps Café" last week. Not the one we went to, but it was a café in the Alps mountains in Austria. I think I told you I went to Austria, didn't I. It wasn't very romantic, though, I couldn't understand a word of the music there.

I love you.
Your Johnny

October 13, 1951
Landsberg

Dearest Viv,

Today I went to the post office and asked for my mail, and guess what? I still didn't have any mail from you. What's the matter, honey? Lose your pencil? Well, I've still got mine and I'm going to torture you with letters until I get one from you. I've got nothing else I'd rather do anyway, than to write you, even though it's Saturday night.

Most of the boys are out getting plastered, except two that are doing the same thing I am, writing to their girls. But they're getting that wild gleam in their eyes, and will probably leave any minute.

I've had a very peaceful evening, so far. I went to the show tonight and saw a thriller, "Folsom Prison," and you know what? The moon is full tonight, and almost as big as it gets in Texas. The only thing wrong is, we're not together. Don't you feel the same way? I miss you more every day, honey, and I think about you all the time. I bet you didn't know you could get under a guy's skin like that did you? These letters probably sound a little corny to you darling, but that fits me.

Today with some friends of mine, I went to the big city of Landsberg, and what a crummy town. I believe the Germans are all crazy. Everybody rides a bicycle, and the streets are like a beehive. It's almost suicide to try to cross one, but the Germans treat an American like a god. Everybody that you meet smiles and speaks. I don't know why, but they do. They would even get out in the street to let one of us pass. They must think we're over here to protect them from the Russians. I can just see me protecting them. All I want is a nice fox hole.

Well darling, the wheel from the orderly room said, "lights out," and so therefore I'll have to close. Honey please answer soon. Will ya, huh?

Goodnight sweetheart. I'll be thinking about you.

I love you, sugar
Your Johnny

P.S. I hope you don't think I'm trying to be smart, but I'm sending you some stamps.

~

October 18, 1951
Landsberg

Dearest Viv,

Your faithful Johnny is back again, and worse then ever before. Two more days have gone by, and still no mail from my darling Viv. One of my friends got

Landsberg
October 16, 51

My Darling Viv,

I finally got some spare time, so I'll write again honey. But dont think anything about it if the stationery is smeared up, cause I'm eating chocolate candy.

I still didn't get a letter from you honey, and I'm getting pretty desperate. The mail clerk is scared of me now, I give him such mean looks every time I go to check my mail which is twice a day, and twice a day I've been disappointed for the last nine days, but I believe I'll get some from you tomorrow. I've been thinking that for the last few weeks days.

My friend from Wisconsin hadn't had any mail from his girl since he'd been here and today, he got 10 letters from you her. He was almost ready to commit suicide till he got those letters. You should see him shine now.

The boys have been telling me that you didnt love me anymore. That's why you dont write, but I dont believe that. You do love me dont you darling? I love you.

Pardon me if I'm writing downhill but you should see the conditions under which I am trying to compose.

They dont furnish writing tables, so I'm lying down on my bunk, eating chocolate candy and trying to write. I'll bet you're getting tired of my silly letters, aren't you, honey? Well, you said you would write until you heard from me, and so I'm going to write until I hear from you. And nothing ever happens interesting here, but I'll try to write something.

You should see the moon tonight honey. Big and bright and beautiful, just like you. Except you're not big. I wonder does the same moon shine here that shines in Texas? I dont think so. It's not near as big here. I wish we could be together again and just look at the moon. I bet you think I'm a big softie, but I dont think so. I'm not the first guy that's been this way. I wonder if things will ever be the same as they were this summer. I hope so. I wish things wouldn't change a bit, but I know two or three years can make a lot of difference. I had more fun in Santone than I ever had anywhere else, and I'll never forget it, honey, or you.

Guess what song I just heard on the radio? "Are You Lonesome Tonight" by Al Jolson. You're doggone right, I'm lonesome tonight, for you.

I bought me a harmonica yesterday to

Keep myself occupied in my spare time, and
you can bet your life all my friends enjoy
my playing. I'll probably have a band of
my own when I come back. I wish you
was here so I could serenade you.
    Darling, I am very tired and sleepy, so
I'm going to get in my little bed.
    Tell your folks "hello" for me, and write
sweetheart, I sure miss your letters.
    Goodnight sweetheart and sweet dreams

                        I love you always,
                            your
                             Johnny

P.S. The "boss" told me today that if I stay
on my toes that I might get another
stripe in January.(Nice of them) Then
it would be, your corporal Johnny,

                    Love, again, honey

four letters from his girlfriend, and another one got three from his girl. They offered to let me read their letters, and make believe it was you saying all those romantic things to me, but that's no good, so I'll just keep waiting patiently, to put the word mildly. I probably would have got some mail from you, but the plane that was bringing our mail over from the States is missing over the ocean. It had 6700 pounds of mail for us boys in Europe. What a blow!!

Honey, please pardon me if I sound a little sarcastic, but I don't really mean to be. I'm just a little perturbed because I haven't had any mail, and my morale has dropped to sub-normal. Today, when I got off work, the Sgt in charge said he hoped I got some mail tomorrow so he could get a little work out of me. He knows I wouldn't work even if I did get mail.

Guess what I just finished doing! I did my washing again, 9 pairs of socks, 4 t-shirts, a pair of fatigues and my unmentionables. I'll make some girl a good housewife when I get out. Or don't you think so?

Last night, I went to the gym with the boys and played basketball about an hour, then lifted the barbells and climbed ropes and just all sorts of things, and tonight I'm so sore I can't hardly move. And on top of that, I've got a nasty old cold. I wish I could give it to you like I used to. Remember the night you said I wasn't going to give you a cold? The next night, you were sneezing. You know what? I'm nuts about you.

I'm getting a weekend pass from Friday night to Monday morning. A couple of boys and I are going to Munich, one of the popular places in Germany. I won't say what it's popular for, but it's popular. We're just going up there sight-seeing. Anything would be a relief from what I've been doing lately. I've only been off the base once since I've been here, and that was only for about three hours.

But, I've about run out of words and I'm getting sleepy again, so I'd better go to bed. I've got a hard day "at the office" tomorrow.

Goodnight sweetheart, and sweet dreams. Take care of yourself for me.

I love you always,
Your Johnny

~

October 21, 1951
Landsberg

Hi Sweetheart,

I had a very exciting weekend. I went with a friend of mine up to Munich Friday night, when I got my pass and we stayed there Friday night until noon Saturday, then we went to Augsburg and stayed until about one oclock this morning. We had a very good time both places, and the people treated us very nice, too, except I don't think they appreciated us much at Augsburg, because the Air Force destroyed nearly the whole town in the last war, but most of them treated us like kings. We went to a hotel last night to eat, and they gave us a free steak supper and asked us to stay and see the show, so we did. I suppose it was a very good show, because everybody laughed. The only thing that we could understand was the women's dancing. They probably thought we were rude because we didn't laugh, but it was all in German. A man we were sitting with could speak English, and sometimes he told us what the joke was and we would laugh, naturally at the wrong time while they were telling the next joke, and that just made it worse. They played a song especially for us, "Dear Hearts and Gentle People." It wasn't like any way I'd heard it played, but we appreciated it.

Guess who came in yesterday? Link. He said there was something you said for him to tell me, but he forgot it. I could have killed him. All he could think of that you said was "God bless you." I showed him the picture you sent me, and on the back it says, "Always be thinking of me, I will always be thinking of you." And that's what he said that you said. Is it?

I am always thinking of you, honey, except when I'm asleep, then I'm dreaming about you. I dreamed about you last night, but it wasn't very pleasant. I dreamed we were roller skating at St. Mary's and you fell and broke your leg. I picked you up and carried you to my car (where I got it, I don't know). When I got you home, your mother told me to leave and never come back if that's all I could do, take you out and break your leg. I was trying to explain that it wasn't my fault, when Link woke me up. When I woke up, I was worried about you. I hope you didn't break your leg, darling.

Link just came in again. I told him to sit down and shut up till I finish this letter. I'd better not tell you what he said. Except he said "Hello, Johnny's Sweetheart." I like that. He said he just never could get around to writing all those letters. He had 16 letters waiting on him from his girl when he got here. The bum. He's trying to read this. He said "Tell her you love her." I love you.

Did Pat get my letter? I haven't heard from her yet, either. Guess what Link just said. You don't know? Well, I'll tell you. He said he thought your sister Syl was cute and when we get back, we should have a double wedding. What a brother-in-law!

Well, honey, I've run out of words again. Write, sweetheart, and tell your folks "hi" for me. I love you, darling,

Always,
Your Johnny

35

My Viv,

Today I'm very happy sweetheart. I got four letters from you today. Two were mailed the 21st, one the 22nd and one the 11th of Oct. They're all a little old, but so are diamonds.

I didn't get your picture yet, but I think I will pretty soon. I had my picture made in my uniform. Hope you don't mind. Do you honey? And your picture <u>is</u> worth something, to me anyway. All the other boys have their pictures of their girls hanging around. I'll show them all up when I get yours.

Guess what song they're playing on the radio? Stuart Hamblen's singing "I'll Find You." I like the part where he says "You know girl, if you should ever stray——etc" I think that's real romantic. Remember one night I tried to say that to you, and you told me to shut up because I didn't mean it. Well, I did mean it, but I guess I didn't have the nerve to tell you then. You asked me what I thought of you. Honey, well if you don't know by now, I'll tell you. I love you very much, and I think you're just wonderful, except when you're mad, and darling I know I want just as much as you do to be back with you. And I'm always looking forward to it, and thinking of you.

Darling, you forgot to put my box number on one of my letters, or I would have got it sooner. Watch that next time young lady.

I went to town this morning to do some shopping and was talking to a German woman about 50 years old. She asked me all about America and all about myself, and asked me if I had a Frauline (girl) at home. I said as a matter of fact, yes I do. She said your name is "Vernain" in German. I like "Vivian" best.

I bought you a present. I'll send it tomorrow or the next day when I get time to go to the post office. I hope you like it, darling. It's not the nicest thing in the world, and I don't know what you would like, but the man said any Frauline would like it, I hope so. It's not a Christmas present, just a love present, and I do love you. I just couldn't keep a secret. I had to tell you about it.

Darling, I have to go to work.

I love you always
Your Johnny

~

Hi Honey,

I'm writing from the service club. They have a writing room for us here, and just about anything else that we want, although I haven't had time to enjoy it. They're already playing Christmas carols. "I'll Have a Blue Christmas Without You" is playing now. I wonder why I always think of you when I hear a Christmas song? I didn't know you at Xmas. I hope to know you for many more to come though, darling.

You know, I told you I bet I would go to sleep on the job last night, well I did, about 4 o'clock this morning. I was asleep sitting down for nearly an hour when the Sgt-in-charge woke me up. No damage done though. The United States didn't get whipped because of it. He just said not to let it happen again. I won't, not before three o'clock tomorrow morning.

The "Grand Ole Opry" is on the radio now. It's last week's program but that's alright. Hank Snow just sang "One More Ride." Come in Hank!

Goodnight sweetheart and always be thinking of me and remember that I love you always.

Your Johnny

~

October 31, 1951
Landsberg

Hi sweetheart,

I got that much-welcomed letter from you today, and believe it or not your picture. The letter was one you wrote the 26th. Honey I was sure glad to get the picture. I went to the P.X. tonight and bought a frame to put it in, and I have it hanging up on the wall now with a "Hands Off" sign on it. That isn't exactly what the sign says, but that's what it means. When I got the picture, it had been opened, and the folder was creased on two corners, and some of the paint was rubbed off your cheeks and lips, but I can't notice it at all a few feet away. The man in the photo lab here on the base said he could fix it up just like new, so I'm going to let him do it next week, so it will be alright after all. And have you been around, honey! First the picture went to Kilmer, then to Sonthofen Germany, then here, they sent it to headquarters at Wiesbaden, then back here again, but I trapped them this time, and got my darling's picture.

Our "Hoochie Coochie" show from Paris didn't show up tonight honey. I don't know what happened to them, but we waited at the "Airmens Club" nearly two hours. Everybody was sure raving about it, including me for a while, but I got tired of waiting and left, another guy and I. He's writing to his "darling," too.

Honey, I can't get my eyes off your picture. You don't mind if I stare at you like I used to, do you? Darling, I'd give anything if I could talk to you, and say the things I want to say.

Oh yes, I forgot to tell you, I made "Sharpshooter" on the firing range Sunday morning, and two more points I would have been "Expert." Just call me "Dead eye Johnny."

I hit the jackpot on mail today. I got a letter from my folks, one from you, one from my wild brother in Memphis, and one from my sister in New Orleans, and your picture, so "Everything's gonna be Alright."

Goodnight sweetheart and sweet dreams. I love you.

Always your Johnny

~

November 3, 1951
Landsberg A.B.

Hello Tex Darling,

I got two letters from you this morning, honey, both mailed the 29th, and I almost didn't get them because I was sleeping at mail call, but one of the boys woke me up in time, because he said he knew I would be uncontrollable if I knew I had mail and didn't get it. And he's about right.

How do you like my Technicolor letter? Don't you think the red stationery is cute? It's a French brand called "Moulin Rouge." Maybe it's a little too sexy, but I like it.

Honey, I am very happy when I get your mail. You'd never know just how happy. I think that's all the most of us over here live for, 11:30 and mail call. I like to get mail from anyone, but honey, you know you're someone special with me. Getting a letter from you is almost like talking to you. I try to imagine you saying the things that you write, and it brings you closer somehow. Pardon the dramatics, but I am happy when I get your mail.

Tell your mother I said "thanks for the prayers." I'll need them if anybody would, and tell her I have been hearing from you, and tell her to take care of "our little girl." That's you. Oh yes, and tell her to take care of herself too, and not get herself all banged up again, or she will look old before her time. Honest, honey, I don't think she looks a day over 29 or 30.

I'll write again tomorrow honey. This won't go out till Monday anyway. Keep writing darling. That's the best way you can make me happy, now. And remember that I love you, sweetheart, and always will. Tell all your folks "hello" for me, and tell Ray "good luck" on his new "career."

All my love,
Always,
Your Johnny

~

Johnny explains later that the "88" seen in the following letter means "hugs and kisses" in Western Union code.

38

88

Hello Baby,

It is a bright, sunshiny afternoon and the birds have been singing this morning, and I didn't even throw rocks at them. For the first time since I've been here, I can see the Alps mountains down south, although it's almost 50 miles to them. Darling, it's a perfect day for us to be together. I wonder if you're thinking of me now? You seem very close to me now. I'll bet you think I'm a pansy poet, but I love you.

I thought us guys in Security Service had been working pretty hard, but I guess we haven't been working hard enough. They've changed our shifts now, and I'll be working six hours on, then twelve hours off for nine days straight. Some days I'll work twelve hours. Wow! But they still only beat me twice a day. Now I know I'll be working Christmas. Boy, am I gonna have fun! Honey, whoever told you that Air Force guys didn't work, were wrong, dead wrong.

Well, I'm out of words sweetheart, and as I said, I've got things to do, so I'd better be doing them, cause it's not long before I go back to the dungeon.

So long for this time darling, and write as often as you can, and remember that I love you always, honey, and I'll be thinking about you.

Your Johnny

~

November 5, 1951
Landsberg Ger.

Hi Viv darlin',

I got your sa-weet letter today you mailed the 30th, and you know what, honey? I'm a very happy fly boy till tomorrow at mail call.

Honey, I'm glad you feel the way you do about me, and I hope you mean it, because I do, darling. Maybe I am lonesome, but I know I love you. And no, I'm not angry with you for saying that, but you know now honey. I don't think it's a joking matter myself, so I don't joke about things like that. I love you honey.

Honey, it's now eleven oclock, and I've got to get up at 5 oclock tomorrow, so I'm going to close. I hate to write short letters as much as I hate to receive them, but I'm out of words.

Keep writing, darling, and I'll write just as much as I can. And I'll always love you darlin. Stay sweet for me.

All my love,
Your Johnny

P.S. I luf you too.

~

November 9, 1951
Landsberg

Hi sweetheart,

I finally got around to writing you again honey, and I'm glad you don't mind getting a short letter, because I just can't write a long one until I hear from you. Today and yesterday I didn't get a letter from you, but tomorrow is Saturday, and I know I'll get one, cause I couldn't wait till Monday. I'm going to write the Secretary of the Air Force and tell him I want more d—— mail.

Honey, what is Catechism? I never heard of the word. You've got a dumb boyfriend, but he loves you.

I'm glad you liked the locket honey. My friend from Rhode Island got one like it for his girl, and put a note in it that said, "Your Locket is my Broken Heart." You know, the song by Hank boy. He didn't really mean it though, just did it for a joke.

My Commanding Officer left this morning for San Antonio. Know where that is? That's where my sweetheart lives. I want to stow away on his plane, but I couldn't manage it! Maybe I can get promoted to Colonel pretty soon, and I can go to Santone every month like he does.

Honey, one of my friends got a phonograph from home and we have several records already, along with Pat Page's "These Things I Offer You for a Lifetime." That song always reminds me of you, honey.

Well, my little one, I'm out of words now, before it gets wilder, I'm gonna close. Always remember that I love you honey and am always thinking of you.

Your Johnny

~

November 24, 1951
Landsberg

Hello Baby Darling,

Darling, I'd give anything to be with you tonight. All by myself and not a thing to do, except go to a sorry show. I wonder if you're as lonesome as I am, you seem so close to me sometimes darling, even though there is over 4000 miles between us. And I hope you'll always feel about me, the way I feel about you. Darling, I love you more than anything else in this world.

It's almost time for the "Grand Ole Opry." I can't make up my head whether to stay here and listen to it, or go to the show. Or would you like to come along, and we'll go to the service club and watch the floor show and drink ginger ale, or maybe you'd rather go dancing at the Waldorf-Astoria?

You can see I've about run out of words darling, but I told myself this was going to be a long letter. And it's almost time to go to the show, I made up my head, so I'll be back before you know it. I love you darling.

I'm back sweetheart. It wasn't a bad show at all, "The Guy Who Came Back." A little bit corny, but still good. Have you seen it?

Darling, I still miss you. The guy that I went to the show with wouldn't even let me hold hands with him, and make believe it was you.

I'm going to church tomorrow morning, and I mean it this time. There's a guy in this room that's Catholic, and he wants me to go with him.

They're playing one of our songs now darling, "I Still Feel the Same About You." Remember? I do, and I'll never forget, that was the first night. The night you wouldn't let me kiss you goodnight.

Remember that I love you and I always will.

Your Loving Johnny

~

December 2, 1951
Landsberg

Hello Darling,

You know what I did last night? I got inebriated. You see, the night started off very smooth. I went to the early show with the boys, then they suggested that we go to the Airmen's club and watch the floor show. Then someone suggested that we have a drink. Well, we did. I started off drinking Ginger Ale and rye whiskey mixed, but after three or four, I decided that I didn't like ginger ale. So, I tried to drink all the rye whiskey in the place. I decided about 12:30 that I couldn't do it, and left, not feeling a bit of pain, and came back to my room. One of the boys had brought a half pint of Italian rum, and I didn't have a thing against the Italians, so I drank the biggest part of that. By that time I was in a happy little world. The boys said after I finally went to bed, I kept them awake till 2:30 this morning talking about you. They said that I said over and over, "she has the prettiest eyes, and the softest lips in the world." I hope you don't mind honey. I was fully unaware of the fact. The rough part was getting up at 5:30 this morning and going to work. I almost didn't make it.

Darling, don't tell your mother I got plastered, will you huh?

I love you darling.

Yours always,
Johnny

~

41

December 6, 1951
Landsberg

Hello Darling,

I am glad you feel that way about drinking honey, even though it makes me feel low. That's the first time I've ever been completely stewed, and it won't happen again. I don't know why it is honey, maybe I'm not human, but after it was over with, I was ashamed to face anyone that saw me drunk. Ninety percent of the boys live only for that 3-day pass so they can get drunk and raise hell, and they forget about it after the hangover is gone. But me, it's been on my conscious ever since, and I know why too. I promised my mother I'd never drink. Believe me, I'm ashamed.

Yours till hell freezes over
Johnny

∽

December 9, 1951
Landsberg

Hello sweetheart,

You know what's playing on the radio now? "Shanghai." That reminds me of the "Cavalier" hamburger shop at the bus stop there on Commerce Street. I used to wait for the bus there and listen to that song and eat hamburgers.

Honey, I'm going to finish this later. I'm going to the show now. "Showboat" is showing. I've already seen it, but I want to see it again. So long now, darling. I love you.

Back again sweetheart, and just in time to finish before lights out. I liked the show—again, and it puts me in a romantic mood, but I don't have a victim handy.

Goodnight my darling. Think of me will you? And remember I always love you honey.

Always yours,
Johnny

∽

December 13, 1951
Landsberger

Hello Darling,

I want to thank you for the I.D. bracelet. It's the most precious thing I have. I love you darling.

Remember the little note you put in the package that said, "Sweetheart, I love you. Your Viv. Merry Christmas Darling"? I've got it framed and stuck on the wall. Everybody thinks I'm nuts. I am, about you.

I hope you didn't mind me opening your Xmas present now, but I couldn't wait.

Your Johnny

~

December 14, 1951
Landsberger

Hi Baby Darling,

Today I went out and dusted the cob webs out of my mail box. That makes a week and a day honey, and I'm getting pretty desperate for a letter from you. One of the boys got a nice sweet letter from his girl, and he let me read it to cheer me up, but that didn't work either.

Have you ever heard the song "I'll Find You"? I told him the words to it, and he wrote it to his girl. He likes to say real nice soft things like that. What would you do if I said, "My Darling, you are like beautiful music to me, when I'm with you a thousand violins are playing, and when I left you, those thousand violins ceased to play, and so did the very strings of my heart, which no longer will resound until our next wonderful meeting." He told her that! You're supposed to read that real slow and soft. That guy is Ben Perea, the one that sent you the Xmas card.

Darling, I love you. Read that real slow and soft.

Guess what I heard today? Frank Sinatra singing "Rose of San Antone." They won't let me alone. Frank and his bride, Ava, are up at Weisbaden now. I heard them on the radio this afternoon.

I think I'll stop doing everything but writing to you. I'd probably write you three months even if I didn't hear from you because I love you so much and believe you love me. Don't try me though honey. I'd be nuttier than I am now if I didn't hear from you for three months.

I miss you and your letters so much. Goodnight sweetheart. I love you.

Your Johnny

~

December 20, 1951
Landsberger

Hello sweetheart,

I just got back from the show and I saw "Warpath," so you better watch out.

I hope you don't mind the GI typewriter, and I know it isn't exactly what Emily Post would do, but I just felt like typing it tonight, or try to, at least.

Thanks for telling me what a cyst is. You're keeping me well informed. I don't know what I'd do without you, and I don't want to do without you, honey.

43

Darling, you know I'm going to miss you Xmas and New Years, and you know what, there's either six or seven hours difference in the time here and there, I don't know which, but I'm going to be kissing you at six oclock and at seven oclock here the first of January. I hope you can feel it, honey. I wish you could feel all the other times I kiss you, too. I love you darling. Even though I'm gripy at times, I love you always. I wish I could stare at you too, I would really be unpolite.

Darling, I'm using the typewriter at the Air Police desk, and the big bad man with the gun said he had to have it, so I'll close for now. I had more to tell you, so I'll write again tomorrow, OK?

Remember I love you honey. Always. And try not to be mad at me for anything I said, although I don't blame you if you are. You know I love you darling.

Your Johnny

~

December 21, 1951
Landsberg

Hello Sweetheart,

I keep coming back like a song. I told you I'd write again today, so here I am, and I love you more than ever.

A guy I know hadn't heard from his girl in about a month, and today he got two letters from her. He was so happy and excited, and he opened the first one, and it was a "Dear John," then he opened the second one, and it was an invitation to her wedding. I couldn't help but laugh when he showed it to me, but I felt sorry for him, too. He sure looks sick.

My squadron is getting a free beer party tomorrow. Everybody gets all the free beer they can drink. I'm glad I'll be working so I won't be tempted. I'd probably be tempted to get plastered, if I wasn't working. They're also giving us a partial payment tomorrow. Thirty dollars for Christmas. They'll take it out of next month's pay though, the bums.

Your loving Johnny

~

December 23, 1951
Landsberg

My darling darling,

I've only got a few minutes, but I'll write a little, cause that mean man with the flashlight will be turning out the lights pretty soon.

We had a Christmas party at the service club tonight, and my friends and I went for a while. We sang Christmas carols, and played games with the officers' wives, and not one of them looks like you. We got tired of it after a while, and went to shoot pool. I'm a bad boy.

Boy, you should have seen this place yesterday. I think everybody was drunk except us guys working. So, you shouldn't have seen it, it was disgusting. And about half of them are still drunk, and will probably stay that way till after Christmas. Honey, why does everybody get drunk on Christmas? Looks like it should be the other way around. Nobody should get drunk on Christmas. Right? One guy in this room came in last night stewed to the gills, and went to sleep on the floor, and that's where he woke up this morning. That reminds me of a song, "Sunday Down in Tennessee"—"I woke up this morning with my head on the floor where I left it Saturday night"——

I hope you've had a nice Christmas, honey, and that you was thinking of me just a little.

> I love you, sweetheart.
> Your Johnny
> Smack

~

> December 26, 1951
> Landsberg

Hello Sweetheart,

This morning the 1st soldier came in my room, and it was a mess from Christmas packages etc, and he got a little mad, and said from now on the room will have <u>three</u> inspections every day. We have to keep the rooms in perfect condition all the time. And if we don't, he'll put us to work digging ditches or something. Nice guy.

I got letters from two girls today besides yours. One girl is 17, and the other is a little older. The one seventeen said she'd be glad when I got back, cause she was sure going to miss me. The other one loves me too. My sister and my mother, darling. Nice girls.

My sister sent me a box of fudge she made herself. I don't think she does want me back.

I thought I had lots to tell you darling, but it looks like I've run down, so I'll turn it off.

Goodnight sweetheart.

> Your Johnny

P.S. Mi amor mandame a decir siacaso allates alguna persona que te diciera lo que te escrivi en Espanol.

~

45

Sandsberg, Dtch
December 25

Hello Honey Baby,

Seems like I'm always writing you at the last minute, but since it's Christmas, I was celebrating, if you want to call it that. I worked today, and after work, I went bowling, then to a stage show at the theatre. It was a pretty good show, the part I understood. Most of it was in French and Spanish, but it was pretty good.

What did Santa Clause bring you honey? He couldn't come to see me, cause he's not cleared to handle Secret information. The only thing I'd want him to bring me, is you anyway.

Mi Querida te quierro y te amo con todo mi corazon, y por favor nunca te olvides de mi.

Honey, I've sure missed you, especially the past two days. I couldn't possibly tell you how much. I love you darling. Thats all I can think of to say and you're on my mind all the time. I dont want you to think I'm looking for sympathy, and trying to cry on your shoulder but these past two days have been the bluest I've ever lived. Maybe I shouldn't feel that way,

46

because there's thousands more in the same boat I'm in, or worse, in Korea, but I can't help feeling low at a time, like this when I miss you so much. I guess I need to grow up.

We did have a little fun last night. There's a couple guys here that play the guitar, and we stayed up till about 3 oclock this morning singing hillbilly music. Do you like hillbilly music honey? I thought you did.

I'm not out of ink. This damn pen just wont write.

Honey, I'm out of news, not that there was any in the first place, but I just wanted to write and tell you I still love you. I still love you.

Goodnight Darling, and sweet dreams. I hope I hear from you tomorrow. A letter from you would do wonders honey.

I love you darling, with all my heart

your
Johnny

Je Vous Aime Viv.

December 27, 1951
Landsberg

My Sweetheart,

Pardon this messy paper honey. I'm eating candy again.

Honey, I didn't know you was so little. 106¼—you are my <u>little</u> girl. But why did the doc put you on vitamins? Are you sick honey? Maybe it's not any of my business. You don't have to tell me. You know how much I weigh? I weigh 180. I weighed this morning. Many more holidays, and I'll be getting fat, too—like you.

You know what happened this morning? The first Sgt. came in the room nosing around. He went to the window sill where I've got your picture, looked at it, then at me, and then back at your picture, and grinned. He didn't say a word, just walked out. I could have slugged him. I don't know what he was thinking, but I didn't like it.

So long for now darling, and remember, your Johnny loves you very much.

Your
J.R.

I love you little girl.

~

January 1, 1952
Landsberg, Germany

Hello Sweetheart,

I just woke up and thought I'd start the day and the year off right by writing you, GI typewriter and all.

What did you do New Years Eve honey? I slept, or at least tried to. I worked last night till ten minutes to twelve. When the old year went out, I was at midnight chow with three boys I work with. At midnight we raised our coffee cups, and said "Here's to the girls back home!" Then I came back and got in my little bed. Everyone was gone but me, and I would have been if I hadn't been working. As I said, I went to bed, but I couldn't sleep, so I got up and got out all your letters and read most of them again. That just made it worse. So you know what I did? I sang love songs to your picture, then I turned on the radio and got some Hawaiian music and did the "hula" for you. You should see me do the hula. I surprise myself sometimes. I do crazy things when I'm alone, and you do too. You talk to yourself, don't you?

Well, I finally went to sleep and the drunks woke me up at 6:45 this morning, so I got your picture and kissed you "Happy New Year" at 7:00 this morning. I hope you felt it. What was you doing at midnight last night, darling? I tried to imagine what you would be doing, but I couldn't, except a few things I didn't want to imagine.

You know what Ben Perea did last night? He went to town, and got about half stewed, and was out with a woman. This morning when he came in, I started kidding him about it, and told him he should be ashamed, and what would his "Rita" think if she knew. Well, he was ashamed, and got her picture and took it to bed with him, and he talked to her about half an hour, apologizing, and now he's sleeping with her picture in his hands. You should see him, he really looks pathetic. Some time I think that guy's got it too bad, but then I look at myself, and see that I do things almost as bad.

Jo Stafford is singing now, "No Other Love." Heard it honey? That's the way I feel about you. You are the only one for me—for always.

Say honey, do Catholics believe in getting drunk? I never thought to ask Ben. It doesn't look very holy to me.

Darling, I've got nuthin else to say, except how wonderful I think you are, and I could never find the words, so I'll schtop. And I love you little girl. You and you alone. Write soon darling.

Yours eventually,
Johnny

~

January 3, 1952

My Baby,

You know what I did? Yesterday I was cleaning out my duffel bag and found an old shirt that I wore last summer with your lipstick on it. I put it back for safekeeping. I'm going to keep it always.

Sweetheart, you've got me puzzled. Once you said that you'd die if I turned out to be a drunkard, and in this letter you said it really didn't make any difference. Maybe I don't know what you mean. You'd rather I wouldn't but if I did it wouldn't change your feelings about me. Is that it honey. I don't know how you feel exactly but I know how I feel about it. I think it's stupid. Even though it does offer some kind of escape from boredom and loneliness, I know what it would do to me. I couldn't stop when I wanted to. It would be alright if I could drink over here when I feel so low, and then stop when I get back over there. But I couldn't do that. I know I'd be a sot. My dad used to drink all the time and it didn't make things so happy at home a few times. Maybe that's the reason I'm so set against it.

I remember the first time I saw you. Jim Hobbs and I came to town together that night, and went to the skating rink. We'd been bragging, just kidding about what great lovers we thought we were. Hobbs saw you first, and said, "If you're so great, let's see you get a date with that one." Well, I did in a crude sort of way, and I never thought it would turn into this. But I cherish the day I met you darling.

I love you.

~

January 8, 1952
Landsberg

My darling,

Here's your sweetheart back again, and as bad as ever.

So the bums have been following you, huh? Well, I don't blame them. With your looks, you should carry a gun. The next guy that bothers you, you tell him your Johnny will break his little head when he gets back. I don't like for guys to mess around with you. Be careful, will you honey? You know I wish I could be there to protect you, but I can't, so you'll have to take care of yourself till I can.

I love you darling. I sit around and stare at your picture, and get so lonesome I could die. I guess you know how it feels to want someone so much you nearly go nuts. That's the way I get when I start looking at you. I never thought I'd feel this way about anyone, but I do. You sure did something to me darling.

I love you and you alone with all my heart.

Your Johnny

~

January 14, 1952
Landsberg

Hello Honey,

Honey, I was happy to get those letters, but the one you wrote New Years eve night made me very blue. Almost sick, believe it or not. I lost a lot of confidence in you. I remember once you said that you hated drinking and you'd rather die than to see me drink, and you was about half gone when you wrote that letter. I can't figure you out.

Remember I promised you that I wouldn't drink? I did that for you, and I haven't drank since. So you said you'd just had two highballs when you started that letter. That's not the first time either, is it?

I love you Vivian, and if that means anything to you, you'll want to please me. I'm not asking much, just please, please don't start drinking and be a nice girl. Will you do that for me?

I'll write you again tomorrow. You know I love you, or I wouldn't have told you these things. If I didn't love you I wouldn't care what you do. But I love you. Always.

All my love,
Johnny

~

January 15, 1952
Landsberg

Hi Sweetheart,

Darling, that letter I wrote yesterday, I knew two hours after I wrote it that I would be apologizing. Honey, I'm sorry I ever talked so rude to you. I didn't mean to be so hateful, and I know I owe you an apology. I did mean what I said about drinking, and I'd rather break my neck than to see you start it. I was in a bad humor yesterday honey, and I hope you'll forgive me.

I'm going to bed now darling. I'm sleepy. Goodnight honey.

Your Johnny
Always

~

January 19, 1952

My Baby,

Through the blizzard the old trusty mail plane brought me two letters from you today and one from your mother. I'll try to answer them all tonight, but if I don't, ok? This is Saturday night, and my hair is getting kinky.

Honey, about my girlfriends, once a month now I'm on a three day pass. Twice since I've been over here I was with a girl. Once at Augsburg and once at Munich last week. Darling, those girls don't mean a thing to me. You should know that. I just see them one night, and never see them again, and never look for them again. Baby, I'd trade 100 of girls like that for one kiss from you. After all, I'm only human honey, and I get tired of looking at a bunch of boys everyday. You don't mind, do you darling?

Well honey, I've run down, so I'll stop and write a little to your good-looking mother, if you don't mind?

I love you darling.

Your
Johnny

~

Letter to my mother, referenced above.

Hello Mom,

I just wrote a letter to our girl, so now, yes now, I'll try to answer your questions.

Oh yes, you know my heart belongs to your little girl. And I would like to take over your job. Just wait till I come marching home. You'll have a hard time getting rid of me.

I know what you mean about temperatures. Even though it was snowing today at mail call, things were pretty warm when I was reading those letters.

And you can be sure Viv is putting those "sweet nothings" also "sweet somethings" in my letters. Not long ago, I left a letter from her laying around, and some of my friends read it. Since then I've been known as "Johnny Darling" by my friends. I don't mind a bit though.

My pencil refuses to write anymore, so tell that little girl I still love her, like I wanted to tell her the night I called from New Jersey, and choked up.

Love,
Johnny

~

January 23, 1952
Landsberg

My Baby,

I meant to write you last night, but they had a good USO show that I wanted to see, so I went and when I got back, it was too late to write. I hope you don't mind. It was a pretty good show. They had eight women and four costumes. Quite a novelty. They've got a pretty good show on tonight, but I'd rather stay and write you.

Honey, I'd give a month's pay just to talk to you tonight, or even to tell you I love you. What a life! I didn't know love could be such torture. Sometimes I can almost feel you in my arms, I think about you so much and can almost feel you thinking about me. Honey, I'm love-sick, in case you didn't know. When I get back, they're going to have a hard time keeping me away from Santone.

Keep writing, and loving me darling. I love you with all my heart always.

Your Johnny

~

January 25, 1952
Landsberg

My Vivian,

I went to the Airmen's club tonight when I got off work, and drank some beer. Too much, I guess. Honey, I guess you'll think I'm one great guy. Bawling you out for taking two little drinks, then doing the same thing myself. Honey, I guess I haven't got an excuse, not a good one, at least. Darling, believe it or not, my job is very hard on the nerves. And I've been sitting around just doing nothing except going to work, eat, and sleep day after day. It gets very tiresome honey. I'm not used to it. So the reason I drank tonight is to try to feel better. I thought I was feeling better, but down inside, I'm not. Honey, I don't want to do this. You know why? Because I want to be worthy of your love. I

52

know I'm not, and could never be, but you love me, and I know I love you, and I'm making plans for us honey. I know from the things you write, that you're thinking about <u>our</u> future, too. I don't think it makes any difference to you, but <u>for you</u> I'm going to stop it, whether it makes any difference or not. I've said that before, haven't I? I'll bet you get tired of hearing me talk about drinking so I'll stop. Just one thing more: I want to apologize again for talking so mean to you in that letter that I wrote answering the one you wrote New Years. I am sorry honey, and I guess I'll be apologizing again when I receive an answer to it. But honey don't ever start drinking. Even if the guy that loves you is a sot. I want you to stay the way you was when I left there. Not change any way.

Honey I wish that dream would come true about me coming home, but it won't, and you're a little off beam about my mother. She doesn't look like you dreamed she did. She's big. Weighs about 200 pounds, has brown hair, or did. It's over half gray now. My dad is about the size of your dad, and has black hair. He's 55, and Mother's 48. I have three sisters, and two brothers. One sister 28 lives in New Orleans. One sister will be 18 day after tomorrow. She's already married and has a boy just learning to talk. They marry 'em young in them thar hills, except we don't live in the hills. One sister is 14. My sisters' names are Louise, Reba, and Joann. I have one brother, 30, lives in Memphis. Name's Roy. I have a brother, eleven, named Tom. So now you're clued in on your future brothers, and sisters-in-laws. Quite a family, huh?

I love you darling, and I'll always love you alone, with all my heart.

Your Johnny

~

January 27, 1952
Landsberg
2:30 am

Hello Darling,

It's two thirty here, and 7:30 Saturday night there, and just about now, I can see you, almost. Getting ready to go out somewhere, with someone. I bet you'll be thinking of me tonight, cause I'm thinking of you. What I wouldn't give to be sitting there waiting on you to get ready. And those dozens of kisses! You know what? I'd give ten dollars just to hold your hand. I'm lonesome, very lonesome for you. That's not hard to tell, is it? Remember when we used to sit at the drive-in and your hair would get in my face? I'd like to smother myself in your hair now.

I love you sweetheart. Always.

Your Johnny

~

My darling,

Vivian darling, I knew when I got an answer to that silly letter I wrote you, I'd be sorry, and I am darling. It makes me see how wonderful you are by the things you said, and how silly it was of me to say the things I did. And it hurt me to know that I hurt you. You'd never know how much. Darling, I've got complete confidence in you, and I trust you completely, and I always will. Anything you say, I'll believe darling. No matter what you tell me, I'll believe. And I don't think I really doubted you when you said you only had two. Honey, I was about half sick, and in a bad humor when I got that letter, and I took everything wrong. And honey, you couldn't know how many times I've been sorry for it.

Honey, "88" means "Love and Kisses." It's used by Western Union, and in radio sometimes to make messages shorter. "79" means "Good night."

Pardon this writing, but it's cold here in the dayroom, and I'm shaking. It snowed again last night. It keeps getter deeper and deeper.

Baby darling, my mind's gone blank, so I'll close, before I freeze to death. I forgot to tell you, I'm a big time singer now. I'm singing the 31st at the service club for "March of Dimes" benefit. I gotta go practice now.

So long for now darling. I'll write the next chance I get. And I'll keep on loving you. You and you alone, with all my heart, all my life.

Your Johnny

P.S. I love you darling. Write every chance you get. I wish you could send yourself in a letter. I'd throw away the return address. I love you my darling.

~

February 1, 1952
2 pm

My Darling,

Yesterday and last night I killed the boredom around here. We had a "March of Dimes" carnival at the gym, and I was over there from one o'clock yesterday to midnight. The 1st soldier got me off work so I could sing. And did I sing! I'm so hoarse today I can't talk. People requested songs for me to sing at a dollar a song, and I took in nearly $200. So I guess I did my part for the March of Dimes. We had a hillbilly band, and a pretty good one too. I sang every song I know, and some of them at least a dozen times. You didn't know I'm a big-time singer, did you honey? You heard Hank Snow's song "One More Ride"? They made me sing that so many times that

I heard it in my sleep last night. And everybody I meet today calls me "Hank."

I'm hoping that I have a letter to answer tomorrow. If I don't, it's going to be the longest weekend I've ever seen.

I love you
Your Johnny 7744

~

February 4, 1952

Hi Honey Baby,

I don't think you're too frank by telling me everything honey. I'm glad you're that way, because I'd rather you'd tell me everything, than to just hint at some things, or just tell part of some things, then leave me wondering. And I hope you will be having <u>our</u> kids someday darling.

Honey, I'm the only guy I know that tells his girl about the girls he runs around with over here. I've told you everything and I'm glad we understand each other. Some of the boys say I'm crazy for telling you, but they just don't understand us. This guy, Perea won't tell his girl about the girls he runs around with over here because she doesn't want him to go with any girls, so he lies to her and says he doesn't see any girls over here. I'm glad we're the way we are honey, and you'd be insulting me if you ever thought that the kind of girls I see ever meant anything to me. There's no possible way to compare them with you darling. You're all I ever want.

I love you.
Johnny

~

February 6, 1952

My Baby,

You know what they're making us do? Take P.T. I went to the gym last night and tried to get rid of a little fat and today I'm so sore. I can hardly move. I'll go over again tonight and work the kinks out. And I am getting fat. I weigh 183. Remember when you told me I should drink milkshakes the last night I was there? Well, I did, 13 pounds worth so far.

Darling, if a Protestant marries a Catholic girl, the wedding has to be Catholic, and their children have to be brought up Catholics, don't they? And they can't name their own kids. Someone else names their kids, don't they? Maybe that's not right, but that's what I've heard.

I just heard the song "Blue Skirt Waltz." Remember when we used to skate to that? We couldn't waltz, but we tried anyway.

55

And that song, "San Antonio Rose," when I get back, I'm going to buy a record of that, and play it over and over, and hold you and kiss you while it's playing to make up for every time it's made me lonesome. We'll show 'em!

I love you little girl.

Your Johnny

~

February 12, 1952

My Baby,

The snow melted enough for them to bring me three letters from you today. And it made me very happy because this made five days that I didn't get a letter from my darling.

Know what the radio is playing now? "September Song." September I left home, and the girl I love (you). When I was on the train to N.Y., it was raining most of the way, and every click of the wheels was putting you farther behind me. And I was saying over and over to myself, "If I don't come back on a one-way track, way down to Mexico, you can find me there or any old where that a tumbleweed will grow. It's goodbye now, you'll never know how I'm grieving."

I love you darling. I'll always love you alone.

Your Johnny

~

February 17, 1952

Darling Vivian,

Boy! I love you! Yesterday, I came down from work expecting a letter from you. I looked in my little box, and guess what? Not one, not two, but <u>six</u> letters from you, three from Pat, one from Mama mio, one from my little sister, one from my cousin, and two Valentines from friends. Fourteen in all. I walked in the room and stuck up my nose at everybody.

Perea hasn't heard from his girl in four days, and this afternoon, I was telling him about how much you write me, cause you love me. I kept on, till he almost cried. So tonight, he wrote her a letter and bawled her out cause I got 9 letters from you since Wednesday and he didn't get any. You keep them coming honey. You'll never know how happy you're making me.

I sing solo, and with a group, too. Most of the time I was singing solo hillbilly songs. Then later that night, I sang with another guy, songs like "In the Evening by the Moonlight," and "Shine on Harvest Moon." Yesterday I got a personal letter of commendation from the C.O. He seemed to like my singing. Big deal. By the way, my C.O. is from Texas! Lubbock.

Goodnight Vivian darling. I'll be dreaming of you. I love you.

Your Johnny

~

My Baby Darling,

Ok, so I had to write and tell you I got promoted. I did, finally, just like you said. I'm proud of it, even though it isn't much. I was about to get an inferiority complex. So, don't insult me anymore by putting "PFC" on my letters.

When I found out I was promoted, I was going out to celebrate tonight but I had another talk with myself. I decided I wouldn't, and we'd both celebrate when I get back. Not get drunk, but just go out and spend all the money we can in one night. But it won't be just one night. I hope we'll be celebrating a lifetime together.

Goodnight my darling. I love you with all my heart.

Your Johnny

~

February 26, 1952
Midnight 30

My Baby,

Honey, I really don't know what nationality I am except a little Indian. And I didn't know I had an Italian name. My dad can't trace his ancestors any further back than his grandfather. It seems some of the Indians were kind of peaceful in those days. My dad shows Indian blood a lot more than I do. I really don't know what I am honey. I'm just a cur, but I'm almost positive my kids are going to be part Italian. A bunch of little dark hair and eye kids with skin like their beautiful mother's. You have the prettiest skin on earth.

I love you darling with all my heart.

Your
Johnny

~

February 27, 1952

My Baby,

Perea hasn't heard from his girl in 16 days. For a while he almost went nuts, but lately I think he's getting bitter. He won't hardly talk to anyone. He'll probably be getting a "Dear John" pretty soon, if he gets a letter at all. There's already been three in this room that broke up with their girls. Those familiar letters, that start off, "Dear John, I think you're wonderful, <u>but</u> . . ." You know what I believe honey? I don't believe they had much between them in the first place. I know there's something between us honey. I don't know how to say exactly how I feel way down inside, but I know our love is stronger than that. It's been

57

tried before and proved positive, and darling I think it will always prove positive. You make me very happy darling. More than you'll ever know, and I know that I'm the luckiest guy alive to have a sweetheart like you.

I love you with all my heart.

Your Johnny

~

February 27, 1952

My darling,

Back again honey and it's after midnight again, but I'm not sleepy. I like to write you in the wee small hours of the morning when it's quiet.

Today I was talking to an Italian guy I live with, about you. I was telling him about how we trust each other, etc. And you know what he said? He said I was nuts. He said there wasn't a woman alive that wouldn't lie to you, especially an Italian woman. He married one and they were divorced, guess that's why he talks like that. I don't tell many people that we trust each other like we do, or they would laugh at me. But I know my Vivian. They could never make me believe any different. I've convinced some of them by letting them read some of your letters. Some of them say "She's just feeding you a line," then I open up my box with all the letters you've written me in it, and they shut up. It would have been a pretty long line.

Goodnight sweetheart. I love you with all my heart, which belongs to you in the first place.

Your Johnny

~

March 3, 1952

My Vivian,

Honey, two or three times I've started to ask you if you smoked, because I was almost positive you did when we were with Jeanette and Jean. But I didn't ask you if you smoked because I was afraid it would make you mad, and I thought if you did smoke it would get on your conscience and you'd tell me about it sooner or later because you knew how I felt about it. And I was right.

I forgive you for it honey, and I believe you from the bottom of my heart that you won't do it again if you say you won't. It didn't make me mad when you told me honey because I expected it. Maybe I'm wrong to let it mean so much to me darling, but it does, and I can't help it. I came from a small town honey, where nice girls don't do things like that, and I can't get over it. Some guys don't care what their girls do, but I'm one who does, very much. I always put girls that smoke, drink, and curse all in one class. You know the class.

Honey, you know I love you, and I also respect you. If I didn't respect you,

I couldn't love you very much. Understand darling? You see honey, I'm thinking about a future for us, and I want you to be the mother of my kids, and I don't want you to change. Right now I think you'd be the best wife and mother in the world. I think you're wonderful darling, and I love you.

I had heard of blanket parties, but the only kind of "blanket party" I was ever involved in was with the boys only. What we (the A.F.) call a blanket party is, when a guy does something wrong or gives somebody a dirty deal that makes a lot of us mad, somebody slips up on him, throws a blanket over his head, then everybody slugs him. He never says anything about it, because he doesn't know who hit him, and if he does tell, he knows the same thing will happen to him again. I guess the blanket party there was <u>quite</u> different.

I love you, and you alone with all my heart.

Your Johnny

~

March 12, 1952

My Vivian,

I just got off work, and I'm going to write you one letter now, and another one tonight. I'm straining myself to do this, but I haven't written much lately and I wanted to make up for it. Even though you don't love me anymore because I didn't get a letter from you today, and I only got seven yesterday.

Honey, I was just reading over those seven letters, and you said I was too good for you. Don't ever say that. I know it's not right. So you did take a couple of drinks once, and smoke a few cigarettes. That doesn't mean you're a "Female Dillinger." Forget that honey. It's all past and forgotten as far as I'm concerned.

I love you Viv. I'll always love you.

Your Johnny

~

March 12, 1952

My darling,

Honey, you say you don't mind me going out with girls over here, then you say you want me to have fun, just so it's clean fun. You don't sound like you know why I go out with these girls over here. I'm afraid to think what you'll think about me if you don't. There's no way to have "clean fun" with these girls. They're all a bunch of drunks and pickups. Every single one of them. They're always trying to get soldiers to buy them drinks, and give them money and worse.

I feel like someone that's in a place that smells like rotten eggs and is trying to get a breath of fresh air, but can't. Did you ever feel that way? I'm always looking for something, but can't find it. What I need to do is see you and talk to you, but I can't. That's what I mean when I say I want you to help me forget a lot of things. I want you to help me forget these ugh! women over here. Honey, I love you so much. Please believe that and trust me.

I was just telling this Italian guy <u>again</u> how much you love me, and vice versa, and he said he was just kidding. He believes you love me, and he knows I love you. He talks with an Italian accent and he says "You love that little Dago, so write to her. Always write to her, and when you get back, she'll be waiting for you." I love you little darling.

Always remember I love you.

Your boy

~

March 12, 1952

My Baby,

I just got back from the show, and I'm gonna write you again. It won't be long cause there's nothing to write about.

I promised I'd tell you everything, so I'll tell you this. There's a girl here on the base that is real nice looking. A blond. I've seen her around a few times, and talked to her once or twice, and she is nice. Her dad is a Captain stationed here, and it sure was nice talking to her after the girls I see in Munich. I had a date with her tonight, but she had to go home early, so we didn't do much talking. I hope you don't mind honey, she's only five years old. I sat beside her in the show and bought her some popcorn, and she told me about the teddy bear Santa Claus brought her. Quite a love affair.

Goodnight Sweetheart. Keep writing and loving me.

Your Johnny

~

March 20, 1952

Hello Darling,

Honey, I've gotten one letter from you in eight days. I thought until today it was because the mail service is screwed up, but today, a big load of mail came in, and everybody, I think, had mail but me. I hope you're not sick darling, but something is wrong somewhere. I've been bluer yesterday and today than I ever have been and at mail call today I was almost sick. The boys are laughing at me honey. They want to know what happened to "that girl that loves you so much."

I'll go nuts if I don't hear from you.

Goodnight sweetheart. I love you.

Your Johnny

~

March 25, 1952

My Baby,

I wasn't expecting a letter today, but I got one, and I was very happy honey. Lately I haven't been worth killing, but I've felt good all day after I got this letter. I love you little baby.

Perea got a "Dear John" today. I told him he would after that mean letter he wrote her. She really "sent his saddle home," and he's about to go nuts. I love you Vivian. I love you. I love you. I love you.

Baby, I hope you pass those exams, and I know you will with that brain. It's going to be good having you honey. At least there'll be one in the family with brains. I'm sitting here looking at your picture and thinking how nice it would be to kiss you again. Even on your little pug nose, and put my face in your hair. Remember when your hair used to get in my face at the drive-in? That seems like years ago.

Goodnight darling. I love you with all my heart.

Your Johnny

~

March 29, 1952
11 am

My Baby,

I just went to mail call and I got two more letters from you. That makes seven in the last three days. Honey, I'll never gripe again.

And I'm in love with you honey. I never fell so hard in my life. I think about you every minute of the day and you're with me everywhere I go. Don't ever worry about me stopping loving you darling, because I know I never will. I've got you so deep under my skin, that you're a part of me. Someday I'm going to be back with you for good darling. Just stay exactly like you are till I get back.

I love you little darling.

Your Johnny

~

April 7, 1952

My Vivian,

I asked you in a letter about two months ago why you didn't ever tell me about your dates, but I guess you didn't get it. You know it's your privilege whether you want to or not, but as I said, I'm always wondering where you are and what you're doing. I don't want to know so I can criticize, but I'm always wondering. I love you Vivian and it's only natural that I would wonder where you are and what you're doing.

Something else you said was "I love you Johnny, please get that in your little mind and keep it there, please darling." I happen to have an I.Q. of 108. That's at least average. Honey, you've convinced me you love me, but I can't see why you make remarks like that. I could think of a different way to tell you I loved you.

Honey will you please send me some of the pictures. I asked you three months ago to send me some snapshots. Will you? You know I only have one pose of you. I'd like to have a picture of you in shorts or a swimming suit. Ok? Please.

I love you Vivian darling.

Your Johnny

~

April 10, 1952

My Baby,

Honey, you know I do trust you and you can feel free to tell me about all your dates. I know before you met me you had lots of dates, and it would torture you more than me if you couldn't have dates now. So please feel free to tell me about all of them, and I'll promise not to ever run you down about your dates. I'm glad my baby is so popular and I hope it will always be just like you say, just friends and I hope none of them ever get "Vivian on the Brain" like I have. Someday, I'm going to make you forget all of them honey. When I get back they're going to have to find another little girl.

Darling, when you tell a guy that you love a guy in Germany and you're going to wait for him two years, I'll bet he laughs, doesn't he? They laugh at me when I tell them you're going to wait for me. They say, "I'll bet she's out with someone else now." I tell them I know you're out with someone else, but you're still true to me, and still love me. And they can't understand that. Honey, I've never trusted a girl like I've trusted you. I know you're one in a million. I love you Vivian.

Your
Johnny

~

April 11, 1952

Hi Sweetheart,

Honey, I noticed on one of your letters you wrote, "Johnny Ralph Cash." I don't remember ever telling you my name was Ralph. Because I didn't ever think of that name. I remember telling you once that my middle name was Roger, because a lot of the boys at Brooks used to call me John Roger. But it's not. I don't even have a middle name. Just the initial, "R." At least that's what my folks say. And that's what's on my birth certificate.

This morning I went to the snack bar and they got some new records on the juke box, and one of them is "San Antonio Rose," by Bob Wills. I played it about three times while I was drinking a cup of coffee.

I love you Viv darling.

Your Johnny

~

Johnny mentions carving "Johnny loves Vivian" again, this time in a tree.

April 13, 1952

My Baby,

Good morning sweetheart. I just got up and now I'm writing my baby. I have to go to work at eleven oclock and work about two hours, even though I am on pass. I went on a two day pass yesterday afternoon, but they told me not to go anywhere, because I'm going to be needed about two hours today. Did I tell you about two weeks ago I was indoctrinated to see Top Secret stuff? They've been working me pretty hard since then.

I did something real romantic yesterday honey. There was about five of us boys sitting out on the grass by the fence. But that wasn't the romantic part. I carved "Johnny Loves Vivian" on a tree. Wasn't that sweet? On a US Government property tree. I love you baby.

Keep writing and stay sweet for me.

Your Johnny

~

April 14, 1952

My Viv,

If you only knew how lonesome I am for you baby! It wouldn't be so bad if I could have a date once in a while, but I can't even do that. I envy those guys that take you out, and I'd give anything if I could be in their place just one night. Honey, do you love me as much as you ever did? I probably sound like a little kid now, but I love you as much as I ever did, and I need a lot of re-assurance. Honey, I can't see how I can stay away from you for so long because I'm afraid I'll lose you. I know you've told me a hundred times that you'd wait for me and keep loving me, but when I think how long it's going to be, I start thinking things again. Vivian if I could, I'd lay down and cry like a baby, because I love you so much and want to be with you so much and know you're mine. Honey, if you only knew how it is over here. It seems I'm just waiting around for something to happen, but I don't know what. Sometimes I get so mad at this place I could commit murder. Sometimes I hate everybody I meet and can't even stand to look at the guys in my own room. I was never this way before, and I hope sometimes I'll learn to like this place, but it seems to get worse all the time.

You told me I shouldn't get drunk too late honey. Yesterday afternoon six of us walked to Landsberg and got drunk. We really got plastered. We stayed in Landsberg till about ten oclock last night, and got the bright idea to walk <u>back</u> to the base too. Then we got a brighter idea to take a shortcut across the field which wasn't a shortcut after all. It was about two miles further which made it about 6 miles. Then we decided to be men of the world and take off our shoes. We walked at least four miles bare-footed, and with our coat, hat and tie off. And when we got here, we didn't take the trouble to go around to the gate to get in. We climbed the fence. In all, we walked about 12 miles yesterday, and to about two oclock this morning. But we still weren't tired, and I stayed up and wrote you a letter this morning, but you won't get it. I read it over today when I got up, and it wasn't very nice. Rather passionate. I surprise myself sometimes and if you'd got that one, you'd never write me again.

I got a letter from my brother in Memphis today, and he saw your picture. Here's what he said "I saw your girl's picture. Pretty girl. Looks like she's got brains with all the extras." He told me once that before I fell in love with a girl with bright eyes, to be sure that brightness isn't the sun shining through the back of her head. I love you, bright eyes.

I go to work at midnight tonight, working till eight in the morning. After a week of that I'll be ready for the grave. I'll try to write every day though.

Remember I'll always love you, Vivian.

Your Johnny

~

April 25, 1952

My Baby,

Honey, in two more months I win a $10 bet. The first of January one of the boys bet me $10 that you'd write me a "Dear John" before the first of July. That's one bet I'm almost positive I'll win. I'll send you half of it, ok?

By the way, today I showed your picture to a guy from Texas, the one of you sitting on the divan, and he said "Now! Who says Texas hasn't got the prettiest women in the world?" He said something else, but I won't tell you.

Baby, I love you.

Your Johnny

~

May 5, 1952
Monday

My Baby,

Darling, they didn't have any graduation congratulation cards at the P.X., but I'll be thinking of you, and you know your happiness is my happiness. I'm proud of you baby. I wish I could be there and see you at all those services. I know you'll be beautiful. If you take any pictures in your gown, send me one will you darling?

Baby, I love you so much. Lately, I've been dreaming about you every night. I used to just dream about you once in a while, but lately I've been dreaming of you every night almost. Last night I dreamed I went home, and my mother met me at the door and said there was someone to see me in the kitchen. I went in the kitchen and you were standing there smiling, but you had tears in your eyes. You know what I did then? I grabbed you and kissed you. Smack! It was so nice baby, then I woke up. I always wake up.

I love you Vivian darling.

Your Johnny

~

May 16, 1952

My Darling,

Honey, I wish I could tell you about my job, but I can't. I'm not trying to sound like a big wheel because I'm not, but I would get 20 years in jail if I told you about it and they found out. I told you I heard of one guy that did get 20 years, and he could have gotten life, or the firing squad. Pardon me for bragging, but this is the most important squadron in Europe, and thousands are depending on us. There are 800 in this squadron, and 50 of us are allowed to handle "Top Secret." And believe me, it is "Top Secret." I'll clue you in about that honey. "Top Secret" is information that if it gets in the wrong hands, could cause serious damage to the whole nation. So I have to keep my big mouth shut. We're only 16 minutes by air from that "dangerous zone" the nun told you about, and as Eddy Arnold says, "You know how talk gets around." So I can't tell you. You understand don't you honey? I trust you with it, but the Air Force doesn't trust you.

I'd like to see you with your shorts and little halter on honey. I'd probably start climbing the walls if I did. I haven't seen a girl dressed like that since last summer. No matter what you wore you'd look good to me. When we're married, I'm going to make you wear shorts all the time. Well, most of the time.

I love you my little sweet baby darling. I love you, love you, love you.

Your every own
Johnny

~

May 24, 1952

My Darling,

I didn't have to stand the inspection this morning, so I went over to the service club and played records. Honey, they've got all of "our" records over there. Honey, they've got "These Things I Offer You," "I Still Feel the Same About You," and a lot more that remind me of you. I played records all morning and thought about you. Honey, I love you so much it hurts. I'll never stop loving you Viv.

In just three days you'll be graduating. Honey, I'd give anything if I could be there to see you, then take you out afterwards. I want to take you everywhere and show the world what a sweet little girl I've got. We're going to show them all when I get back darling.

Your Johnny Forever

Honey, now they're playing "No Other Love." Darling, I love you so much.

~

May 25, 1952

My Sweet Baby,

I'm sitting in the hall writing this. Maybe you can decipher it. It's just like a circus out here watching all the drunks come back from town and the Airmen's club. They all want to know what I'm doing. I told one I was writing poetry.

Darling, I'm sorry this is so short, but there's not a thing to write about. I just wanted to tell you I love you. It would take this whole box of stationery to tell you just how I felt about you. Honey, don't ever stop loving me.

Your Johnny

~

May 26, 1952

My Darling Viv,

Yes, I think Perea and his girlfriend made up honey. He got three letters from her last week, and another one today. He got her picture out, and he takes it to bed with him every night now.

I think Perea was a little mad at me. You see, when Rita wrote him the "Dear John," he bought a little doll in Landsberg and set it up over his bed, and every time he'd leave the room, I'd turn it upside down. It had real bright green panties. He didn't like that because he said that was the only girl he had left. He would turn its dress down and tell me to leave her alone because his little doll is modest. I think he got pretty mad about it a couple of times. But now he doesn't care because he got his Rita back.

Yes baby, we're going to make up for lost time when I get back. We're going to have the rest of our lives.

I love you with all my heart always.

Your Johnny

~

May 28, 1952

My Sweetheart,

We're having a party Saturday night. It's for all us guys that work on the shift I'm on, four or five officers and their wives, and girls that boys bring along. We're having it at a guest house down in the mountains on a lake. I don't know exactly what kind of party it is going to be. Probably a drunken brawl. I wish there was something to do besides something like that. I wouldn't even go but one of the officers asked me to be on the entertainment committee. There are three of us. Two that play instruments and myself, to try to sing. I'll tell you all about it when it's over honey.

I love you always and always.

Your Johnny

~

June 1, 1952

My Darling Viv,

We had the big party last night, such as it was. I got disgusted and came back last night at midnight. I think all but about 3 or 4 were drunk, and believe it or not, I was one that wasn't. Four of us didn't drink a thing but Coke. There wasn't any girls there except two or three hags someone drug in, and there wasn't a thing to do but drink. I sang myself hoarse and at midnight a few wanted to come back, so I did too. They wanted me to stay all night but I couldn't see it. The guy that drove us down there was too drunk to drive back last night, and I was the only sober one that came back at midnight, so I had to drive the truck all the way back. I was nearly dead when I got to bed this morning. So that was our big party honey. I danced once or twice with a waitress that looked like Dracula's mother. Some fun.

Honey, I can't see how boys can go out and get plastered, fight and raise cain, and say they had fun. I'm no angel, but it disgusts me to see something like that "party" last night. Maybe I'm still a kid, but if these are men that I run around with, I hope I never grow up. Even though I have drank, I hate drinking and I'll always hate it. I don't think it was meant for me to be in a place like this. I should be with you.

I love you Viv. I love you with all my heart.

Your Johnny

~

June 2, 1952

My Sweet Baby,

Honey, how much does that silver set cost in all? How often do you have to make a payment on it? Next month I'll send you some money honey. And I want to pay for the rest of it if they'll take the payments at the time I can send the money. I don't want anyone else to pay anymore on it. I want us, or myself to pay for it. Ok?

Some of the boys said I was crazy. They said I won't be back for two years, and you're buying a silver set for Vivian and some other guy. But they don't know my Vivian. I love you darling, and I think you're the most wonderful girl on earth. I'll always love you honey.

Your Johnny

~

June 4, 1952

My Baby,

I didn't get a letter from you today either honey. I've only gotten one letter in six days. Don't you love me anymore? I miss your letters so much baby. I nearly go nuts when I don't hear from you.

Pretty soon, Monday I think, I'm going on a special assignment. I don't know where I'm going and couldn't tell you if I did, but I'll be gone about ten days or two weeks. I can write you, and I can get your mail where I go honey, but it will be a few days late. I'll let you know all I can about it before I leave honey.

I love you darling.

Your Johnny Always

~

June 5, 1952

My Darling Viv,

I finally got a letter honey. In fact I got four long ones. I'm very happy again baby.

Darling, I'm sorry I made you feel like a heel. You're not, and I didn't mean to make you feel like one. Darling, I wish I could talk to you, but I can't, so I'll have to write it the best I can. Viv, you are deserving of my love. Anyone would

JUNE 4TH
3 AM

MY DARLING VIV,
     I'M ABOUT TO GO TO SLEEP ON THE JOB HONEY, SO I
DECIDED TO WRITE YOU BEFORE I DO. THIS JOB IS A
PAIN IN THE NECK, OR WAS UP TILL ABOUT ONE O'CLOCK.
ALL THE DRUNKS COMING IN MAKING NOISE, AND# I HAVE
TO TELL THEM TO SHUT UP NO MATTER HOW BIG THEY ARE.
I HAVEN'T HAD ANY TROUBLE YET THOUGH, AND THE CQ
USUALLY DOES. THINGS ARE REAL QUIET NOW AT LAST.
ALL I HAVE TO DO IS ANSWER THE PHONE AND WRITE MY
BABY. AND YOU SHOULD HEAR SOME OF THE PHONE CALLS
I GET. MOST OF THEM ARE GERMAN GIRLS CALLING SOME
GUY IN THE SQUADRON. THEY WANT ME TO GO WAKE UP
THEIR BOY FRIENDS SO THEY CAN TALK TO THEM, BUT I
USUALLY JUST HANG UP. I GOT ONE CALL TONIGHT FROM
THE STATES. A WOMAN IN HARTFORD, CONN. WAS CALLING
HER SON TO TELL HIM THAT HIS SISTER HAD A BABY, AND
ALL WAS WELL. I DIDN'T GET TO TALK TO THE WOMAN.
THE OPERATOR JUST TOLD ME THERE WAS A CALL FROM THE
STATES FOR THIS GUY, AND I HAD TO GO GET HIM.
     DARLING, I DIDN'T GET A LETTER FROM YOU TODAY.
YOU DON'T LOVE ME ANYMORE. JUST A LITTLE MAIL CAME
IN, SO MAYBE YOUR LETTERS DIDN'T COME. I SHOULD
GET TWO OR THREE TOMORROW, BECAUSE I ONLY GOT ONE
IN FIVE DAYS.
     I LIKE MY NEW ROOM JUST FINE HONEY. EVERYTHING
IS A LOT QUIETER WHERE I AM NOW, AND THERE AREN'T
QUITE AS MANY IN THE ROOM AS THERE WAS IN THE OTHER
ONE. I SHOULD GET #### ENOUGH SLEEP FROM NOW ON.
     VIV, I LOVE YOU. I'VE BEEN THINKING OF YOU ALL
NIGHT, AND GETTING MORE LONESOME FOR YOU EVERY MIN-
UTE. EVERYWHERE I GO, AND EVERYTHING I DO, YOU'RE
ALWAYS ON MY MIND. VIVIAN DARLING, WILL YOU MARRY ME?
IN TWO YEARS, THAT IS? I JUST WANTED TO ASK YOU NOW,
THEN ASK YOU AGAIN WHEN I GET BACK TO YOU. DARLING,
I THINK YOURE THE MOST WONDERFUL GIRL ON EARTH, AND
I'M THE LUCKIEST GUY ON EARTH TO HAVE A GIRL LIKE YOU,
AND TO KNOW THAT YOURE GOING TO BE MINE SOME DAY.
     BABY, I LOVE YOU.
HONEY, I CAN'T THINK OF A THING TO WRITE SO I MIGHT
AS WELL STOP. I'LL BE LOOKING FORWARD TO A LETTER
FROM YOU TODAY.

GOODNIGHT SWEETHEART. I LOVE YOU. I'LL ALWAYS LOVE
YOU VIVIAN. DONT EVER FORGET THAT I LOVE YOU.

                              YOUR JOHNNY

70

be. I know I've done things worse than you have. Even though I say I hate drinking and dime-a-dozen girls, I've been right in with the motley crew before. It makes me sick when I take a look at myself sometimes honey. If I could be there with you I could be decent. Over here nobody cares. Boys grow up fast over here honey, and 95% grow up on the left side. I've been trying to be part of that 5% that don't, for you, so I would deserve your love. I'm not too good for you, Viv, and will never be.

Honey, someday we're going to be married and happy. I'll be the happiest guy in the world when I start living with you.

Vivian darling, I love you with all my heart and soul.

Your Johnny

~

June 13, 1952

My Darling,

Viv, I've never told you much about my family, but since you've been writing my mother, I think you've learned a little about it. Since we're planning on getting married, I think you should know a little about it. Up till about four years ago when my dad quit farming, we didn't exactly live "high class," as a matter of fact, we were in misery part of the time. Not cold, and never hungry, but every penny had to go for essential things. Since my sister married, and I left home, they've started to live a little comfortable. It's always been a respectable family, that is, for the last eight years since my dad quit drinking, but a poor family.

Honey, remember when you said you didn't think boys noticed things like you and your mother kissing. I'll tell you why I noticed it. Because I never saw it in my family except when one of us would be gone a long time, then come back to visit. My parents love us all, and always did, but they weren't the kind to show it all the time. I remember when my brother died, and I thought my mother would never get over it and that was the only time I ever saw my dad cry. Up to that time my dad was hard hearted and cruel, but since then he's changed.

Since I've been in the Air Force is the only time they've really shown their affection for me. When I went home on my first leave my mother said to me one day in the kitchen, "Did you know I love you?" I knew she did, but she never told me before. Then when I left you and went home, my dad said, "We've never shown you kids much affection, but we think a lot of you, all of you, and we're proud of you." I know my face turned red.

Maybe it was mostly our fault that there wasn't much affection in the family. I never showed my parents much, and I would do anything for them, and love them both.

Honey, maybe you don't want to hear all this, but I thought you should know about the family now. Oh, I'll go on. There's one of my sisters honey that I've never kissed in my life. The one that's 18. We grew up together, worked in the fields together, and fought every day. I don't think there were many kind words between us until she got married.

When I "grew up" I wanted to let her know that I thought a lot of her, but I didn't know how, and I didn't even have the courage to kiss her when I went home on leave. I didn't even kiss her when I left to come over here. I've thought about it so much, about her, my parents, and my other brothers and sisters that it nearly drives me nuts. I did one decent thing, though. About a month ago I wrote my sister and told her how much I loved her, and was sorry that I'd never treated her like a sister should be treated. She answered back and said about the same thing I did. I feel a lot cleaner inside now, honey. I never fought with my older sister. We were almost like brother and sister should be to each other.

Honey, I don't think you know yet just what the family is like, but you know a little about it now. I was trying to show you the difference in our families so you'd know what kind of family I've got. The way I lived is 100% different from the way you live honey. It's a little different now honey. My folks even start my letters off "Dearest" now.

So you know now that I wasn't raised on Park Avenue. I was raised in a cotton patch. You never asked me anything about my home life or how I was raised. So maybe it doesn't make any difference to you. That you love me is the only thing I'm interested in. I believe I can make you happy. I know I love you, and I'll always love you darling.

Honey, I sent in a request to the "Cowboy Roundup" for you today. I hope they play it for you Friday night. Listen to the words if they do, honey. I mean every one of them.

Honey, I guess I've run down, so I'll close. I'll write again tomorrow, baby. Keep those precious letters coming darling.

I love you Viv. I love you with all my heart and I'll always love you darling.

Your Johnny

~

June 15, 1952

My Darling Viv,

Darling are you actually happier since you gave up dates? I hope you are, and I'm glad you're serious about it. Honey, I really do love you more all the time, and because I love you more, that's why I'd resent anyone else being with you. I can't help it. I love you so much it hurts. But darling, what are you going to do when your hope chest fills up? I hope you never get as lonesome as I am.

I don't believe you could stand it, and I don't see how I can. I thought when spring came that it would be different but I don't think it is. I've tried to laugh and have fun, but there's no fun to be had. I get out and play ball for a couple of hours, and that's a couple of hours that I can forget everything else, but when I come back in, I have to look at the same faces, do the same things over and over. I'd rather be in jail. It's enough to give a person claustrophobia.

One of my buddies is in here playing the guitar honey. He's playing "Santone Rose." He's just trying to make me blue. I feel like bawling already.

So long for now darling. I love you.

Your Johnny

~

June 19, 1952

My Darling Viv,

Darling, you'd better look in the mirror again. You're not horrible. You're not even gruesome. Baby, I think you're beautiful. I know what I'm getting, or I think I do. You've got what it takes honey, and on you it looks good. I don't know exactly what you've got, but I know I'm a lucky guy to get you. I was looking at your picture the other day honey and thinking how small and sweet you are, and what a beast you're getting. But as Jack says, "That's the way the ball bounces."

I love you darling. I love you with all my heart.

Your Johnny

~

June 21, 1952

My Sweet Baby,

Baby, I'm going to write you, then I'm going back to bed. I didn't get enough sleep because they made us get up and go to a lecture of the "Marshall Plan." I care about as much about the Marshall Plan as I do Roy Acuff's dog.

Darling, I've done gone to the Air Force and made good. I'm a "senior" now on the job. The orders came out on me yesterday. That means that I can be trusted to handle any job no matter how important it is, and it also means that I'll be eligible for Staff Sgt on this tour of duty. Big deal. I'm a big wheel.

I love you with all my heart. I'll always love you sweetheart.

All my love all my life,
Your Johnny

~

June 22
midnite

My Darling Viv,

Baby, I just got off work and I'm going to write you a little then going to bed cause I'm tired.

Viv, I love you so much, and miss you more every day. If only I had you darling, everything would be alright.

Baby, I got a pleasant surprise last night. Myself and two other guys were picked out of about 40 to train for "Trick Chief." You dont know a trick chief from Adam, do you? Well, on my job, the "trick chief" is in charge of operations. There's about 50 men under him. The other two that are training ~~are~~ have been here longer than I have and one of them is a staff sgt, so I dont think I've got a chance to get

74

the job, but at least it will be two
weeks that I wont have to work much
And it makes me feel pretty good
for them to pick me out of that
many. I trained last night and tonight, and so far I think I'm
doing alright.

Baby, I was thinking tonight of
those driveins we used to go to, when
we'd sit on Wayne's car and smooch.
I've thought about that so much
that holding you in my arms would
be like a dream. I'd give my left
ear if I could hold you in my arms
now. Honey, I never thought I'd
love anyone as much as I love you.
I'll always love you V.V.

Baby, I'm going to bed now.
I'll write you again sometime
tomarrow.

Goodnight sweetheart I love

75

YOU.

your
johnny

I love you darling.

My Sweet Baby,

Honey, I just got off work again and took a shower and I'm writing you before I go to bed. I don't think I'll have time when I get up because I've got a lot to do. Honey, don't be surprised if you see my name in the paper for murder someday. These guys are always griping about me writing so many letters. And sometimes it makes me a little mad. I'm living in a room with a bunch of dumb, conceited, selfish, buffering Yankees, and I'm thinking about reviving the Civil War.

Today I was arguing with one of those guys, a "hot rod" from California, and I was sitting in the window calling him names, and he threw a wooden shower clog at me. You should see him now baby. He's got a big blue spot under his left eye where I hit him with my little hand. He's sitting over there griping now because the lights are on, but I've got to write my baby.

I love you.
Your Johnny

~

In this letter Johnny told me about the death of his brother Jack.

July 1, 1952

My Darling Viv,

Honey, it's easy to be true to you. It's no sacrifice at all. There will never be anyone but you Vivian, and I think it's only natural that we should be true to each other. You make me so happy darling when you say that you do want to. I get so lonesome I could go nuts, but I can wait for you honey, and I will.

Yes, honey, I lost a brother. Viv, I want to tell you something so you'll know about a few things. I won't go into the details about it, but I want to tell you why I hate drinking. He was 14 at the time and was working in the high school shop for the agriculture teacher so he could have a little money. That was May 1944. He was jerked into a swinging saw, and cut deep. Everybody knew he wouldn't live, and everybody in the whole town visited him in the 8 days that he lived. He was a paper boy, and everybody knew him. My oldest brother was working in Port Arthur, Texas and he came home. Up to that time, my dad had been anything but decent, but the night before my brother died the next day, my dad prayed all night. I sat and listened to him crying and praying, and several more men and women there, crying and praying. I was only 12 at the time, but I promised myself right there that if I ever got married, there wouldn't be any drinking in my family. It's been eight years, and I still feel the same way. Now you know why I raised so much cain when you told me you had two shots New Years. And that's why I'm not drunk every pass I get, and that's why I'm not in town tonight where most of the boys are.

I don't suppose there's all that much sin in drinking itself, but all my life drinking has been associated with hungry kids and unhappy homes, so for me, it's taboo.

Darling, I like it when you talk about old times, our wonderful times together. I've relived them all a dozen times. Honey, we're both going to be lonesome for a long time, but when I get back, we're going to make up. I want to show the world that you're mine, and that I love you. I'm going to kiss you in anybody's drive-in, or taxicab. I'd give anything just to kiss you once now, darling.

Honey, the G.I. Bill of Rights was passed and when I'm discharged, they'll give me a $300 bonus and I'll be paid $110 a month till I get a job. Pretty neat, huh? We'll have something to start on sweetheart with what I can save. Viv, I wish you'd spend your money on yourself, and things you want. I appreciate your saving for us, but you're doing enough by filling that hope chest. After all, I'm supporting you and I'm wearing the pants in the family. See? At least I'm wearing the longer ones.

Baby, I'm going to close for now and I'll write again tomorrow.

Yours always,
Johnny

～

July 2, 1952

My Sweet Baby,

Honey, a friend of mine went down to the French Zone last night, and met some girls, and is going back tonight and wanted me to go back with him and meet them, but I'm not going. He said I was crazy because I'd been away from girls five months, and these are good looking. I wouldn't go if they were queens. They may be nice looking, but I told him I wouldn't go. I'm going to stay here and go swimming this afternoon, and to the show tonight, then play pool a while and come back and maybe write you again. I'd rather sit and just think of you, and write you than to be out trying to have a good time with someone else. I don't want any French girls, or any German girls. All I want is one little Italian girl named Viv. You know anyone named that darling?

Your Johnny

～

My Darling Viv,

Tomorrow is the 4th of July, and you know what I'm going to do? Work. I'll be thinking about you darling and wondering what you're doing. I'd give anything to spend one day with you. Your dad wouldn't call you off the porch at midnight because Viv wouldn't be there at midnight.

Honey, that night you were talking about, when you and I, Pat & Wayne were on the lawn. I didn't think you enjoyed that night. I never will forget the expression on your face that night. Every time I kissed you, you'd blink your eyes and stare at me, with that expression on your face "I'm just a little girl." That was a wonderful night darling, and I told all the boys back at the base about it. That was a night when you made me so happy darling. Remember when Ray came back and he asked me why you and I didn't show Pat and Wayne how to kiss. You put your arms around me and closed your eyes. I'll never forget that darling, or you.

Baby, I wish I could be with you and call you darling to your face and tell you how much I love you. You're the only one I'll ever call darling.

Goodnight sweetheart. I love you.

Your Johnny

~

July 4, 1952

My Darling Viv,

I went swimming today after work and tonight I'm writing letters. Big July 4th!! You know what I did darling? I've been watching a woman in a bikini bathing suit. She's out of the pool and we've got a telescope, and we've been watching her. I'm a bad boy. Have you got a bikini bathing suit honey? I'd like to see you in one. I'd like to see you, period.

I love you Viv. Baby, I'll always love you, and I love you always. Does that make sense?

Your Johnny

~

July 5, 1952

My Darling Viv,

I think I do know what you mean about me trusting you darling. I'm glad we trust each other because I mean what I say when I say "No more girls." When this guy tried to get me to go down to the French Zone the other night, and I told him I wouldn't go, he said "What Vivian doesn't know won't hurt her." But it would hurt me to know that I lied to you or kept something from you. I'll never keep anything from you, Viv, and I hope you won't.

Honey, you should take care of yourself. I'm preaching. Get plenty of sleep, drink plenty of milk, and milkshakes, little girl. It's not natural for you to lose weight, and you don't need to lose any. Not that it would make any difference to me, cause I like you slim, but you don't need to lose weight. Have you ever heard the saying men have about skinny women. I'm not going to tell you because you wouldn't tell me those jokes. Besides, it's not nice.

I'll always love you baby.

Your Johnny

~

July 6, 1952

My Sweetheart,

Viv, unless something changes, I'll probably leave here May 1st, 1954. I cringe every time I think about that, but that's the way it is. 21 months darling. If you wait for me that long honey, I'll work my fingers off to the elbow to make you happy. I love you.

Baby, I love you so much, and miss you all the time. I can't sleep for thinking about you. Darling, don't ever stop loving me. You're all the sunshine I have.

Your very own,
Johnny

~

July 8, 1952

My Darling Viv,

Honey, there's something I meant to tell you today at noon, but I forgot. Guess what baby? I'm going up for promotion to Buck Sgt. this month. It was a little hard for me to believe at first, but my officer-in-charge told me this afternoon. I suppose they'll start playing games again, but since I am going in for it this month, that means I'll make it for sure by September. The promotion board doesn't meet till the last of this month, the 26th I think. That means I can save more money for us honey.

Honey, one of the boys was asking me about you and how often I write you. When I told him that we write each other every day, he almost fainted. He said I had it made because if you still write me every day after 10 months, it must be true love and I shouldn't worry about a thing. I do believe in you honey. I'd trust you to the end of the world.

I got an answer to the letter I wrote my sister honey. I'm sending it along for you to read. Honey, I'm sorry my family is running down the Catholic religion, but you wanted to know what they said, so I'm sending it for you to read. Do you know why my family doesn't like the Catholic religion honey? Because they believe in moderate drinking. When it comes to that, we're both going to be good Protestants, if we're married. Honey, tell me the honest truth do you believe in moderate drinking, and do you have any desire to drink?

I don't want to make you mad honey, but I want your opinion on these things. I just wondered what your parents had taught you about it. And do you think I can mix in with your family and friends without drinking a little? Please tell me just exactly what you think about it.

I love you with all my heart, Viv.

Yours always,
Johnny

~

July 11, 1952

My Darling Viv,

I went to Munich yesterday about noon with another guy. I won't lie to you honey. I got drunk. I got so drunk I couldn't walk. I couldn't stand it anymore. I couldn't have any fun, so I did it. There wasn't any girls involved honey. There were lots of them there, but I didn't go with any of them. I almost got in trouble over a girl. One came up and sat down by me and started begging me for drinks and money and I was ignoring her and she started calling me names. I hit her with the back of my hand and knocked her out of her chair flat on the floor. The Germans called the police, or MPs, rather, and they came out and got me and took me to the train station and told me to stay there until I could get a train back to Landsberg. I stayed there till 4:30 and caught the train. So that's what your future "ideal husband" did last night. I thought the MPs would arrest me, but they said they wouldn't since the Germans wouldn't lock up the street walkers.

I don't know what you'll think of me, but I couldn't lie to you, and darling, I didn't touch a girl except the one that I hit, and that isn't on my conscience a bit. She should have been hit. There were several more GIs in the place and they were all for me.

I suppose you think I'm a big fake after what I said about drinking. Maybe I am honey, but I still hate it. I hate every drink that I took last night, and if I was in a place where I could have a little clean fun and happiness, it wouldn't happen.

I love you Viv, I love you with all my heart.

Yours always,
Johnny

July 13, 1952

Darling,

Honey, sometimes I get to thinking, and I must have rocks in my head for ever griping at you for anything. You've taken more off me than any girl ever would, and you still love me and treat me like a king. You're wonderful Vivian, and I only wish I could be more like you in some ways. I'll try not to criticize you or your parents or anyone, none of your friends anymore honey. After what I did in Munich, I haven't got a right to say a word if you get a job as a strip teaser. I know you're wonderful and sweet, and all that a guy could ask for, and it hurts me when I know I've acted so silly. I'll keep trying darling, and for sure, I'll keep loving you. Until I can be back with you and make you my wife, try to have fun and be happy honey. I'm going to be living the rest of my life just to make you happy.

Take care of yourself for me Viv. Do what that doctor says, hear? I'm preaching again.

Your Johnny

~

July 14, 1952

My Little Darling,

I had a crazy dream about us last night. I dreamed I was back with you, but you didn't love me anymore. I dreamed that we met every night on the river where we went walking, and I'd talk with you to see if you had a change of your mind, then one night you brought all the letters I'd ever written you, and threw them in the river. When I woke up, I could still see the letters floating in the water. Then I went down to the mail room and I had three letters from you. You make me so happy baby, and I love you more every day.

All my love.
Your Johnny

~

July 17, 1952

My Vivian,

OK, darling, I'm ashamed of myself for watching the girl in the bikini. I won't do it anymore. I'm glad you didn't know what a bikini is honey.

Thanks for sending the words to those songs honey. They do fit us. I heard the song "It Had to be You" just the other day darling, and was thinking of you. It had to be you darling, and will always be <u>you</u>.

I'd give anything if I could just be with you and tell you "I love you." Someday darling, I'll have the rest of my life to tell you I love you, and prove it.

Yours for life,
Johnny

~

July 18, 1952

My Darling Viv,

Yes, I wish we could be married soon too honey. But we've got a long time. I don't know what to do to make the time shorter. Viv you can still wait that long, can't you? I shouldn't ask, but I want you to keep telling me.

Darling, last night at work I had a "Stability Under Pressure" test. When I went to work, I thought that h—— had busted loose. The officer on duty and two or three S/Sgts started bawling me out about every little thing. No matter what I did, they'd bawl me out and tell me it was wrong. About 10 oclock they put me off "Trick Chief" training and put me back to work, and they still bawled me out, said all my work was wrong. I was about ready to end it all when I left that place last night. I got mad a few times and started to tell them off, but I was lucky I didn't. I even laughed at them once last night. This morning I went back up there and expecting them not to even speak to me, but the S/Sgt in charge called me over and told me what was coming off last night. He congratulated me for holding my temper through all that, and showed me a letter of recommendation that he wrote up on me for Buck Sgt. It made me blush honey. One thing it said on there was "This man maintains a calm attitude and even smiles under the strongest pressure." He recommended me for the job of Trick Chief and Buck Sgt. In all, he wrote up nearly two pages on me, and if I can live up to all that, I'll be a Superman. He really laid it on thick. I also found out that I have the least time in grade for any man in the squadron that's going in for Buck Sgt. this month. I don't think I've got much chance, even with that letter he wrote.

Honey, I'm on pass now, and these guys are trying to get me to go to Munich, but I'm not going. I've had all of that place I want. I'll stay here and go to the movies and write letters. Darling, I guess I'll close now and go eat. I'll write you again tomorrow sweetheart. I love you darling with all my heart. I'll always love you Viv darling.

Your Johnny for life.

~

July 19th

My sweet Baby;
   Honey, I got up and it was too
late for mail call, so I went back to
sleep, and got up again, and we've been
singing, and drinking milk. No, we aint,
we've been drinking Hasenbrau beer,
and singing Hillbilly songs. Darling
what else can I do to have fun? I
try my best, and nothing I can do
around here is any fun. I think about
you all the time, and I nearly go nuts.
Honey, will you forgive me? Viv, I
promise darling, that I wont make
a habit of it. I thought I was going
to be above this, and I try Vivian,
please believe me when I say I try.
I do hate drinking, I hate the taste
of it. I hate the effects of it, and I
hate it that I do it. I'm just plain
stupid to do it when I dont want
to. I use the brains of a two year
old sometime. Viv darling, why does
God make people this way? To be lonely
and blue, and cant find any peace within
themselves? Why didnt he make a
man so he could be contented alone
when he had to be alone? I cant
understand it.

84

Dont worry about me honey. Nothing is going to happen to me. I'd never do anything to harm myself no matter how blue I get. Darling, I was reading in a book where a woman said, "Dont ever think of your troubles, God will take care of them, Think only of your happiness." Most of my happiness is hopes. I try to do what that woman said. I guess I'm lucky after all. I've got you to look forward to as long as you love me, and I'm healthy. Even though I'm full of this stinking, rotten beer, I'm healthy. Viv you dont think I'm bad do you? Honey if you only knew how much you help me. You're helping us both. You're a good influence for us both; I want to do right Viv darling, and as long as you stay as sweet and wonderful, as you are, we can live a happy life. You're sweet and pure Vivian, and I thank God every day for you. Always stay like you are Viv. Let the rest of the world rot, but dont you change. You'd probably laugh if you could hear me say that wouldnt you? You dont think you are because you lose your temper sometimes, and but when you do you're h--- on wheels, but I think you're sweet when you're mad.

Honey, when we're married, I promise
that I'll be above the average as far
as moral living is concerned. I wont
drink honey, and I'll try to give you
a nice home and make it happy
for you. Honey, if you only knew how
many men step out on their wives,
it would make you hide from the
human race. Viv. I know nothing
like that would ever happen as far
as I'm concerned. I couldnt run
around with other women if we
were married if I hated you. It's
not in my blood honey. I dont even
do it now. I'll always be true to you
Viv and give you all my love as long
as you want me.
    Darling, I'm going to sleep now.
I'm completely happy when I'm asleep.
    Honey, I promise I'll write, Syl,
your mom, pat, and Denise in the
next two days. I promise.
    I love you Vivian darling. I
love you so much it hurts. Please
believe in me and understand me
honey. I love you so much.
                    yours forever
                    Johnny

        I love you.
        I love you.

86

July 20, 1952

My darling Viv,

Honey, I just got up and went to chow and took a shower and now I'm writing you.

Darling, I don't know what you'll think of me after yesterday. I hate to even face you today. I hope you won't think too hard of me Viv. I'll try not to let it happen again. I'm so ashamed of myself, but the worst part, I had to write you that silly letter yesterday. I don't expect you to believe me anymore when I say I want to do right and not drink, but I'll keep trying darling if you'll forgive me, and I'll try not to let it happen again.

Honey, in just 14 days, its been a year since I left you. It sure doesn't seem that long since I left you. I guess it's because I've felt so close to you all this time, and I love you more every day darling. I don't think time or anything else will ever change my feelings for you darling. You're wonderful Viv and I love you.

Baby, I've got your big picture sitting here on the window sill. You're looking out the window. I don't know what you're looking at, but you sure look sweet to me.

Yours always,
Johnny

~

July 22, 1952

My Vivian,

Baby, I still can't sleep. When I got off work this morning, I was so tired I was numb all over, but I couldn't sleep over three hours today. If I can't sleep tomorrow, I'm going over and get some sleeping pills at the dispensary. I don't know what it's caused from. I guess I smoke too much and drink too much coffee.

Darling, I don't think I explained it too well about going to school when I get out. You see, under the GI Bill, the Government will pay me about $50 a month to go to school on.

I'm not going to college, but I'm thinking about going to some kind of training school that they will pay me while I train. Like refrigeration mechanics, or something. I've got a long time to think about it and decide.

I love you darling, with all my heart, and I'll always love you.

Yours for life,
Johnny

~

July 23, 1952

My Sweetheart,

Honey, they're playing "Blue Skirt Waltz" now. Remember when we used to skate to that? I miss you so much baby. I'd give anything to be with you tonight.

Honey, did you ever hear the song "River of Roses"? I heard that today too, and of course, I thought about you. It seems like just a few days ago that we walked on the river, but it's been a lot of lonesome days and nights ago. Darling I want to be back with you so bad. I don't know what I'll do without you for so long. Honey, it makes me feel so good to know that you're waiting for me. We'll have the rest of our lives together baby to make up for all this time.

Honey, remember when I kissed you on the river? No, I mean I kissed you on the lips, but we were by the river. We had been sitting on the bench and just got up to leave, and I tried to pull you to me and kiss you, and you held back because you thought someone would be watching and get the wrong idea. You let me kiss you just a little one anyway, and you smiled at me and dropped your head. Honey, I think I was in love with you then. You're the first girl that I wanted to kiss in a public place. No, I mean on the lips, but didn't care who saw it. I remember going home on the bus that night I even wanted to kiss you on the bus. I mean on the lips. Baby, I love you and miss you so much.

I probably sound silly and corny to you, but I'm so lonesome for you darling. I'd give anything to hold you and kiss you right now.

Yours always,
Johnny

~

July 26, 1952

My Darling Viv,

Darling, what do you mean that you hope there's nothing wrong with moderate drinking when you're married? Do you mean for us? Honey, I can't hold it against your family if they honestly believe it's alright. If they believe it, maybe it's alright for them. But I don't believe in it, so it's wrong for me, and I won't do it at all. Darling, you don't have to drink to be sociable, at least I know I don't. Remember Jim Hobbs? He was one of my best friends and he got drunk nearly every time we went to town. The buddy of mine in Alaska was the same way, and I never drank a drop when I was with them. I had as many friends as anybody, and never drank over three bottles of beer in my life before I came over here. I just hate it honey, and I can't help it.

I love you Viv. Keep writing and take care of yourself for me honey. Darling, I love you.

Yours for life,
Johnny

~

My Darling,

Yes, honey, I'd like to get a job in San Antonio, and I'm going to try to. But I don't know exactly what I'll do yet. It could be anywhere. Honey, the reason I asked you that was because of what a guy told me. He asked me if I was going to marry you, and when I told him I was, he said "I feel sorry for you marrying an Italian girl. You'll never get her away from her mother." I know you'd leave your mother honey, but I know anyone hates to leave the place they've lived all their life. We've got a long time to talk about that darling.

I love you Vivian darling. You're the only one I'll ever love Viv.

Your Johnny

~

August 10, 1952

My Vivian,

Darling, I think you're wonderful and I get to thinking sometimes about all of the things you've done for me and hate myself for saying anything hard or sarcastic to you. I know you could have a date every night if you want to, but you gave them all up for me. You could have gotten married, but you'd rather wait two years for me. And all the other things you do. Like the silver set and the hope chest. Darling, I love you so much. I wish I could repay you. I wish I could hold you in my arms and tell you I love you. I'm the luckiest guy alive Vivian, as long as I have you.

Darling, I love you. Always remember that. I love you Vivian darling, with all my heart.

Your Johnny

~

I should explain here that my father was never entirely supportive of my decision to stop dating, and he finally insisted that I get out and meet other boys. Two years, he said, was a long time to stay home, simply waiting for Johnny to return. Johnny graciously accepted the inevitable. I started dating again.

August 11, 1952

My Darling Viv,

After six days without a letter from you, then I get one saying you're going to have dates again, I felt a little bad honey, but you're right, and your dad is right, you should have dates. It's too long for you to not go out with boys. I'll try to look at it as someone grown instead of a jealous 10 year old. I was going to tell you to have dates when you wanted to so you could have a little fun instead of staying home all the time or just going with the girls. But there's something I can't understand honey. I can't understand why your folks want you to have dates unless it's to look for someone else. I wish you'd told me why they want you to.

Go ahead and have dates if you want to honey, and try to have fun. I'll keep the promise I made to you Viv. I won't go with those pigs over here.

But there's something I want you to promise me. I want you to think about it before you do and stick to it if you do. Maybe you won't want to, but I'm asking you to please don't go with one guy more than two or three times. And please, please don't go with that guy, Jay, again. Will you do that for me Vivian? Especially the latter? I know from the way you talk he's been trying to date you again, and if you go with him again, I couldn't stand it Vivian. No matter if he doesn't mean a thing to you.

Honey, I got 33 letters that you wrote in July. Do you think I'll get that many in July next year darling? I guess it will be my fault if I don't. I'm sour as a grapefruit lately.

Yours always,
Johnny

~

August 15, 1952

My Darling,

I'm sorry I couldn't write yesterday honey, but the night before I went to the show, then we came back and got our hillbilly band together and went down in the basement and stayed till daylight. I stayed in bed all day yesterday, till nine oclock last night. I didn't get drunk. I just didn't feel good.

Honey, I've got a buddy from Arkansas that sleeps here next to me. Last night he cracked up just before we went to work. He went to take a shower and came back in the room and started shaking and crying. I asked him what was wrong, but he wouldn't talk, he got worse and worse, so I called an ambulance and we took him to the hospital. By the time we got him over there, he was completely out of his head, but they gave him a shot to knock him out. I went over to see him this morning after work and he's better, or seems like it. I think it's mostly from the morphine they gave him to quiet him.

I guess a lot of things could have caused it. He works too hard for one thing and drinks every minute he's on pass. He's not a drunkard, but he just drinks to "get away from it," I guess. He was the most pitiful thing I've ever seen honey.

Vivian, do you love me as much as you did? I want to know honey if you started having dates again just because your dad wants you to. I want to know the truth no matter what it is. I've felt like crawling in a hole these last few days, and I want to know just what the score is, no matter what it is. I'm getting tired of disappointments and if there's going to be any more disappointments, I want it all at once. You know I love you Vivian, so be honest with me.

Yours always,
Johnny

~

August 15, 1952

My Darling,

Vivian, I'd like to trust you and believe everything you tell me, but when you tell me that you're going to have dates again just because your dad wants you to, I'm sorry but I can't believe it. I guess you do get blue, disgusted and lonely by not having any dates after you've been used to having so many boy friends.

It didn't make me mad honey, but I was a little disappointed and hurt. You had said that you honestly didn't want to have dates because you didn't care anything at all about going out because you love me so much. You said you were happier and you know that I certainly was.

Honey, I'm not mad at your parents or have nothing against them, and I think they're very nice, but I can't understand the reason that they want you to go out when everything was going smooth. We'd both said we'd be fine, and you said you weren't going to have any more dates. I know that they knew about it, but they still want you to go with other boys. I've never heard of a girl's parents insisting that she had dates whether she was in love or not.

Honey, I feel so low. I wish I could just take you away from everybody so we could run our own lives and not have anybody tell us what to do. But I guess it will never be that way from the way things look.

I love you Vivian. Always remember that I love you and you alone.

Yours always,
Johnny

~

August 16, 1952

My Vivian,

I didn't hear from you today. Honey, when you start having dates, then the letters stop coming, how can I help but feel something has changed? Something has got to be wrong somewhere. I've got no reason to gripe I guess after all the letters I got before, and I don't want you to write any more than you want to, but I just want to know why you don't write like you used to. It doesn't make me feel good and I want a reason.

I'll write again tomorrow darling. Till then, I'll be thinking of you. I love you with all my heart.

Your Johnny

~

August 19, 1952

My Vivian,

Honey, I've got a date tonight in Augsburg. Do you know why I'm doing it honey? So I won't have any more reason to gripe because of your dates. One of my buddies met three girls at "The American Way" in Augsburg. Three of us are going with them. He says they're high school girls and all of them are nice girls. They've never been with Americans before and don't speak any English except what they learned in school books. If I didn't think she was a nice girl I wouldn't go with her honey, and I'll do what I asked you to do. I won't go with her more than two or three times.

I don't know what you'll think of me honey, but I'm not having the date just to show you I could if you could. I don't care how good-looking the girl is, or how nice she is. I don't care a thing about it. No one can take your place Vivian.

I'm glad you got the glasses and dishes honey. I wish we could be using them together now. All my troubles would be over.

I guess I'll close now honey. I'll write tomorrow. I'll tell you about the date.

Yours always,
Johnny

~

August 20, 1952

My Vivian,

I had that date last night and had a pretty good time considering everything. The girls met us at the train station and we went to a German movie first, then to a club and danced awhile and saw a pretty good floor show.

All three of them were nice girls honey. They weren't beauties, but at least they were decent. I didn't make a date to go with her again. I don't know if I'll go with her again or not. I don't care anything about going with her, or anyone else.

Honey, I guess I'm spoiled because I got so much mail, and now I don't get so much, but lately, I sure haven't been too happy. If you're not going to write as much as you did before, please tell me so I'll know what to expect.

I love you Vivian. I'll always love you with all my heart.

Your Johnny

~

August 21, 1952
6 PM

My Darling Viv,

Hello Sweetheart. Remember me? I'm the guy you used to write to. No letter again today and day by day it's making me more unhappy. Every day I go and look in my little mail box and there's nothing in it. You know what the guy in the mailroom used to say? Every day I'd get one or two letters from you and he'd say "I wish you'd tell that woman to slow down. She's making me work too hard." But you know what he says now? He don't say nothing. He just sneers at me. Darling, I'm going to tell you in words of one syllable. I wish to hell you'd write. Darling, I'm not mad at you, but I am so blue and puzzled that I don't know what to do. I wish I knew what you were up to.

I love you Viv. I love you with all my heart and I'll always love you.

Yours,
Johnny

~

August 25, 1952

My Darling,

I haven't written for four days honey, because I haven't heard from you. I didn't intend to write until I did, but I changed my mind. I was a little angry last week when I didn't hear from you, but since I didn't hear from you today, after the weekend, I decided it was a little silly to be angry when it wouldn't do any good.

Please write me a long letter and tell me everything that's happened. And tell me why you don't write. It's no fun just living from one day to the next for mail call then being disappointed every day.

I love you. Please try to understand that.

Yours,
Johnny

~

August 27, 1952

My Vivian,

I don't know whether you want me to keep writing or not Vivian, but I'll keep on till I hear from you. Darling it's been eight days since I heard a word from you. It's hard to believe that you'd just stop without giving me a reason. Vivian, I try to take it, but it nearly drives me nuts. I love you Vivian. Just write me and tell me what's wrong.

Honey, I can't think of a thing to write. Maybe I'm a fool to write if things are the way I think they are, but I'm going to keep my end of the bargain.

Yours always,
Johnny

~

My Darling,

Honey, I don't understand it. It all seems like a bad dream. If you were sick I know someone would have written me. It will be ten days tomorrow since I've heard from you. I don't know what to think anymore.

I don't want to hurt you honey. I've hurt you enough already. I hope you won't hold anything against me, even though you've got a right to, you've got a right to hold a lot against me. I'm not worth two cents to anybody and never will be. It's stupid to try to pretend that I'm any better than the worst of these people, and just lately I've had the sense to realize how stupid it is to tell <u>you</u> what's right and wrong when I belong in the gutter myself.

I love you and I'll always love you.

Yours,
Johnny

~

September 1, 1952

Hello Honey,

That letter finally came Saturday after nearly two weeks.

I wish I knew what was wrong with you too honey. I wish I knew how you can go so long without writing and still say you love me when it means so much to me and you know it. You're tired of writing and waiting, aren't you Vivian? You've proved that. I can't blame you for it. I can't blame you a bit, but honey, don't you think it's a little dirty to do the way you did? Maybe you didn't do me dirty. Maybe you've got a right to after the way I've treated you.

All those days that you didn't write, you had dates, didn't you? You don't have to answer that. When you go so long without writing and have dates besides, I can't see too much love. How many boys would stand for that Vivian? No one would unless they loved the girl like I love you. I'm a liar when I say I've got pride. I haven't got a damn bit. I'd let you beat me with a bull whip. But I'm not taking it anymore. If you still love me, you can write like you used to or we're through. It's probably what you want from the looks of things. You'd be free then. You could have a date every night and not have to tell anyone about them.

Vivian, I wish I had a chance to show you that I can be as good to you as anybody, but I guess I've got too much competition. I wish to hell every boy in San Antonio would get sent to Alaska.

I might as well close darling. I've run down. Vivian, please don't wait so long to answer. <u>I love you. I love you</u>.

Yours always,
Johnny

~

September 10, 1952

Dearest Vivian,

I don't know what to say honey, but I wanted to write anyway. The last letter I had from you was two weeks ago tomorrow. You said you'd write the next day, but I guess you changed you mind.

Vivian, will you please write me just one letter? Don't you think I have a right to know why you stopped after all you mean to me? I know I do, and I can't see why you'd do this way unless you hate me.

If I don't get an answer to this letter, I'll not bother you anymore Vivian. Anything else I said would just make it worse I guess, but the least you could do is keep your end of the bargain, and give me the reasons why you stopped.

Please answer soon. I'm tired of waiting and wondering.

All my love,
Johnny

~

After some weeks, I came to realize just how much Johnny meant to me and how much I wanted to reciprocate his love, whether my parents supported us or not. I resumed writing, assuring Johnny of my true feelings.

October 18, 1952

My Darling Viv,

The mail came in today for the first time in five days. I got seven letters from you and one from your mom. I don't know exactly what to say Viv, but I don't think I've ever been happier in my life. Certainly I'll take you back darling, and you don't have to beg. I wish I could take you in my arms, but that's impossible so I'll try to make the best of it on paper.

Darling, I've been trying to forget you, but it's impossible too. I'd been spending all my passes drinking and fighting and telling myself that I hate you and every other woman in the world, but it doesn't work. The last two days especially have been the worst I've ever lived, I think. I've thought of you every minute I was awake, and dreamed of you at night. I knew something had to happen, then I get these letters today. It seemed like a gift direct from God Vivian. Honey if you've been praying that I'd take you back, then God must believe in us too, because he's filled me with love for you.

Vivian, you don't have to do a thing to regain my love except <u>be mine</u>. The dates are alright honey. I want you to go out and have fun, but darling, please let's don't have anymore of these "Wait awhile till I look around" deals. We're both old enough to know what we want, and have the reasoning power to reason things out for ourselves. I think a lot of your parents, your brother, sister and Pat. Your parents are wonderful and you're lucky, but honey it's been proven that we love each other. Now will you please let everyone know that we're in love and going to be married and for everyone to please let us alone? I'm going to try to treat you so good that you'll never want to look around again.

Darling, you seem to feel convicted or hurt because of all this trouble, I don't want you to feel that you're the cause of it. I'm willing to forgive and forget everything if you are. I'm asking for your forgiveness now Viv. I'm asking you to forgive all the hard and sarcastic things I've said to you. I want us both to forget every other thing except that we're deeply in love. Will you forgive me completely Vivian, and we can start all over again?

I'm going to do everything in my power to prove to you that you're the only one I love, and I want you to believe me when I say that I'm going to be good to you. I love you Vivian. I love you with all my heart. It seems silly to think of spending my life with anyone but you. I want you to be my wife. I'd do anything in the world for you, and I'll be hoping with all my heart that we can stay together until I get back with you to make you my own.

Goodnight my darling. Thank-you for being so wonderful to me. I can't explain how much I love and appreciate you, but I do know that I am going to bed a happier little boy than I've been in a long time. I love you Viv darling, with all my heart and soul.

Your Johnny for Life

~

October 19, 1952

My Darling Viv,

Yes, I made Buck Sgt honey. I forgot to tell you when I wrote. That means I can save more money for us honey, for our life together. Thanks for the congratulations sweetheart.

Darling, I've read these seven letters at least a half dozen times each. I don't see how I could stand it without your letters again. Please write every chance you get.

Honey, I hope the doctors report comes out alright. Take care of yourself Viv. Someday you're going to be a mother and my wife, and you need a little more weight. You're just right for me darling, but a baby inside you might get you down. Take your vitamins, eat plenty, sleep plenty and take care of yourself. Hear me?

Goodnight honey. I'll write tomorrow. I love you with all my heart.

Your Johnny.

~

October 20, 1952

My Little Darling,

Honey, I went to town about a week ago, and a couple of my buddies and myself were playing and singing at this restaurant. My two buddies left about eleven o'clock but I stayed to get drunk. Three Polish guards that work at the base came in. They were off duty and we were all sitting there together, and trying to talk to each other. One of them stole a carton of cigarettes from me and sneaked out. I started asking the other two about it and we got into an argument, then a fight. I didn't even get a scratch, but one of them, I knocked out four of his teeth and broke the other ones nose. I finally got out and back to the base, but they reported me the next day.

The 1st Sgt called me in Saturday and said I'd probably have to pay for getting his teeth fixed, and the other one's nose set, but the C.O. called me in this morning and said they investigated and the Polacks aren't supposed to have been in town. They didn't have a pass, and when they are in town they're not supposed to associate with Americans. I didn't even get written up for it. The C.O. just told me to watch myself.

I guess I was lucky, but I got to thinking and decided I might not be so lucky next time. I promise I won't get drunk anymore Vivian. I have no reason to. I'm not mean and dirty Vivian. I'm so ashamed of myself I could die. I don't know why I'm telling you all this, but I don't know who else I'd tell it to. Please have faith and confidence in me darling. I love you and I want to show you that I can be good to you and provide for you as well as anyone. I love you Viv, and I want your love more than anything else in the world. I need you Vivian. I need you like I need air. Knowing that you love me and that you're all mine makes all the difference in the world in how I feel, act and think. I love you. Please stay mine.

Yours for life,
Johnny

~

I'm always thinking about what you and I will do the first night I'm back. We'll probably go driving around in my new car. Well, maybe it won't be new. About a '48 Ford I guess. Maybe we'll go dancing, or to a drive-in or something. Then we'll go to a nice moonlit spot and park. You know, just like in the movies. There'll be a lake, and trees, and bright moonlight. I'll hold you in my arms and tell you over and over how much I love you.

Remember that you're always in my mind and heart.

All my love,
All my life,
Johnny

~

October 29, 1952

My Darling Viv,

I was over at the Service Club a few minutes ago with Link. He was playing a new concerto for me that he learned. The officers' wives were having a party of some kind, and I think nearly half of them were drunk, or getting that way. I wanted to take a gun and clean the place out. It's none of my business, but they make me sick they know they don't do things like that in the States, and they come over here and raise cain. I hope someday I'll stop worrying about what other people do and ignore them, but it still makes me sick.

Goodnight, darling. I'll write again tomorrow.

Yours always,
Johnny

~

November 6, 1952

My Darling Viv,

Honey, I saw one of those Polacks today that I had a fight with up by the PX. I expected him to brain me the next time he saw me, but guess what he did? He shook hands with me. I sure feel sorry for him and ashamed of myself. He looks like an old man when he smiles. If I could, I'd buy him some teeth.

Honey, I don't know why I talk like this. I'm so puzzled sometimes and want to be with you so bad I could die. I've been finding it more and more true every day just how hard it is to be away from the one you love. It seems like the whole world is against us. I'll keep hoping and praying that something will bring us together. I get so tired of just working, eating and sleeping. I actually get so starved for fun and excitement that I feel like breaking all the windows, picture and light, then go to bed.

I guess our time is coming though, but it sure seems á long way off. Someday, I'll be turning over and saying, "Darling, wake up. It's time for breakfast," instead of saying, "Tex, get the hell out of that sack! It's time to go to work."

Yours till then,
Johnny

~

November 10, 1952

Hello Sweet Darling,

I just finished washing some clothes and took a shower and now I'm writing you before I go to work. I hate to think how my clothes are going to come out. I didn't have any bleach or starch and I just threw them all in together. I bet I'm going to have some technicolor underwear.

Darling, once I asked you what you wanted out of life. That was at a drive-in one night, I think you said "Just to be comfortable." You're wonderful Vivian. I'm going to work my fingers to the bone to try to give you more than comfort, and with God's help I'm going to have you and your love all our lives.

"Hillbilly Gasthaus" is on now honey and Eddy Arnold is singing "Molly Darling." I think that's a beautiful song. The name of it should be changed to "Vivian Darling" as my song to you.

No, sweetheart, when we're married you'll never sleep on the couch. If you do, I will too. Nothing is going to keep me away from you when we're married. I hope we never have to write letters to each other after I'm back.

All My Love,
Johnny

~

November 19, 1952

My Darling Viv,

I woke up about one oclock this afternoon honey and went down to check my mail. I was happier than I have been in a long time Viv. I got seven letters from you.

Yes, darling, if you send me a St. Christopher's medal, I'll wear it and respect it. Perea has two and I wore one once or twice. I'll wear it and treasure it because it's sacred and because <u>you</u> gave it to me. Things like that seem to bring us closer together Viv. Something that is of God and from you.

Honey, that new job sounds like a good deal. I hope you will like it sugar and won't have to work so hard. I'm glad I'm getting a woman with lots of brains as well as good looks. You can support us if I get lazy. No darling, I'd work twelve hours digging ditches to support us if I had to. I'm going to make a happy home for you and our kids in spite of everything.

Bye for now Viv honey. I'll see you tomorrow, by parcel post that is. I'll be thinking of you and loving you till then Viv. Always remember that I love you and you alone with all my heart always. You belong to me darling and I belong to you. Wherever you are, I love you.

Yours, now and all my life,
Johnny

~

November 20, 1952

My Darling Vivian,

I got another sweet letter from you today sweetheart. The one with the picture in it. You make me so happy Viv. I don't know how I ever did without you before I met you. I love this picture honey. I know you're not devilish, I think you're sweet. Keep sending pictures like that darling. I want to see more of you.

Sweetheart, I want to send my money home and save it. It cuts out a lot of so called recreation, but I'm not going to be broke when I get back. The first thing I do I'm going to buy a car and pay cash for it. I'll get $300 discharge bonus and with the G.I. Bill, we can have enough to start on. I don't want to be broke when we get married. I'm always going to know where the next meal is coming from at least. You've been happy at home and have been comfortable and as these Negroes say, "There ain't gonna be no change, man."

No one will ever take your place Viv. That's something you'll never have to worry about, my going out with other women. A lot of men do it after they're married, but I wouldn't even if I hated you. Marriage is sacred to me, and even though a lot of people take it lightly, I won't be one of them. I'll always belong to you Viv and I'm going to make you happy.

Honey, the time does seem to pass fast over here. I can make it from now on. I was just thinking about that last night. About all the guys that got "Dear Johns" from their girls. Most of the ones that broke up, it was in the first year after they left, and I feel so good because you and I are going stronger than ever. None of them had a girl like I do though. They didn't have true love in the first place and didn't have a girl as true, sweet and wonderful as you are.

Your future husband,
Johnny

~

My Sweet Viv,

No letter today honey, but I guess I'll forgive you. That would be sweet of me since the mail didn't come in, wouldn't it? I'm still reading over the letters I've gotten from you the last few days. I read all of them at least three times, then I hate to put them away. I've got them all stacked up by the months and I've just about got my box full, but I can always get a bigger box darling. One month, September, I think, I just got four letters from you. I was looking at them last night, and just had to laugh. For June and July I've got a big stack, a middle-sized stack for August, and September is a little bitty one. I think you're sweet honey but don't pull that stuff anymore. I hate those little stacks even if they are cute.

Your Very Own,
Johnny

~

November 22, 1952

Hello Sweetheart,

This one letter that you put, "To My Darling" on the outside, the mail clerk sure gave me a funny look when he handed me that one. He was checking over the letters in my box to see if they were all mine because there's another "Cash" in this squadron, and when he came to that one he said "Here you are, 'Johnny Darling!' "

If you think you've been too frank with me, then I should hide my face for some of the things I've said darling. I don't think you could be too frank with me Viv. After all, we belong to each other, we're going to be married and spend our lives together, so I can't see where anything you could say to me to bring us closer together would be wrong. Just the thought that I have you to tell things to, and I know you'll understand because you love me. I know you wouldn't tell another boy what you told me about being so proud if you were pregnant. It makes me love you more darling to know that I'm getting a woman that will be so devoted to her children. I couldn't help but laugh when you said you'd start wearing a maternity dress before you had to, so you could let people know darling. I think you're sweet and wonderful.

Yes, honey, I'll give you a kiss every morning before we get up. I'll probably be the first one awake every morning because I don't think I could sleep very late with something like you beside me.

Goodnight, my darling. I love you very much.

Always yours,
Johnny

~

My Sweet Darling,

I've just been down washing my clothes again darling. Someday we'll be washing our clothes together honey, or let one of our maids do it. I remember when I was a little kid, I used to say that when I grew up I was going to buy my mother a washing machine so she wouldn't have to work so hard, and that when I got married I was going to have maids so my wife wouldn't have to work. It's a pity grown-ups can't be all optimists like all little kids are. Including myself now.

I'll write you tomorrow darling. I'll be hoping for a letter then. Keep writing honey, and keep loving me. Goodnight sugar. I love you always,

Your Own,

Johnny

I love you sweetheart, sweet dreams.

~

December 1, 1952

My Vivian Darling,

Honey, I got served breakfast in bed this morning. Not by a woman though darling. Five of my friends came in drunk about 6 o'clock this morning and woke me up to get me to sing for them. They'd been to the mess hall and stolen some cereal and milk and bananas and brought it to me. They drug me out of bed, made me clean up and play and sing for them till they sobered up which was about ten o'clock. I wore off five sets of fingers on that guitar. I've got a bunch of Rebel buddies that crave hillbilly music when they get drunk. They'd have to be drunk to listen to me.

About six of us are getting together tonight and have a hillbilly party tonight in the basement. Two S/Sgts are going home tomorrow that have served their time here and want us to sing and play for them for the last time. I wish they were playing for me and I was going.

Your very own,

Johnny

~

December 2, 1952

Hello Darling,

We had quite a time last night honey. We sang and played down in the basement till about midnight then the CQ made us stop. I'd rather stay here than to go out when I can have fun here, and it doesn't cost anything. I don't know what I could do to have any fun if I did go out. I certainly can't be happy drinking, and that's all there is to do around here.

Yours always,
Johnny

~

December 5, 1952

My Little Sweetheart,

I got five sweet letters from you today honey and I wouldn't take a million dollars for them. You're sweet darling.

I'm glad you like your Christmas present honey. I know it doesn't seem much to me but I just hope you like it as much as you sound like you did. They told me it's the best in the world and that's what I want for you always. That perfume is supposed to do things to men honey, so be careful who you're with when you wear it. I want you to wear some of it when I get back and see what it'll do to me. You could do more than the perfume though.

I love you Viv.

Your Own Always,
Johnny

~

December 6, 1952

My Sweet Viv,

Yes honey, I got the letters addressed "To My Darling" and I thought it was sweet. I don't care who sees it or what they think Viv. Sometimes I feel like going around all over the place, telling everyone "Viv Liberto loves me and she's the sweetest girl in the world." They'd think I was nuts, though. I'm so happy now Viv. I feel like bawling because I can't be with you but it feels wonderful to know that you love me and you're all mine.

Your own always,
Johnny

~

December 31, 1952
Landsberg, Ger

Hello Darling,

You're not the only one that can't sleep at night. Seems I've got Vivian on the brain. You're all I can think of honey, and I'm losing sleep over you. I had to get a new pillow Saturday, I squeezed all the feathers out of the other one. Seems like I get just like you when I don't hear from you. All the boys were glad when I heard from you. They said maybe they could get along with me from now on.

I love you little girl.

Your Johnny

~

This is first time Johnny addressed me as "My Wife to be." I so loved the sound of it!

January 26, 1953

My Wife to be,

Darling, this morning at 8:00 the C.Q. woke me up and said I had a call from San Antonio. I jumped out of bed, put on my fatigues and shower shoes and went down to the desk and the operator said you had placed the call, and I would get to talk to you Saturday 31st at 12 AM. My heart was in my mouth honey. I thought I'd get to talk to you this morning, I was so happy and excited I couldn't go back to sleep. Just five more days honey and I'll hear your voice.

Viv, I think it's wonderful that you'd wait for me. You're the sweetest, most wonderful thing in the world. I think of you all the time darling, and of the happy days and nights we'll spend together.

Darling, I'm going to bed now. I'll write tomorrow. Goodnight my darling. I love you with all my heart and soul.

Your husband to be,
Johnny

~

January 27, 1953

My Darling Vivian,

Honey, you've probably seen girls like Martha before, and you know how 100% of them always end up. There's something wrong with her mentally darling. She may dress nice and seem to have good sense sometimes, but she's not a bit better than the Mexican girls that walk the streets at night. They just go at it in a little different way. She may think she's having fun and think she knows all there is to know, but someday she'll be hurt bad. I can't see how she can ever plan on two kids, unless they're illegitimate. I don't see how an average man could have any love for her.

Darling, what I'm thankful for most is your <u>natural</u> decency. I'm so thankful for your firm belief in what's right and I'm thankful that your parents have made such a wonderful girl out of you.

104

What I want is to raise my girls just like your mother has raised you. I'm glad it disgusts you to hear Martha talk about her boy friends darling. I think you're wonderful. Viv darling, don't ever change. I don't know why I deserve you but with God's help you're going to be mine.

Honey, it's a shame that there are people like Martha in a country like the U.S. If some people could just see how people over here live. Millions behind the Iron Curtain would give all the money they ever had if they could just worship freely. God has blessed the people over there so much its pitiful, and it's a shame that people won't try to at least do half way what God asks.

Your husband to be,
Your Johnny

~

January 31, 1953

My Darling Vivian,

Honey, I was in the 1st Sgts office this morning at 1 oclock when the operator called and said they couldn't make connections. I was sure disappointed and I know you were too. Everything was quiet and I was all set to talk to you. The operator said it would probably be next week before I got to talk to you, but I'll be here anytime the call comes through.

No honey, I haven't been drinking so much coffee. To be perfectly honest darling, for the last ten days I couldn't afford it. Everybody was broke. Don't worry baby. I won't drink too much coffee.

I won't get drunk anymore either Vivian. Thank-you darling for being so sweet about it. Honey, it gets almost unbearable to stay in that room sometimes. I'm nervous in the first place and that room is crowded. I've stood it a long time and I guess I can from now on, but sometimes I get to where I don't care about anything. It gets to where nothing interests me, and I have to force myself to even sweep the floor.

Darling, last night I saw the grade book the Control Chief has kept our grades in for the last five months. They grade us in efficiency, attitude and appearance. The way they grade is "1" is very poor, "2" is poor, "3" is average, "4" is above average, and "5" is excellent. I don't want you to get the idea that I'm conceited or bragging in telling you this, but I have all "5"s honey, and I'm the only one that has. Very few have any fives at all. That's why I got to be Trick Chief after this six weeks.

Darling, when I get back, I want to go to church with you and thank God for all he's doing for us.

I love you my darling, with all my heart.

Your future husband,
Johnny

~

February 1, 1953

My Wife to be,

Darling, I just hung up the receiver and I'm waiting for the operator to call me back. I don't know why we were cut off honey. If they make connections again, maybe we can hear each other better.

Darling, I was up in one of the offices for 5 hours tonight, and the third time the operator said she lost communications, I went to the room, I told the CQ to call me if the call came thru, and a few minutes later, it did. I'm sorry it was so messed up honey, and that you were caused so much trouble.

Were you disappointed darling, or disillusioned? My voice must have sounded horrible, but darling, when I said "I love you," I meant it from the bottom of my heart. Don't think I would sound that way when I'm with you. I love you Vivian and you mean everything in the world to me.

Darling, I have to go to work in an hour, so I'll close this one and write again tomorrow. I don't know if we'll get to talk to each other again or not. But I hope so. I want to tell you again that I love you. Someday I'll whisper it and you'll hear me darling.

Goodnight Viv darling. I'll be thinking of you and loving you. I love you my darling.

Your husband to be,
Your Johnny

~

February 2, 1953

Good morning darling,

I just got off work and I wanted to write you the first thing honey. I've been thinking of you all night, and I feel so close to you Viv.

Darling, last night I was disappointed because I couldn't say what I wanted to about sending you a ring. Vivian, I feel like a heel because I haven't sent you one. I've been thinking of it for a long time, and made up my mind a long time ago that I would send you one instead of waiting till I get back to give it to you. Darling, I meant to send it so it would get there around your birthday, but after talking to you I've decided I want to send it just as soon as I possibly can. Maybe by March 1st. You've waited too long without one now, and I want you to wear a ring for me.

Darling, what I tried to tell you last night was if there's a certain style you like, send me the picture and I'll try to get what you want. Viv honey, it's something you'll be wearing, and something you only have once in a life time, and I want to get just exactly the kind you want, if you know what you want honey. I want you to be happy with it darling.

You told me you wanted white gold didn't you honey? And didn't you say size 5½? And you don't want a solitaire, right? Darling, you better send me a ring card, you know what I mean, and mark the hole that fits your finger, or a piece of string the size of your finger so I'll be sure the size is right. Honey a solitaire has one large stone, doesn't it? I just want to be sure to know what not to get.

Vivian honey, it hurts me that I can't be there to put the ring on your finger. That's one reason why I didn't send it sooner. I'd give anything in the world if I could just put it on your finger and kiss you. It's not the money that was holding me back honey. It doesn't make a bit of difference in the world to me. I want you to tell me just what you want if you can, and I'll get it.

Vivian, in a way I've been worried since that call last night, and I won't feel easy till I get a letter that you wrote after last night. I've been wondering what you think of me now. I know I sounded hateful, but darling it was because I had to yell. It isn't very romantic to say, "I love you" in a tone that sounds like you're angry. You didn't sound that way darling. All night I've been saying over to myself, "I love you too," trying to remember just how you said it. It sounded sweet and wonderful Viv, and as many times as we've called each other "honey" and "darling," it sounded wonderful to hear you say "honey." Even though you did say "Honey, I can't hear you," I felt like it was natural to call you that. Darling last night made me realize just how true and strong my love for you is. Viv, if I ever lose you, I'll have nothing to live for. You're everything in the world to me.

Oh Viv, I wish I could talk to you this morning. I love you so much and feel so close to you. There will never be anyone but you Vivian. I swear I'll never love another woman as long as I live. It will always be just you, Vivian darling, as long as I live. You're going to be my wife, Vivian, as long as you're willing.

Bye darling. I love you with all my heart and soul.

Your husband to be,
Your Johnny

~

February 3, 1953

My Wife, someday,

Darling, after I wrote you yesterday morning, I meant to write again in the afternoon, but I went to town. I only stayed in town about 30 minutes, but

I hadn't slept since day before yesterday at 4:30 PM. I was dead tired when I got back here so I went to bed and didn't wake up till this morning.

Honey, I looked at some rings yesterday and didn't see anything I thought you'd like. A friend of mine is going to Munich tomorrow morning, so I'm going up there with him and look around. I'm not buying it till I hear from you and see if you send a picture of the kind you want, or give me an idea.

Darling, I guess I should have made all the arrangements before I asked you to wear one, but as usual, I didn't think. I guess I'll keep you guessing when it will get there.

Honey, I wish so much that we could pick out the ring together like we're supposed to. I hope you'll like my choice darling. It will be yours to wear for a lifetime, and I hope so much that you like it.

The ring will bring us even closer together Viv darling, if that's possible. People say engagements and even marriages don't mean anything these days, but this one will be an exception. The ring means that it's just you and I, and that there will never be anyone else as I see it. I think the ring will mean as much to me as it will to you. It will make me happy to know that you love me and are waiting for me. The ring will show everyone else too.

Vivian darling, I love you so much. Since the phone call I've had you on my mind so strong that I can think of nothing else. You will always be the only one for me honey. Someday you'll be my wife and you'll be mine to love and take care of the rest of your life. I love you so much Viv. I'll never even look at another girl. God has given me the best woman in the world and I'm going to keep you.

Your very own,
Your Johnny

~

February 3, 1953

My Darling Vivian,

I just got back from the movie, sugar, and I'm going to write you a little before I go to bed.

Honey, I just remembered something I meant to tell you today but I forgot. Yesterday in Landsberg a German girl stopped me on the street and asked me to take her and buy her a drink. First, I asked her if her father was a magician. She said no, and I asked her if she ever lived in San Antonio, Texas. Of course, she said no, then I said "You don't look the least bit like her, and as a matter of fact she doesn't even drink." I know she thought I was crazy as a bed bug. I walked off and when I was two blocks down the street she was still staring at me.

Darling, there will never be another girl for me but you. I mean that from the bottom of my heart. I love you Vivian, and it will always be just you.

Your husband to be,
Your Johnny

I love you darling.

~

February 4, 1953

My Sweet Darling,

I've been playing pool since I got back from Munich honey, and I came up to write you before I go to bed. I got back from Munich at 3 oclock today darling. In all I didn't stay there over three hours. I think I found what I was looking for. A woman in the PX recommended a German jewelry store for me and I went there. They seem to be half way decent people honey and I believe I can get you a good ring. Darling, the man said they could make any style of ring you wanted. I'll wait to see if you give me an idea of what you want, and if you don't, you'll have to trust my taste honey.

Honey, I had the cutest little girl friend today. I met this American woman on the train. She had her little girl and boy with her, and the little girl could talk the horns off a billy goat. She was asking me all about cowboys and especially "Hopalong Cassidy." I told her a long, crazy tale about why he's called "Hopalong." I think she fell in love with me honey. She wants me to come to Florida and see her when I get back. You don't mind, do you sugar?

Someday we'll have kids honey. We'll be the happiest family on earth Viv. I love you Viv darling. You'll always be the only one for me. I love you so much. I'd give anything to be with you sweetheart.

Your Johnny for life.

~

February 5, 1953

My Wife to be,

Darling, I got the box of stationery and the ink today. Honey, you shouldn't go to so much trouble for me. I'm not worth all you do. You know I appreciate it though Viv and I thank you from the bottom of my heart.

Darling, I finally got the cyst taken out this morning. They didn't put me in bed, but the doctor gave me permission to stay in my room today and not go to work. It took them exactly 45 minutes to cut it out. They froze my jaw, then cut it and the doctor bursted it before he got it half way out, then he had to cut it out by pieces. After about 25 minutes the feeling started coming back in it and I thought I would die. I asked him to put me to sleep but he kept saying "I'm almost through," so I stuck it out for about 20 more minutes. It doesn't hurt me now and the doctor says it won't leave hardly any scar at all. I thought a few times he was trying to cut my head off, but I guess it's not as big as it felt. He only took four stitches and I get them out Saturday.

Don't worry about me honey. I feel fine now and I believe it will heal nicely. Bye darling. I love you baby darling.

Your husband someday,
Your Johnny

~

February 7, 1953

My Darling Vivian,

Sweetheart, you made me very happy again today. I got four letters from you. Two of them were written after we talked. What made me happy was because you were so happy Viv.

Viv, it will be so nice engaged to you. It will bring us closer together and just the thought that you're all mine and waiting for me makes me so happy. Darling I feel sometimes that I'm already married to you. When things go wrong and when I feel blue and lonesome, I've always got you to talk to and rely on. Vivian darling, if I ever lose you I honestly don't want to live. You mean that much to me.

Viv, once is all I ever intend to be engaged, and once is all I ever intend to be married. I have all the faith and trust in the world in you darling. That's why I want you to have a ring. We should be together during our engagement but by doing this I can prove that I love you and trust you completely. Sixteen more months before we'll be together. I know you'll respect the ring for what it stands for. I'd like for you to think the ring is me, and I'll always be with you wherever you go.

Vivian darling, I'm soft as a grape sometimes. I could cry I feel so blue and lonesome for you. I need you with me Vivian. I need your lips and I need your arms at night. Someday my darling we'll be together as long as God lets us live. I'll continually thank Him that he gave me your love and pray that He lets me keep it. I love you Vivian.

Please stay mine darling. I belong to you always. God bless you my darling. I love you.

Your husband to be,
Your Johnny always.

~

My Sweetheart,

Viv honey, I was just thinking, do you think I should write your dad? I wondered if I should talk to him about marrying you since we're getting engaged. I don't know if I should write him or not. Maybe I should wait till I get back. I guess he already knows a lot about me. I don't know what to do honey. Tell me.

I guess I sound a little crazy, but I am happy about everything honey, and most of all I'm happy about the wife I'm getting. I think you're wonderful Vivian. You're clean and sweet and you'll be the best wife in the world. I love you Vivian darling. I love you with all my heart and soul.

I love you with all my heart.

Your Johnny
All your life

~

February 10, 1953
My Wife to be,

Sweetheart, I just got off work and I'm going over to the service club to play bingo. I wanted to write you before I go. There's a $500 jack-pot and I'm going to try for it.

Sugar, Amesbury came up where I was working today. He was on C.Q., and said I had a phone call and I thought it was you again. My heart was going 90 mph, but it was for the other "Cash" in the sqdn.

Honey, I'm going now and win that $500. We'll buy us a <u>new</u> car when I get back if I do. Bye for now sweetheart.

Your husband to be,
Your Johnny

~

February 11, 1953
My Sweetheart,

I didn't win that jackpot last night. I knew I wouldn't but it was something to do. We can buy an old Ford anyway honey.

I don't want you to work after we're married darling. A lot of girls do when they first marry, but you're not. I'm bringing home the bacon someway. I know you'd be happier just keeping house and so would I.

I love you Vivian. Stay sweet and remember you're mine.

Your Johnny always.

~

My Vivian darling,

I just got back from the movie, and I wrapped you a little present that I bought from the traveling salesman at the mess hall. I'll mail it tomorrow darling. I hope you'll like it. I couldn't wrap it very well, and you'll probably have to press it when you get it.

Sugar, there's a peanut wrapped up with it. You see, I was wrapping the package and I was eating peanuts and wondered if you'd like to have one. Don't eat it all at once darling.

One of my buddies just came back from his pass honey. He was in Munich last night. He's been over here about three weeks and he was telling me yesterday what a sweet wife he had and about his little girl. He vaguely remembers where he stayed last night in Munich. He was in here just now almost crying, wondering how he was ever going to face his wife again.

I don't think some of these guys love their wives in the first place when they'll go out and stay with anything they can pick up. It would make me want to kill myself. If I can stay away from them while I'm single, I know they could since they're married. I can't see how some men can be so dirty. He must have been plenty drunk to do it, or else he doesn't have any feeling for his wife and kid. If I were that dirty I'd want someone to shoot me right between the eyes.

I'll be glad when I can get out of this hell hole, and won't have to be around things like that.

'Night sugar. I'll write tomorrow. Stay just as sweet as you are Viv. Don't change ever. I love you my darling.

> Your husband someday,
> Your Johnny

~

February 16, 1953

My Own Sweetheart,

After we've been married awhile darling, you may want twin beds. I toss and turn all night every night. Every morning when I get up usually both blankets are on the floor and I've got the sheet wrapped around me every which way. Yesterday morning when I got up one blanket was on the floor and the other one was next to me with the sheet on top. I just do a lot of wrestling and fighting in my sleep. Maybe we won't have to get double beds darling. You can just wear a suit of armor to bed every night.

Vivian darling, you'll never know how happy you make me when you say "The next date I have will be with you." Honey, I guess that's what I've always wanted you to say, and now that you have, it makes me feel kind of funny. You know I appreciate it darling. I appreciate it from the bottom of my heart. That's certainly doing a lot for a guy. Someone said, "Two people deeply in love never feel worthy of the other's love." I feel that way and I guess that's why I feel so funny when you tell me that. No words could tell you how much I love you for it Viv.

One thing I can do for you, which won't be a sacrifice, I'll do the same for you Vivian darling. I won't have anything at all to do with any woman except you. I mean it Viv. It's a promise. I believe that you believe me so that's all that counts. Other guys can't understand and would say I'm crazy, but no one on earth has as wonderful a love as yours. Don't listen to anyone when they say I'm not. I am Viv and I always will be true to you.

I love you sweetheart.

Your Own always,
Your Johnny

~

February 19, 1953

Vivian darling,

I dreamed something last night that worried me nearly to death till mail call. It was only a dream, but it was so plain that it scared me. I dreamed that an old man with long whiskers pointed his finger at me and said, "Tomorrow you will get a letter from someone dear to you that will make you very, very unhappy. Check your mail twice." That's all I dreamed then I woke up. I was waiting at the mail room when it opened, and in all I checked my mail five times today, but I just got these three letters from you and they certainly didn't make me unhappy. I'll be restless till tomorrow. Even though it was a dream it still got under my skin because my dreams, some of them, have come true. Just before my brother had his accident I dreamed he died, and a few days later he had the accident that killed him.

Vivian sometimes I want you and need you so bad that I'm nearly nuts. Although there's never been nothing more than a kiss between you and I, I feel like a husband to you because I know there will never be another man for you. I feel positive now that I will always be the only one, and it makes me happy.

Viv, down at the PX today I was looking at the February horoscope and it said that for a man born in February, he would be best mated to a woman born in April. It does honey, but I already knew that.

I will probably be Trick Chief another 20 or 25 days darling. I sure like the job, and I know I haven't made any mistakes. I've been getting along with all the boys just fine. The only one I ever have any trouble with is Link. He resents it because he has to work under me, but so far he hasn't gotten very far with his resentment.

Yes, honey, I like fried oysters. Not as an everyday dish, but I do like them and eat them once in a while. My favorite food is black eyed peas and corn bread. You can't take the "country" out of a country boy darling. My next favorite food is chili, so I won't be hard to cook for. I can eat most anything honey, and right now I'd eat kangaroo tonsils if I could sit down with you and eat them.

I love you.

Your husband someday,
Your Johnny

~

I suggested to Johnny in one of my letters that we start having a weekly prayer at the very same time, so that we could feel a special bond of closeness during prayer.

February 21, 1953

My Sweet Wife to be,

Vivian darling, you're the sweetest, most wonderful woman on earth. I think it's a wonderful idea, what you said about praying together. Honey, how about 9 oclock every Saturday night? It would be 9 PM here and 2 PM there Saturday afternoon. Will that be alright with you Viv? Around that time is the only time of day or night that I am never sleeping, no matter what shift I'm working. If that's alright with you, then I'll be praying for you, for myself, and for us at exactly 9 PM here every Sat. night. On the 5 to Midnight, I'll be working then, but I can easily get off a few minutes darling to be with you to talk to God about us. No matter how far apart we are Viv darling, we will be together at that time.

Vivian, I think it's a wonderful idea, and I'm so happy honey to have you. I love you so darling. You're so sweet and wonderful and clean. You could never know how happy that made me for you to suggest that. I love you darling. I love you with all my heart.

Honey, I wonder how many other boys and girls in love, together or apart, would think of asking God to guide their lives. People would laugh at us, but I wouldn't take all the money in the world for what there is between us Vivian. Honey, let's keep it this way. Let's don't let the coming months make any change at all. We can beat this loneliness Vivian and come out on top. We've got what it takes darling, and I know we can make it.

Honey, I discovered something yesterday that made me so mad I could scream. I've got another cyst. It's on my left cheek right in the same place the other one was, except on the opposite cheek. It's so small it can't be noticed yet, but nevertheless, it's a —— cyst. It will have to be cut out sooner or later, but I'm going to wait till I get over the anger of the other one. They cut one out, and another one will take its place. It makes me mad. The other one is healed up honey. I can even shave over it now. The scar isn't very big.

> Your husband someday,
> Your Johnny

~

February 23, 1953

My Vivian darling,

Honey, every guy that is on this base on his 21st birthday, the Airmen's Club gives him a $20 bottle of French Champagne. I'm going to get it the 26th and my buddies and I might celebrate my birthday. It depends on how I feel. I don't like it at all and I may sell it. I could use the money more than I could the Champagne. I'm a capitalist aren't I darling?

Honey, do you know what I'd like for a birthday present? One little kiss from you. It would be the best present I ever got.

> Your husband to be,
> Your Johnny

~

February 28, 1953

My Sweet Darling,

Here I am again sugar. I'm in the 1st Sgts office waiting for you to come through. I went to Munich today darling and got the ring and at 2 PM, just as I was coming back, the operator called and said the call would come through at 9 PM. It's now 8:15 PM.

We've been apart 19 months Viv. Even though there's been so much loneliness and heartache, it's wonderful that we've stayed together Viv. We'll make it alright now, won't we honey? We'll show the world what true love can do. I wish I could just tell you how much I love you and appreciate all you're doing for me Vivian. I love you darling.

Honey, its 9:30. I just called the operator. She never did call me. She said there's no connection. I'm going to bed darling. If the call comes in, the CQ will come get me. Honey, this sure is getting disheartening. I know it's causing you a lot of trouble. Have you been losing any time at work sugar? I'm sorry Viv. Maybe we'll have some luck somewhere, sometime.

This letter that Johnny wrote to my parents is one that I've always cherished.

Feb 27th

Dear Mom & Dad,

I got the birthday card today. It was very nice. Thanks a lot for remembering my birthday.

I'm sorry I didn't write sooner, but thats just the way it goes. I'd probably lie if I tried to make excuses, so I'll just let well enough alone.

I'm sitting in the 1st Sergeants office now waiting for Viv's call to come through. This is the third night. Maybe we'll be lucky tonight.

Mr. Liberto, do you find that daily your mail box is flooded with letters addressed with green ink? Do you know that there is a deep-rooted reason behind all those APO postmarked letters?

The reason is that Vivian likes green and so do I. There's another reason before I forget. Your daughter Viv and I are nuts about each other. To be perfectly honest with you, we're google-eyed over each other.

We're planning to be married when I get back Mr. Liberto. We've been making plans for a long time now. From what Viv tells me, you and Mrs. Liberto approve of our marriage, which

116

makes me very happy.

I realize that with our difference in religion there are certain problems that we will have to work out, also certain "sacrifices" that I will have to make. I'm perfectly willing to go along with the laws of the Church, and any religious difficulties that may arise, I think Viv and I have the ability to talk things over and work things out sensibly.

I know that we love each other very much and it takes that for it to work in any marriage.

I'm a country boy and I've still got a little of the cotton patch dirt between my toes, but I've got the ambition to get ahead and I think I can give Vivian a comfortable and happy home. You'll always find me working and trying.

All my people are Missionary Baptists and the largest part of them live in the state of Arkansas. I'm proud of them of course. All of them are decent people, even though one of my uncles is known to be the biggest liar in the solid south, he's a decent liar.

I'm going to get Vivian's ring tomorrow. I sure wish I could be there for our engagement, but as they say in the Navy "That's the way the

117

wind blows." I've still got quite a few months left over here and I want Viv to wear my ring while she's waiting. They say theres nothing like putting it on her finger in the moonlight, but again, the Navy.

I sure like the present Viv sent. Its something I can really use, although you shouldn't let her spend so much money on me.

Well, I'm going to start Viv a letter. I hope to talk to her before I finish it. You all take care of yourselves and write when you can.

With Love,
Johnny Cash

Johnny, 1951:
the first photo he gave me

My senior picture, 1952

Mother and Daddy

Johnny going "ape" over my photo

From one of my many photo sessions for Johnny

Johnny acting a fool

No mail today

"Here's your big fat sailor, darling."

Johnny and his ten-dollar guitar

"Honest, honey,
I caught bigger ones
than this."

Johnny's working girl

"On the train coming back—
I'm not as mean as I look."

March 1st '53

To My Darling Vivian,

I hardly know what to say Vivian. If we were together at this occasion I'd probably be choked up, so I guess it's best to try to say what I'd like to on paper. There are no words that could tell just how I do feel.

It's hard darling, to have to give it to you this way. It hurts to be denied the joy of taking your hand and putting the ring on your finger. It would be so wonderful just to be near you.

Try to feel me there beside you Vivian darling. Even though we're miles apart, you know that in our hearts we are together at this moment. My darling, every word of love I've ever said to you, I wish you could feel at this moment. I wish you could understand just how much pure love comes with this little ring.

Thank you for saying that you will be mine Vivian darling. Thank you for being so sweet and wonderful, and for waiting all this time. With Gods help I will make you happy.

Wear this ring darling to tie our hearts together the long months we will be apart. Wear it as a token of my love, and to show the world someone loves you. Someone does love you Vivian. More than any man ever loved a woman.

Wear it sweetheart until the day I can put the wedding ring on your finger that will make us as one as long as we live.

God bless you my darling, and keep you safe for me until you're in my arms.

I love you Vivian. I never meant it any-more than I mean it now. I love you with all my heart.

Your husband some day,
Johnny

July 4, 1954: the day Johnny
returned from Germany

. . . Our wedding day
was well worth
the wait!

Finally, Mrs. Johnny Cash!

Goodnight my darling. I love you Viv. I love you so very much sweetheart. I'll always love you Viv darling.

Your Very Own,
Johnny

~

March 3, 1953

Hello Sweetheart,

I didn't get a letter today darling and I only got seven yesterday. I don't think you love me anymore.

Honey, thank you for the compliments, but if I were as clean and decent as you talk, I'd be an angel, and I'm far from it. Darling, I just want you and I to be above the average as far as being morally clean is concerned. I want us to have a home and family we can be proud of. What I'm so thankful for Vivian is that I've got a girl that's so clean and decent. Never let loneliness or anything else bring you to the point where you don't care what happens to you. You'll never regret being what you are darling. People have never lived as dirty as they are now. Everybody's mind is in the gutter. There'll be a big breakdown sometime.

Darling, you know I told you that you and I would pray together at 9 oclock on Saturday? Well, Saturday night at 9 oclock I was waiting for the call. I prayed from 9 to 9:04, for you and I, our folks, for everything that concerns us. It made me feel so good Viv.

Viv, by the time you get this you should have gotten the ring. I hope it made you happy darling. Now we're officially engaged, aren't we sugar?

Your husband to be,
Your Johnny

~

March 4, 1953

My Darling Viv,

Sweetheart, tell me if the ring fits OK. It sure seemed small to me. I couldn't even get it on my little finger. You're a little girl though aren't you darling? You're just the right size to sit in my lap and lay your head against my cheek. You're perfect in every way. I love you Vivian.

Honey, I've been thinking about what I'm going to do when I get out and I know something I'm going to try. I'm going to try to get a job with the Air Force as a civilian. On Brooks Field they have what they call "Iron Curtain Block." It's part of Air Force Security Service and civilians work there. The pay is good, but I don't know if I can get a job there. I know a few that have, after they were discharged. You have to have a Top Secret and a perfect service record. I've got that,

March 1st

My Darling Vivian

Honey, I feel so good. Talking to you
boosted my morale 100%. I'm so happy darling.
I've just been in a daze since we talked. It
all seems like a dream that I finally got
to tell you things that I've been wishing for
so long.

Sweetheart, I love you so. you made me
so happy. telling me you loved me. I just
couldn't get enough of it darling. I heard
you every time you said it, but I wanted you
to keep saying it. I'm the luckiest person in
the world to have you.

Sugar it was no joke when I told you that
you were the sweetest girl in the world.
The way I said it must have been kind of
funny, but I didn't exactly know how to tell
you what I wanted to. You are honey and
I love you.

Sweetheart, there's one thing I said that
I think you got the wrong impression. The
way I said it, you couldn't keep from it though.
When I said, "If I had you in my arms, I'd
probably go crazy," you said "No, I wouldn't
let you." I probably embarrased you to

120

death. I didn't mean it that way darling. I'm just lonesome for you, and I miss you so much. You know how I think of you Viv.

Honey, please don't think anything about my having the ring special made. The price is the same either way. Besides, you're getting just what you wanted darling and I think the style you picked is perfect. I'm so happy about our engagement that I think I've just about shown everybody in the squadron. It's not all that expensive, but I have to let people know how we love each other darling.

I'm sending it tomorrow afternoon Viv, and all my love comes with it. That's a lot of love darling. I love you more than any thing in the world.

Honey, I just got two letters last week. I sure hope the mail service beats that this week.

Viv, I hate for you to have so much expense, but I can't send any money for at least a couple of months. Honey, I want you to tell me honestly now, can you pay the customs tax and phone bill? If it will hurt you to pay it, or if you'd have to get it from your folks, I want you to tell me and I'll write home for some of my money. Its *our* money in the bank darling, and if you need it, I'll get it for you. Please tell me if you need it darling. I'm going to send it to you later on anyway so if you need it now, tell me.

Sweetheart how much did the call cost? I'm a little afraid to ask. We talked 15 minutes, didnt we?

Viv darling, I doubt if I can sleep tonight. I'm so happy honey. It still seems like a dream. I wouldn't trade this afternoon for anything.

Honey, dont worry about me staying in so much. I will get out more from now on Sugar. Its getting warmer and I can play ball, etc. I'll make it alright honey. And I meant it when I said I'd make it alone. It will always be only you Vivian darling.

Viv I could talk to you all night if I could find any thing to say. You made me so happy this afternoon darling. I love you so very much. You're sweet whether you think so or not. I'll bet you've got sugar between your toes. Look and see.

Baby darling, I'm going to bed now. I'll

122

write tomorrow night honey. I sure hope
I hear from you tomorrow.

I love you Viv darling. I love you so
very much. I'll always love you Vivian.

your husband to be,
your Johny

and if I can keep my record straight, I may have a chance to work there. Of course, I won't know till I get back but I'm going to try it then.

Keep those precious letters coming and keep loving me Viv. I need you.

Your husband to be,
Your Johnny

~

March 6, 1953

My Darling Vivian,

Yesterday afternoon, the Control Chief and the other Trick Chief had to go to a meeting and I was left alone in charge of everything. It was OK most of the time, then a Major and Captain came in inspecting. We were short four men because two had to go to the hospital and two had to go to basketball practice. I explained to them six times that two men had to be in the hospital and the commanding officer let the other two off. The major told me to get some more men somewhere, he didn't care. So I called the Control Chief and he came out and argued with them for about an hour and they finally realized that there was no way of getting more. We didn't need them in the first place.

They finally calmed down and then they wanted to know when I got my haircut. I got it cut yesterday morning on my lunch hour, but just couldn't make them believe that I didn't take time off from work to get it cut. The Control Chief again argued with them about an hour, then after that they wanted to know why I was Trick Chief when I was only A/1C. I told them I was appointed by the C.O. and they forgot that part. I was beginning to think I was getting another "Stability under Pressure" test, but they finally left me alone and got on the Control Chief about the floor being dirty.

Then honey, when I got off work we swept and mopped the room. That wasn't all though. I went to bed and at 2 AM three of the boys came in slobbering drunk and woke me up to play pinochle. I can't play pinochle. They kept me awake for an hour and when I started getting a little angry, we started arguing. What made me so mad was that they brought whisky into the room and if they'd been caught, I'd be the one to get in trouble because I'm room chief. I turned out the lights right in the middle of the game and they got up and left, so mad they could kill me. They were alright today though. We're all still friends.

I'd rather be dead than see another day like yesterday. I'm beginning to see why 90% of the boys are drunkards when they come back from overseas.

Goodnight Viv darling, I love you.

Your Johnny

~

My Darling Vivian,

Viv darling, don't feel guilty when you go out and have fun. I do feel the same way when I have a little fun, but it's not wrong because I only have fun with the boys. If I went out and had fun with the girls now, I'd feel like killing myself. I want you to have fun Vivian. The happier you are, the happier I am. If you can be happy without boys, then I'm happy Vivian. There's never going to be another girl for me, but you Vivian. I will try to have fun Vivian. I'll do my best to be as contented as possible alone. Another woman would be revolting to me. I couldn't lay my hands on another girl. God made us for just each other Vivian. He made our hearts for each other and our bodies for each other.

Vivian, please go out with your girlfriends and have a good time. Do anything to occupy yourself and don't get so lonesome. When did you quit going roller skating honey? I just wondered why you haven't been lately. Try to have fun darling. I love you so much and want you to be happy.

When it comes to you Vivian, I don't think there is a dirty side of love. I worship you Vivian and anything between us would be wonderful. Even so, I'm glad you and I never had relations together. We will love and appreciate each other more when we're married, bedsides, it's what God wants. I think He's proud of us now and if we do what he asks maybe our prayers will be answered. I know when we're married, it will be because we love each other and not because of a heat wave between us. I love you Vivian darling. I want you to be my wife because I love you. I love you more than anything in the world.

One of my buddies asked me to go to Munich and meet a "lady" he knows. I asked him didn't he remember that I just got engaged, and he said "Oh well, come on and go, Vivian doesn't have to know." I told him I was going to tell you what he said darling, and I told him you'd be mad at him. So I did darling. These guys say I'm crazy for passing up these women, but there's nothing that would make me touch a one of them. You'll always be the only one Vivian darling.

Vivian honey, if I hadn't wanted you to have the kind of ring you want, I wouldn't have asked you to send a picture. Now that you have the ring you see that it's not too expensive after all. If it had cost $10,000 I wouldn't mind Vivian. I knew how much I was going to pay for a ring before you sent the picture and honey, please believe me, the cost wasn't any different. If you hadn't sent the picture, you would have gotten a German style and they're old fashioned and ugly. Darling, please don't feel bad. I asked you to do it, so don't feel that way. I can't see why you feel the way you do. I just want you to be happy with what I got darling. I hope with all my heart that you like it. It's not expensive, so forget the cost. As far as thinking you're a gold digger, if anyone ever said you were, he'd have me to fight. You're perfect Vivian, and I love you with all my heart.

Your husband to be,
Your Johnny

I love you Vivian

~

March 8, 1953

My Sweetheart,

I got up at 10:30 this morning darling and it took me two hours to clean up the room. Those guys really hit a new low last night. Whisky was spilled all over the floor, cigarettes and ashes were on everything, and it looked worse than a pig pen. I cleaned it up and it looks half way decent now.

It will be so nice when we're married Viv. We'll have a clean house, home cooked meals and it will be wonderful living with you. I won't be going to bed wondering what time the next drunk will wake me up. I get so disgusted I could start swinging. I'll never forget last night. I was sitting in the window watching the show. Everybody was drinking, yelling, cursing and vomiting. I can't see why people have to be the way they are.

Honey, this morning I was listening to a preacher on the radio. He said that one of God's weapons against sin is anxiety. He said that sometimes when people get too worry-free and happy and contented, they are inclined to do just what they want to, and forget God because they've got what they want. He said God makes people sad, lonely and unhappy so they'll stay closer to Him. Maybe that's why we have to be apart Viv. Maybe God makes us this way so we'll stay closer to Him. We'll have to remember to keep on worshiping Him and depending on Him when we're back together and happy.

Honey, I remember when we were coming over on the ship and I was telling Perea about you and that I was in love with you. I told him that I was going to keep writing you but I said I knew that I'd not have you when I went back because it would be too long. I loved you then Vivian, but I never dreamed it would last like this and we'd be so close to each other and love each other so after 18 months.

Your husband to be,
Your Johnny

~

March 11, 1953

My Wife to be,

Darling, didn't I tell you that an A/1C has to have 12 months in grade to make S/Sgt, or did you know? Well, we do, but there's one way to beat it.

126

That's to be put in as "outstanding." I don't believe it, but he told me tonight that I was going in for Staff Sergeant. He said he would submit my recommendation next month. I only have six months in grade then, but he says I'm going in then anyway. If I do I'll be the first one in this sqdn that went in that way. It makes me feel good, but I'll have to see it to believe it.

Your husband to be,
Your Johnny

~

March 12, 1953

My Darling Wife to be,

Are you going to announce our engagement in the paper honey, or are you supposed to? I just want people to know. I think I'll tell Mom to put it in one of the papers there.

Honey, I'm so happy that you're working under pleasant conditions and that you like the people you work with. Sugar I'm going to have a job for you some day and I hope with all my heart that you like it. You won't have to do much darling. Just keep house, have kids and sleep with me so I won't be so lonesome at night.

Darling, last night I must have been dreaming of you, but I don't remember it. Anyway, I woke myself up saying "Viv darling . . . Viv darling." I had my pillow in my arms and was caressing the top of it where your head is supposed to be, and kissing you. I sure felt silly, honey, but I was a little disappointed.

Darling, it made me feel so good that the Control Chief was putting me in for Staff Sgt, but I feel kind of dirty about it. It will be six months before Louie and Bob and Perea can go in. Us four came over here together and I feel kind of dirty to go in under "Outstanding" conditions. All of them have still been my good friends and haven't resented it because I was made Trick Chief, but I wonder how they're going to take this. I've just done my job like everybody else, but the Control Chief thinks I've done it better than anyone else. I just hope I don't lose any friends over it.

I start training tonight to learn more about Teletype machines and another big complicated machine they've got here. They'll probably decide soon that I'm not so outstanding.

Your husband to be,
Your Johnny

~

March 17, 1953

My Wife to be,

Darling, I'm at work now and felt like talking to you. I think this is the first time I've written you at work since I've been here. I shouldn't, but I've got this paper hidden and I'm watching for the wheels out of the corner of my eye. I don't have anything to do for 25 minutes anyway. I'll tell you if I get caught honey.

Darling, I just had to talk to you. I feel so close to you, and I've been thinking of you all night. Sweetheart, I didn't say much today about the letter I got from you when you got the ring, but I sure was happy darling because you seemed so happy. Viv honey, I love you so much. If I ever lost you I wouldn't want to live. I need you so darling.

Darling, tonight I dreamed that you and I broke up. It was horrible honey, and when I woke up and realized it was just a dream, I was so happy. It was so realistic though that it wasn't funny. I dreamed that you wrote me a short, not too sweet letter one Monday, and the next one you wrote was Friday and you said, "I'll be perfectly honest with you Johnny, I've been dating a boy from Randolph and will continue to do so."

Then the letter I wrote you back, I remember it so plain, I could even see the green ink in my dream. I told you how bad I hated for it to happen, but if you continued to go with this guy, then the next time you'd hear from me would be the day I came to get you the very day I got back. I told you that you were going to be mine if you were married or not. It was horrible honey. I wish I wouldn't have such crazy dreams. I know things like that would never happen.

God is going to keep us together darling. We've been through a lot. We've still got a lot of loneliness to go through honey, but we can make it. We'll be the happiest couple in the world darling. With the love we have for each other, it will be wonderful. I love you so much my darling. You're so sweet and wonderful to me, and I love you so very much Viv.

Sweetheart I guess I better get to work. If they caught me writing a letter I'd probably not be smiled upon.

I love you Vivian darling.

> Your husband someday,
> Johnny

~

March 21, 1953

My Darling Wife to be,

I got two sweet letters from you today sweetheart. They're kind of short but they're awfully sweet. Just like you darling, you're kind of short, but you're awfully sweet.

Honey, thank you for making me some cookies. I appreciate everything you do for me Viv, but you shouldn't go to so much trouble packing and having them mailed. But I am anxious to get them darling. It will be the first time

I eat your cooking. I bet they'll taste wonderful. I love anything that has anything to do with you Vivian.

I'll be up at nine oclock to pray with you sweetheart. We'll be together for a few minutes with God. See you then honey.

Your husband to be,
Your Johnny

~

March 31, 1953

My Sweet Darling,

I just got back from Munich honey and I'm sure glad to be back. It's been raining most of the day, and of course Munich was in its usual glory. The "ladies" in Munich were out in force today. They know the GIs get paid and I bet we said "No thank you" a half a dozen times. It's disgusting.

Vivian darling, I love you and miss you so. I'm all alone tonight. The other guys are out in Munich and Augsburg, most of them. I think only four of us on my shift are here. The two that went to Munich with me are down in the next room playing records, and the other one is a married guy that's true to his wife, believe it or not. He's really a nice guy. He's been here nine months and hasn't been untrue to her yet. I'm true to my wife to be too. It makes me feel so good to be true to you Vivian. I love you so much darling. I love you with all my heart.

Your husband to be,
Your Johnny

~

April 7, 1953

My Sweet Wife to be,

Honey, sometime this month I'm going to wrap all the letters you've written me and mail them to you. Darling I want you to promise to keep every one of them for me. I want them as long as I live. My box is full and I don't have anyplace else to keep them so I'll send them and you keep them for me honey.

Viv, when I look at those letters I have all kinds of feelings. Pain, because you've spent so much time on me and trouble. I'm not worth all that. Sometimes when I look at them I could cry because I'm so happy that I have your love and have had it so long and never held you in my arms and told you I love you, but still, Vivian was there writing and waiting.

I love you with all my heart.

Your husband to be,
Your Johnny

~

April 8, 1953

My Darling Wife to be,

Sweetheart, I got the cookies today and I'm sitting here eating them and writing you. Honey, I don't know what you thought was wrong with them. They sure are good darling. It's all I've eaten today. I got up when the mail room opened and I've been munching them ever since. They were a little beat up and mashed in the mail, but they're good. Thank you darling. You're so sweet. It will be wonderful if I could eat them while they're hot darling. Someday I will.

You're mine Viv darling.

Your Own,
Johnny

Thanks again for the cookies, Mrs. Cash to be

~

April 17, 1953

Darling Wife to be,

Honey, I'm going to be leaving here within the next two weeks for some country about a thousand miles south of here, I think. I'll be there about five weeks, I think. I don't know much, do I darling? Well, you see, it's this way. My officer in charge told me I was going on temporary duty for about 5 weeks. He said "soon" and that's all he would tell me honey. The last time something like that happened, four guys went to this country for 5 weeks, wore civilian clothes and stayed in a nice hotel and got paid $9.70 per day. I'm just keeping my fingers crossed that's what it's going to be darling. Our headquarters asked for four men from this squadron, one from each trick, so they picked me, because I've had experience. I'll tell you more if I can when I find out more honey.

Goodnight my darling. I'll write tomorrow night, and I'll be praying with you tomorrow nite at nine Viv.

Your husband to be,
Your Johnny all your life.

~

April 24, 1953

My Darling Vivian,

Honey, no mail came in today, but I have the one I got yesterday to answer.

Viv, I'm sorry about that letter last night. I know I was silly and made a fool

My baby Darling,

Happy birthday honey. Many happy returns. Darling, Willie and I have been to the club celebrating your birthday.

Honey, now don't be hurt cause I've been drinking just beer and Willie and I are plased. Baby I'm going to tell you something and you can figure it out. I had 70¢ darling. Thats 14 nickels, and they sell beer for a nickel tonight I've got 15¢ left, so how many beers did I guzzle?

Honey, some Nigger got smart and I asked him to go outside and he was too yellow. He thought he could whip everybody in the club but he wouldn't ever fight me. He's yellow coon.

131

Honey, we got vaccinated yesterday and willie said, "lets go outside and mash each others vaccinations." Willie is crazy darling.

Vivie, I love you sugar. Happy birthday. Darling I love you. You're so sweet. I wish I had you with me baby darling. I need you in my arms so much. Honey, I'm nearly drunk, but you know it's been a long long time since I drank any and I promise I won't anymore. Please keep on loving me vivie. I want you to be my wife, and I promise with all my heart and soul that I wont get drunk when were married. baby darling I promise, I love you.

Viv honey, tomorrow when I get up I'll take a shower and get a cup of coffee and I'll be alright so don't worry my darling. I'll be just fine tomorrow, I'm just fine tonight honey too.

I can't keep anything from you Viv, I love you so much and I wouldn't lie to you for anything in this world. I know you don't like for me to get drunk, but Viv, I don't like to either darling, but I just couldn't stay in the room alone anymore. You know I wouldn't go out with a girl for anything in the world Viv, so I didn't do any harm tonight. I wouldn't ever be untrue to you Viv my darling. I went with Willie, and Willie is never unfaithful to his wife. We both just had a few beers and came back to the barracks. Viv honey, I'm going to bed as soon as I write you darling. I'm wasted.

Honey, I'll write tomorrow I'm so very tired. I'll see you in my dreams tho. My darling, I love you. I love every ounce of you from the tip of your head to the bottom of your toes. You're so sweet Viv, and I love you so very much. I do my darling I love you. I love you.

yours All your life
All yours,
Your Johnny

134

of myself. I'll try not to drink anymore darling, and if I do I promise I won't write you when I do. That was the first time in a long, long time darling, and I just couldn't stay here alone. I'm sorry I was drunk, but my conscious doesn't hurt so much because at least I was true to you. No girls were there except for waitresses, and I came back and went to bed as soon as I wrote that letter.

Viv, maybe you don't mind so much, at least I think you'll forgive me, but I'm so sorry darling for not holding my will power and staying sober. When I opened my eyes this morning I wanted to jump out the window, or hide. I'm sorry Viv. Please forgive me for acting such a fool.

I didn't do anyone any harm except maybe myself. Although I nearly had a fight with some smart Negro at the club, which wasn't my fault. He came in the door pushing everybody, and walked down the aisle jigging when he walked with his collar turned up. When he pushed by me, I pushed him. He finally calmed down and sat down after I asked him to go outside. They're not so mean and tough when it comes to actually doing something.

It will be wonderful living with you darling. I need you for my wife Viv, and you're the only one that would ever do. I could never share my life and love with another woman. It's wonderful the way I love you Vivian. It's hard to understand the feeling between you and I. Viv, it will be wonderful the way we love and understand each other. Darling I love you so much.

Your husband to be,
Your Johnny

~

April 25, 1953

My Sweet Darling,

Viv, you make me so happy. I'm glad you're so proud of your ring honey. I'd do anything in the world to make you happy Vivian. There's nothing in the world I wouldn't do for you.

Honey, last night I dreamed that we were married and you'd just had a baby. You'd been back from the hospital about a week but you were still sick and weak, and lay on the couch by the heater. I dreamed that everyday you seemed to lose weight and get pale, so one sunny day, I picked you up in my arms and took you out in the back yard and sat down, then sat you down in my lap. You said the sun felt good but you were so weak and could hardly lift your arms. I started kissing you on the face, lips and eyes, and you felt better then you said that you thought that was what was wrong. I hadn't been kissing you enough. When I woke up, I had my hand on the back of your head and was pressing my face to your neck. Honey, I don't know why I'm always dreaming about you having a baby. Maybe it's because I think about it a lot.

Vivian, I owe more to you than to any person I've ever known. I'm not bragging on myself, but it's all because of you. Tonight at nine I wonder where all my buddies will be. I'll be with you praying and they'll be out drunk or worse. I never say anything about it to any of the boys, but Vivian I'm so thankful that you're keeping me just halfway the way I want to be. I know I got drunk the other night, but there was no reason for it and I've promised myself that it won't happen again.

Your husband to be,
Your Johnny always.

~

April 29, 1953

My Sweet Darling,

Honey, it sure is a dull day. It's misting rain and cold. It's a good day to sit here where it's warm and write you and think about you. I wish you were here with me sugar. The other boys are down in the basement shooting pool or something. If you were here honey, I'd get my guitar and sing you a song, and maybe I'd even read you Shakespeare. I know that would just thrill your soul.

Darling, I read in the paper that an Italian girl had a man arrested for kissing her once, and now he's in jail for 18 months. I don't believe it was worth it, although I know one little Italian girl that's worth it. To kiss you once I'd spend 18 months in jail, that is, if they'd let you come to see me every two or three minutes all the time.

Honey, I sure had a crazy dream last night. I dreamed I went home, and I was wanting to go to San Antonio to see you, and all my old school friends came. One of the girls asked me to marry her and I said I would, not realizing what I was saying. Two minutes later she was over with one of the boys flirting with him, and I began to realize how silly a mistake I made by promising to marry such a fickle girl. I knew that she'd never be true to me because of the way she was acting. Some way, I got away and the next thing I knew I was on your front porch, and you came out of your house with a broom in your hand. You sure looked cute honey. Your hair was tied up on top of your head, your face and blouse was dirty, and your skirt was hanging down in front about 3 inches more than it was in back. You were embarrassed and I was so tickled because I caught you that way. I wouldn't let you get back in the house. It seems we were the only ones there, and I stood there talking to you. We hadn't kissed, or said anything about how lonesome we'd been for each other. We'd been talking about just little things, then I stopped and stared at you and said, "Vivian, I love you," and we both jumped at the same time. I held you up off the floor and held you tight and kissed you hard, then stood you back up and smeared the dirt on your nose.

Darling, it all seemed so real and it was so wonderful to be with you, even though it was a dream, I've felt so close to you all day Vivian, and I've missed you so much. I've been thinking all day how lucky I am to have a girl just like you were in the dream, instead of like the other one that would mean nothing but misery. I love you so much my darling. You mean all the world to me. You'll be the sweetest wife in the world. I want the whole world to know I've got a girl that couldn't be beat anywhere on earth. You're wonderful Vivian and I love you with all my heart.

Bye darling. Remember that every ounce of your sugar belongs to me, and I'm all yours.

Your husband to be,
Your Johnny

~

May 1, 1953

My Darling Sweetheart,

No mail today sugar, so you're not going to get much. I'm mean aren't I honey? There's really not much to write about, except that I wanted to tell you I love you. I love you darling.

Honey, you know something? I love you very very much. I'm sitting here writing with your picture in front of me telling you I love you on paper, and whispering it to you too. You look so sweet. If I could just hold you once and kiss that smile on your face, I'd be in heaven.

Honey, I was thinking last night that some night next summer you and I will take another walk down the river. We'll pick a night when it's nice and warm, and late, so there won't be many people around, and walk down the quiet river together, talking and holding hands. We'll sit on the bench where we did before and talk about old times, and say how much we love each other. That will be just next summer honey. No more we don't have to say, "Just two years darling." It's next summer. 8 more months and it will be, "This year."

Darling, it's seemed like an eternity already, and we've still got lots of lonely nights ahead of us, but darling, the time will fly, and we'll be in each other's arms again.

Yours for life,
Your Johnny

~

May 3, 1953

My Darling Vivian,

Honey I don't know how to start. I feel like a dog, but I'll tell you everything and hope for the best.

I haven't been untrue to you Vivian, but what happened last night wasn't

137

any better. Honey, I got up too late yesterday morning to go to Munich and get my clothes, so I didn't go. Yesterday afternoon I went to town to get a chair for our writing table, and met three boys that just got here, and they were going to Augsburg and asked me to go with them.

We caught the 5:30 train and when we got to Augsburg we went out to this club to see the floor show. We ate supper and when we finished I looked at my watch, it was 9:45. I missed our prayer together Vivian. That's one thing I did that I was so ashamed of. It hurt so much to know that I had let you down, and you had prayed alone. I certainly needed someone to pray for me.

Honey, the boys started drinking beer then, so I did. We sat there and watched the floor show, and when it was over at 11:00 we went to another joint. We started drinking cognac then and got drunk. Those three guys halfway behaved themselves, but I didn't. I must have had a guardian angel last night because any other time I would have come back in two or three pieces.

The town was full of Army guys, and I think we were the only Air Force in town. I called them all "Doggies," and called the M.P.s "Ground Pounder Cops." I called every 1st and 2nd LT, "Louie."

To top it all off, we got a taxi and started back to the hotel at 1:00. We stopped at the train station for a few minutes and a Negro called me a bus driver. As soon as he saw I wasn't afraid of him, he started walking off, and I called him every name anyone has ever given a Negro. The further he walked away, the louder I yelled, calling him "Coon," "Nigger," "Jig-a-boo," and a few others. I yelled for a full 30 minutes that I could whip any Negro that walked on the face of the earth. None showed up so we went to the hotel and went to bed after waking nearly everybody in the hotel with our noise.

This morning I was sick, and so disgusted with myself that I want to die. I drank a lot of coffee and vomited it back up.

Vivian, I don't know what you'll think of me now. After promising just a week ago that it wouldn't happen again.

My darling, I love you. Please forgive me and forget this and give me time and I will prove that it won't happen again. Vivian, I know I'm not worth an ounce of you, and I don't deserve you. Viv, please forget and forgive me honey. I know I've no right to ask for forgiveness again, but darling, you know I tell you everything. I couldn't have kept this from you. Vivian, I'll prove to you that I'll do better. I'll prove without you even asking me that this won't happen again.

Oh honey, I'm so sorry I made such a fool of myself. And missed our prayer last night. I've prayed already for forgiveness, and will continue to pray for guidance.

Viv honey, don't let what I do change the way you feel about anything. Honey, please keep on praying for us and for me. Keep on going to church and stay the wonderful girl you are. Vivian, you can straighten me out and keep me that way.

Darling, you mean so much to me. I need you so. Please keep on loving me Vivian darling. No matter what I did, I wasn't untrue to you Viv. I remember all that happened, and I didn't even as much as talk to any girls. I didn't even go by the place where that girl that I went with last fall. I didn't even see her. I'll never be untrue to you Viv. None of the other boys went with any girls either.

Viv, maybe you're not asking me to apologize. I wish I could talk to you. I need you so Vivian darling. I wish I could hold you in my arms and tell you how sorry I am, and how much I love you.

Honey, I'm going to get some sleep now. I'm not sick now but I want to get some sleep before I have to go to work at midnight.

Goodnight Viv. I love you my sweet darling. I love you with all my heart and soul. Please keep on loving me, Viv, and keep those wonderful letters coming. I love you and need you so Viv. I love you my darling.

> Your husband to be,
> Your Johnny

~

May 4, 1953

My Darling,

Viv, someone came in today and told me I didn't get any mail, but when I woke up tonight there was a letter from you lying beside my bed. I guess some more came in and he brought it to me.

Honey, those personalized pillow cases sound nice. You're sweet darling. Although there's going to be two heads on the one marked "Vivian." For awhile we won't need but one.

Vivian, I guess I'm superstitious or worry too much, but after I got so drunk the other night and missed our prayer, I was afraid that God would punish me, or us. I was a little afraid that something would happen to us. Viv, I guess it sounds silly to you and maybe it is, but I'm going to keep praying for us. And I promise that nothing like that will happen again darling. I'm so ashamed of myself, Viv.

Viv, I won't go to Africa. When and if I go, I'll go to Turkey, I think. But don't tell anyone that honey. That's the place the last four went. I wish I could find out more about it, but they still haven't said a word. If I don't go pretty soon, and get back, my leave will be shot.

Honey, this morning I went over to see a buddy of mine in the hospital. He went over yesterday to get something for his nerves, and they put him to bed. He's got high blood pressure and shakes like a leaf. He works too hard for one thing, and he's worried sick about his girl. He goes home in five months and his girl has waited 27 months and has started going steady with another guy now. She hardly writes him at all now and he goes to the mail room three or four times a day, or did. He told me the doctors asked him if he's been thinking of committing suicide, and that's got him stirred up even more. He always was very emotional and has some wild ideas and beliefs. If they'd leave him alone over there and treat him human he'd be alright, but those dumb doctors do him more harm than good. I know he never thought about suicide, but now he thinks the doctors think he's crazy and he's mad at the whole bunch and there's no telling what will become of him. I told him I'd get his mail for him everyday if he gets any.

Honey, I hate to think about what I'd do if I lost you. I don't think I'd do like that guy, but I don't think I'd want to live. You're a part of me and I don't want to live without you.

Your husband to be,
Your Johnny

~

May 6, 1953

My Sweet Darling,

Viv, I found out a little about my trip this morning. The Capt. called us four guys in and gave us the story, part of it anyway. I like what he said honey.

Get this darling. The Air Force is buying me civilian clothes. He said they were going through the red tape now to get our clothes. Where we're going, we will wear civilian clothes only, and live in a hotel, and get paid $9.70 per day. Honey, I was keeping my fingers crossed and it worked.

He gave us the glory story about how proud of us four boys he was that we were chosen out of so many (150). Of course he wasn't any happier than I am. I'm sure lucky to get something like that.

Honey, he wouldn't tell us when or where exactly we're going. I have an idea, but couldn't be positive. I believe it won't be over ten days or at the most, two weeks before we leave.

Viv, I might be gone four or five weeks, but it could be 3 or 4 months, so if I find out it will be over four or five weeks, I'm going to call you before I leave here.

And honey, if and when I do call, don't say anything about the trip. I can tell you when I leave here and when I think I'll be back, but I won't and don't you say anything that anyone at all could figure out what we're talking about. There will be lots of people listening sugar, and I'm not ready to be shot.

There is something you can tell me though, sweetheart. You can tell me how much you love me. I think I'll make you tell me first this time because I told you first the other two times.

Honey, I sure am sleepy. I'll be glad when the mailroom opens and I can get my mail from my darling, if it came in, then go to bed. I like to read a letter from you when I go to sleep. It's just like a long goodnight kiss because your letters are so sweet and wonderful. Someday I'll hold you and kiss you goodnight darling, then all night you'll just be whispering distance away. It will be wonderful loving you and living with you Vivian. I love you so much darling. The Bible is sure right when it says "Man should have a wife." Someday I'll have a wife, the sweetest, most wonderful wife in the world. I'll always love you, Vivian darling.

Your husband to be,
Your Johnny

~

May 9, 1953

My Darling Wife to be,

I got up this afternoon, went to the first movie, then came back and prayed with you at nine. We've been playing and singing ever since and its after midnite now. We had a nice time honey. I think we woke up half the people in the place.

Viv, maybe God has a reason for keeping us apart. He knows how we love each other Vivian. All we can do is hope, pray and want. Sometimes I need you so bad I could scream, but if we can't be together soon, I can wait. You're certainly doing your part darling. Vivian, I wish I could tell you how I love you and how I appreciate all you do for me. I love you so much my darling.

Your husband to be,
Your Johnny

~

May 10, 1953

My Darling Viv,

I finished wrapping all the letters from you honey, and I'll mail them tomorrow. You keep every one of them for me honey. When I get back we'll sit side by side and read about old times. Most of our "old times" are in those letters Viv, but it's been wonderful having your love even though we've been apart. We'll make up for every minute of the time we spent on those letters darling. We'll have a lifetime in each other's arms.

Honey, I think there's about 500 letters in that box, and if it had taken you 40 minutes to write each letter, it would have taken you 15 days if you had written them all without stopping. 15 days of telling me you love me without eating. I'll have to remember that darling. I'm going to spend a lifetime taking care of you and trying to make you happy. I love you so much Vivian darling. And from the bottom of my heart I appreciate everything you've done for me. I'll never forget it honey. There will never be anyone for me but you Vivian. You're all I ever want and will always, as long as I live, be the only one.

Your Johnny,
All your life.

~

May 11, 1953

My Darling Vivian,

Honey the people at the Post Office laughed at me today. On the customs card, under "Description of Contents," I put "500 Love Letters." They are love letters, and those people probably thought they were just the average run-of-the-mill love letters, but they're priceless to me.

I love you Viv honey. I love you so very, very much.

Your husband,
Your Johnny

~

May 15, 1953

My Darling Wife to be,

Honey, I set a record today at work. An all time record for efficiency. I was kind of proud of myself. It wasn't very good for me though. I sat in one place from 7:30 in the morning to 5:00 this afternoon. I got up <u>once</u> to eat dinner. The record I set was "259," the most that has ever been gotten before in the last 3 years is "256." You don't understand do you sugar? Well, I'll tell you all about it in 20 years, OK? Just so you know, I set a record that beat everybody including a few hot Staff Sgts.

Honey, I'm going to bed now. I'm very tired. I wish I could snuggle up to you and go to sleep.

Your Johnny
All your life

~

May 16, 1953

My Sweet Darling Viv,

Honey, do you have a record player? I bought us one today. One of my buddies was flat broke and had a record player he just bought a couple of months ago for $35 so I bought it from him for $15. It broke me, but I've got one now and I've always wanted one. I want to keep it here till nearly time to go home, then I'll send it to you honey to keep for us. We'll buy all our favorite records. I can't get many records here that I like, and they don't have any hillbilly records at all, but some of the other guys do.

I'm back honey. I just prayed with you. I could almost feel you beside me darling. Honey, where do you pray? Do you go in your bedroom alone? I always thought that's where you went.

Goodnight my Viv.

Your husband,
Your Johnny

~

May 20, 1953

My Very Own Darling,

At the lake the other day we took a lot of pictures and if they're any good I'll send you some of them. Darling, we sure met some nice German people at the lake. One little girl about six and a boy about 12 asked me all about the States. They had learned a little English in school and I think I was the first American they had talked to. We gave the kids gum and the older ones cigarettes and got in solid with them. The little boy got my address and said he would write me. The little girl said she wanted to go home with me, but I told her I'd have to have a wife to adopt her. They all were cute honey and sure treated us nice.

The two guys that I went with are new here and this was the second time they'd been out. Both of them are married, but one of them didn't seem to know it. He was always wanting us to go with him to meet some girls. We didn't, of course, so he stopped trying.

Honey, I just can't get over things like that. It seems that half of the guys that are married don't care. I want to kick a guy in the pants when he mentions going out with one of these girls while he's married.

When we were in the hotel, this guy was talking about his wife and telling us how fast he'd ditch her if she ran around on him while he's gone. I asked him what he thought she would do if she knew what he did, and he said, "Oh, she would forgive me." I sure feel sorry for his wife. I don't see why he married her in the first place when he intended to degrade her by running around with one of these pigs.

I suppose there's a lot of things I can't understand. I only know I'd die before I'd do something like that.

Remember I love you Vivian. I love you more than anything in this world. You mean everything to me Viv. I love you so.

Your Johnny
All your life.

~

My Darling Vivian,

Vivian, I read something today that was very disgusting and very disappointing. It was a little book on "Mixed Marriage." I'm not going to send it to you unless you ask me to because it's discouraging. It's urging Catholics not to marry Protestants and Protestants not to marry Catholics. If my life were going to be as this book says, I'd be in misery all my life living with you. I don't believe it and even though it's a Catholic publication, I know you wouldn't.

Vivian, there's something in it that disgusted me. It said that before a Catholic can marry a Protestant she will have to sign an oath saying that she will always try her best by word and example to change her mate to Catholic. Is that right Vivian? Do you have to sign that, and do you intend to do that?

I don't want to start any confusion but once you promised me that you'd never try. According to this, you're going to be forced to "nag" me until I submit. Tell me about that will you darling? I want to know everything now.

Vivian, doesn't the Catholic Church believe that anyone else will go to heaven? Do they honestly believe that people of other faiths that are married are living in adultery? Vivian, you can't believe all that they teach. You couldn't love me and want to spend your life with me if you didn't believe in me.

Honey, when I was 12, I was converted, baptized and joined the Baptist church. I was forgiven of my sins, and accepted Christ as my savior. When I die, I'll die a Baptist, and when I die, I'll go to heaven. I'm not throwing anything in your face, Vivian. I was just showing you my belief.

Is it asking too much to ask to be left alone? Why do they have to be that way? I was so torn up over it that I couldn't sleep last night. If people could only live the way they want to. In the end there is one God to reckon with and one God rules our lives now. Whether he's Baptist, Catholic, Jewish or what.

Vivian darling, I honestly don't think you deceived me. When you made that promise, I believe you meant it. Do you still mean it now that you know this, if you didn't know it already?

I found out another sacrifice I'll have to make that I didn't know about. That in case of death all children will be buried in a Catholic cemetery. Why is that honey? Even if the wife is Catholic, is that so? Can't they respect a man's family name and tradition?

One reason I know the guy that wrote the book is nuts is because of what he says about love. He says love is just a fever that lasts only a few months, maybe a year after marriage. Ask your Mom if she loves your dad. Ask my mom if she loves my dad. She'll say yes, and they've been married 30 years.

This guy also has the wrong idea about sex too. He thinks Protestants have a dirty minded attitude toward sex. I don't worry about that though, because

I know you have more faith in me than that. I've never said dirty things to you. But if this guy would ask me what I thought of sex, I'd tell him this: It is something God given that only married people have access to, and only to their mates. God made us the way we are so we can marry and love. Maybe I've said dirty things about it, but I realize that it's holy. When two people are married, and <u>in love,</u> they are close to God when their bodies are joined together. That's the way I believe, and if it's dirty to believe that way, then I'll admit my sin.

Honey, you know yourself that you know girls, Catholic and Protestant, that are filthy minded about it. I know boys of both faiths that are the same way. I hear boys stand around and freely talk of their most intimate relations with their wives. They talk about taking their wives virginity as if it was some prostitute they met.

I suppose I'm talking out of turn Vivian, and judging other people by the guy that wrote this book. I'm sorry if I said too much. But it stirred me up and made me so angry that I couldn't see.

Vivian darling, you still believe we can make it and be happy, don't you? I still say I'll do anything for you to make you happy. I'm going to forget this, and never read one of those books again.

Vivian, I know you have faith in me and don't believe any of those things about me. Honey, I need you and I want you to be my wife. I'm going to have you and happiness too, if I have to take you to the South Sea Islands. I need you my darling and I want you. I'll love you as long as I live. Vivian, I know I will.

> Your husband to be,
> Your Johnny

~

May 23, 1953

My Sweet Darling,

Honey, I hope you did have a nice time when you went skating. About the boys bringing you home, I don't care because I know you were true to me. Of course I trust you darling, and I thank you for telling me even a little thing like that. Be careful though darling. You know some very strong romances can get started at that skating rink.

Honey you said you knew I'd approve of those guys. Darling, I trust you, but trusting someone else is a different thing. I wouldn't trust any guy with you unless I knew him well. Engagements don't mean a thing to some guys no matter how they talk. Of course, I believe that they treated you with respect and I'm thankful for it. Anyone would treat you with respect if they knew you like I do, but those guys don't owe me anything, and being away from their girls, well, I just don't trust anybody honey. I trust you and I know that you'd put them in their place if you ever saw them and they got out of line, so that's what matters. Just don't ever let anyone forget that every ounce of you is branded "Cash," and just one Cash at that.

Yes, I do hope very much that our first born is a boy honey. It always seemed to me someway that a family was out of order if the oldest child wasn't a boy. I suppose it's silly, but I think that way.

I'll always be with you Viv. Especially during your pregnancies, to take care of you and get you pickles, hot dogs, ice cream, peanuts, watermelons, etc.

I love you with all my heart and soul Vivian. I need you so.

Your husband,
Your Johnny

~

May 25, 1953

My Darling Sweetheart,

Viv, I found out a little about my trip. They told me this morning that I would leave here the 10th. I'll take a train to Frankfurt, Ger. and from there I'll take a plane to Rome Italy. I won't know my final destination till I get to Rome. I'll probably be relieved of duty here the 3rd or 4th, and will start to clear the base and get my civilian clothes. I'll be gone approximately 3 months honey.

What do you think about the trip honey? Don't you think it will be nice? I'm sure lucky to get something like that. I wish we could make a trip together like that. Of course I'm going to work and not to sightsee, but I think it will be nice anyway.

I love you Viv. Keep on writing darling, and remember you belong to me. All of you is mine darling.

Your husband to be,
Your Johnny

~

May 26, 1953
Kaufburen, Ger

My Darling Viv,

Honey, I've got a confession to make. I threw rocks at the crows today. You see, there were some crows in a tree, and the other guys threw rocks and sticks at them. All the time I was thinking about what Viv said, "Johnny, don't throw rocks at the birds!" Well honey, I just couldn't stand it. The crows just sat there. I just had to make them fly, so I threw 3 wittle wocks at them and they

146

fwew. Fwee is all I fwowed, honey. I fwowed fwee 'n 'ey fwew. I pwomise I don't do it anymoah.

Your husband to be,
Your Johnny always.

~

May 25, 1953

My Very Own Viv,

Viv, when I opened this letter today and saw the heading "Dear Johnny," I got weak in the knees. For just a little second, I couldn't see the last "ny" on my name. I saw "Dear John," but then I knew it was silly. When I read the letter I was so happy because it was so sweet and wonderful, but so hurt because you had to suffer so (at the dentist). I love you Vivian darling.

Your husband to be,
Your Johnny

~

May 27, 1953

My Darling Wife to be,

Viv, I came back to Landsberg this morning and I had a long, sweet letter from you. Honey, I also got the packages you sent. My darling, I wish I could explain to you how much I appreciate the things you sent, and how I love you for it.

Viv, everything fit perfect. I couldn't ask for a better fit. Honey, you're wonderful. You know just when to do everything just right. You couldn't have given me anything that I would have needed more, or at a better time. I can use these on my trip honey. The socks fit perfectly and I just love them. These are the first ones I've seen like this honey, and I sure do like them. Everything is perfect. I love you so.

Viv honey, I got my orders today. More or less, they say this: On the 10th of June, I will leave here by train for Frankfurt, Germany where I will catch the first available aircraft to Rome, Italy. I will get my orders there. I know where else I'm going honey, and it's good. I won't even leave Italy though. I'll be on the East coast of Italy for 3 months, the four of us rather.

Darling, I get my civilian clothing allowance tomorrow. The officer said we could get any kind of clothes I wanted. I'm going to get one of these "Botany 500" tropical suits, two or three sport shirts and pants, and some work pants, socks and underwear.

Honey, this officer said we were the luckiest four guys in Europe. He said we're going down there to give the people the idea that we're just four Americans on vacation. We won't wear any G.I. clothes anytime. Of course, we have

147

a job to do and will be on orders, but we're on our own practically all the time. He said it would be three months vacation for us.

Honey, I also found this out, and I believe it's positive this time. I'll get $13.00 a day for that 3 months, besides my base pay. You realize honey that's about $520.00 per month for three months, which is $1560.00 for the 3 months! He says living costs are high, and we'll pay for our own room and food, but I really believe I can save five or six hundred dollars for you and I.

Darling, it will be miserable being in such a pretty place without you. Honey it would be heaven if I could have you there with me. I'll save all I can and you and I will go off somewhere alone when we're married darling. Even if we were broke it will be heaven being with you. Vivian, I love you my darling.

Viv, I don't know how the mail situation will be yet, but I'll find out in a couple of days and let you know. But keep on sending my letters to this address honey and they will be forwarded to me.

I can't describe my happiness Viv, but I'm so <u>completely</u> happy, and just because I know you're mine. Darling I've had two or three girls to say they loved me, while I was home, but I never realized that sharing a love, and a love so pure, and clean and wonderful as yours could be so heavenly. That's what you are to me, Vivian, heaven. Every letter from you makes me so happy. Every thought I think of you is wonderful.

I just thank you for being mine, and promising that you always will be mine. You know I'm always yours wherever I am. That isn't saying much, but this is a partnership, and you can always be sure it's complete here.

Viv, thanks again for the shirts, socks and candy. Honey, I appreciate it from the bottom of my heart. As long as I live there will never be any woman for me but you.

Your husband to be,
Your Johnny always.

~

May 29, 1953

Viv, I wrote you about three hours ago, then they got me up to go get interviewed on this job I'm going on, so I thought I'd write you now, then sleep till time to work tonight.

Honey, I found out a lot. The Major that talked to us is the one that's supervising the trip, so what he told us should be right.

First darling, he said we're only going to be there one month, then come back. He says it isn't going to be any picnic. We're not going to get any days off to mess around. We leave here the 10th, take a plane to south Italy from Frankfurt, and take a plane back a month later.

Honey, one thing he said wasn't too good. I won't be able to receive or write any mail at all. It will be one whole month that we won't be able to get mail from each other darling. I'm sorry, but that's the way it is. We'd have to send our mail through Italian channels, and because of our job and status, we can't do it.

Honey, I know you trust me, but just so you know I'll be true to you that thirty days, around all those good looking Italian girls, they've fixed up everything. Here's what the Major said sugar: "You will not at any time, or any circumstances talk to the Italian women." The reason for that is, he wants just as few people as possible to know that we are Americans. He said we'd be court martialed if we got caught with the girls there. That doesn't affect me though, because I've got the best little Italian girl in the world, including all of Italy, and I don't care. So I can't write you, but I'll be true to you darling.

Viv, I know it will be a long hard month for both of us, but honey, you know my feelings for you would never change. Even though I can't write darling, you know I'm thinking of you and loving you.

Darling, there's no need in you hurting yourself writing so much while I'm gone. Of course, it will be here waiting for me when I get back, but I know it will be awfully boring for you writing a month with no mail from me. It's up to you how much you want to write, or feel like, but you don't need to strain yourself.

But darling, you'd better not get out of the habit, cause when I get back I'm going to make you write every day, or spank you when I get back.

Viv, I'll probably place the call to you in a couple of days. I want so much to talk to you darling. You mean so much to me Vivian. You're the most wonderful girl in the world. I love you so very much.

Your husband,
Your Johnny

~

May 29, 1953

My Darling Vivian,

Honey, I got paid $490 yesterday. That's my clothing allowance, and money to live my first month in Italy. I feel like a millionaire carrying around that much. I get paid today, the regular payday too. I believe I can save a lot for us darling. We may get a new car after all.

I love you Vivian.

Your husband to be,
Your Johnny

~

June 2, 1953

My Darling Wife to be,

Honey, it's almost midnite. I went to the first movie, then sat around and read and played records for a long time. I'm staying up till 3 AM, then I'm supposed to talk to my darling.

Honey, I placed the call this morning. I wanted to place it for 2 AM, but the operator said it would have to be 3 AM. Darling, I sure hope the call goes through. I want to talk to you so bad Viv. I love you so much.

Darling, I guess I've lost the lighter you gave me. Honey, I stopped by the snack bar on the way to the movie and lit up a cigarette. That's the last time I remember seeing it. After the movies I reached for it, and it wasn't there. I went back to the theater and had the guy turn on the lights, but it wasn't there. Then I went to the snack bar and asked the Manager if a lighter had been found. None had, so he said check back tomorrow and see if it had turned up.

Viv, I'm sorry I'm so careless. No money in the world could have bought that lighter. It meant so much to me. I'm going to post a notice here in the squadron that I lost one, and maybe it will turn up. One of the German waiters in the snack bar probably has it now, and I'll probably never see it again.

Honey, I sure hope that call comes through at 3 AM. I can hardly wait. It will be so wonderful talking to you. I sure hope we'll have good connections. It will help us both I know, to talk to each other.

I love you my sweet darling.

Your husband to be,
Your Johnny for life.

~

June 3, 1953

My Darling Vivian,

As you know honey, the call didn't go through last night. I was in the 1st Sgts office at 3 AM, and the operator called and said there were no connections. I told her to try again tonight at 2 AM, so I'll be down there waiting.

Honey, I got my lighter back. I went over to the snack bar this afternoon and one of the German girls had found it and turned it in to the mgr. I sure was glad to get it back darling.

Honey, I hope you had fun at the movies, swimming and the picnic. Where did you go swimming, and on the picnic honey? I sure wish I could have been with you. I hope you had a real nice time darling.

Honey, I got a letter from Mom day before yesterday, and she said "I love Vivian as if she was my own daughter." Don't say I told you this honey, but she said she'd been thinking of asking you to come visit her, but she didn't know if you'd think of coming without me there.

Vivian, she's has so much trouble, worry, pain and heartache that I'd want to kill myself if I ever hurt her. She says she approves of our marriage, and we'll have it where you want, but I want you to promise me something. For my family's sake, or just for my sake, I don't want any intoxicated drinks served at the wedding, or the wedding reception, or dinner, or supper, or anything.

Yes, honey, I want to help you plan everything. You probably know more about it than I do, but I want to talk over everything with you, who we invite, etc. I want it to be a happy, holy occasion darling. Just as it should be.

Sweetheart, I paid for our phone call yesterday. We're going to talk ten minutes for $30. I can make it alright Viv honey. Thank you very much for offering me the money though hon. If I ever need some I know where I can borrow it. "Viv Liberto Loan Agency." Thank you very much darling.

It will make me feel so much better if I can talk to you tonight Vivian. I feel so all alone, and lonesome for you. Just sitting around with nothing to do makes it worse, but if I can just hear you say "I love you" tonight I'll be alright for a long time. I love you Vivian darling.

Darling, I'm going to sleep if I can, and have the CQ wake me up about one oclock.

Your husband,
Your Johnny

~

June 4, 1953

My Darling Wife to be,

Honey, the operator came back with her same report last night, no connections. The call was supposed to have gone through at 2 AM, and at 1:50 she called and said she'd call me back as soon as they had connections. I sat there by the phone until six oclock this morning, and she didn't call, so I called her. She said that at 5 AM she had called me, but no one answered the phone. I told her she must have called the wrong number because I'd been there in the same room waiting for the phone to ring for 4 hours. And I was. I sat there and read the Sears Roebuck Catalog, and I know the phone didn't ring.

Maybe it will go through at 1 AM tonight darling. That's when she said she'd try again. Honey, this is so disappointing. I wanted to talk to you so bad. I sure hope it goes through tonight.

Darling, did you see the movie, "The Lawless Breed"? I saw it tonight. The woman in this movie waited on her husband 16 years while he served a prison term. Sometimes it seems that we've been that long apart. This year is almost half gone sweetheart, and then we'll be together the next one. It's been so long darling. You've waited so long, and have been so wonderful to me. I love you Vivian darling.

Darling, our record player will play all sizes, and all speed records. It will play 33⅓, 45, and 78 RPM records. So if there are ever any records you want to buy for us and keep it doesn't matter what size. The guy in the room with me has lots of records, and I bought four at the PX the other day. They get in records here at the PX about every 2 months, and if I'm lucky I can get the ones I like.

Darling, I'm glad you lock yourself up, and no one knows we pray together. I usually pray in the toilet too, or go down in the basement. It's better to do it in secret. I love you Viv. Surely God will answer our prayers and bring us together some way sooner. I need you so my darling.

Well, little darling, I'm going to take a shower, then go down to the snack bar and get something to eat, then go wait on the call. I'm taking another book with me tonight. I get tired of Sears Roebuck. There's no plot to any of their stories.

Your husband to be,
Your Johnny

~

June 5, 1953

My Darling Wife to be,

Viv, I've had you on my mind every minute since we talked last night. I couldn't go to sleep for two hours after I went to bed. I lay there for so long, thinking of our conversation, and of you, and wanting you in my arms so bad I could die. It made me feel so wonderful darling. You seemed so close to me, and I love you so much.

Darling, I bet anyone listening in thought I was a lovesick punk. I guess I am, but can't help it. I love you so much Vivian darling.

I felt so good and was so happy because I talked to you, and we told each other how we love each other, but afterwards my heart was bleeding for you Vivian. I lay in bed thinking and praying that we would be together soon.

Viv, when you feel that way, there's nothing I can do except tell you I feel the same way, and I do sweetheart. I think of you all the time, and love you with all my heart. You've always got me Vivian darling. Wherever I am I'm yours. No one will ever take your place.

Honey, my cyst hasn't given me any trouble, but darling, I promise that as soon as I get back off my mission I'll go see if the doctor thinks it's big enough to cut out. I promise darling, so please don't worry sugar.

Viv honey, I'm going to tell you a little secret about that pin you've got around your sweet little neck. I first used it to pin up a hole in the side of my shorts. You still going to wear it around your neck darling?

Honey, I'm sending this book you asked me to. I don't know what you'll think of it. I'll just hope for the best. I've never heard of the guy that wrote it, but I don't believe him, that is, part of it. I feel sorry for his wife. He's admitting that he doesn't love her, and that she's just a friend that satisfies his sexual urges. I'd never listen to anyone that believes like he does. He contradicts himself every other sentence.

I don't want to ever argue about religion honey. We both worship the same God and we can't take our advice from people that are preaching to people in general. Darling we've loved each other so long, and meant so much to each other, and have been so close in heart, that we are definitely for each other. From now on I'm going to be careful how I let anyone's advice affect me, no one, or very few would even try to understand or try to see how we feel. People would judge us by others.

Yes, darling, I know it's going to be hard for you not getting any mail. It's certainly going to be hard for me too. I'm going to take all the letters from you with me and read them over.

Stay sweet Viv, and keep praying and keep your chin up honey. Try to be happy my darling. Your happiness means so much to me Vivian. You're all I ever want and if I have you, I'll have a prize. Last night after I went to bed honey, I was thinking about what you said over the phone, "You'll have me as long as you live, darling." Then I will have what I want in life Vivian darling. The most wonderful girl in the world.

Your husband to be for sure,
Your Johnny

~

Note: Because of his mission, there was a thirty-two-day "break" here in our letter-writing.

~

July 7, 1953

My Darling Wife,

Viv honey, I've missed you so much today. I wish I could make you understand how I love you and need you. Oh my darling, I need you so much. I love you Viv. I love you with all my heart and soul. Darling there will never be anyone else for me as long as I live. If I could only have you in my arms for a few minutes I could make you understand how I love you. Hon, I need you so.

I start back to work tonight at five oclock honey. Back into the old routine. Darling, I sure do miss you today. The weather is so pretty and warm, and it would be so nice if we were together. I love you so much sweetheart. I know this is short angel, but I guess I'd better get ready to go to work. I've got to shower, shave, and shine my shoes.

Your husband,
Your Johnny

~

July 13, 1953
9:30 PM

My Darling Viv,

Honey, I just got back from the lake about an hour ago. I got five letters from you today darling.

Honey, we had a fair time. We took guitars, etc. out with us, had a big dinner and went sailing. It was too cool though. I almost froze out on the lake. I think only about half the boys got drunk. I drank some wine again. I've decided wine is the only drink I actually like the taste of, and I only drank that when I ate. I guess I'm still a little boy honey, but I hope I never grow up.

You're going to have to stop playing poker though. I don't like for you to honey, at all.

Darling, speaking of differences, I suppose or knew that with your beliefs, you think it's silly, but my dad would probably kick me out on my ear if I started playing cards at home. My mom would burn them up. It's against our religious beliefs. I don't know the first thing about any kind of card game.

Maybe it's no sin at all, but it's just as easy to leave alone if you're in doubt honey. Viv, sometimes I wonder and worry so much about how I'll ever fit in with your friends and your way of life. I have no doubts about fitting in with you. We were meant for each other, but how can I ever accept New Years open houses, "card parties," and drinking as "right." Do you ever worry about me darling? Do you ever wonder if you can actually live with and put up with my beliefs. Darling, I'm not a fanatic. I know I'm not. I try my best to live by what my religion teaches, and God himself wants me to do that.

Vivian darling you're a wonderful girl. You're the only girl in the world. You were born to be a perfect wife and mother. I know you're very intelligent and a very clean, sweet girl, just what I've dreamed of. But darling, how can I fit in? Remember the night Jean Mitchell came in when I was there, and said, "Oh what the hell. I've already had three (burp) beers."

I guess you're going to have a nut for a husband darling, but he loves you and believes in you. I only want you, and I should say to myself, "Take Vivian and let the rest of the world rot." I'm going to take you darling, because you're the only woman on earth for me as long as I live, but I've just wondered a lot what our social life is going to be like.

I love you so very much.

Your husband someday,
Your Johnny

~

Nearly two years into his tour in Germany, Johnny surprised me with the following letter.

July 16, 1953

My Darling Wife to be,

Darling, I have a lot to tell you. I hope it will make you happy, and I hope you're willing.

Honey, I've talked to the Chaplain and the 1st Sgt, and I still have to talk to the Commanding Officer. Every one has encouraged me. I went to town yesterday morning and put an ad in the German newspaper for an apartment. I want you to come over here Viv.

I know you wanted to come a long time ago darling, and as nothing has been said about it in a long time, I don't know if maybe I'm taking a lot for granted by writing this letter, but you can give me the answer after you read it.

Honey, I was planning to ask you to come before, but my trip to Italy postponed it. We still have plenty of time though. If you come I want you to come around the 1st of September and we'll have till next May here. Viv it isn't as simple as it may seem now. There is so much red tape that it's pitiful. I went to different places in the last few days and I think I've found out practically everything.

First of all, and most important, you will have to have written permission from both your parents with their signatures on it before you can come. That will have to be mailed to me, and I will turn it in at the Orderly Room, and to the Chaplain. There has to be three copies of that.

Next you have to have a medical certificate from your doctor, 3 copies, sent to me, saying that you are in good physical health and saying that you are ready for marriage, also a blood test. Next you have to send three copies of your birth certificate, and when you come, bring your certificate of Baptism.

Viv honey, the Chaplain told me to stress on your mind that it isn't going to be so simple. He said to tell you to be sure you understand that there's going to be a lot of trouble and red tape. Of course, nothing will keep us from getting married, but there's just a lot of legal red tape to go through. I talked to the Catholic Chaplain, and he said he thought it would be a nice deal, but to tell you not to expect living conditions to be like those in the States. Maybe I'll be lucky and can get a nice apartment for us, which I will do my very best to do.

But if I'm not so lucky, I want you to be sure that before you come, you'll be willing to accept what we can get. I put the ad in the paper for a two room apartment with kitchen and bath. A lot of people haven't been lucky enough to get rooms with bath, and that's what I mean, that I'll have to accept what I can get, and fix it up as best I can. He also said that a few couples are living in apartments that don't have adequate heating, but I can always buy a couple of electric heaters. And don't be surprised if there's no running water.

That sounds crummy I know darling, but the Chaplain said that some American girls have come over and have been disgusted and sick, but others have hit it lucky. I'll do everything in my power to make you comfortable darling, but please be prepared to live in crowded quarters, and for a lot of inconveniences if we have them.

If you come, we'll live in Landsberg because that's the only place we could live so I could catch the bus to the base to go to work. A lot of American women live there. Dependents quarters are there, but the reason we can't get Government quarters is because no one under S/Sgt can get them. We may not live near any Americans, but again we might live next door to some.

If you come, as soon as you get here, we have to go see the "Burgermeister" in Landsberg. He's the German Justice of the Peace. We have to register, and sign our names about a hundred times and give him all the information about ourselves. Then we have to go to Munich and register and sign our names a few more times at a place there.

The Chaplain said we definitely couldn't get married as soon as you got here. There are too many things we have to do. He said it may be 3 or 4 days before we can get married. I'll have the apartment fixed up for you to stay in the meantime hon.

Here's something else darling. We have to get married twice. The Chaplain said we have to get married in town by the "Burgermeister" then come to the base and get married here in the Base Chapel the same day. The reason for that is that the German Government will not recognize us as man and wife unless we get married by German Law, and the American Govt won't recognize a German wedding as legal for Americans. The Catholic Chaplain told me that.

Honey, you're going to have to go and apply for a passport. I think you go to the county courthouse. Or maybe you can apply for it at a travel agency, such as "TWA" ticket office. I want you to come by plane if you want to, or will honey. It costs a little more than by boat, but it's only 18 hours from there to Munich, and there isn't near so much red tape to go through there if you come by plane. I think you can get a plane right there from San Antonio to Munich, or maybe you will have to go to Frankfurt. You can find out about that hon. Anyway, I know that you have to wait two or three weeks for your passport after applying for it. And I would like for you to come just as near Sept 1st as you can if you can be ready that soon.

Now about money darling. There is a regulation that any man who brings his wife overseas will have $300 invested in "Airmens deposits" all the time that his wife is with him overseas. I wrote home today for the $300 to put in the bank here. I have to have that money in there before you come.

I hadn't reckoned on that before and if it wasn't for that I could pay for your ticket here, but with that $300 gone I can only pay for part of your ticket. I think you have a little money saved, but I'm sure not enough for a $360 plane ticket. I told my folks to tell me how much I had besides that $300 I have to put in the bank, and when they tell me I'll have them send you all but what I'll need here for our apartment, etc. But if you don't have the money to pay for part of it, don't borrow it anywhere Viv. I'll get it somehow and send it to you.

On my status, an A/1C, married, wife o/seas with me, I'll draw $65 per month, plus $60 for separate rations, and you will draw about $135 per month honey. On that we can live easy. We'll have about $260 a month, and our rent won't be over 25 or 30 dollars per month if I can get that apartment I advertised for.

Because I'm just an A/1C, we won't have commissary privileges. We'll live off the German economy, but the food is just as good and cheaper. We can get everything we need to eat except a few rationed items, and I can always get some S/Sgt to buy things we need out of the commissary.

But even in the main P.X. we can get most any kind of canned goods we want and they have a meat counter anyone can buy from. And in the P.X. you can get anything you need Viv. They sell all "ladies needs."

Vivian darling, I want so much for your parents to approve. Talk to them and explain everything to them. I'm going to write your dad tonight or tomorrow and explain everything to him and your mom and just hope for the best. I know they'll hate for you to go. To be in a foreign country and so far and so long from home, but if you want to come honey, please explain everything to them and don't argue and hurt them.

I think it will be a wonderful thing for you. You'll get to go to countries you'd never hope to see any other way later on unless we were rich, which is very doubtful. I'm doing it for that reason mostly, because I think it will make you happy. Of course another reason is because I want you with me so bad I could scream but it is a wonderful opportunity for you if you're willing. We'd have just about the right amount of time over here. We could go to a lot of places and see a lot of things. And still you won't be over here so long that you would get sick of it, I hope.

I intend to put in for a 15 day leave that will start the day you get here, and if we can get married in time, we'll go somewhere, wherever we want to, if we have the money, and then we'll take another leave early next spring.

That's why I need to know exactly the day you'll be here darling, if it's possible, I need to know 15 or 20 days in advance. You'll have to go soon and make reservations for the plane, if you'll come on a plane. And honey, I think you only have to make a deposit on the ticket, then pay for the rest of it when you leave.

Well angel, I hope I've told you everything I meant to. I'll write you again tonight or tomorrow, and maybe I'll think of something else.

Viv, you can wait till a week or so before you leave to send the three copies of your medical certificate but get the three copies of your birth certificate and three copies of your parents consent soon.

The parents consent has to be like this honey: TO WHOM IT MAY CONCERN: WE, THE PARENTS OF MISS VIVIAN LIBERTO, DO HEREBY GIVE HER PERMISSION TO GO TO GERMANY TO MARRY A/1C JOHN R. CASH. Or something like that. Just so it says they permit you to come overseas and marry me. That's for all people under 21 honey. If I were under 21, my parents would have to give me permission to bring you over here and marry you. Both our signatures have to be on that.

Viv honey, please talk to them and explain things. I wouldn't hurt your parents for anything in the world. I'll write your dad tomorrow morning and you can wait till he gets the letter before you say anything to him if you want it that way.

Another thing, I don't think, and the Government doesn't think that there is any danger of anything happening over here. Of course no one knows, but everyday hundreds of American women and kids come over here to stay. You certainly won't be isolated here at Landsberg. There are lots of American women here that you can make friends with.

Well, darling, I've got to get some sleep before I drop. I'll write tonight if I have time sweetheart. I hope this has made you happy Viv. I hope you want to come as bad as I want you to. I need you so much my darling. I love you Vivian darling. I'll love you and only you as long as I live.

I'll be waiting for your answer darling. Just be sure that you are willing to accept the poorest living conditions if we have to. Make sure honey.

Bye darling. I love you with all my heart and soul.

Your husband soon,
Your Johnny

~

I was giddy with excitement, dreaming of going to Germany to marry Johnny. Johnny wrote my father the next day, requesting parental permission for me to go.

Landsberg
July 17th '53

Dear Mr. Liberto,

I hardly know how to start sir, but there's a lot I'd like to tell you and explain to you. Vivian has probably told you that I've asked her to come over here and marry me.

I didn't do it by impulse. I've talked to a lot of people as to what the situation would be like, and made a lot of plans. Of course the plans could be changed if Vivian isn't willing to come, and if you and Mrs. Liberto won't permit her to come.

Vivian and I are very much in love. We've been apart two years, and we're still the same. Of course we could wait the rest of the time, but I honestly think it's for our good that she comes since we were planning to be married when I return.

I know how you must feel about your daughter being away in a foreign country for so long. I know she's precious to you as she is to me. I'll do anything in my power to make her happy and comfortable here. I've put an ad in the German newspaper for an apartment. We would live in Landsberg, three miles from the base.

I'm sure we can get a decent apartment. There may be inconveniences that she wouldn't have there, but we're willing to try hard. I'll get the best I can possibly get and make it comfortable for her.

There are dozens of American women living in Landsberg. Even men with less rank than I have live there with their wives. As it stands now, we would live off the German economy. If I ever make Staff. Sgt. we can get government living quarters, but it could be even better this way. German food is cheaper, and so are living quarters.

Vivian will have to come over by civilian aircraft, and again, if I can make Staff sgt, she will come back with me on the ship next May.

With her over here, we would draw a total of $260 per month, and I'm sure we could live easily on that and put some in the bank.

I think it would be a wonderful opportunity for her Mr. Liberto. I don't know when she'd ever have another chance to see Europe. I intend to take a 15 day leave starting the day she gets here, and we will go somewhere if we can get married in time. Then we'll take another leave next spring.

I intended to have on appartment fixed up for her to stay in, until we could get married, but one of the men I work with told me this morning that he had an extra bed room, and his wife would be happy for Viv to stay with her until we could get married. We'll be married by the Catholic priest here on the base.

I believe this is the right time for her to come. If she had come sooner she might have gotten tired of Germany, but as it is, we'd have just enough time to go to all the places we'd like to.

I dont believe there is any danger of trouble over here. The government brings hundreds of American women and children over every day so the families can be together, and they do have an evacuation plan for dependents in case of an indication of trouble.

Sir, its compulsory that I have your and Mrs. Liberto's written permission for her to come. I know she's a grown woman, but thats the rule for all people under 21. I want you to approve of this. I dont want to go against your will, but I hope that you will trust me and believe in me. I love her very much, and I promise to always take care of her, make her comfortable, and see that shes treated right always. I'll do everything under the sun to make her stay over here happy.

I'll be looking forward to your answer.

John Cash

July 17, 1953

My Darling Wife soon,

Honey, I haven't had a letter from you the last two days, and I'm staying up for mail call again this morning and writing you in the meantime.

Darling, I just wrote your dad. It was sure a hard letter to write. I didn't know what to say, and may not have said the right things. I'm just keeping my fingers crossed till I hear from him.

I'm just counting the days till I get an answer from the letter I wrote yesterday. Viv, I want you here with me so bad. I know we can make it alright. It will be so wonderful having you here. You've just got to say you'll come Viv. I love you so very much my darling.

Vivian darling, I love you. I love you so much it hurts Viv. It will be heaven if I can be with you. Honey, when I found out all the things, and found that I could bring you over, I felt as if our prayers were answered. We prayed that God would see a way to bring us together, and I believe He has. Oh my darling, I need you so.

Your husband to be,
Your Johnny

~

July 18, 1953

My Darling Vivian,

Darling, I didn't write this morning after work because I went to town to see about the apartment, and when I got back I was dead tired so I went right to bed.

Honey, no one called the paper saying they had an apartment. I suppose it was a little soon though. The ad was just in the paper yesterday. I'll go back Monday or Tuesday and check again honey.

But in the meantime I have a chance for another one. Last night one of the boys asked me if I was looking for an apartment, and I told him I was. Then he told me about this deal. He was supposed to marry a French girl soon and was getting this apartment from a guy that just made S/Sgt and is moving into government housing. Now his girl has postponed the marriage till next fall because she wants to go to a modeling school, so he says I can have the apartment.

We're going to go look at it tomorrow morning darling. It's right in town in Landsberg, and he says it's very, very nice. It's the whole upstairs part of a house, and there's a living room, bed room, kitchen, and bathroom, completely furnished for around $30 a month. If I can get that, we'll have it made angel.

Vivian darling, you've just got to come. Maybe I'm planning too much, but

I need you so my darling. I think you'll be happy Viv. I want so much for you to be happy. I'd do anything for you my darling.

Honey, one of my friends, A/2C that works the same shift as I is going to bring his wife over in October. He's buying a jeep, and he said he and I will go and come to work in it. You can make friends with her and you two can get together and gossip while we're at work so you won't be so lonely. He says his wife is sure a nice, sweet girl. (Naturally) She's only 18. I'm sure you will have a lot of friends here angel.

I'm glad you liked the things I sent you darling. You're welcome. Soon I'll be buying all your clothes for you sweetheart. Maybe I'll even buy you a dress already made. A store bought one.

Viv, I enjoyed praying with you down in Italy in that field more than any other time. It was a beautiful clear night. The moon and stars were shining, and I was all alone, and it was quiet as a church. I prayed with you tonight too angel. I thanked God that He had seen a way to bring us together.

Darling those 45 RPM records cost me 65 cents apiece. If you're coming honey, you can mail your records if you want to. We'll listen to them together in our own apartment and read our old letters over darling. I love U.

Vivian, what if I weren't willing to sign that paper at our wedding? What would happen then? No darling, if I <u>have</u> to sign it to have you, then I will, then I'll keep on praying and trying my best to be happy that way. Faith and trust in God can do anything, and I'm going to keep my faith and trust strong as long as I live.

Viv, I'm so proud of you. I'm sorry you missed a day on your novena honey, but I'm glad you're doing it, and glad that you're still going to do it all over again. You couldn't be too religious for me. With both of us praying to <u>our one</u> God, we can't go wrong. He'll make us happy if we keep trusting in Him. Don't ever change Vivian. Don't ever in your life let anything at all change you. You'll never be sorry.

Your husband soon,
Your Johnny

~

July 20, 1953

My Darling Sweetheart,

Honey, still no one had called the paper saying they had an apt. I told the woman to run the ad two more days. I asked for two rooms with bath. I still think I can get the apt. my friend was telling me about, but I just wanted to be sure of another one if that deal fell through. I'll find us a place darling.

Viv honey, I don't know what our wedding will be like here. It will probably be quite simple. I honestly wanted you to have just the kind of wedding you wanted Vivian. I know it won't be the same without your folks there and your friends. I guess you're getting cheated on that part darling. But Viv baby, at least none of your friends can say they got married to the same man twice on the same day.

Honey, I've wondered if a Catholic wedding is like or much like a Baptist wedding. Does the priest say, "Do you, Miss Vivian Liberto, take this man, etc. etc." Then you say "I do." And does he ask me about the same thing, and then at the end say, "I now pronounce you man and wife"? I just wondered honey if those few lines are in the Catholic ceremony too. I'll talk to the Chaplain about the arrangements honey. We'll have as nice a wedding as possible. It's not the ceremony I'm thinking of though. It's the wonderful woman that's going to be beside me that makes it so heavenly. I love you Vivian darling.

Honey, you know, I told you about my friend that is bringing his wife over in Oct. He went to town with me today, and we were sitting down in the restaurant eating ice cream, and for about an hour at least we sat there and just talked about you and his wife. He sure thinks the world of her. He said he knew you'd like her honey. She doesn't drink or smoke and she just loves to gossip. I told him you two would hit it off just fine then. I'm not picking your friends darling. But I know you won't know anyone here at first and if you like this girl, you two can stay together a lot while Chuck and I are working. We both work the same shift all the time. They're from Arkansas.

I told him how we met, how we fell in love, about all our letters, about a couple of our quarrels when I acted such a fool. I also told him what an industrious girl you are, and what a pure clean girl you are, and most of the wonderful things about you.

I'm so proud of you Viv. There's not a girl on earth that would compare with you. You'll be the best mother and wife in the world, and I'm so thankful to God that He made you just for me.

Viv honey, I don't like to bring up things about religion that might cause confusion. But there's something that I'd like to understand that I don't. I know you say I can talk to you about anything, but I don't want you to think I'm taking advantage of that because we're that way to each other. Angel, what I want to ask you about is Catholic belief on birth control.

I know you don't believe in it, and for that matter, neither do I, or any devout Baptist, except in some cases. I know it's wrong to practice birth control if the parents do it just because they aren't, or think they aren't financially able to have children. God will provide a way to take care of them if you want them. Or if the parents just decide they're too old and have had too many kids already.

But honey, say in a case like this: If you had a baby, and the doctor told you that it would be dangerous for you to have another baby, or dangerous for the baby if you were in poor health. Then honey, would you be permitted to allow your husband to use contraceptives, or would you just not sleep with your husband till you're in good health? Are there any cases such as that where you can use birth control?

Vivian darling, with the love we have for each other, I know that love will continue to grow, and we can always talk things over and reason them out. I can sure see my mistakes for getting angry and saying things I shouldn't have and that's just the way I <u>don't</u> want to ever be. We have differences in belief, and as time goes by, you're going to have to explain things to me in detail, so I can understand and not criticize. I suppose I was born to criticize. But Vivian, living with you, I think I can get over it. The last thing I want to do is criticize God's word and some of the things I've raised cain about was because I didn't think it was God's word. There's a lot to life. There's certainly a lot to understand.

Maybe in the next two months we'll have each other Viv. It will be so heavenly coming home to you. Just you and I alone. Eating together, talking, playing records and making love. And telling each other in person, "I love you." Viv honey, I love you so angel.

Your husband soon

~

July 21, 1953

My Very Own,

Viv honey, those medals I got July 7th aren't anything hardly at all. I didn't mean to give you the impression that I was all decorated darling. The hash mark just shows that I've been in service 3 years, and the European Occupation Ribbon just shows I did Occupation duty in Germany. I'm eligible for the good conduct ribbon because I've done 3 years service without getting in any trouble that went on my records. Of course, I knocked a Polack's teeth out, but it didn't go on my records. I don't know when I'll ever get the good conduct ribbon. They haven't put out any orders on them lately, but if they ever do, I'll get it.

Viv, I don't know if you think you can afford or will have time to go see the folks, but I sure wish you would if possible. I don't like for you to travel alone either honey, but if you could make the arrangements and tell her what time you're supposed to arrive, she'll meet you. She usually does the driving now and she could go to West Memphis to meet you and save you a lot of trouble. No, I've got my wires crossed hon. I don't think she could meet you in West Memphis if you went by train. She could if you went by bus. Which had you rather ride darling? Look honey, I'll write mom and tell her to write and tell you where to buy the ticket to. I'll let her work that out with you darling. She'll meet you somewhere so you won't have to be alone anywhere in a strange place. Don't be afraid honey. You can sit with other women who are going the same place you are. Just tell those wise guys that flirt with you that everything you have belongs to J. Cash, and he's very particular how people treat his sweet-heart.

Goodnight angel. Keep those precious letters coming till we're in each other's arms.

Your husband soon,
Your Johnny

~

July 22, 1953

My Darling Wife soon,

Honey, what club was it that you went to after work? I'm glad you enjoyed yourself, Viv, but I still don't like for you to go where everybody is drinking. I appreciate you not drinking Vivian but I <u>hate</u> for you to go to those things. Maybe it was all harmless and everybody behaved themselves, but I don't like for my future wife to patronize such places at all. Maybe soon you'll be away from those people and they'll leave you alone.

I want you to have fun. I want you to be the happiest girl in the world, but things like that, cocktail socials, etc. do not fit in with my way of life, and they can't fit in with <u>our</u> way of life if it is going to always be "<u>us</u>" and not "you and I."

Vivian honey, just do that for me. Stay away from those damned places. People will respect you and envy you for it whether you believe it or not. Please Vivian darling.

Vivian I know you've done nothing for me to get up in the air about. I know it must have been hard for you to sit there 4½ hours and not drink when everyone else did, and I appreciate you doing that, but I'd hoped you wouldn't go back to one of those things.

Honey, do they have a dance too, or just sit there and talk? I don't care how decent the place looks and how clean you think it is, I wish you'd stay away. It's no place for a girl like you.

I suppose you don't think I understand, or try to understand, and maybe you're right. I only know I love you more than anything in the world. I think you're the most wonderful person in the world, and I don't like for people to cheapen you. You don't belong in groups like that.

Vivian, I always feel like kicking myself after I talk to you this way. I love you so much, and I'd like so much to just talk things over with you.

Honey, you know what I want ourselves to be like. I want to make you happy. I want to take you out and show you a nice time, and make you comfortable and contented, but drinking and dancing where there is drinking, is <u>OUT</u>. When a man won't hold up for what he believes in, he isn't much of a man. You know what I believe in. Do you think you're going to be happy Vivian? I can make you happy with the above things left out. I'd feel like killing myself if they were an active part of your life.

Honey, I was thinking today about when we get married. I'm going to borrow someone's car if I can. We'll be married in town, then come to the base and get married, then go somewhere. We'll drive around if it's pretty, and go to some nice place down in the mountains and eat supper, then come back to our apartment.

If you want to, I want us to spend our wedding night in our apartment. Don't you think that would be starting things off right honey? Of course we could find a nice hotel somewhere, but I think it would be best to stay in our "home" the first night honey, do you? If we stayed in a barn it would be heaven.

Angel, I'm going to take a shower and go to bed. I'll write tomorrow nite honey. Till then stay sweet and God bless you my darling.

Your husband soon,
Your Johnny

~

July 23, 1953

My Darling Viv,

I went to the first movie tonight honey. Did you see "Come Back, little Sheba"? I sure liked it, especially the moral. He was an alcoholic honey, and his prayer daily was "God, give me the serenity to accept what I can't change, the courage to fight what I can change, and the wisdom to know right from wrong." Isn't that good darling?

Viv honey, I just wonder what a girl like Kate thinks of my not wanting you to drink at all? I just wonder if the class of people you mix with think I'm crazy.

Goodnight my sweetheart. Maybe this time two months from now we'll be side by side where we belong. I love you Vivian darling. Stay the sweet girl you always were. Keep on loving me and stay mine. I need you so much.

Your husband soon,
Your Johnny

~

My Sweet Darling,

I just got back from town honey, and it's 9:30 PM. I went in to check the paper again, and this time I had some luck.

Two people had written the paper answering my ad. One of them was from a little town out about 4 miles from here, but I didn't even look at that one because I'd have no way to come to work.

Honey, I went out to see the other one, and at the present time there is an airman and his wife living in it, but they leave next week, so I'm getting the place for you and I.

Darling, I don't know if you'll like it, but I'm going to take it because I'm afraid it's all I can get. It's one large room, and a small kitchen darling, a very small kitchen. The living room is pretty large though. There's plenty of room to move around in. It's furnished and there's a clothes cabinet, dining table, chairs, curtains and a table for a table lamp, and also a big dresser, and the bed. Honey, when I first walked in, I didn't think too much of the place. But this guy and his wife both told me I was sure lucky to get it. They said they were proud of it after some of the things they'd lived in. The furniture is good and strong, but it isn't so modern.

Darling, they furnish a coal stove for cooking, but I'm going to buy us a double hot plate with an oven. I don't want you to cook on a coal stove. Besides a hot plate, the kind I want to get, is a lot better. In the kitchen there is a cook table, a dish cabinet, and a place for the stove, and that's about all the room there is in it if you want to be able to move at all. This couple there now, are using a hot plate and they say they make it fine.

The living room is heated by a coal stove, and they say it keeps the room plenty warm. The lady that runs the house will order our coal for us.

Honey, there are three people living in the house. The German man is in the Police, so you'll be well protected. His wife is the one I saw. She seems like a nice old woman. She speaks a little English and her daughter, about 22 speaks good English. She works out here at the P.X.

Honey, this guy said they are very nice people and would do anything in the world to help us. We can decorate or paint our rooms anyways we want.

Darling we have to share the bath room with those three people, but they said there had never been any confusion. He said they're very clean, and we can put our things in the bathroom and they'd never touch a thing. And he says they never at all came in their part of the house uninvited.

Darling, I'm going to pay for the apartment in advance payday and have it looking as good as possible for us when you get here. It's only $20 a month and we pay half the light bill, which will be about $3.

Sweetheart, I hope so much that everything works out for us. I need you with me so bad. You've just got to come.

Your husband soon,
Your Johnny

~

July 25, 1953

My Darling Wife soon,

Honey, no mail came in today either. I sure am anxious for a letter, but I'm expecting a letter Monday for sure in answer to the one I wrote asking you to come.

Darling, I sure worked hard today, and I'm sure proud of my day's work. I accomplished something very important to us, and even to Washington. I went to work at 7:30 and didn't get out of my seat till 12 oclock to eat dinner, then I came back at 1 oclock and didn't move again until 4 oclock, when the Trick Chief got a relief for me. I was pretty nervous but I didn't want a relief. He insisted that I go and not come back today. So I went to the snack bar and ate. I kind of hated to leave because I'd accomplished so much and I wanted to get the credit for it all, after I'd done 9 tenths of it. But he said I'd worked enough for one day. I sure feel good about it honey. If I get a commendation, I'll tell you.

Boy, I don't sound too conceited do I? But honey, I did have two or three officers around me throwing compliments right and left. One said I deserved a medal, if they made medals for it.

Darling, last night the woman told me to go see her daughter and talk about the apartment, because she speaks good English, so I went up there for a couple of minutes at noon, and told her that I wanted for sure, the apartment. I thought it was mine, but there's a chance I can't get it.

She said that some guy has asked for it before, then said later that he probably wouldn't take it. I begged her, and told her to be sure to tell her mother we want it. She said there's 99% of a chance that it's ours, and she'll tell me for sure Tuesday. I think we can get it hon, if not I'll find another one someplace.

Those people sure asked me a lot of questions about you. They had rented it before to a G.I. who said he's married and he brought a German girl in there to live with him. The people didn't know for 3 days that they weren't married, then they kicked them out. There was a lot of trouble over it, and the man almost lost his policeman's job.

I haven't told them that we aren't married yet, and won't until I make the payment on the rent. I'm sure they'll let me have it if I can explain to them that we don't intend to live there together before we're married. I think everything will be alright hon. I sure hope I can get the place for us.

Viv honey, this guy that is in the place now said they furnish just enough plates or dishes and silverware for two, so if you have some thing we might need, send them. Anything you want to send that you have now, I'll take it down to the apt as soon as it gets here. I think that we'll need those blankets honey. They'll probably hang down to the floor on both sides as small as that bed is. But the woman that lives there now said it was large compared to some places they'd been. It's plenty big enough if you keep on loving me angel. There's sure no place to sleep if you ever get angry with me. You can't sleep on the couch. There isn't any couch darling.

Before you come I'm going to buy you a rocking chair so you can sit and read or sew while I'm gone. There's no chairs except the straight chairs. Also I'm going to get some pictures. I might paint the kitchen green too honey. Would you like that? The woman said we could paint or decorate it anyway we want. That is, if we get it. I sure hope so.

Your husband soon,
Your Johnny

~

July 26, 1953

My Darling Wife to be,

Before long we'll be doing our washing together honey. Or at least we'll be sending it off together. It would probably be hard washing our clothes in the bathtub.

Honey, there's another thing you should know. Before we can take a bath, we have to build a fire in the little heater under the water tank and heat the water. Mary, the woman that lives here now said tell you that you're going to get mighty tired of having to heat water to bathe and wash dishes.

I'm not trying to discourage you darling, but I just want to make sure you know what to expect. I'll do anything to make you happy and comfortable angel, but some things you'll have to take. It's far from being as nice as it is over there.

My 1st Sgt told me the best way to start a marriage was from the bottom up, and I suppose that will be our case. I'm willing to do anything to be with you though Vivian, so if you and I can get over the rough spots at first we'll make it alright. Compared to your home there, this place is going to be a pig pen, but we can work together at it and make it half decent.

Vivian darling, I want so much to make you happy. I wish I could give you the best of everything in the world. I'll work hard Viv, and always do my best for you. You'll just have to bear with me for awhile. Your husband to be is just a little old A/1C. A peon.

I love you my sweetheart. Keep on loving me till I can make you my own. Then you're trapped.

> Your Johnny for life.
> I love you Viv hon.

~

July 27, 1953

Honey, I got that letter I was expecting, and another. They're going to be kind of hard for me to answer too Viv. I hardly know where to start.

I'll start by saying I love you more than anything in this world Vivian darling. I wish you only knew how I love you Viv honey. I need you so.

Do you think it's good for you spiritually and morally to spend so much time around girls like Kate and Anna? Vivian, maybe Kate is a clean girl. From what you've told me, which isn't much, she is a clean girl. Honey, Kate has been disappointed in love and marriage. It hasn't worked with her and she must be a little bitter. Even if she isn't bitter, I can see that it isn't good for a girl like you to be with her so much. And as far as Anna is concerned, I feel like crying when you tell me about running around with her. She swears, talks filthy and drinks.

Viv darling, I've prayed for you so much, prayed that you would stay just the way I left you. You were just a school girl then, and I wasn't exactly growed myself, but you were a wonderful, sweet girl, and you still are, and always will be if you'll only use your head and don't be influenced the wrong way. I want you for my _wife_ Vivian. Not as a partner to raise hell with.

My darling, please keep on loving me. If I ever lost you, I wouldn't want to live. You're my life Vivian. You're all I live for Vivian darling. I mean that Viv, you are. You control my thoughts and my actions. I've really got you under my skin Vivian. And there will never be another woman for me but you as long as I live.

> Your husband soon,
> Your Johnny

~

July 28, 1953

My Darling Wife to be,

Vivian, last night I went to bed, and about one AM one of my drunk buddies came in and woke me up and talked to me about an hour. After he left, I couldn't go back to sleep, and I lay there for at least another hour thinking of you. Vivian darling, I was miserable. I wish I could explain how I felt. I needed you so much that I didn't see how I could stand it another minute. Hon, please understand me. I wanted you with me, to talk to you the way I want to talk to you. I did all kinds of crazy things. I lay there imagining you were right up close to me asleep and were breathing in my face. I could almost feel your breath. I held my hands together, making like we were sleeping, holding hands.

Honey, I think there was a change in me last night. I prayed that God would straighten me out and make me stop treating you dirty. I think He has. I had no reason to say some of the things I did to you. And I had no reason to preach to you.

All day today I was thinking and wondering how any woman could be happy with me. I'm usually so grouchy and sarcastic that it's a shame. I've just realized today what a shame I am, and I'm not going to be that way Vivian. I'm through criticizing people.

I picked up the bible today, and read about where God said something about people always trying to clean the "moat" from their neighbor's eye when they have a "beam" in their own. It made me think of some things I've said, then I thought of my own self. I felt like crawling in a hole. As dirty and vulgar as I talk sometimes around these guys, and the things I've done in my life, then the things I've said about other people. It's time for me to change and try to realize that I'm not an angel. There's going to be a change too Vivian. I'm going to "hold fast to the right" and try to live right, but I'm through finding fault with people.

Sweetheart, you've just got to come. I love you so. Honey, I want to take you everywhere. It will be a nice experience for you. I'll take you to Rome for sure honey, and I think you can get an audience with the pope. One of my buddies went down there, and it wasn't any trouble at all. We'll talk about that later though.

Your husband soon,
Your Johnny

~

July 30, 1953

My Darling Wife to be,

Viv honey, I got that letter today that I had prayed wouldn't come. I don't know what to think or say to you Vivian. It was such a setback that it stunned me.

Darling, I'd be a liar if I said it didn't hurt. But what hurts more is to know that you were hurt so much.

I'm not angry Viv, not at your parents, but I just can't see why it has to be this way. Maybe they're broader minded than I am and can see that it is wrong. I can't. I've seen in to everything, and I have things ready for you now. But if that's the way its got to be, I'll accept it Vivian darling.

172

Honey, I wish you could have been able to talk to him so I'd have an idea what the reason is. I can't help but think it's because he's afraid you won't get a Catholic wedding, or that you can't worship as you should.

If I could only talk to him. It's always been this way. We've never been able to talk things over since we've been in love. There's always been a misunderstanding. We need to be together. We <u>need</u> to.

Alright honey, I'll forget our plans. But how can I forget how you're hurt. I didn't mean for you to be hurt, but I should have known that if you couldn't come it would nearly kill you. Every single letter I've written up to last night is going to break your heart in two.

I know things would have worked. We could have been happily married here and we would have opportunities to see things together that you will never see. I hope your dad has taken that into consideration, how much happiness he's keeping from his daughter.

I'm sorry darling. I sound like I'm angry now, but I'm not. Maybe it would be taking a too big chance all around. I'd never forgive myself if you came and war started and something happened to you. But if I'd been anticipating something like that I'd have certainly never asked you to come.

Vivian darling, please, please don't let this affect you too much. Keep on loving and living with your parents. Don't leave home Viv. I know you're a grown woman, and 99% of girls your age would revolt and run away, but Vivian darling, promise me that it won't change you. Stay the wonderful girl you are. Please Vivian, do it for me darling.

Vivian darling, I need you so. I wonder how long a man can go without a woman. I know I can make it though. Vivian, pray for me like you've never prayed before. Pray that I won't be bitter, and change. I feel so silly saying that, but Vivian you know I have always been yours, and I always want to. Pray for me darling.

Vivian, I won't be able to sleep at night till I get a letter from you and your dad telling me why. And even yet, I'm going to pray that he will change his mind. I'm not going to tell that girl I don't want the apt. for at least two or three days.

My darling, I want you to know how much I appreciate how you've taken this. I know you're hurt honey. But I appreciate you being so good and understanding about it. I could have cried I was so happy when you said, "Darling, it just must not have been God's will." Most girls would have fought their parents and someway forced them to sign and give permission. I know you wanted to come. I believe it hurt you even more than you showed.

Vivian, let's keep on like we always have. Let's don't let this slow us up. Let's keep on writing every day and praying together for strength. If the whole world is against us, we'll be together and married someday. No one will take that happiness away from us if God will take me back to you. And He will

Vivian. Let's keep praying Vivian darling, and please, honey let's stay like we always have been.

Angel, if it's definite that you can't come, then I'm going to call you. I may place the call within the next two or three days. I've got to talk to you now. I think it will help us both Viv. Oh hon, I need you and love you so very much.

Viv honey, give my love to both your parents. Tell them I'm sorry things didn't work out, but there are no hard feelings whatsoever.

Bye angel, I'll see you tonight. <u>I love you.</u>

Your Johnny as long a I live.

∿

I was devastated when Daddy would not consent to my joining Johnny in Germany. I refused to speak with him for a week.

∿

July 31, 1953

My Darling Wife to be,

Honey, I got 3 more sweet letters from you today. One of them was written the 25th, when you were still making plans, and the other two were written the 27th.

Darling, I feel a lot better now, because you feel a lot better. It isn't going to be so hard to take I guess. I'm just happy that you're taking it as you are.

My darling I love you so much and wanted you with me so bad. You've just got to tell me the reason Viv. I'm tired of tossing and turning at night, and walking the floor in the day. Sweetheart, please tell me.

Yes darling, I suppose all we can do now is wait for each other, but it hurts. Viv, you will be 20 when we get married. Darling, do you have any regrets about waiting that long to get married? Do you feel like you're missing much in life? Oh darling, if we could only be together. At least honey, we'll both be old enough to know what we're getting into. Viv I do feel like I'm missing a lot. I need you for my wife so very much, but one thing, we'll have more money saved, and we won't have to start out from rock bottom like some couples.

Your husband,
Your Johnny

∿

August 2, 1953

My Darling Sweetheart,

Hon, I had the nicest dream last night and I wish I could remember more of it. When I woke up this morning I missed you so much and felt so close to you darling.

174

Anyway, we were lying side by side on our back on an army cot somewhere listening to records. The record player was over on my left side and you were lying with your head over my right arm. I'd just reach over with my left arm to change a record. I don't remember the first of the dream, but where I remember from, you had on a skirt that you'd made with the material I sent you from Italy, and you were holding the bottom of it tight between your knees. I think I'd been trying to caress your legs and you'd decided I'd better stop. I was ashamed of myself and I turned my face to your cheek and kissed you all over the side of the face and was apologizing to you. The only thing I remember you saying was "Honey, I love you so much, but be careful till we're married."

I think I'm getting pretty dirty minded honey, I've sure had some dreams lately that I'm ashamed of. The service and a place like this sure fixes a person up good. But I will be careful till we're married sweetheart. I love you too angel. I love you with all my heart.

Your husband to be,
Your Johnny

~

August 3, 1953

My Very Own,

Viv honey, I didn't get a letter from you today either. I hadn't heard from you since last Friday. Darling, I'm worried sick about you. Maybe it's just the mail. I sure hope so, but honey I can't keep from thinking something has happened to you or you've left home. Honey, if that call don't come through tonight I'm going to be crazy. Vivian, I love you so much sweetheart.

Honey, I went ahead and let the other guy have the apartment today with the promise that I'd get it back if you decided to come. His wife isn't coming till Sept.

Sweetheart, I bought us some more records today. Five hillbilly. "Kawliga" by H. Williams, "Going Steady" by Faron Young, "RUB-A-DUB-DUB" by Hank Thompson, "How's the World Treating You" by Eddy Arnold, "That's Me Without You" by Webb Pierce. Someday we'll be side by side listening to them darling. And speaking of side by side, do you think you could get the record "Side by Side" by Kay Starr? Have you heard it, and do you like it hon? Get it and keep it for us if you can, and if you like it, will you sugar?

Viv honey, I was looking at the first picture you ever gave me tonight. The one you had on the mantle at home. I was looking at the small one in my billfold and thinking how wonderful you are, and how wonderful it is loving you and having your love. Vivian, I'm so thankful that we've stuck it out so far. The time won't be long now angel, and we'll be together for life.

Hon, I'm going to close now. The operator should call any minute now. Goodnight angel face.

Your husband to be,
Your Johnny

~

August 4, 1953

My Darling Sweetheart,

Viv honey, I just talked to you and I just had to write you now.

Hon, it hurt so much that you thought I was angry with you. Viv please don't think I was, I had to yell to make myself heard. I wasn't angry with you honey, and I'm _never_ going to be angry with you again. I mean that Vivian darling. I'm never going to hurt you again. Vivie, I love you my darling. I love you so very much my darling. Oh Viv please don't be hurt. I did want to know the reason for your dad's refusal, but honey, I wasn't angry. I wasn't darling.

Honey, I just wrote mom and told her you were coming the 8th. I'm sending the letter and this one through German mail. It's supposed to go faster.

Vivian, I love you my darling. I love you so very much. Go to mom's, and be happy Viv. Try to be happy my darling. I love you so much Vivian. Oh my darling, I need you.

Honey, I meant every word. I'll write every day till we're in each other's arms and I'm going to make you happy. I love you my wonderful darling.

Your husband,
Your Johnny

~

August 4, 1953

My Darling Vivian,

Honey, I just talked to you about an hour ago, then wrote you a letter special delivery, and I'm going to send this one to my home, I guess.

Angel, I hope everything works out and you are at Mom's when this comes. Vivian, I know how it must be for you being so far from home and in a strange place, but try your best to be happy there and stay as long as you like. I want so much for you to be happy.

Angel, remember I told you I thought I might get a commendation for the work I did last Saturday? Well, I did honey. I went to work tonight, and everybody started calling me "sir" etc, acting a fool. I asked what it was all about, and they showed me the commendation.

It wasn't just a personal commendation. It was on the bulletin board. The squadron had gotten a commendation from Washington because of my work, and they gave me one, the squadron did. I'm not allowed to take it because it was classified, but it was sure something. It had my name, rank and serial nr. at the top. Owen told about what I did, and how important it was, etc. One thing it said was, "Because of Airman Cash's untiring efforts, this squadron is one large step ahead in the completion of its mission." "He is to be commended for his outstanding efficiency."

I'm a big wheel now honey. Don't believe it darling. I'm not a wheel, but it makes me feel a little good anyway.

Honey, I'll be hoping and praying that you make it to Mom's and back alright. I feel kind of bad about you traveling alone too honey, but I know you'll be careful. Just be careful who you mix with traveling darling. I'd give anything if I could be making that trip with you honey. I know how lonesome you're going to be. Some day we'll be going and doing everything together. I love you so much, Viv.

Your husband,
Your Johnny

~

August 5, 1953

My Darling Viv,

I got a letter from you today honey. A long sweet one, and I got one from mom. Darling, I hope you don't mind, but mom sent me the letter you wrote her saying you couldn't come. Viv, I never read such a sweet letter. Honey, I didn't know you talked to mom like you do, but I'm so happy you do sweetheart. I think it would sound more appropriate if you called her "mom" honey. You seem so close to her. Vivian, I love you so much.

Honey, I sure hope you get to go see them. I'm mailing this letter there, then I'll mail the rest of them to San Antonio, I guess.

Viv, it's nice to think of you being there, in the house where I lived 15 years, probably sleeping in the same bed I did, eating at the same table I did. I can imagine you will be miserable for me honey, but I feel the same way.

Have you ever been on a farm hon? From what they tell me, that farm isn't much because of the drought, so I'm sure glad dad isn't farming. Don't let them put you to chopping cotton or plowing darling. I can just see you driving a team of mules.

Sweetheart, thanks for the lock of hair. It's worth a fortune to me just because it's part of you. It smells and feels so sweet Viv. I'll keep it as long as I live because it's part of you. Oh my sweet darling, I love you so very much. Thank-you my Viv, from the bottom of my heart.

Viv darling, I'm not kidding, this lock of hair brought back so many pleasant memories. As soon as I touched it, and smelled it, I automatically thought of the times I used to hold you in front of me at the drive-in, and put my face against your hair. It's lovely Vivian, and you're lovely and wonderful in every way.

Viv, I don't mean to make you think I was dead set against card playing. I used to play Rook a little myself, but that's the only thing I ever learned to play, and now I've forgotten that. My parents never said anything against me playing Rook, but they were against the other kinds of cards. Somehow I've always hated the word "poker." I don't believe there's any harm in card playing where there's no gambling involved, but hon, you know yourself that harmless card playing 90% of the time, will at some time lead to gambling, which I am definitely against. I know myself honey. I know that when I get in a habit of something, I overindulge. Like smoking or drinking coffee.

It's so hard to talk to you in a letter Viv. I wish I could explain it to you like I want to. I'll always listen to your point of view Vivian, and we can always talk things out, but I'm just going to pray that God will make you see my way on certain things. You're a wonderful girl Vivian. You're clean and sweet and I love you more than anything in the world. We will always talk things out. Vivian darling pray for me that I will be that way. I've come more and more to understand you Vivian, what I want to do more then anything, completely understand you.

No honey, I've never slept in anything more than shorts and T-shirt. I used to sleep with a T-shirt on at home, but since I came in the service, just shorts. If you want me to honey, I'll try to sleep in a T-shirt, then when I come home, I'll buy some pajamas. But I doubt if I can wear it. I always get so restless, and tear it off or pull it off in my sleep. I don't know why it is, but it sure bothers me. I'm not very civilized honey, but your cave man loves you.

Viv, if that's the way it was with your dad, then I won't say another word. If they prayed so hard, and left it to God, then who am I to be angry over it. Sure I understand Viv hon. I won't worry about it anymore. It doesn't bother me now at all. Don't worry about me being hurt, Vivian. What hurts me is that you're hurt. Honey, please forget it. I love you so Vivian. Don't worry about it angel.

Vivian darling, take care of yourself and be careful honey. You know there are some dirty people in this world. Don't take chances while traveling. Watch out for men that want to be extra helpful and nice to you.

I love you so very much my sweetheart.

Your husband to be,
Your Johnny

~

178

My Happiness,

Honey, I got two sweet letters from you today and one from your mom. Viv, they made me so happy they were both long sweet ones, and I've read them over and over.

Viv, this letter from your mom made me feel so much better. It was so sweet. I'm going to have a wonderful mother-in-law. Of course she didn't explain things to me, the reason for their refusal, so I'll be looking forward to your dad's letter.

Viv honey, the reason I asked you what if I didn't sign those papers was because you kept asking me if I was sure I was willing. Honey, how else could we get married if I didn't sign them? Any other way you'd be ex-communicated wouldn't you? Vivian darling, you should know how I feel. Naturally I resent the Catholic Church telling me how to run my life and raise my children, but to have you, I will. There isn't any other girl but you Vivian. There just isn't.

Viv when I said pray for me that I won't change, I don't know exactly what I meant. When I got the refusal, a couple of times after that I felt like writing and telling you to put the ring away and stop writing. It was such a blow at first that I felt like the very life had been taken out of me.

And I was afraid your dad didn't want me to marry you at all. I thought about last fall when he asked you to go with other boys, then the first letter I wrote him that he didn't answer, and I was afraid that this refusal had sealed it. Of course we could get married without his consent when I get back, but we don't want it that way.

I'll be alright Viv. Praying about it has helped me so much. I know I can make it easy. I'll do things to keep occupied and stick it out. I could never stop longing for you and thinking of you so much, and will till you're in my arms. You will be someday.

I love you my sweet darling. I'll love you as long as I live Vivian and as long as I live there will never be anyone for me but you.

Your husband,
Your Johnny

~

August 13, 1953

My Darling Vivian,

Darling, I found out how much money I'm going to have to pay back from my Italy trip. It's only $214 honey. I certainly got beat on that deal. They said I was only allowed $5 a day for my time in Germany, 4 days in all, and $9 a day for my time in Italy. I was paid $13 a day for 30 days and was only gone 23 days, so I have to pay back $214. I didn't get my base pay for the month of June, so that's $80 off the total. I won't get paid at all this month, and I'll only draw about $30 Oct 31st, and that will take care of it.

Vivian I'm proud of the things you believe in and the way you think. Once that I thought your running around with Kate changed you was when you said, "Kate is divorced honey. I know that doesn't sound nice, but she's really a sweet girl." I know you didn't mean it the way I took it at first, but it seemed to me as if you had decided divorce was alright because Kate is a sweet girl.

Vivian darling, I know exactly what kind of a girl you are. You're clean and pure, and to me, the most wonderful girl in the world. I don't suppose it's my business who you mix with but I can't help but be concerned with who you do mix with, because your staying the same as you are is all I ask for.

Maybe Kate is of the 10% that remain a lady after being divorced. I hope so, but under the circumstances it doesn't seem probable. Divorced, and in a G.I. town, living alone with no one to take care of her and advise her. She'd have to be a strong-hearted woman.

Viv, what else could I think except that she was a second class girl when she came in cussing and bragging about the beer she drank. One time like that was enough to set an opinion of her. Even if all she does is drink a beer occasionally and say "damn & hell," you're too good to be around her.

Women are supposed to be mothers and teachers. They're molding the future of the world. It's always best to be sure you're teaching what's right by influence or directly. If you're in doubt about something, leave it alone, or as <u>our</u> God's Bible says, "Shun the very appearance of evil."

Vivian, I love you darling. I hope I haven't hurt you or bored or disgusted you. Honey, I've prayed so hard that God would show me, and "give me the wisdom to know right from wrong." I believe in what I've told you in this letter. I hope you will honestly consider everything. Maybe I don't practice everything I preach, but I believe in everything I preach honey.

I love you so much my darling. Keep on loving me angel and remember you're mine.

> Your husband,
> Your Johnny

~

August 13, 1953

My Darling Vivian,

Sweetheart, I got the pictures yesterday, and darling, I think I've looked at them a hundred times. Thank you so much Viv honey. I love every one of them sugar, and they made me so happy. Honey, you've got a beautiful little body. You're the loveliest girl in the world. Such pretty dark skin. You look so sweet Viv.

Sweetheart, I have no way of comparing then and now, but it seems you've developed quite a large bosom, haven't you honey? You don't have to answer that angel. But they do look larger than they did before. Every bit of you is lovely.

Honey, I can't see where you need to gain any weight. You're beautifully slim. You look perfect to me. You've matured and everything is in the right place.

Viv, I don't know what to think of the letter your dad wrote. Did you read it honey? He gave me one reason. That if you lost your passport you might be isolated here for months. And he said there are lots of things that you'd have to fear here that you wouldn't there.

Viv, I'll try to forget about it and not worry, as long as you say everything is alright, and that nothing will change. I could never hold anything against your dad, and I don't want to be angry with him. I suppose he'd be justified if he was against me marrying you. He loves you and wants you to be happy. I suppose it's up to me to convince him that I will make you happy.

Vivian darling, don't ever let anything change. If I'd ever lose you Vivian, I'd want to die. I love you and I need you my darling. You've got to be mine Viv. I love you so very much. My sweetheart, I love you. I love you with all my heart and soul.

Thank you for being true to me at the skating rink sweetness. I'll be true to you, too. As long as I live, I'll be true to you, Viv.

Honey, I'll be looking forward to those other pictures. You're going to have to send me lots so I can fill my "Sweet Vivian" album. I've already got these in the album. The album is small hon, and only 2 pictures this size go on a page, so if you'll send all those pictures I'll have it about half full, then you won't have to send too many more. Isn't that sweet of me hon? Send those pictures, gal.

Your husband,
Your Johnny

~

August 14, 1953

My Sweet Vivian,

Hon, I sure hope you made it to mom's and back safe and sound. I'll be so worried about you till I know for sure. I've prayed for your safety honey. I hope nobody tries to harm my little darling. Tell me if anybody bothers you.

Honey, my friend Chuck is having his wife sell his car before she comes, and he got a letter from her yesterday about it. She went with the county sheriff in his car to the state capitol. He was so nice to her, helping her get her passport, etc. In the letter yesterday she said she was to meet the sheriff at 9:30 that night and he was going to drive the car and tell her how much he thought she could get for it. She was telling Chuck how nice the sheriff was to go out of his way to help her, and would even take time at night to try her car out.

Today Chuck got a letter and Alice started off, "Honey, I don't know how this letter is going to turn out. I feel so sick and disgusted with everything." She didn't mention why she felt that way, and didn't mention the sheriff and what he thought about the car.

Chuck is about to go crazy over it. Naturally the sheriff tried something with her. He wasn't able to write a letter in time to tell her to stay away from the sheriff since she first started telling about the sheriff going to help her. Chuck has certainly got murder in his heart for a sheriff. He's so torn up he's in a daze, and of course not knowing anymore than he does makes it worse.

Chuck says Alice is only 18 and is the kind of girl that would never believe there are men that would try anything with a married woman. He says she puts all the faith in the world in a perfect stranger. I suppose she knows a little more about what men will do, now.

Honey, hearing things like that makes me worry so much about you. I know you know enough to not let strangers be that nice to you. Living in San Antonio you've probably had to put guys in their place before. But there's a million guys with a million different tricks. And when a guy starts being extra nice and going out of his way to help a strange woman, he's after one thing. Real life isn't quite like it is in the movies.

It would kill me if something like that ever happened to you Viv. I know there are men that hang around every train and bus station just waiting to help a lone woman, and they've got a smile and soft line a mile long. Watch yourself especially when you're away from home darling. It's alright to have faith in people, but the way the world is today you can't have faith in any stranger.

I'll be so happy when I know you're back safe honey, and I hope so much that you enjoyed yourself. Mom said she sure wanted you to come, but she said she was so ashamed for you to see the place the way the heat has ruined it. It sure must be bad.

Honey, tonight at 8 oclock the Air Force band will be down town. They're going to play down there in the town square from 8 to 9:30, and Chuck and I are going I think. I think we will enjoy it. They're a very good band. They're going to play and sing German Folk songs tonight. I suppose we'll go down, then come back as soon as it's over sugar. We're going to come back and play the guitars, so I guess we'll have something to do on this break after all.

Your husband,
Your Johnny

~

August 18, 1953

My Darling Wife to be,

Honey, I'm so happy that everything turned out alright. I'm so glad you like the family. I just hope everything will go off as smooth as it did that first day. I want so much for you to be happy Vivian and especially enjoy that week there. Of course there isn't much to do there but it's a change for you and I sure hope you enjoy every minute of it.

Honey, this seems so funny, "Miss Viv Liberto, Rt.1, Box 138, Dyess, Ark." It seems you're my wife already. Although I don't think that will ever be our address. I'd starve to death trying to make a living farming.

Honey, you and Tom seemed to have hit it off good together. They say he's grown up a lot. I hope he doesn't steal my girl. He isn't that big is he honey? Nobody better try to steal my girl. You belong to me baby darling.

Vivian I need you so. It will be so wonderful when I'm with you and we're married. I'm so lonesome for you especially at night Vivian. Everything would be complete if I just had you beside me at night. Someday my darling and the time is getting closer.

Your husband.
I love you Viv. I love you so.

~

August 19, 1953

My Very Own Viv,

I guess it's alright for you to call me "Pooch" honey. But I wish you hadn't heard that. Can I call you "Snooks"? Darling, who is "Sam" that is so sweet. You better be talking about my dog angel.

I don't think it would sound right for you to call me J.R. honey. I've been called John and Johnny for 3 years. I don't think it would sound right for anyone to call me that. I always hated the "name." I sure get messed up. No real name to call my own. Isn't that pitiful? But you can call me anything you want to Viv. I like it better if you call me honey. And darling I'll be so happy if you've always got that tone in your voice that says you mean it when you call me honey or darling.

Angel, I sure hope they didn't tell you the name my uncle Russell calls me.

I love you Viv. I love you.
Your husband.

~

August 20, 1953

My Vivian Darling.

Sweetheart, I got two more letters from you today. You make me so happy

Viv, and I love you so much. So they did tell you what my uncle Russell calls me. I was afraid of that.

Darling, I know this is awfully short. It's nearly nothing, but I'm so tired honey. I worked so hard today, and it's getting late. I'm going to shower and go to bed honey. Tomorrow is my last day on the day shift, and I'll write a long letter tomorrow nite.

Goodnight Vivian. God bless you my darling. I love you with all my heart.

Your husband, Your Johnny

~

August 21, 1953

My Darling Vivian,

Honey, is it alright with you if we change our prayer time to Sunday instead of Saturday? There's no special reason I guess, but it seems to me it would be best to have it on Sunday. I don't remember if it was you or I that suggested Saturday, but if it's alright with you, let's change it to Sunday. Sweetheart, it doesn't make all that big of a difference to me if you don't want to, but if it is alright with you tell me. I'll pray this next week on Saturday and Sunday both at 9 oclock, and you tell me if you want to.

Honey, I got some more records. I now have 18 records 45 RPM, and 4 albums of 33⅓ RPM. I bought an album of Cowboy spirituals by the "Sons of the Pioneers" and an album of Gospel songs by "The Chuck Wagon" gang, and an album of 8 different hillbilly songs. Most of the 45 RPM are hillbilly. One by Hank Snow "A Fool Such as I." One by Eddy Arnold, "How's the World treating You" and "Going Steady." I think I told you that. I'm going to make a rack for all my records to keep them till I send them to you honey.

Your husband
I love you my darling angel

~

August 22, 1953

My Very Own,

Dad certainly does like you Viv. He wrote me a letter, the first in about 4 weeks and said a lot about you. He said everybody that met you was nuts about you, and he told me to hurry back and hook you while the hooking was good.

Sweetheart, I think you'll be the one that won't want your stomach massaged after 6 or 7 kids but if you'll let me I sure will. Even when you're going to have your 10th one angel. You'd still look the same to me if you'd had 15 kids Vivian. You'll still be the same wonderful girl I love so much. Your little body might be all out of shape from carrying so many of my kids, but that will just make me love you more.

Honey, I didn't go anywhere at all today. It's rained all day and I've just sat around in the room. I've missed you so much Viv. I've read your letters over and over and looked at all your pictures. I need you so much my darling.

Your husband,
Your Johnny

~

August 24, 1953

My Darling Sweetheart,

Honey, Chuck got a letter from one of his buddies today and the guy told him that the talk was all over town that his wife was seen out parked with the sheriff more than once. He also got a letter from her and she talked like she was all broken up. She told him about all the gossip about her and the sheriff, and said there wasn't a thing to it. But still she said she had to go back to the state capitol and with the sheriff was the only way she had to go, so she was going with him the next day.

Chuck is certainly hurt and torn up, and angry. He said he'd never in his life mistrusted Alice, but this was too much. The whole town is talking about her, and she still won't stay away from the guy.

I don't know why it is honey, but Chuck always brings those letters for me to read. I tell him it's his business and to keep it to himself, but he insists I read them. I sure don't know what to think of his wife. He's always been so much in love with her, and has always thought she was a perfect angel. She's supposed to be over here about this time next month and Chuck said she was going to have to clear up this mess and straighten him out when she got here, and if she wasn't telling him the truth, she was going right back home and he was going to divorce her.

Vivian darling, when I think about other girls, and how they act, and can't even wait for 5 or 6 months, then think about you gladly waiting 2½ or 3 years, it makes me want to get down on my knees and thank God that he made one perfect girl with a true honest love, and gave her to me.

I love you my sweet, wonderful darling. I love you so.

Your husband to be.

~

August 29, 1953

Honey, I just got off work again and wanted to write and tell you I love you before I go to bed. I'm here all alone now honey. All the other boys are down playing cards again. I sure am lonesome for you Viv.

185

Vivian I would never have asked you to stop writing and put away the ring. I just felt like dying there for awhile. Nothing seemed to matter anymore. Vivian, if that ever did happen I'd be down on my knees begging you not to. Vivian darling if anything ever happened between us, I'd <u>never</u> get married. It's going to be you or <u>no one</u> Vivian. I mean it. I could never love anyone but you. I would be miserable even going with anyone else. It's always going to be just you Vivian, and if you ever changed your mind I honestly wouldn't want to live. I could never find a girl that would halfway compare with you. God threw away the mold when He made you Vivian.

Yes angel, Uncle Russell calls me "Shoo Doo." I'll swear I don't know where he got that name. He calls Roy "Screw Driver" because he's a mechanic, I think. You can call me anything you want angel.

Your husband,
Your Johnny

~

Sept 6, 1953

My Snookie Pootsie,

Isn't that a killer sweetheart? I'm not drunk honey, I just dreamed up that name.

Honey, I bet you don't know where I am. I'm in our house. Chuck asked me to come down with him and stay here tonight, so I did. It's 12:30 honey. And I've really had a nice time.

About 8:00 Chuck and I brought our guitars down here and the lady that owns the house cooked supper for us, so we ate, and started playing and we just stopped a few minutes ago.

Honey, I've missed you so much. I'm sorry for bringing it up darling, but this would probably have been our wedding night if you'd come. Instead, Chuck is sitting here beside me instead of you. Chuck made the coffee instead of you, and there's G.I. underwear in the chest instead of ladies things. It could almost be enough to make a person bitter honey.

Honey, I was with you at prayer tonight. I went in the toilet and prayed. I love you sweetheart.

Your husband

~

September 8, 1953

My Wonderful Darling,

I got three sweet letters from you today Viv honey. They're all so wonderful.

Honey. Someone really did one of the letters dirty. It was dirty, greasy, all bent up, and had a big black foot print on it. I should have taken it to the P.O.

claims dept, but forgot about it till after I'd opened it. Someone really messed it up honey, and it made me a little angry.

Sweetheart, that gown and negligee you said you were buying for our wedding night, I know you're doing it to make me happy hon, but let me tell you frankly what I'd really like honey.

First of all I think modesty in a woman is the most wonderful thing in the world. On our wedding night when you reveal yourself to me for the first time I want you to be yourself honey. I don't want you to have a lot of expensive negligee honey. I want you to look lovely, but simple. A pair of panties and bra and something thin to wear over that if you want, but that would be perfect for me darling. Of course, if you want to dress up, if that means a lot to a girl, OK honey, but I just want you as you are.

Honey this guy I know goes home in December because he's married. He had never been untrue to his wife, till last night. He went to Munich to buy his Christmas presents, but he bought something else too. He met some pig and stayed with her last night, and came back about noon today. I never saw a worse looking guy. He thinks he's diseased now. He hasn't said a dozen words since he's been back. I sure feel sorry for his wife and any kids he might ever have. I'd just as soon as be dead as face what he's facing.

I'll write tomorrow angel. God bless you and keep you for me.

Your Johnny

~

September 11, 1953

My Little Angel,

Honey, have you heard "Lead me Gently Home, Father"? I've got the record hon, and I'm playing it now. Someday He will lead me gently home, back to you, the one I love. Let's keep praying Vivie. He'll answer our prayers.

Your husband to be,
Your Johnny

~

September 14, 1953

My Darling Wife to be,

Honey, I thought you were sending a book in that envelope, but it was the 50 page letter. Darling you made me feel so wonderful. You're so sweet Viv. It makes me feel like a king when you do something like that for me. I love you so much my darling.

Angel, did you ever hear of King Ludwig? I didn't either till I got over here. Anyway, I forgot to tell you that tomorrow I'm going to his castle. As a matter of fact, 40 of us are going. We went on break tonight, and our Control Chief has chartered a bus for us and we're all going out there tomorrow to tour the castle. I don't know if there will be anything to it honey, but I think I'll go and take my camera along and get some pictures.

Darling in the paper it said "Miss Vivian Reberto of San Antonio, Texas spent a few days with Mr. & Mrs. Ray Cash this week." That's all honey. I don't know how it got in the paper, and how they messed up your name. Someday you'll have a name everybody is familiar with honey. "Mrs. Cash." It sounds perfectly in order angel. It fits you perfectly.

Your husband to be,
Your Johnny

~

September 17, 1953

My Darling Wife,

Darling, I had such a wonderful dream last night about you, and for once there wasn't any trouble. The places were all messed up as usual. I dreamed I was in Memphis, and Memphis was here in South Germany, and you were in Frankfurt working as a secretary. Joann was with me, and I told her she'd have to go home alone because I was going to Frankfurt to see you. Joann said I shouldn't because mom would be worried about me, but I told her I was going because I hadn't seen you in over two years, and I was going. I was on a 3-day pass honey and the next thing I knew I was in Frankfurt looking for you. I knew what street you worked on honey, and I walked down the street stopping at all the houses. It was about 6 PM and I knew you'd be home from work. The last house I stopped at and asked for you, the woman said, "I'll tell you where she is for 5 American dollars." So I shelled out and as soon as I did you walked out of the house and said, "Honey, I'm sorry it cost you $5, but she would have beaten me if I came out before you paid her." Then I got really angry and said "You're not going to work in Frankfurt anymore, and you're not going to live in this house Viv. You're going to live in Munich so we can be together on our B day breaks, and if they ever try to beat you, I'll burn this house down." Then you pulled up the side of your skirt and showed me marks on your legs, and said "Johnny darling, they already did." Then I took my cigarette lighter and set fire to the curtains, and we ran out with the old woman screaming, and when we stopped running and looked back, the house was about half burned up.

Then we walked along real slow and it started raining and you started crying and said all your clothes and all your money had burned up. I don't know where I got the money darling, but I kissed you and gave you $800 and said we'd go buy you some clothes the next day.

Then you said you were cold, so we found a hotel and got one room and went to bed with all our clothes on. I wrapped you up with blankets and lay down beside you and held you tight. Your hair was wet honey, and I kissed you all over your face, and you finally went to sleep, and I lay there thinking that I was going to stay just like that with you until I had to go back to the base the next night. It was so wonderful honey. I felt so bad when I woke up and found it wasn't true.

Angel, some more mail came in and I got the package. Sweetheart, I wish you knew how happy you've made me. My darling I thank you from the bottom of my heart. Oh honey I love you so much. Vivie you're so wonderful darling. You're so heavenly. Yes angel, I can sure use the socks and handkerchiefs. I can use any color handkerchiefs with my uniform darling. And the socks I can sure use. Honey, how do you do it? You always know exactly what I like best and need most. Angel you're so wonderful. And you got all my favorite records honey. I love every record you sent. You got our record too angel. "These Things I Offer You," and "I Still feel the Same." Vivian darling, you've made me so happy honey. I've got the best girl in the whole world. How could any woman ever come close to halfway comparing with you. Viv I feel like bawling. I want to tell you so bad how much I love you and how much I appreciate all this. You do so many wonderful things for me.

I got up too late for dinner, so my darling sent me some candy. I ran out of stationery, so my darling sent me some. I'm going on leave, so my darling sent me some socks and handkerchiefs. I couldn't buy any records, so my darling sent me all my favorites. Vivian, I love you sweetheart. I love you so much it hurts.

Your husband,
Your Johnny for life.

~

September 21, 1953

My little Angel,

Honey, I guess I did you kind of dirty yesterday. I didn't write darling and I'm sorry. I got up early and went to church, then I meant to write that afternoon, but I went to the movie, and was going to write after work but I was just too tired angel, and I went right to bed. I'm sorry sweetheart.

No honey, I know your parents don't tell you what to do. I guess I took that deal all wrong. I can see now that you were the one that was broadminded about it. I would have put up a fight but you knew that it was best not to. I couldn't understand why you didn't if you really wanted to come, but I do now. You did exactly right as usual. It's all over with now and I guess it's for the best.

Darling, if Kate cursed at all it's more than she should have. God didn't mean for women to be that way, or men either. But it just kills my soul to hear a woman curse. Kate must have put sugar on herself if she was "sweet" honey. I can't see how a cursing girl could be sweet. With all due respects to your friends, she sounds like a typical divorcee to me, and I'm glad she's gone.

Vivian, I love you so much darling. You're all the world to me sweetheart. I love you and want you for my wife. Please try to understand how I feel about these things and don't ever think I'm silly. Vivian darling, you're going to always be persecuted for being good and doing good, but it has to be that way. Good people will always be persecuted by the evil and filthy people. But it's worth it darling. You know it is.

Your husband to be,
Your Johnny

~

September 22, 1953

My Darling Angel,

Chuck went to meet Alice at Munich yesterday honey. He told me yesterday morning that if he didn't come back last night, I'd know Alice came. He got off four days from work. He didn't come back, so I suppose Alice got here alright, and they're down in our little honeymoon apt. There's happiness there anyway darling, even if it isn't ours.

Well darling, I was planning on you quitting work when I get back, since I will be discharged as soon as I get to the states. I'm going to get a job as soon as I can, then we'll get married. We're going to have to arrange everything for our convenience Viv. I'll be discharged around June 1st and not July 7th as I was originally scheduled. I don't know yet honey. If you do keep working for awhile after I get back, wait till we're sure of the day I'll be there before you take your vacation. But I don't think it will be convenient for us for you to keep working.

Angel, I've got to rush now or I'll be late for work. I'll write tomorrow sweetheart.

I love you my darling.

Your husband,
Your Johnny

~

September 23, 1953

Vivie, you know what honey? I saw Chuck and Alice today. They're so happy Viv. She's sure a sweet girl darling and they both love each other so much. They're so happy. And I wish it was us honey. Chuck brought Alice to the base this afternoon and I met them. I told them all about my Viv. I love you so much my sweet little darling.

Honey baby, I didn't get any mail today or yesterday. I feel so badly when I don't hear from you. Honey I know it isn't your fault but I feel so bad. I need mail from my darling little angel.

Vivie, I love you. If we were married I'd be with you now and we'd be in each other's arms and I'd be kissing you honey. I'd kiss you and hold your little face close to mine. I'd caress you and love you so much cause I know you're lonesome for me too, aren't you little angel? I'd kiss you so much and I'd kiss your lovely breasts too because you're my girl and you'll be my wife, but when you're my wife, I'll do that. Because you won't mind me kissing your breasts because you love me and if you're my wife you won't mind darling.

I know I shouldn't talk like this Vivie and I'm sorry. I know I never said that to you when I wasn't drinking, but that's what drinking does Viv and I shouldn't talk about your breasts until we're married.

But you're wonderful and I love you so much. Don't be angry Viv. I didn't talk dirty to you. I just love you. I don't just love you because you've got a beautiful figure Viv. You know I don't, but I just love you and need to kiss you honey.

I've got to go to bed now little darling, but don't worry because I'll be alright tomorrow because I can sleep late as I want to because I'm on pass. I'm not going anywhere because I'm true to you. You know I am don't you Viv? You sure do.

> Your husband to be,
> Your Johnny

~

September 24, 1953

My Darling Vivian,

Honey, I suppose I should apologize for that letter last night, but I don't know how. I'm so sorry for what I did that it hurts, but I guess I couldn't help it.

I loaned Chuck my record player yesterday and was alone here from 3:30 yesterday afternoon till 9:30 last night when I went to the Stag room with Willie. I sat here and read, and listened to the corny programs on the radio till I was sick of it. I started thinking of Chuck and Alice here together, then started thinking of you and I just couldn't stay here any longer. We didn't leave the base. We just went to the Stag room here on the base, then came back around midnite. Maybe it was later than midnite, I don't know, but we came back to the room and I wrote you and went to bed.

I wasn't going to write you but when I got back I decided to. People say "what she doesn't know doesn't hurt her," but I can't be that way. I can't keep anything from you honey, and I never will keep anything from you no matter what. I want us to always be that way with each other and I'm not going to start wrong.

I love you Vivian. I know you don't feel as bad as I do when I do something like this. I feel like a punk because I want to abstain completely and I didn't. I'm just sorry. That's all I can say. I'll try to not do it anymore.

Bye honey. Keep on loving me and always remember that you belong to me. You do belong to me Viv. Every ounce of you.

Your husband to be,
Your Johnny

I love you Viv.

~

September 27, 1953

My Darling Angel,

Honey, I sure envy Chuck getting to go home to his wife every morning after work. It would be so wonderful to go home to my little Viv. She'd have breakfast all ready for me. I'd sit down with you, and we'd eat breakfast and talk, then go to bed. It would be so wonderful, so nice and quiet. Then lie down with my lovely wife and go to sleep with her (you) in my arms. Then about noon I'd wake up as I usually do, and you would give me a few "kisses," then I could sleep soundly the rest of the day. I could sure use some of your kisses after working this shift honey.

Angel, it's time to pray with you. I'll be back in a few minutes hon. I love you my sweetheart. I love you with all my heart and soul.

I'm back angel. I prayed with you for 9 minutes. Were you with me honey? I think you were because I felt so close to you.

God bless you and keep you always for me my darling.

~

September 28, 1953

My Darling Vivian,

Vivian, there's no use in me trying to be happy here. I can't be happy till I'm back with you darling. You're my whole life. The time is getting short and that helps a lot. I can't stand drinking and the only thing on the base worthwhile is the movie. I haven't got the money to travel on my passes. I'm saving it for my happiness with you. That's all I'm looking forward to honey, being with you. That's when I'll be happy. Don't worry about me being unhappy, Viv. I've been unhappy 2 years and I can stand it another 8 months, then things are going my way for awhile.

It doesn't seem real that in just a few short months you're going to really be mine. I've thought of you every minute since I've been away, and have longed for you and needed you for so long.

It doesn't seem real that your love, your sweetness and kindness and your lovely little body are actually going to be mine soon.

Goodnight Viv. God bless you darling and keep you mine.

Your husband to be,
Your Johnny

~

September 30, 1953

My Darling,

I'm going to Munich tonight. They're having a big carnival that's been going on for about two weeks. I'll probably stay in Munich two days honey.

Honey, I was never hurt so much in my life this morning. Chuck came in my room and looking like he was about dead. I asked him what was wrong and he told me that Alice broke down and confessed. She gave herself to that sheriff on 4 different nights. He's so hurt. I've never seen him like this. He cursed and cried till it was pitiful. But he still loves her, and said he might even forgive her and not divorce her. I can't see how he can, and he said he can't see how he can ever trust her again although he loves her. After all she lied to him, and even scolding him for acting like he didn't believe her at first. He was crying every word he told me. He told me everything in detail how the sheriff seduced her the first time, then she seduced the sheriff the other 3 times. After adultery 4 times and all those lies, he still loves her. He's nuts. He sure talked about women though. He said there wasn't a woman on earth any better, cleaner, purer than Alice was when they married, and said all other woman are under Alice even yet, and if I ever in my life halfway trusted one single woman I was a stupid so and so.

I can't get over it. Why does something like that have to happen always to the best of people. I've never known a guy that could halfway compare with Chuck, then him get a slut for a wife. As true as he'd been to her, and as much as he believed in her, and loved her. They went together about 3 years before they were married. It doesn't seem possible that such a good guy should have to face a life of misery.

I'll write when I get back from Munich. I'll be true to you Vivian. I'm going for just what I said Vivian. Nothing else.

I love you with all my heart and soul.

~

My Darling Sweetheart,

Viv, I finally got back from Munich. It's 7:30 pm now. I got back this afternoon. Honey, it's been two long days, but they were enjoyable. Day before yesterday I went to Munich with 4 more boys. We went to the carnival and stayed there till about midnite then three of us went to the G.I. hotel and went to bed. I don't know where the other two boys went. We haven't seen them since.

Then yesterday morning we came back to the train station and two of the boys came back to Augsburg but I met Chuck & Alice in the train station and they asked me to go with them, so I did honey. We went to the P.X. and they shopped around all afternoon, then we ate supper in the snack bar at the train station, then went out to the carnival. We stayed out there till 10:30, then we all went to the G.I. hotel. We met another friend of mine at the carnival. Chuck and Alice got a room in the hotel, but my buddy and I had to sleep on the couches in the lounge. All the hotels in Munich are full and even the G.I. hotel was full last night, but Chuck and Alice were lucky enough to get a room.

Honey, we had a nice time. Especially last night. Night before last I was dead tired. I only slept a couple of hours before I went up there and I was miserable. But I slept till noon almost yesterday, and we had lots of fun last night. And I was true to you Vivian. I didn't even talk to any girls.

Darling, I got the long, wonderful letter from you today, and the one you wrote the day after. Darling you made me so happy.

Honey, I feel so sorry for Chuck I could die. He walks around in a daze. He's beginning to get bitter. Yesterday he and I were alone for a few minutes and he told me he thought he would go nuts before this is over with, which will be a divorce probably. He loves Alice. That's what hurts him. He wants her and loves her so much, but he said if he lived with her he could never respect or trust her. He said that every minute of his life he was going to be miserable. When he said he mentioned divorce to her the first time, she screamed and cried and fainted about six times. She loves him so much it's pitiful. He said she told him that she would follow him on her knees the rest of her life if he left her.

Vivian, I wish you could meet her. I can't figure her out. She's just turned 18, and acts like she doesn't know what life is all about. She's like a kid at times, but she isn't. She knew what she was doing and knew it was adultery, but didn't have the sense to know the heartache it would cause. And she has. It's pitiful what it's done to Chuck honey. He looks at her with just a blank stare in his eyes as if he actually can't himself believe what she's done to him. She looks at him every time with a sheepish, pleading look. You can tell that she worships him. How she could have done what she did, I don't know. It doesn't seem possible that this could have happened to them as young as they were and as much as they loved each other. I suppose that will stand between them forever. I think Chuck loves her less everyday. He called her some dirty names that just made me cringe today. Not to her face, but we were in the restroom and he said, "Well, let's go find my little whore and see the rest of the carnival."

Angel, say a few prayers for them.

Goodnight hon. God bless you always. I love you so.

Your husband,
Your Johnny

~

October 3, 1953

Honey, I forgot to tell you, but I bought a nice corduroy shirt (green) when we were at the PX in Munich. I had it on here last night and it sure will be nice for my leave. I also won a big blue teddy bear at the carnival honey and I will send it to you when I send another package. I think I'll take it to bed with me when the other boys aren't looking. It sure is nice and soft, just like my little darling.

Sweetheart, whatever you want to wear on our wedding night, you get it, OK? I want everything to be perfect for you Viv. I guess it means a lot to a girl, more than to a man. And to a girl like you, I guess the wedding night is everything. I just didn't think honey. I told you what I'd like best, but who knows, maybe I'd like you better in what you choose. You could wear a flower sack to bed, and you'd be just as heavenly and lovely darling.

Yes honey, I know what you mean by butterflies. I get them too. It will be heaven darling. It will be wonderful to make you "my woman." And I'll be so lucky and happy that I'm getting you. It will be so wonderful when we're married and can give all ourselves to each other and not be ashamed.

Honey, when I think about these things, the jokes about sex, and the dirty books and movies and everything seem so stupid and silly. The way we love each other, making love to you will be just what God asks, (when we're married). It will be everything sacred and holy and wonderful. It's a shame we humans can't see it always the way two people deeply in love like you and I, and not degrade themselves and others. It's wonderful if we could always see it as God wants us to.

Angel, I never heard of "fuchsia" color makeup. But then I never heard of many kinds of makeup honey. Whatever it's like, I'll love it on you. When I come back, I'll buy about 20 different kinds of makeup, and you can put them all on, and I'll kiss them all off, then I'll tell you what kind I like best. OK sugar? Alright baby.

195

Good night my Viv. God bless you and keep you wherever you are my darling. Always carry my love in your heart.

Your husband to be,
Your Johnny

~

October 6, 1953

Hello Angel,

Honey, I broke my watch today. I took it to the PX tonight, and I get it back in 6 days. Honey, I sure broke it in a crazy way. I'll try to explain it to you. When I got up this morning, the radio announcer said, "It's now 6:42," and my watch was 1 minute fast, so I set it, then he said, "I'm sorry, the correct time is 6:37," so I set it at 6:37, not 6:47. I pulled the stem out and set it twice. Then he said, "Ladies and gentlemen, I got up too early. The correct time is 18 minutes until 7, that's 6:43," yes, 6:43, 18 minutes till 7. That was the last straw honey. I pulled the stem out too hard to set it the last time, and when I pushed it back in it wouldn't run. It was my own fault honey. I got annoyed at the announcer, and pulled it out too hard. It needed cleaning and oiling anyway, I guess, but I sure hate to do without it six days. I'm sorry I was so rough with it honey, but the announcer and I both got up too early.

Honey, do you think playing BINGO is gambling? I mean, paying, to play for the jackpot? I guess it is, and I never thought about it till last night when I played. Honey, after I wrote you last night, one of the boys asked me to go to the club to play Bingo. It only lasts an hour so I went. I bought a card for a dollar and played, and lost of course. Anyway, the jackpot was $475.00, and I prayed that I'd win because the money would help you and I so much. I guess it was silly honey, but I promised God that if I won I'd give $50 to the church. When the last number was called, I only needed one more number to win the $475.

When I walked out I was thinking and wondering why I didn't win it, then the thought struck me, "You'll never do any good, doing any wrong." And I realized it was wrong then and that I was asking for divine assistance in something that was wrong from the beginning.

It was just a mistake darling. I didn't realize it was gambling till God woke me up. I'm sorry, and I won't play Bingo again for money.

I love you more than anything in the world Viv.

Your husband to be,
Your Johnny

~

My Darling Viv,

Honey, I know I'll sound like a conceited punk, but I'll tell you one thing that's been wrong for a long time. Out of the 50 boys I work with, I've got the hardest, most important job there is. Because it's so important, I work harder than anybody there, and <u>every single day</u> that rolls around, somebody has something sarcastic. One guy especially is always calling me "Airman of the Month." Or somebody is always asking me when I'll make Captain. When there's something unusual comes up, and the officers run over and watch the work I turn out, I can see two or three guys looking at me with a smirk on their face. They think I kiss all the officers' tails because I like my job, and I don't like <u>any</u> job unless there's a lot of work. I've got plenty of work, and it's the kind I like, and they, two or 3 or 4, ridicule me for it. I've worked hard ever since I got here, and as long as I've been here, there's been from 1 to 4 that think I work hard just to get in good with the officers and get promoted. I thought I'd never live it down when I got that last commendation. Most of the boys congratulated me, and said it was really nice to get a commendation like that, but those 3 or 4 had something wise to say, and if it wasn't for losing everything I've made since I've been in the service, I'd have knocked somebody's teeth out long ago.

Honey, things like that bear on my mind and make me want to crawl in a hole. I can't stand for somebody to dislike me that I have to live with and work with. It worries me so.

Goodnight and God bless you my angel.

Your husband,
Your Johnny

~

October 27, 1953

My Precious Darling,

Yes angel, we do want a big family so there will be more of us to be happy. Honey, I was thinking the other day how much more wonderful it would be with kids too. I was thinking how you'd act and feel if something happened that we couldn't have kids. I know it would nearly kill you but you'd go on from day to day loving me and living for me to make me happy, and still praying your heart out for children.

I'm sure we'll have lots of kids honey. But we'll pray for that too. God will give us children. They really do make a house a home darling. And love and decency makes a house a home.

Goodnight hon. I'll write tomorrow night. God bless you my sweet darling and may He keep you always safe and guarded for me.

I love you so much.

Your husband.

~

October 31, 1953

My Darling Wife,

Honey, I got three wonderful letters from you today. They made me so happy Vivian. I felt so good after I read them. A guy brought them up to me while I was working honey, and I just stopped. I told Sgt. Richards I'd have to read them then, so I went out in the section lounge for about 20 minutes and read them.

Sweetheart, when I get such wonderful sweet letters, I feel like a million dollars. I acted a fool all afternoon. Of course I did my work but I was so happy.

Honey, Joann, the girl you work with must realize she's nothing special, or she'd trust her husband in Paris, or maybe her husband couldn't be trusted. It's not me Vivian, it's you. You're something special. I could be true to you anywhere. I'd just have more chances with pretty women in Paris, that's all. I had plenty of chances honey, but I was true to you, and I'm a little proud of myself. When I came back the boys asked me how I liked the French women, I said I didn't touch any French women, and they wouldn't believe me. They said that even though I did have a girl like Vivian, I shouldn't let you tie me down in a place like Paris. But I argued, and they'd shake their heads in disbelief. But I couldn't live with myself if I'd been untrue to you Vivian. I believe most boys would have gone ahead, and never told their girl, but I've made too many promises, and if I were untrue to you I'd want to die. The only physical love I want is with you, when I've got our marriage license in my pocket Vivian darling.

Yes hon, Perea was kidding. He's always asking, "How's Viv and the kids," because I told him you and I were going to have about 15, then later on I'd say, "Well, Perea, congratulate me, Viv and I are going to have another baby, our 12th one." Then he'd say, "Well! That's fine. How's Viv getting along? Is she up yet? How does she feel?" And I'd say, "Oh she feels fine. She's so happy. She wants a little girl this time and I do too. The last 5 were boys." We were always acting a fool like that hon. You had so many babies that you didn't know about angel.

Baby darling, when you said something about sleeping curled up to me, I had the funniest feeling, because I thought so much about that this morning. I woke up just freezing, about 4 am this morning, and it was at least an hour

Johnny and me as newlyweds

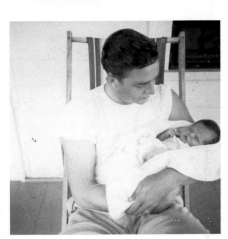

Marshall Grant, Johnny,
and Luther Perkins

Johnny and Rosanne, 1955

Johnny always wore white in those days.

I was so proud of Johnny.

Johnny and Homer
at play

Rosanne and Kathy
all dolled up for church

With Lorrie Collins
(of the Collins Kids)
and Stu Carnall

Poolside fun
at home in Encino

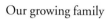

Our growing family

Johnny in bad shape

"Ole Jessie,"
the infamous camper

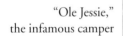

In our front yard at Casitas

Unhappy times, 1962

My wedding to Dick,
January 11, 1968

Christmas 1968
(*standing:* Rosanne;
sitting left to right:
Cindy, Tara, and Kathy)

Rosanne, Kathy, me, Tara, and Cindy in the eighties *(Photo: Ron Keith)*

Me, Tara, Cindy, Johnny, and Kathy, July 2003

Annie and me

Johnny and me

Sitting at "our bench" along
the River Walk,
San Antonio, 2004

before I went back to sleep. I lay there cold, and thinking how nice it would be to have you in my arms. I crooked my body and drew up my legs and imagined you were lying with your back to me, and I had my arms around you holding you close keeping you, and myself warm. It would have been so wonderful if you had been honey. You're so lovely, and I bet you're so soft and warm when it's cold. Someday angel.

Honey, just what is a wedding reception? Is it after the wedding, and who is supposed to come? I've heard people talk of how drunk they got at someone's wedding reception, but I know ours won't give them the opportunity. Where will ours be, and what will it be like honey?

Sweetheart, with God's help, you will marry me. I couldn't think of either of us ever living with anyone else. We were meant for each other.

Yes, it would be horrible to get a Dear John, but I don't worry about that anymore. I have all the confidence in the world in your love angel. You know you'll never get one from me either Viv. It would be like a divorce. We don't believe in divorce.

Goodnight lovely. God bless you and keep you always for me. Say your prayers with me hon. I'll make believe you're with me when I say my silent prayers and you will be. I love you my sweet wonderful angel.

Your husband,
Your Johnny

~

November 2, 1953

My Precious Darling,

Vivian I'm so sorry to hear about your dad honey. Oh sweetheart, I feel every thing you do. When you're hurt or worried I'm the same way. Sweetheart, I hope so much that there's nothing serious wrong. Yes honey, I'll pray hard for him. Tell him I hope there's nothing wrong and that I'll be praying for him. I told Chuck too honey. I told him to tell Alice, and for them to pray for your dad. Then a few minutes ago I went down to another room where three boys sleep, and asked them to pray for him. These three boys are about the only three I know that I could ask honey. They all go to church, and don't drink and smoke. I asked them to pray for your dad and they said they certainly would. So honey, in all there will be six of us over here praying for him.

Yes, sugar, it is pretty cold here. It would be so wonderful if we could keep each other warm. If we were married, my little Viv could put on her pajamas and we'd get under two blankets and snuggle. I'd hold you close to me and kiss your sweet lips and cheeks and eyes and hair. You'd be so warm and soft angel. Just like a little bunny. Someday we'll do that angel. We'll be in each other's arms all night, every night.

199

I'm going to take a shower, then say my prayers and go to bed honey. I'll write tomorrow angel. Goodnight my sweet darling. Keep on loving me and stay my little girl. I love you Viv. I love you and need you so much it hurts.

Your husband.

~

November 3, 1953

My Precious Darling,

Remember I was talking about dreaming of you honey, and I said I hoped I'd have a dream about you last night? Well I did sugar, and it's been on my mind all day. I've just got to tell you about it angel.

It started off, I was in a city somewhere. I had no idea where I was, and I was ashamed to ask anyone what town it was, and I was walking along the street, and I saw a theatre named "The Hippodrome." I was awfully tired and so I started to go in the theatre, and right under where it said "The Hippodrome," it said "San Antonio's Finest Theatre." And it sure surprised me that I was in San Antonio. I bought a ticket and was going in when it struck me that you lived in San Antonio, but I couldn't understand how I could be in S.A. because the Hippodrome is a big theatre in New York. But I walked down the street to where I used to catch the bus to go out to your house when I had a date with you. When I got to Commerce & Navarro I remembered that I didn't know which bus I was supposed to catch, and I had to catch a bus because I didn't have enough for a taxi. Then I woke up honey. I was so disappointed I could die, but I went back to sleep after about five minutes and honest darling, I started dreaming and I was getting out of a taxi in front of your house. I wanted to continue the dream so bad that while I was awake I started thinking of taking a taxi to your house and when I went to sleep I'd gone all the way from up town to your house, and the dream continued.

Then I went in your house and your mom met me and she didn't recognize me, but then you came out of the kitchen. Darling you looked beautiful. You had on high heels and stockings and a brown corduroy suit, and a little tan hat. I started toward you to kiss you and you said, "No Johnny, you can't kiss me for 3 days." Then your mom told me you were married but getting a divorce in 3 days, then I could kiss you.

The next thing I knew the 3 days were up and we were married, and as we were leaving your house, you mom came out and said, "Johnny, Viv wasn't really married, but I just told you that because I didn't want you to take her away." Then I put my arm around her, and told her I wouldn't have taken you away soon if she didn't want me to. Then she just cried and cried honey. When I asked her what was wrong she said, "All my life I've taught Viv to be a good girl, and she's always been nice and sweet and has taken care of herself, but now all of a sudden you're going to take her off and ruin her." Then I told her you were my wife and I loved you, but she kept saying, "You're going to ruin her and spoil her after she's been such a good girl." We were both trying to talk to her and console her when I woke up darling, and I couldn't make the dream go any further. I don't think I ever did get to kiss you honey, but it was still a wonderful dream, seeing you. I felt so lonesome when I awoke. I wanted you so much sweetheart.

I love you Vivian. I love every ounce of you sweetheart.

Your husband

~

November 9, 1953

My Precious Darling,

Honey, I got three little sweet letters from you today. Angel, I couldn't live without you.

Viv, I'm so happy too that your dad is alright. I was worried before we started praying for him, then it didn't worry me at all. I know prayer is all that did it honey. I'll tell Chuck and the other three boys, and I know they'll be happy too. I feel so good about it all Viv.

I know you'll look lovely in that evening dress angel. I'd give a million dollars to see you. I hope you have a chance to make some pictures like last time.

I'm living for the day I'll see you in a gown when you're the star of the show. I know you'll look heavenly. It will be so wonderful Vivian darling. The day can't come too soon for me precious.

Right now I've got to shower and shave and get ready for work love. I'll see you tomorrow angel.

Your husband.

~

November 9, 1953

My Precious Darling,

Viv, I just got off work and I just had to talk to you before I go to bed.

Honey, I love you. If only I could be with you tonight to show my love for you. Oh my precious darling, I love you. Sweetheart, I need you so. Viv, can't you see how much I love and need you angel?

Viv, I had the most horrible dream I ever had last night, and it's been so strong on my mind all day and night. I know it's silly, but it was so vivid and realistic that I was shaking when I awoke. I was also the happiest guy in the world to find it wasn't real. It was a horrible dream about you. Honey, I feel so silly, but I still worry. Sweetheart, be careful and take care of yourself. If anything happened to you I'd want to die. You're so precious to me Vivian darling. I hate to think of trying to live without you. I couldn't do it I know. I couldn't possibly go on living without you. Vivian you're my life, can't you see darling? Oh my sweetheart, I love you and need you so.

Viv darling, I'm on that 2 day pass now starting a few minutes ago, but I'm not going anywhere. I'll stay here and clean things up. I've got a lot of clothes to wash and I can keep busy.

I love you my little wife. I love you so very much.

Your husband,
Your Johnny

~

November 10, 1953

My lovin' darlin',

Viv, I got a wonderful sweet letter from you today sugar. Just like you angel, wonderful and sweet. I think you're the sweetest girl in the world, and you'd better not laugh this time.

But honey, some of the mail is really behind. This letter was written the 5th, and the latest one yesterday was written the 2nd, and I know you wrote between that because in this letter you answered some of my letters that I wrote about the day I sent the pictures, and in that one the 2nd, you hadn't answered my first letters yet. So, all evidence points to the fact that I, Johnny R. Cash, am overdue some mail which should, beyond a shadow of a doubt, come in tomorrow if the mail comes in. There should be two big fat sweet letters from my little bunny. But considering the circumstances existing lately, there is a chance that the said mail will be delayed, which will probably depress the dickens out of me. That's the breaks I guess. Another "thumbs down" for the Post Office department.

I bet you look lovely in the skirt honey. Not because I bought it, but I just wanted you to have a skirt like that. I remember you in one skirt like that I think. It was a full one, and when you'd turn around it would spin. Viv, if I could just see you I'd be so happy. It would be so wonderful just to see something as lovely and attractive as you are, after staring at these four blank walls and all these boys. I feel so good when I get a picture of you. It makes me feel so good that such a lovely girl, and such a pure, wonderful sweet girl is going to be my very own. Sometimes I can't believe that God is so good to me. I love you Vivian darling. I love you so much it hurts.

Your husband,
Your Johnny

~

Most all of Johnny's letters were handwritten. This is one of the few typewritten ones he sent me.

November 12, 1953
2:30 AM

Hello Chicken,

I bet you don't know where I am do you sugar? I didn't think you did. I'm at work, and hon, don't tell anybody, but I'm not very busy. I'm supposed to be slaving away, protecting my country, but some days you just don't feel like it.

I'm sitting right in the back of the room so I can see anybody that is coming, so I won't get caught.

Sweetheart, when I think back over all the time we've been apart, it seems like it's been centuries. All that time you've waited for me. I was thinking today about the last two years. I remembered the first New Years Eve I was here and stayed in my room alone, wanting you so bad I almost bawled, then the night I sat out in the hall writing you. I thought of that first id bracelet you sent me, and I remembered going down town and buying those earrings for you, and then the second id bracelet you sent me. Then I thought of today, sitting in my room, lonely and wanting the same girl, only worse than ever.

Sometimes it's bitter for me to think back over all of it, Viv. Not for any sacrifices I might have made, but for you. If I thought I was worth all that, I would be different, but I know I can never make you happy enough to repay you for all you've done for me. I think I can make you happy, but you've sacrificed so much.

Honey, it will be so wonderful the night we're together, the first night, I mean, and all of them. I'm going to plan something special for that night just for you and I. We'll take a long drive, maybe go up to Blytheville, or West Memphis to a drive-in, or something else. The first night, I don't think we'll want to be around a lot of people anywhere. We'll have to be alone, go somewhere and sit on a river bank, or lake or something where it's quiet and romantic, so we can get used to being together, and make what we're expecting be real. It's going to be a wonderful night angel. I'll figger it all out.

Honey, I should have been busy a long time ago. If it got caught doing this, I know I'd lose every stripe I've got, so I better close.

Night angel face. You can bet your sweet little pug nose that I'll be thinking of you every minute I'm awake honey, and hoping to dream of you too.

I love you my sweet wonderful darling. I love you so.

Your very very own

～

203

November 16, 1953

My Wonderful Darling,

Ever since I asked those guys to pray for your dad I've watched my language because I didn't want them to think I'm a hippocrite. It's helped me a lot Viv honey. I've taken some of the filth out of my mouth. I'm going to keep trying and praying and someday I hope to compare with you in that.

But darling, one thing, I've <u>never</u> broken the commandment that so many people carelessly break. I have <u>never</u> said "goddamn." Most people wouldn't believe me, so I never tell anyone that, but I <u>know</u> that in my whole life I've <u>never</u> offered that word. I can't say much for the rest of my speech, but I've never said that, not even when I was mad.

Honey, Bob has a sign on his wall locker that says "Speak Gently: 'Tis better to rule by love than Force." Although he's a poetry fiend, it almost seems that he put it up there for me. He doesn't think I've even noticed it, but I have, and it helps me.

I love you so much my Viv.

Your husband.

~

November 19, 1953

My Darling Vivian,

Vivian, ever since this mail came today, I prayed and prayed that God would show me what was right to say, and let me say just exactly what I should, and not worry about anything I shouldn't. What I say, I think is right and honest for me to say.

You're right honey, if a month and a half ago you'd told me about the guy that came over to see you, I would have been angry. As it is, I'm hurt and disappointed. Not because of him coming to see you and taking you out for "coffee," but because of the circumstances.

At first I was angry that some guy thought he could make out with you, then that turned to hurt. I want to be happy in our love and trust you to the end of the world Vivian, but you're not helping me too much.

Vivian, I tell Chuck & Alice, and everybody that I don't even want to <u>meet</u> or talk to any girls. I tell them I'll never go out, but you don't do that do you honey? You don't let the men you work with know that you definitely wouldn't go out. If so, that guy wouldn't have told his brother in law about you. What do you think he told him about you honey? Why do you think the guy came to see you?

And another thing that hurt was that you didn't tell me anymore than you did. I wish you'd told me where he took you for coffee, what you talked about, etc. Why didn't you serve him coffee at home honey?

Vivian, you didn't write that night just because you were lazy. I know you didn't do a thing wrong, but why did you cover up so. Why didn't you tell me that you didn't write because you were up so late talking to him and going for coffee? I can't stand for you to cover up. When things don't make any difference in the world anyway, why don't you tell me all about it? It isn't hard to see that the reason you didn't write and answer my letters was because you were talking to him. Not because you were lazy.

I'm glad the guy wouldn't appeal to you in the least honey. Vivian, I don't know if you're serious, or what your point is, but you know as well as I do that that guy wouldn't go to all the trouble of looking up your name and telephone nr. just because he wanted someone to talk to. You know that Vivian. You said this guy at the office gave him your name, so he looked it up in the phone book. Then he called you, did he? And you asked him to come over. You said once that he called, and then you said he just came over, and you didn't know why he came over.

If you'd tell me everything straight Vivian, it would be so easy to believe you, but you're so afraid of something that you won't tell me straight.

Vivian you're too smart to think this guy is innocent. He's 27 years old and knows what he's after as well as you do. You know better than to trust him, or think his intentions are honorable.

Vivian, when I was in London, I got on a street bus. It was the night Perea took this girl home, and I went back alone. When I sat down on the bus, a woman sat beside me. She knew I was an American and asked me how long I'd been in London. I told her, and she wrote down a phone nr, and said, "I'm working at night myself, but this is my cousin's nr, and if you'd like to meet a nice girl, I'm sure you'd love to meet her, and she could show you the town." I thanked her for the nr, and as soon as she stepped off the bus, I tore up the paper, then went to my hotel room, and wrote you and went to bed so lonely for you I could die. When I did that, I said, "I know Vivian would do the same for me." Now I wonder if you would.

I'll never be happy this way Vivian. Not as long as you're the way you are now. For quite awhile now I've been wonderfully happy. I've felt so close to you and thought of you as an angel. Now I can't say how I feel. I didn't think anything about it when you went to the movie with Beck, or had dinner with him, or sat up till 2 AM talking to Sylvia's 2 boy friends, but this hurts too much. It makes me wonder what other men think of you. What would that guy tell his brother-in-law about you to make him go to so much trouble to call you, and come to see you. And what makes you act like its perfectly innocent. And your covering up and making excuses and contradicting yourself kills me, when there's no need for you to.

Vivian, if you just can, I want you to tell me what that guy's idea was, and

205

why this guy at the office ever gave his brother-in-law the idea he could make out with you. If not, when I come back I'm going to find both of these guys and find out myself just what's going on. I'd like to see this guy Gipson and talk things over with him, and straighten out a few of his ideas. I know what he's after whether you'll say you do or not.

Now do you understand what I mean about getting too friendly with the men Vivian. I know that when you're around the office there you're friendly and always talking to them, and this guy got the wrong idea about you. You know it.

I wanted to be happy, and I wanted more than anything to be good to you, but you won't let me. You didn't have to tell the guy he could come over in the first place, and you didn't have to go out with him. My prayers aren't being answered Vivian. I've prayed for our love to be kept strong and for me to be good to you. But you let a guy you've never met before come before me, and you will as long as I'm over here, and you can meet a new guy and talk to him and just do enough that you can't exactly call it a "date."

I want you to tell me what kind of idea these people have about you, why they think you're just anybody's girl when you're so clean and decent. If I were in San Antonio now two men would tell me something or get their brains blown out. You belong to me and nobody's going to toss you around and talk about you. If you're going to be mine Vivian, you've got to be all mine, and not hide things from me. If you can be that way we'll be happy because I don't need anyone but you, even to talk to. If you can be that way to me Vivian, we'll be happy. If you can only be close to me and tell me everything honestly no matter what happens.

If you can talk to me like a husband, and let people know what the engagement ring means to you, and tell me everything honestly, I'll show you how good I can be to you. I'll pray like I never prayed before, and I'll show you how much I love you and how much you mean to me.

If not then I'll take the only life I could ever live without your love. Drunkeness and cheapness as long as I live. I'm not asking for perfection. I'm only asking for honesty and for the faithfulness I know you can give me.

I'm sorry this had to come up. I lay in bed last night praying and thanking God for our love. Now I feel like I have to start all over again, trying to bring you close enough to talk to me honestly.

I suppose the more I talk, the more I hurt you, but I don't think you could be as hurt and disappointed as I was today. You couldn't be.

Vivian, I'm going to pray now and go to bed. I'm going to pray harder then I ever did because if I'm tormented all day tomorrow like I was most of today I'll go crazy. How can you be so friendly with the men and interested in them

Vivian as much as we've meant to each other? How can you treat our precious love so lightly? How can you do it?

Goodnight my darling. I love you so much it hurts.

Your husband.

~

November 19, 1953

Honey, I'm not sleepy, so I thought I'd answer a few of your letters, or part of them, till I get sleepy, then answer the rest tomorrow night. It's getting late, but I'm still not tired.

Vivian, I prayed hard tonight. This all seems like a bad dream. It doesn't seem actually that I got angry again and hurt you because I tried so hard. But that letter just tore me up honey. If it had been a young guy, 19 or 20, it would have been different. But someone 27 years old, and you seemed to think nothing of it. Vivian will you tell me whether or not he got fresh with you? There's not a doubt in my mind what he came to see you for Vivian so I want to know if he tried anything. Is that what you covered up honey? Were you afraid to tell me that he got fresh? Vivian, if you'll tell me everything, honestly, I promise I'll never see the guy, but if you don't I will.

Darling, I'll send the coaster with your Xmas presents. And honey, I'll also send my ring, so you can have my wedding ring made the same size as it. It fits perfect honey. I believe that's the best way to do it.

Hello angel, I'm back again. It's 5:30 PM and I just got off work and ate supper. I'll try to answer all your letters tonight darling. I got one from you today. It was short, but sweet and wonderful. It pepped me up so much, and I was so happy when I read it.

Viv, I bought my gun when I was in Italy. It's a .25 calibre pistol that's so small it fits in the palm of my hand. Darling, it's in the bottom of my footlocker under some books, and it's been there since I came back form Italy, except the one time Chuck & I took it out.

Honey, it is against regulations to have it, but when I bought it in Italy, we were in a town that was 90% communist. We worked out alone, in a wheat field, and at that time we had no guard. People were always coming around to see what we were doing and they weren't friendly. They never bothered us except for that, and I asked this major one day if he cared if I bought a pistol to take out to work, just to scare people away in case they bothered us. He said, "It's against Air Force regulations, but I've got one myself. Go ahead and buy it, but keep it hidden, and never tell anybody that I know you've got it." So I bought one honey and 3 more boys did too. Honey you don't have to worry. I'll never use it for anything but killing snakes. I know better than to ever try

207

anything with a gun angel, and when I said last night I'd blow those guys brains out, I didn't mean that.

I'll <u>never</u> harm <u>anybody</u> with it honey, but I love guns. I want this one to take home and use for sport, and killing snakes in those ditches, etc. You hate guns honey? I was thinking of teaching you to shoot it when I come back. I don't think you'll mind it sweetheart. I get you haven't been around guns much have you? If you really hate them honey, maybe I'll give it to dad, or sell it when I come back if you want me to.

Honey, I'm going to write my folks now and go to bed. I went down and drank a cup of coffee and read the paper just a few minutes ago honey, but I didn't tell you because I knew you'd miss me.

Viv, keep on praying hard for us, and that we can be together soon. Honey, God will surely answer our prayers and bring us together. He knows how much happier we'd be and how much better we could serve him if we were together. Pray hard with me Viv.

Your husband,
Your Johnny

~

November 21, 1953

My Precious Darling,

Honey, I met the sweetest little girl tonight. I went to the movie, and there weren't any seats except down close with the kids, so I sat down beside a little girl about 4 years old. She was with her brother, he was 9 or 10. Before the movie started I told her if she didn't be a good little girl, I'd bite her ear off. I didn't mean to scare her, but I guess I did, because she moved over towards the other side of the seat. The movie was "Abbot & Costello meet Dr. Jekyll and Mr. Hyde," and she got scared to death. Hon, about halfway through she put her hand on my arm and said, "I'm scared and mother isn't here." So I took her hand and held it for awhile, and she got more scared, so I took her in my lap, and everytime there'd be something scary, she put her hands over her face, and turned against me.

She was so sweet honey. I felt like squeezing her to death. I thought of you so much Vivian and how happy we'd be to have our own kid to take care of. I could almost feel you there beside me. I felt like a father to her, and I sure missed her mother.

Vivian honey, you are like a wife to me. A wife that I love very much. I want you all to myself. I don't want anyone to touch you. I love you so much my darling. I'd be so happy if you were my wife now. Someday you will be sweetheart, but it's wonderful imagining you are now.

Darling, I don't know if mom told you, but dad sold the farm. They don't know where they're moving to yet. Mom and Tom & Joann want to buy a house there in Dyess, close to school, but Dad wants to move to Osceola, and make a down payment on a home there. There's nothing to Dyess, but I certainly hope they stay around there. I know they wouldn't be satisfied anywhere else after 20 years at Dyess. There's no point that I can see in them moving to Osceola, but I didn't give them my viewpoint.

So when you come there honey, I guess you'll meet me at a new place. It won't be like going home though. I know I'll always feel like I didn't quite make it home if I go to a new place, but I guess sentiment is out when it comes to necessity. I'll be happy though if they can be comfortable.

Angel, I'm going to bed now. I've got to get up for work tomorrow. Goodnight precious.

I love you so.

Your husband,
Your Johnny.

~

November 23, 1953

My Precious Darling,

Angel, I was so blue for awhile today. The mail came in today at noon, and I think there was mail in every box but mine. I sat and waited and watched him put it up, and when he finished my little box was bare. So I went back to work, and an hour later I went down, and I had 3 cute little letters from you. I grabbed them and sat down and read them and I was so happy sweetheart. Angel, these three were written the 15th, 16th and 18th. Old 17 must have rested awhile.

Sweetheart, I'll sure be looking forward to those pictures. Thank you so much hon. You know how much I want pictures of you sweetheart, so when you're around a camera, be a pig and have a lot taken of you.

Darling, I got a letter from mom today too. She said the farm is definitely sold. They've got paid for it by now. They're still undecided to move up "town," or to Osceola. She said she breaks down and cries every time she thinks of leaving there. The place has so many memories.

I was walking back from supper tonight, and I stared thinking about it too, and I honestly got tears in my eyes. I thought I was going to cry out loud. I know it was silly, but that's the closest I've come to crying in a long time. Every tree, stump, bush or every square foot of that place has a memory for me. I remembered especially once when my brother Jack and I were so small. I couldn't have been over 4, and he was 6. We carried a little tin bucket of drinking water to my dad who was over in the field plowing. We found an old rusty quarter lying on the ground, and we were so happy when dad said we could

209

keep it for our very own. Every inch of that place makes me think of something different, something wonderful and precious that happened. I could walk over that place and think of things I'd never remember any other way. I can remember Roy and Louise and Jack and Reba so well when they were all kids. It's even sweet to look back over the hard work I did there with them.

Goodnight my lovely darling. Stay just as wonderful and heavenly as you are.

Your husband.

∼

November 25, 1953

My Precious Darling,

Honey, I'm going to eat Thanksgiving dinner here on the base, then go out there to Chuck's. Chuck had Mrs. Schriner's piano tuned and I guess we'll play & sing.

Hon, do you like to do things like that, playing & singing? I remember just one time you played the piano honey. I asked you if you could play, and you sat down and played, a lullaby, and I said, "I just love that song. My little sister used to play it." Do you remember that honey? Can you play very well darling? How much?

Honey, did you see the movie "Houdini"? That's what was on tonight, and I thought of you so much. He loved his wife, and was so devoted to her. I thought to myself that I would be the same way, if I could just be with you.

Sweetheart, if you were my wife tonight, I wouldn't let you wear pajamas to bed. I'd only let you wear a cute little pair of lace silk panties, and bra. I love you and need you so much. It would be so wonderful to be married, and hold you in my arms and love you and kiss and caress your lovely little body. It's so wonderful to know that you're mine and that no one has ever put their hands on you. You're so sweet and wonderful. I love you so much my darling. I worship you.

Angel, I'm going to bed now. It isn't late, but there's nothing to do. I want to be with you so much.

Your husband,
Your Johnny always.

∼

November 26, 1953

My Sweet Darling,

Honey, I think I must have gained about 10 pounds today. I ate dinner here on the base, then at 3 oclock I went out to Chuck & Alice's. We sat around the room and talked, and beat the piano, then ate supper, then came out to the base at 7 oclock to see a stage show at the theatre. After it was over, they went home, and I came back to my room. I was here alone till a few minutes ago, but Bob came in drunk and is passed out now. People can sure pick some nice holidays to get drunk on.

Honey, John Calvert was the M.C. of this show tonight. This one wasn't half as good as his show last year. He only had one woman in the show, some red head named Anne. He did a lot of magic, and there was a good quartet. The rest of the time he was telling us about all his movies he's made. He is a good showman though, and he could sure beat the show he had with him tonight. It was barely an hour long.

Honey, you know, I think Chuck has gotten over all his hurt. He seems so happy and contented. They seem like a couple of kids that have just fallen in love. They went shopping the other day and bought shoes, shirts and sweaters and jackets just alike. They call each other "honey" and are so good to each other.

Viv, something you said just before I went on leave has bothered me. Remember you said, "I know how Chuck must feel, sleeping with her when he knows another man has touched her. I'd feel the same way." Darling, do you mean you'd feel the same way if you were Chuck, or would you feel that way with me, knowing I'd touched other girls? Vivian, I'll never lie to you about anything. I'll tell you anything you'd want to know. Before we fell in love I had other girls. I wanted you to know that. I didn't want to make you think I hadn't. I'm sorry for it but I can't help it now. I didn't realize how serious my wrong doing was until you came along. You've opened my eyes on lots of things. Vivian honey, can you forgive me for it, and not have any resentment or disgust for me for it? How do you feel about it darling, about the things I did before I met you?

Guys have told me about confessing to their wife their relations with other girls before their wedding, and the girl would usually say, "Forget it. It doesn't matter," or something like that, but I know what kind of a girl you are and I'm worried as to what you'll think of me and the things I've done.

Vivian, I'm sorry honey. I'm very sorry. I wish I could undo everything I've done. But you know I've been yours since I've been here, and I'll be yours for life. I'll never touch anyone but you. To break up with you now would be like a divorce, and to be untrue to you, I'd suffer the same as if I'd committed adultery.

Maybe I was wrong in bringing it up honey, but I had to know how you felt, and how you'll feel toward me.

My darling, I love you. I love you so much it hurts. You're everything in my life Vivian. You're all I live for and all I ever want. Without you I couldn't live you mean so much to me.

Your husband,
Your Johnny

~

November 30, 1953

My Wonderful Darling,

Viv, you told me something that made me so happy I could cry. When you said, "I don't want to be rich honey. I wouldn't know how to act and wouldn't want to know." I wouldn't have thought that God made a woman that feels about that just as I do. I'll work my fingers to the bone to make you comfortable, but I don't ever want to be rich. I want us to live comfortable, but if there was a choice to take, I'd rather be poor than rich. I was always so proud that I was a plain country boy. When I'd see some big shot driving a new car, smoking a cigar, I'd automatically breathe a prayer of thanks that I was poor. My life's ambition was to walk up to John D. Rockefeller and tell him rich people don't go to heaven.

Vivian, you don't need clothes to make you pretty. No matter what you had on you'd be the loveliest girl in the world to me. If you were ragged and dirty, underneath those rags and dirt would be a pure, clean, sweet, honest girl. You are pretty outside too honey. Why do you think I stared at you so? You've got the sweetest smile, the prettiest eyes, and the loveliest complexion in the world. I'll never be disappointed honey. I'm so happy you're mine that I want to lock you up where no one else can touch or see you.

I was always that proud honey, but it wasn't till you sent me these last pictures that I knew I was getting a girl with a body like Venus. I saw Venus in Paris honey, and I'd take you any day if I didn't know you.

I never cease wondering, that God gave you such pretty looks, and such a perfect figure, and then gave you such a wonderful mind. Most girls that He gave such a pretty figure, he didn't put any brains in their heads. He gave you both and made you understand that even though your body was lovely and attractive, it was still sacred. Then He gave you to me, the most wonderful thing that ever happened to any man.

Your husband,
Your Johnny

~

December 3, 1953

My Precious Viv,

Honey, we had to go see a V.D. film today. I don't know why they make us see those crummy things. Did you ever see one darling? In the states they have them. They call them "Road Shows." They have a sexy movie, then they show diseased men and women that are half rotten, but still alive. If you get a chance to see one darling, <u>don't</u>. It's sickening. I thought I was going to vomit when

212

I walked out of that theatre, and so were about half the others. They aren't fit for humans to see. The reason they make us see them is so we'll see how horrible venereal disease is so we'll be careful what kind of women we pick up. I don't need to see it. Don't let any of the girls talk you into going to one of them darling. As horrible as they make it look, you couldn't forget it if you tried.

Honey, the folks have decided to move "up town" there at Dyess. By now they've already moved Viv. They were supposed to have moved Nov 30th. I'm glad they stayed at Dyess. It isn't much but it's home. From the way mom talked they got a nice four room house. As a matter of fact, dad says it's the nicest, newest house in town. But of course it still wouldn't have to be too nice to be the best. So that's where we'll be together when I first get back angel face. Of course it won't be home, but we can make it home I guess. Anywhere that you are will be heaven. I'll be at home anyplace you are. You're my home. You're my very life darling.

Your Husband,
Your Johnny

~

December 7, 1953

My Darling Wife,

I'm so glad your mom and dad are improving honey. I think our prayers are being answered and I'll keep praying hard.

Viv you say it's no sin if they don't get drunk, but still you're praying so hard they'll stop all together. You're doing it for my sake aren't you honey? You don't know it honey, but you're also doing for your sake, and Sylvia's and for any little kids that might see them drink. I've always been taught that it's all wrong sugar, and I can't believe any other way. I've seen it proven so many times. I can see the sin just from what you said darling, "It's no sin if you don't get drunk." I think someday darling that I can make you see.

I know your belief is natural honey. You've been taught it's no harm, and I've never seen an Italian that didn't at least drink wine. It would have been different 2000 years ago when Christ was on earth. Wine was the only intoxicating drink, and it was considered a food, and used like food. Today it isn't. It leads to every kind of sinful drink, and every kind of sinful drink leads to every kind of sinful act. I could see nothing wrong with drinking a <u>little</u> wine with a meal if that's all you ever drank, but you can't show me a person darling that will leave whiskey alone if he drinks even wine.

Honey, I know just how your church feels about that because I read something that the pope himself said. He said "<u>Wine in itself</u> is a good thing, but the world over, people over-indulge, and let the wine lead to other types of sininducing drinks."

I hope I can make you see my way angel, but if not I know we can work it out. It's nothing to have hard feelings about. I'm happy at least that you don't like it, and love me enough not to touch it, because I'd rather die than see you touch a drop.

I hate French kissing too darling. It's so filthy, but when I kiss you darling, I don't like to close them up tight. You know angel, just open them up about half an inch so I can taste your sweet lips. We'll have to start practicing all over again when I'm back honey. It will probably take us 70 or 80 years to get it just right hon.

Darling, you took it wrong about that woman in England. In England honey, a guy can meet a "nice girl" on the streets. England's moral standards are even higher than the United States. Decent girls think nothing of talking to strangers. When this woman told me about the girl that would show me the town, that's just what she meant. She didn't mean she was the kind of a girl I could go home with. If I had gone with her, everything would have been decent. That's what I meant when I said I wondered if you'd do the same for me. I didn't mean that I wondered if you'd do something wrong.

Goodnight my love. God bless you and keep you always for me.

Your husband,
Your Johnny

~

December 8, 1953

My Precious Darling,

You don't know where I've been today do you angel? I've been to Munich. I meant to tell you last night that I was going today darling, but I forgot. I went to have a record made for mom. She asked me long ago to have one made for her for Christmas, so I did. I left here this morning and caught the 10:30 tram to Munich, and caught the 4:20 back this afternoon.

I went alone hon. I had to wait about two hours at the recording studio because they were busy, then after I had the record made, I walked around window shopping till time for my train. I certainly get fed up with that place fast. It's one town that I can't stand. The people are so inconsiderate and snobby and stupid. I didn't have any trouble honey, and not one girl propositioned me, but I just hate the place.

I did talk to a girl though darling. At the record studio where I waited about two hours and drank about 9 cups of coffee, I talked to the girl that worked there. When I went in and sat down she started asking me all about myself and I told her. She was so stupid. She was thrilled to death to meet an Airman because she usually meets Army guys. I sat at the table, and she stood behind the counter and we talked nearly an hour, then she went and put on what she thought was a sexy dress and about six pounds of lipstick and came back out. I just glanced at her when she came back out and it killed her filthy little soul. About 4 pounds of lipstick dropped off when her face fell.

She stood there trying to look sexy and carry on a conversation but in a few minutes the man came out and said he was ready for me. I made the recording and came back through the restaurant part without stopping, and went out the door, saying only "Auf Wiedersehn." Then I heard the other 2 pounds of lipstick drop off.

I don't sound too conceited do I darling. But she was trying to snag me and my money, which I didn't have because she asked me if I was staying in Munich overnight. When I told her I wasn't, she asked me why I didn't stay since I had a 3-day pass. I told her I had to come back to Landsberg because my wife was having a baby and I was expecting a call or telegram any day. In her cute, sweet English, she said, "Oh, what the hell, you've got a 3-day pass. Have fun." I didn't say anything. I sneered and looked out the window and was wishing I had a shotgun to put some lead in that screwed up head of hers.

Boy, I sound rough today don't I honey? Well, that's just the way I felt. I got so fed up with her I could have died. These women can be so vulgar and so stupid when they start trying to pick up a man. It makes me sick the way they curse. She thought she sounded big I guess. That's a prostitute's way of impressing someone.

Honey, you'll never have to worry about me being untrue. I can't stand the way they talk, that much makes me sick, and the rest of their filth would kill me.

Vivian, I love you and want you darling. When I meet someone like that, my heart just cries for you. I feel like a baby after something like that. I want to run to you and hold you and ask you, "Why didn't God make all women like you?" Just one little wisp of a thought of you is wonderful in a case like today when I was sitting there listening to that pig talk. Oh Vivian honey, how I love you and need you. You're so sweet and wonderful and I need you so much.

Darling, I had 3 precious letters from you waiting on me when I got back. And I got the wonderful pictures. Thank you so much darling. You're so lovely. I've looked at them over and over and I just can't take my eyes off them. In this one where you're all dressed up in heels and have on the white hat, you're so pretty honey. Oh if only I could have my arms around those precious little shoulders. I love you so much.

I trust you only made one copy of these pictures hon? Don't give anyone but me those "cheesecake" pictures darling.

Goodnite Viv honey. God bless you and keep you for me. Stay the wonderful angel you are Vivian. You're God's pride and joy I know. I love you my darling.

Your husband,
Your Johnny

December 15, 1953

My Darling Wife to be,

Darling, I bought us some more records today. I guess I shouldn't have, but I knew if I didn't get them now I probably never would. I bought an album of Homer & Jethro, one by Hank Williams, "I Can't Escape from You," and one by the Maddox Bros. & Rose, "On Beautiful Mexico Shores," and "Is Zat You Myrtle," by the "Carlisles." I also got an album of Eddy Arnold, 4 songs. We're getting quite a stack sweetheart.

Darling, I'm so tired and sleepy. I've got to get some sleep. I'll write tomorrow afternoon. I love you Viv honey. I love you so.

Your husband,
Your Johnny

~

December 19, 1953

My baby Viv,

Honey, I tried and tried but I can't stay in the room alone. I get so tired of it and I can't stay and walk the floor anymore. I had to leave honey. I went to the Airmen's club and drank Russian whisky. I don't care Vivian. I just don't care and I can't help it.

A lot of mail came in today Viv, and I didn't get a letter. I don't know what's wrong honey but I didn't get any mail from you and I was so blue. I can't help it Vivie. I tried but I can't. I didn't want to get drunk honey, but I can't help it. I didn't want to drink cause I didn't want to ever drink. Honey darling, you won't will you?

Viv, I'm sorry I'm so mean to you. I don't want to be mean to you honey. I love you so much. I do I do. I love you so much. Please don't drink cause I did. Viv I can't help it honey. I love you my baby darling.

Vivie do you still love me? Honest honey, do you love me? Viv, you must love me cause it you didn't love me, I'll go to the Zugspitz and jump off of the top. That's the highest mountain in Germany, and if you don't love me I'll jump off of the top. You've got to keep loving me Viv cause I love you so. I love you so very much.

Baby darling you know this is Saturday night don't you? On Saturday night they have a floor show at the airmens club and honey it was a strip tease. Viv I don't know what you'll think honey, but I saw the strip show. Please don't think I did anything wrong cause I didn't. Honey they had a strip tease show and there was two women in it and honey they took everything off of their breasts.

Honey they didn't have a thing on from their waist on up. Please don't be angry with me Viv. I didn't know there would be a strip tease show. The women had something on down at the bottom honey but they didn't have a thing on their breasts. I have to be honest with you. I can't help it if you get angry with me honey darling. I didn't know the show was going to be on when I went up there. Honey it wasn't nasty. Do you understand Viv honey? The women wore something around the middle and that's all. Please don't be angry Viv. You know I was true to you. I'm always true to you honey. I never have any girls honey. You know I won't ever Vivie. I won't ever have any girl but you honey.

Darling do you know what time it is. It's one 30. I don't care though. I'm going to sit up and talk to you all night. I am honey. I don't care how late it is. I just want to talk to you. I love you so much my baby. I love you so very much. I don't care if I don't get a letter, I still love you cause I know it isn't your fault cause you love me don't you Vivie? If your letters don't come I know it isn't you fault cause you write me every day. You're so wonderful. If your letters are short I don't care honey cause I know you love me. I know you're so nice and sweet and want to be true to me don't you. I love you my Viv.

Honey, you know I haven't drank in so long but I couldn't help it. I couldn't stay inside my room alone. Vivie honey please don't you ever drink honey. Please don't. I love you so much my baby.

Baby I know what time it is where you are. It's 6:30 and you're probably eating supper. Then I know what you'll do. You'll write me a sweet letter then you'll take your little bath and put on a sweet little bra and a sweet little pair of panties and your pajamas and curl up in the bed with Syl and go to sleep.

Honey please don't think I'm nasty. I know I saw a strip tease show but I'm not nasty with you am I honey? I know you're my wife to be and I'm don't dirty with you Vivie. If you was my wife tonight and you was with me I'd go to bed with you honey. I'd be nice and sweet to you and I'd take all your clothes off of you and kiss and love your little breasts and I'd kiss your lips and your breasts and your stomach and your side. I would darling cause I love you so. No boy has ever done that to you and you love me so you would let me. I'd take your little panties off of you and caress you so much. Cause I love you so much my little Viv. If you weren't my wife I wouldn't do that Vivie. If you weren't my wife I wouldn't do anything but kiss your lips. I love you too much to take your precious little virginity. Oh my little baby I love you so much.

Honey, I've got to go to bed. I'm so tired. Goodnight my baby doll. I love you so much & love you. I love you.

Your husband.

~

My Sweetheart,

Viv, I went out to Chuck's at noon today, and ate dinner with them, and came back about 6 oclock tonight. We didn't do a thing all afternoon except play the guitar a little and just sat around and talked.

Vivian honey, yesterday afternoon I felt so bad and disgusted. I told myself I was going to get drunk and stay drunk on every pass I had. I changed my mind though, and came back to my room after work. I stayed here alone for two hours honey, and I got so nervous and tied up inside that I couldn't stand it. I went to the Airmens Club and met about a dozen of my friends up there. I started drinking and drank till about midnite.

Honey, they had a show on at the club too. Mostly women with not much on. Viv I honestly didn't know there would be a floor show when I went up there. Of course I didn't break my neck leaving when I saw what it was, but I'm sorry I went honey. It wasn't exactly filthy. The women were filthy as usual, but all they did was show themselves. They weren't completely uncovered. Vivian honey, I'm sorry for seeing such a show. I feel that I was almost untrue to you for seeing something so filthy. Please forgive me Vivian. I promise I won't see another one Viv and I honestly didn't mean to see that one last night.

Everything I did last night, I'm sorry for honey. I know I wrote you a long letter, and I remember a few of the things I said to you. I want you to know Vivian, I do take advantage of your understanding. There was nothing clean and holy in the intimate things I said to you.

Anything I said to you intimately wasn't sacred & holy, because I was drunk. I wouldn't talk that bold to you I know if I was with you so I took advantage of you in a letter. It will never happen again Vivian darling. Even if you're sweet about it and say, "that's alright honey, I understand." It won't happen again. I'll never be that bold and dirty with you again. Please forgive me Viv honey. Please forget it and forgive me.

Darling, our prayer is in 45 minutes. I know I'll be with you tonight honey. I've been looking forward to it today. I have so much to ask for and ask forgiveness for. Vivian honey, it will do me good if you're angry with me, especially for the dirty things I said. I'm going to ask forgiveness for that honey because I know it was a sin to talk so intimately with you, when you're pure. I know it's an awful sin no matter how sweet you could be about it.

Vivian, I love you honey. I love you so much it hurts me. Darling, I don't know how I ever got so messed up inside. I know I'd be straightened out if I could be with you. I guess God has His reasons though.

Vivian darling, I love you honey. I love you more than life. I'd do anything for you my sweetheart. I love you more than anything in this world. I do Viv. I love you so much it hurts. Goodnight my love.

Your husband,
Your Johnny

~

December 25, 1953

My Darling Wife,

I just got off work, and I'm going to write you, then go to bed.

Darling, I did get in the Christmas spirit. I had a very nice time sweetheart. Last night after work I went out to Chuck's and we had roast duck for Christmas supper, just Chuck & Alice and I. It was awfully nice and peaceful. We sat around and talked till about 4 AM, and honey, the German lady that owns the house had a bed all fixed up for me, even before I went out. She just wouldn't let me come back. When I got up this morning she invited me in for coffee and cookies. There wasn't anyone there except the old woman honey. The man works night shift, and the girl was gone to visit some friends. When Chuck & Alice got up we had breakfast, then I came back.

Last night my control chief Sgt Richards asked me to come visit them this afternoon, and see his little boy, 5 years old, so when I was coming back from Chuck's about 1 PM, I stopped by there. When I walked in, Richards and 3 more of his friends were sitting at the table drinking, and his little boy was down on the floor playing. Mrs. Richards was lying on the couch, passed out from drinking, and her clothes were messed up. Richards was too drunk to care. I didn't stay over five minutes hon. I talked to the little boy and he showed me what Santa Claus brought him, then I told him I had to leave.

Viv, don't you think that's horrible? I was so sick and disgusted I was ready to die. I can't see how anyone could be that way, and on God's birthday.

Oh Viv honey, you've got to stick with me and steer with me away from those things. I just can't live in something like that. I know you belong with me Vivian darling, and I know we belong in decency because we want to be. I was thinking of the kind of Christmas my folks would have today, and I got so homesick I couldn't stand it. I'd give anything to be back where I could see Christ's birthday celebrated with actual tribute to Him, instead of drunken slobs blaspheming His name.

Viv, I had the most wonderful dream about you last night. My room was so dark and quiet, and I went to bed thinking of you. I dreamed you were lying beside me honey, and you were snuggled up so close and you were so little and soft and warm. I kissed your lips and your cheeks and held your head close to mine, then I felt tears on your face. I asked you why you were crying, and you said, "Johnny I love you so much, and you don't even know how much I love you."

I was trying to think if I'd said anything wrong to you and I woke up. It was so wonderful Viv. I could almost feel your sweet lips on mine. I love you so much my sweetheart. I love you so much it hurts.

Your husband,
Your Johnny

~

December 26, 1953

No mail today darling, so I'll have to sweat it out till Monday. I don't see how I can make it. I just go crazy without your letters Viv.

We probably would have had some mail, but the mail clerks were drunk last night, and didn't even get up to go get the mail. The mail room is supposed to open at 12:30 on Saturday, and at 1:30 the 1st Sgt went up to see whey they hadn't come down, and they were still in bed. By then the post office was closed. If they don't lose their job now there's something wrong.

Viv, I don't know what you'll think, but a lot of times lately, I've thought of you as being like Mary Magdelene. I know you're only human honey, but you're pure, your language is pure, and you're so lovely. That will probably surprise you darling, me thinking that of you, but it's the truth. If nobody bothered you and you weren't around drinking and dirty talk, and some of the people you have to be around, you'd be a saint. God put purity and holiness in your heart and body, and if you were treated right, you'd be another Mary, on earth.

Please keep on loving me, and stay mine, and stay as perfect and wonderful as you are.

Your husband,
Your Johnny

~

December 28, 1953

My Viv,

I got two letters from you today Viv honey. I must say they were short as usual, but they were very sweet honey, so I guess that's all that matters. To be honest, it made me very unhappy honey. I thought I would shake myself to death, I was so nervous and upset till I got out of the room and stopped wondering and worrying. It's midnight now and I'm glad I waited to answer your letters because I feel a lot better.

Viv, I'm not looking forward to you answering my letters honey. Every day you say, "I'll answer them tomorrow for sure." That's been going on for weeks now. I can't believe you anymore, and it's bad to have nothing to look forward to honey, so I'll try my best to stop worrying about you, and wondering why you can just lay my letters up and forget them. I don't like to think of you being that inconsiderate about my happiness.

Vivian I have worried myself sick. I had to talk to someone about it. It's bearing on my mind, and all I can think of is you, who's bothering you, why you're this way to me lately, and why you won't tell me what's wrong just to give my mind a little ease. I talked to Chuck about what's going on with us lately and talking to him helped me. He said that when I had something to worry about like he has, I could really start worrying, but that if I loved you the way I do, I should take anything from you till I got back.

Viv, your letters in themselves are wonderful. I love for you to tell me how much you love me. But this isn't like being engaged Viv. You don't talk to me. You don't tell me about the things that happen every day at the office, or you don't tell me about the people that come to see you or anything about them.

Viv honey, whether you're doing this on purpose or not, I've been going through mortal hell over you. You're killing me darling by not talking to me and telling me what's wrong. You won't give me anything to look forward to. Every day it's the same story honey, and every day I can almost be sure that the same is coming tomorrow.

Yes, Viv, I know you work hard, and have a lot of church activities, and some days you're too tired to write much. I'm not talking about those days. It's the other days that you don't answer my letters just because you don't want to.

Honey, who was the company there the night he came home? Evidently it was your company, because you didn't write. Vivian, I've thought of everything honey. Did Jay or Dick, or even Wayne or any of your old boy friends come back. Somebody's been taking up all the spare time you have honey. Is it Elmer, or one of the men at the office, coming over to see you and talking? Anybody at all darling?

I got the Christmas card today darling. Thank you. Next year is our Christmas honey. We'll be together then, for life. All my worries will be over then honey. I won't be living for mail then. It will seem impossible that I can get up and kiss you good morning instead of looking at my watch to see how long it is til the mail comes in, wondering if I'll get a letter.

Yes, honey, I'll be glad when the holidays are gone too, but will that make a difference Viv? Your short, straight to the point letters, started when you met Elmer Gipson. Will the quietness after the holidays make you think of me more, and less of other things?

Darling, I'm going to bed now. I wanted to go to bed late so I can sleep late because I have to work at midnite.

Goodnight my darling. I love you so. I love you so much it hurts Vivian.

Your Johnny,
Your husband

~

My Precious Darling,

Viv, it seems like it's been a month since I've written you, although I guess I only missed two days. The last letter I wrote you, I told myself that I wasn't going to write you again until I could write you a kind letter. I thought it would take me longer than this to get straightened out, but I think I can now. I can't go on like this. I've got to write you and tell you how I feel about you.

Honey, Bob went on leave 3 or 4 days ago and I've been here alone. I can't describe the hell I've gone through. I never thought I could suffer so much. I broke down two or 3 times in the last few days, here in my room, but I made up my mind to not let it get me. I started praying, and God has helped me. I haven't slept Viv. The last two nights I worked midnite to 7:30, and I haven't slept over 4 or 5 hours in the last two days. I've lay in my bed tossing and turning till I have to get up and walk around.

Sweetheart, I guess I should have appreciated your short letters because I haven't been getting any at all lately. I guess I deserve it honey. I griped and griped about them and now God has made me realize just how wonderful it would be to get even a short one. The last one I got from you was wonderful Viv. It's the one you wrote the night Ray came home. I've read it a hundred times, and because of the letter I can still hold my head up. You were so sweet in that one, and I do believe you still love me. Honey, that one was mailed the 21st, and guys got letters today from all parts of the states mailed the 26th. I got up at 2 PM this afternoon, but my box was empty.

Two nights ago I prayed that I could forget you Viv. I thought I'd stopped loving you. I took your picture down and put it in my foot locker. I put away practically everything in sight that reminded me of you. But at 2 AM I came running down from work and put it all back up again. I couldn't stop loving you for 1 minute. Sweetheart, how could we ever forget one little thing there has been between us? Neither of us would ever be happy with anybody else. There have been too many precious things that have tied our hearts together Vivian darling. Remember our walks by the river? Remember all our sacred talk about babies, the ones we're going to have? Remember the hundreds of letters we've written? Remember all the good times we're going to have at my home when you meet me there? All that and a thousand more things would haunt us the rest of our life if we parted. I've got to have you darling. I know I couldn't possibly live without you.

Angel, when I told myself I didn't love you anymore and went to work, I sat there praying. I said, "God show me a sign. Show me some way whether or not she's the one for me." And Viv, it wasn't 15 minutes till a guy came back to me with a can of plums in his hand. He'd gotten a box of all kinds of food and fruit for Christmas, and he brought a can of plums to work with him. He offered them to me, and I looked at the name of them. They were "Vivian Brand." I knew that was it darling. I was thinking how sweet plums are, then I thought how sweet Vivian is.

Angel, tomorrow is the 1st of January 1954. I thought the day would never come honey, but it's just a few hours off. It's our year Viv. The year all our hopes and dreams are coming true. We've waited a lifetime for it honey. God is going to make us so happy angel.

Oh my precious darling, I love you. I love you I love you. Vivian can't you see how I love you sweetheart? I do honey. I love you so much it hurts. I love you my darling. I love you so.

Vivian, let's keep our love strong honey. It's only 5 more months angel, and if our love is strong and we're happy it will only seem like 2 months. Can't we do it angel? Won't you please have confidence in me again? With such a short time to go I should naturally straighten up and be happy Viv. Please don't think of me as being sarcastic and unapproachable Vivian honey. Please give me one more chance to show my love for you. Please have confidence in my love for you darling. I love you so very much.

In my anger and suffering, I told myself I'd never beg you for anything else, but I will Vivian. I'd beg for your love from now to the day I die. For just a smile or a tender word from you I'd get down on my knees and beg. There's nothing I wouldn't do for you, I love you so much.

I won't tell you that I've changed Viv. I built you up and let you down too many times, but please believe that I am trying.

Sweetheart, I'm going to close now and I'll write tomorrow night. Tomorrow is a big day Viv. It's the first day of our year.

I love you very very much Vivian.

Your husband,
Your Johnny

~

January 1, 1954

Happy New Year Precious,

It's our year darling. The year when all of our dreams are coming true.

Angel, I just got off work and its 8 oclock here, so it's 1 AM there darling. An hour ago at midnite there, I was thinking of you so strong honey. I was praying for us, for our happiness.

Oh darling, I want to be with you so bad. I needed you in my arms so bad. Next year we'll celebrate New Years together angel, and I'm going to hold you tight and kiss you so hard. But I won't squeeze you too hard sweetheart because I don't want to hurt the baby that is on the way. There's just a few more holidays to go by angel, and we'll be in each other's arms. We'll be together for always in about 5 more months angel. We'll go everywhere and do everything together.

Sweet darling I'm going to bed now. I'm so tired and sleepy. It's about time for you to go to bed too sweetheart. You be a good little girl and hit the sack.

Vivian, I'm just going crazy. I guess it isn't all your fault since the mail has been messed up, but I know I should have heard from you. In the letter you wrote the 19th, you were going to write the next day and answer my letters. I guess you didn't honey because it would have gone out the 21st with this one the 21st, and lots of guys have gotten letters two days ago mailed the 26th. Viv honey, you must have some of my letters unanswered that I wrote in November. Honey, I can't understand why if you love me, but I'm past asking questions anymore. All I'm interested in is do you love me.

Honey, from this last one you wrote, it was so sweet and you seemed so close to me. I can't believe yet that you stopped. I couldn't bear it honey. I wouldn't take it. If I don't hear from you by Monday, I'm going to call you because I know I can't last much longer this way Viv. I've made up my mind that I won't turn to drinking this time because I'd only be more miserable. If you aren't writing, and if we can't get straightened out by talking, then I'll take every cent we've got and I'll fly home to see what's wrong. Can't you see Vivian darling. We can't go on like this. I can't possibly live over here if I lost you. I just wouldn't do it. I know I'd go crazy in a week.

Honey, I can't believe we'd ever break up. We mean too much to each other. I think I know what's wrong now Viv. One reason you can do this is because of that horrible letter I wrote you. I can see why what I said to you could be unforgivable. But I'm sorry Vivian. I didn't mean it. I'll always pray for forgiveness.

I think the reason you can go for a month without answering my letters is because I asked you twice again about Elmer Gipson. Honey, you always felt that other men around you was no concern of mine if you were true to me. Maybe someday honey you can realize how I feel, the same way any man would feel. If you're mine I've got perfect rights to resent any man bothering you. But I think that's why you didn't answer my letters honey. You thought I was accusing you of being unfaithful.

I've talked to other guys about it Viv. I told them exactly what happened, and every one of them felt the way I do. Every one of them felt that he was a crumb to mess around with you, with me over here. I'm right too Vivian and you can feel sorry for the one that's caused me all this misery when I get back. I'd be a very poor man if I didn't fight for this girl that I love.

For all the month of December, all I was looking for was a letter from you, saying, "Johnny, Elmer did keep bothering me, but I told him to leave me alone because he was endangering our happiness." Darling, if you do love me you should tell any man to leave you alone, that our precious love isn't to be bothered.

Honey, I'm still not sorry that I went to Paris & London and didn't touch a girl. I'm still glad I took my stationery along and wrote you every night instead of going out with them. Because if you'll just be mine, I'll be fully repaid for that with one kiss from you. That's how much I love you Vivian darling and that's how much I'll always love you.

Honey, I still say that if I don't marry you, I'll never marry. My life won't be worth two cents. I can't believe it would be my fault if I lost you because you haven't understood me, but if I do and it is my fault, I won't live. I absolutely won't face a life of misery and torment Vivian. That's why I've got to know what's the matter even if I have to come all the way back to find out.

Darling, I love you. I want you and only you. I've got to have you. I need you Vivian darling. I know I can make you happy if you'll let me darling.

Bye sweetheart. I love you so very much. God bless you and keep you wherever you are. I love you with all my heart and soul.

Your husband,
Your Johnny

~

January 2, 1954

My Darling Vivian,

Honey, at 11 oclock the mail was put up. It's very unusual that the mail came in on Saturday, but it did honey, and I got 3 letters from you. Darling, they were sweet, and eased my mind a lot. At least I thought they did. I went to bed at 11:30 AM trying to sleep. I lay there till 2:30, just a few minutes ago, and didn't sleep a wink. I'm so tired I was numb and feel worse and worse but I can't sleep, so I won't lie in bed and go crazy.

Darling, one of these letters was written the 20th, one the 22nd, one the 25th. They were all mailed the 27th. Why Vivian? It's no wonder I didn't get but 1 letter for 10 days. Darling, did you just write them and lay them up and forget them?

I'm sorry you were sick and didn't have a nice Christmas Viv. I'm sorry you were sick. Did you have the doctor over darling? Did he say it was food poisoning? Take care of yourself sweetheart.

Yes darling, it's 1954 now, the year when all our dreams are supposed to come true. There's one thing that's endangering all our precious happiness that we've counted on so long. That's drinking, and that crowd you mix with. Surely you didn't have to work Christmas eve Vivian, so the thing you went to the office for was the party wasn't it? When I walked into Sgt Richards's house on Christmas day and saw his wife lying on the couch drunk, I said "Thank God Vivian doesn't drink." But now you told me about lying on the couch sick while the others were passing out presents. Were you drinking honey? How much did you drink? If you'll remember back Vivian, to two years ago, you promised me you'd never drink. You drank since then, and then you promised me again that you wouldn't drink. You also promised you wouldn't go to another office party. You know how it kills me. You know I'd rather die or be dead than for you to touch a drop, but you drank till you were sick Christmas eve didn't you Vivian? It doesn't make any difference I guess. If you drank one, or if you drank six, it hurts me all the same.

Now darling, what do you want to do. Do you want to choose a life of drinking and running around with those drunkards and filthy talking people, or do you want our marriage, our happiness? Are you going to let a few drinks kill a lifetime of happiness? I want to know now Vivian. It's either our love, or your social drinks. If we're going to stay together and keep planning on the wonderful things we have in mind, you won't touch a drop. It wouldn't be hard to tell your friends, "I don't drink," when doing so would kill everything there's ever been between us. And it will Vivian. If you want our love and happiness, tell me that you'll never touch another drop as long as you live. If you want to ever touch another drop, we're finished darling.

My wife and the mother of my children will be the kind of woman that will say, anytime, and anyplace, and to anybody, "No thank you, I don't drink." My parents would disown me if they knew you were anything but that kind of a girl. I couldn't stand before God if I had a wife that drank. You're not pure when you're drinking Vivian. You're filthy and unpure and unclean when you've got a drop of that in your naturally pure body.

Yes darling, will we get out of bed together with a kiss next Christmas morning, and give our presents to each other, or will we be hundreds of miles apart, waking up to another day of misery? Are your friends and your drinking going to keep us from wonderful things like that? What's your choice Vivian? If you're going to let me live, or if you're going to kill me, I've got to know now. There is no alternative.

I'm going to bed now darling, and I'm to pray and pray and pray that God will make you see that it's best to follow His path, the way, instead of stepping over to the left side for a ticket to Hell.

I love you my darling. Please try to understand how I love you. Please think about every word I said and make a choice you can keep.

I love you more than anything on earth.

Your husband,
Your Johnny

~

My Darling Sweetheart,

Vivian darling, if we could be together for about 10 minutes, and be in each other's arms, I know the world would be beautiful to me. I'll never forget the time we've been in each other's arms darling. I felt so wonderful when you'd put your arms all the way around my neck and squeeze. It made me feel like you'd never kissed a boy like that before. Soon you'll be in my arms again sweetheart and it will be the most wonderful thing on earth, to squeeze you tight and kiss your precious lips. It won't be long now Viv. The days are ticking off. You can think back to five months ago and that's how long it will be till we'll be in each other's arms sweetheart. It won't be any time at all and we'll be together for a life time.

Your husband,
Your Johnny

~

January 3, 1954

Hello Darling,

Yes Viv, I had a fairly nice Christmas. I got off work at 9 oclock and went to Christmas services. I had a nice time at Chuck's after work, just Chuck & Alice and I. We had a nice quiet time. We ate roast duck, then sang Christmas carols till about 4:30 AM, then I went to bed thinking of you and praying for us. I went to bed sober. There was no drinking. We celebrated our Lord's birthday the way we thought He wanted.

Vivian darling, 2½ years ago tonight I left you. Does it have to end like this? Does drinking have to tear down all the wonderful dreams we've built? I've told you what you must do to save it Vivian, so tell me what I must do if you want to save it. With only 5 months left apart can't we strengthen our love again? Can't you go back a little and stay the same wonderful, precious, holy girl you've always been?

Darling, tomorrow 10 of us are going down to the mountains. Most of them are going skiing. I'm not going to ski, but I'm going just to get away from everything.

It's 8:15 honey. I was going to the movie tonight but I didn't go because I want to be with you at prayer. I'll be with you at prayer every Sunday. Pray for me if you can Vivian.

Your Johnny

~

January 6, 1954

My Darling Wife,

Sweetheart, we got back at 3 PM this afternoon. Viv, just as I was leaving Monday the mail room opened and I got 3 wonderful letters from you. Oh darling it made me so happy. I took them to Garmisch and read them over and over. One of them was the long one you wrote the 26th & 27th and answered most of my letters. I took that as a special favor from you Viv, because it made me so happy.

I'd been so unhappy for so long, then I got these letters and I changed completely. It seems I hadn't smiled in a month, but because of you, I had a wonderful time the past two days. Thank you Vivian darling.

Yesterday we got up early and went up on one of the mountains and went skiing. Darling it's hard to describe the beating I took. I never thought skiing was so dangerous but it is if you don't know how, and I don't know how. I did good for my first time. I could ski good and fast, but the only trouble was I couldn't stop myself. The only way I could stop was to fall, and I fell no less than 100 times. I knocked the skin off my right knee, and it's all skinned up and blue today. I sprained my left leg and my thumb, but the worst thing I hurt was my rear end. I was going about 40 miles an hour and both skis went out from under me, and I fell on my back and my tail rammed into a rock, solid. I couldn't move at first it hurt so much, but I finally got up and rested awhile then skied some more. I fell about six more times and that's all I could take. I was so weak and sore I couldn't move.

Yes angel, we will have a house full of kids. They're going to have the sweetest mother in the world too. I'm so lucky Viv. You love kids so much, and I want to give you a lot of them. That is your happiness Viv. You'd never be happy unless you had a home, security and lots of children. You were born to be a perfect mother. Please don't change that Viv. Please stay what you are and let me give you that home and those precious children. We'll both be so happy.

Honey, I think the song "I'd Rather Die Young" on the back of "A Dear John Letter" is better. That "Dear John Letter" makes me tremble. And I'd rather die young than live without you Vivian. To not have you would be to not have life, because you are my life and my happiness Vivian. I love you so much it hurts Vivian darling. I'll always love you as long as I live, and I'll never touch another woman but you. I love you so.

Honey, it isn't any harder for a married man to do without his wife than it is for me, or any single man. Drinking causes most adultery over here. Believe me Viv, 85% of the married men that step out on their wives, they do so when they've been drinking. These guys go to Munich or someplace and start drinking and lose all sense of reasoning. The women are there, and a few drinks will make them forget their wives. I can stay away from women over here, and I know these guys could if they wanted to be halfway decent. If they were away from their wives 10 years they still wouldn't be justified in committing adultery darling.

I'll tell you what I've seen Viv, that really makes a man pay for being unfaithful. I know of two married men that have children by a German girl. In one case the German girl proved that this man was the father of her baby. She took it to court, and for <u>18 years</u> this man has got to go send this girl $35 a month to support that kid. Can't you just see that Viv? When that guy goes home to his wife & children, he's got to tell her, "Well, honey, I don't think we can get that TV set yet. I've got to send $35 per month to my kid in Germany." For 18 years he's got to do that. I know his wife is going to be proud of him. I wish it would happen to more men. Maybe they'd remember more of God's laws and standards of decency.

Honey, on the record I made to mom, I sang and talked. She always wants me to sing. It isn't expensive Viv and I'll have you one made, but you can depend on it being silly darling. I can never think of anything to say, and if I write it down, it doesn't sound right. The next time I go to Munich I will honey.

Darling, that sounds like it's a nice anklet your mom gave you, with our initials on it. We'll always be together darling. When I come back I'm going to tattoo my name all over your precious little body. Would you like to have my name all over you angel? I don't suppose you would sugar, but just so I know you're mine.

Honey, I should have been in bed long ago, but I had to stay up and talk to you. I love you and want you so.

Your husband,
Your Johnny for life.

~

January 17, 1954

My Darling Wife soon,

Honey, I made a little chart of the days up till the 1st of June. I made two of them and I'm tacking one up in my locker and cross off the days as they go by. Here's one for you angel, if you want it. I made it small so it won't look like there's very many. By the time you get it you can cross off some more sweetheart.

It really isn't long baby darling, and every day that goes by brings us closer to being in each other's arms again. Before we know it our arms will be around each other. Our lips will be together. We'll be going out every night having lots of fun. We'll be having those long drawn out goodnight kisses, then in just a little while longer we'll be in each others arms all night. Oh my darling, it will be so wonderful, sweet, wonderful you in my arms beside me all night. I love you Vivian darling. I love you so very much honey. It's going to be heaven taking that precious love you've saved for me. I don't think I can ever turn you loose once you're in my arms. I love you so much Vivian.

Goodnight my precious darling.

Your Johnny
Your husband soon.

~

January 19, 1954

My Darling Sweetheart,

Vivian darling, we've got a little over 4½ months apart. Between now and then, there aren't any holidays that call for drinking. You've told me lots of times that you hate drinking and don't even like the taste of it. Honey, up to the time we fell in love, according to what you told me, you hadn't drank a drop in your life. That's the way I still think of you, as unchanged in any way at all. Vivian honey, in the kindest, lovingest way I know how, I'm asking you to not drink another drop till we're together. Darling, remember once nearly a year ago you went to an office function and ordered a 7up when everybody else ordered whiskey? Vivian darling, will you do that for me again if the occasion comes up?

Hon, I hope it was one of the girls that gave you the garters for Christmas, but I guess a girl wouldn't do something like that. Did you ever find out who it was sugar? Let 'em know that anything concerning your legs concerns only one Johnny Cash angel face. Tell them I've got a contract to buy your garters, stockings, underwear or anything you might need. No, you don't have to tell them sugar, but let them know that you're mine from your toes to your scalp.

I love you Vivian. I love you so very very much darling. Please stay mine. I love you and need you so.

Your husband.

~

January 19, 1954

My darling I love you.

I was talking about you tonight to one of the boys, all about you. We were talking about San Antonio, and he asked me where I met you, and for a long time I talked about you. The more I talked, the more miserable I became for you. You're so wonderful. You're so precious to me, and I love you so very much. Vivian, I do honey. I love you so much it hurts.

Darling in this picture of you and the baby, you've got the most precious smile on your face. I'd give the next 4 months pay to kiss that smile on your lips. Oh how I need you Vivian darling. If I needed you anymore I would go crazy. I guess I haven't got a right to desire your physical love the way I do when we're not even married, and maybe it's even a sin. Do you think it's a sin honey? Maybe it is darling, but my life is yours, and you are all mine, so I'm only desiring what's mine. Having another woman but you <u>never</u> enters my mind. I get so ashamed of myself at times when I lie in bed thinking of you, and let my mind go wild. I start needing your body so bad I actually ache. I guess I keep forgetting that we're not married, that you're not actually my wife yet. It seems you are Vivian. It seems only natural at night to want to kiss your lips and breasts and love and caress your legs and body. Then the next day when I think of what I was thinking before, I'm so ashamed of myself. Since I wrote that dirty letter when I was drunk, do you resent me telling you how I need you Vivian darling? Tell me how you feel. Oh darling, I love you so much.

1–20–54 Hello Sweetheart, how's my darling today. You having any labor pains sugar? Let's eat breakfast, then I'll massage your stomach darling. I know it must hurt honey, but it won't be long till the pain will be all over and we'll have a little angel. Take it easy today, Viv, and don't strain yourself in any way. You be sure and call me if you start hurting more during the day, and I'll be home in ten seconds.

That's what I'll be telling you soon Viv. We'll be so happy and we'll have several little angels. I love you so much.

Honey, you're right-handed aren't you? That's the hand I want to hold when I get back, the one that's written me so much love and sweetness. I'm going to kiss it a million times.

Your Johnny for life.

~

January 30, 1954

My Wee Wee Ann,

Baby, it's Saturday night and it's cold. Isn't that a sweet way to start a letter? It is cold and I'm here alone and I'm freezing. I want you Viv, but I guess I just can't have you yet, can I honey? I can dream though.

31–1–54 It certainly has been a dead dreary day. It's just dragged by, and with no mail, Sunday seems like a lost day.

On top of all that honey, I was late for work this morning. Last night after I went to bed, about 10 oclock, I tried to sleep but couldn't. I finally got up about midnite, and went to the snack bar and got something to eat. I went back to bed and finally went back to sleep about 2 AM I think.

This morning one of the boys came down and awoke me at 7:45. Sgt

Richards didn't say a word to me all day honey, but one of the boys said he wrote me up. There were 4 of us late. Two boys got back from Munich at noon today, 4 hours late. One was 15 minutes late, and I was 25. Richards wrote us all up, and we've got to go see the operations officer tomorrow. Richards was mad because the other boys came in at noon, so he wrote us all up. I didn't say a word to Richards all day, but I'm sure going to make him feel little about that. He's always been a personal friend of mine as well as my control chief. I know he likes me, and I know he should have given me another chance, but I'm certainly not going to say a word to him, about that. I'm going to work harder than I ever did, and I'm going to be nice to him. Within 2 weeks I'm betting he'll apologize to me of his own free will.

I don't know what will happen honey. I don't believe they'll do anything to me. I haven't been before the Captain before so I don't believe he'll do anything but tell me to be on time from now on.

Honey, I forgot to tell you, I got the good-conduct ribbon yesterday. Isn't this a nice time to get in trouble? The orders were in my box yesterday, and I went down to the orderly room and the 1st Sgt gave me the ribbon. It wouldn't surprise me if they took it away from me.

I love you so very much.

Your husband soon.

~

February 2, 1954

My Precious Little Darling,

That's just what you are too, precious. You're the most precious thing on earth to me.

Yes, hon, that's my guitar in the picture, and it IS a very good one. I was really lucky in getting such a good one. Some guys have tried to buy it from me, but I won't sell it. I'm going to send it back when I come, and keep it.

Yes, darling, we sure will have lots of fun this summer. I've been thinking and planning things for us. I can take you away from that officer crowd, their mixed dancing & drinking, their filth and everything. I have enough confidence in myself and my love for you that I think I'll make you the happiest girl in the world. That's my ambition Vivian darling, to hear you say, "I love you, Johnny. I'm the happiest girl in the world." You'll see sweetheart. I'll make you happy.

Viv, I'm sure I know a lot of things that were wrong. First of all honey, it was my scolding. You couldn't show your love for me when I did nothing but hurt you. Second, it was the people you have to be around. You know that that crowd aren't the kind that fit in the kind of life we have planned. I don't think we have any champagne parties and dances planned. I don't think we want to be close friends with dirty people that curse around decent girls, or mix with couples that live like they're married before they really are. It isn't your fault you had nothing to turn to. As I said before, it's the fault of the Air Force. You indicated you lost a lot of sleep about that time honey. I don't know where you went with those people, Betty, Jean or who, but it doesn't make any difference now I guess.

But that's what it was Viv. You have two lives you can live. One is a calm decent, give and take life with me, or the other one is a life with those people. I'm glad you didn't go too far down the rut darling before you came back to me.

Vivian darling, I'm not going to let myself believe that anything has changed. I'm going to keep on believing that you're the same perfect, pure girl you always were, that you don't curse or drink. A man has got to be <u>proud</u> of his woman. Some men are proud of their woman if she is a good bed partner honey. Some men are proud of their woman if he can say, "She can drink as much as I can without feeling it." Some men are proud of their woman if she can curse like a sailor.

You know how I'm proud of my woman Viv. I'm proud of her because she loves children, and home and decency. I love her for being the old fashioned, down to earth kind of a girl that would wait 3 years. And I'm proud of you because you're mine, that you've saved yourself for me.

Goodnight my love. God bless you and keep you for me. I love you my Viv.

Your husband soon,
Your Johnny

~

February 3, 1954

My Precious Sweetheart,

I got another little bit of heaven from my angel of happiness today. Surely it must have been stamped by God because there was something heavenly about it. I think I'm beginning to have a monopoly on "happiest man in the world." Viv if those sweet letters like this one just keep on coming, I could make the rest of the time over here standing on my head. Time goes so much faster when we're happy, and I'm the happiest person in the world tonight because I think I know how much you love me.

I'm glad you didn't go skating too honey, if it would have kept me from getting this heavenly letter. That's being selfish I know honey, but you can't imagine how much it helped me. This afternoon I didn't have a worry in the world. I was always laughing and joking and carrying on. All the boys knew how happy I was too Viv. One of the guys asked another one if he got a letter from his girl, and said, "No! Is my name John Cash?" Darling, they were all laughing at me when your letters were short and far between. Now I'm laughing back. Help me to keep on laughing back will you darling? I write 1 a day, so you write 1 a day, OK honey? Fair enough? OK sugar.

Your husband soon,
Your Johnny

~

February 6, 1954

My Precious Viv,

I just got back from Munich honey. I made the record for you, and I got a bunch of empty reels, 9 in all for the recorder. I bought a few other things too. A present for my precious darling, a flash light, a pair of wire pliers, a screw driver, stationery, 3 T-shirts, and I think that's all. That was enough though.

Viv honey, after you play the record the first time you'll probably throw it away. On one side I talked to you honey and on the other side I sang you a song. Isn't that nice of me? Viv, please don't judge my singing by that. I was tense, the guitar was no good and out of tune, and it was cold in the room and I was shaking. If anyone else hears that part of the record honey, tell them what's wrong, will you honey?

I'm mailing the record Monday with your Valentine box honey. I hope it gets there by the 14th Viv. Maybe it will honey. I'll send it airmail, and it will have six days. I hope you like it honey.

Honey, that same girl wasn't at the studio today. Thank goodness I didn't see her. But I saw plenty more. Ted and I must have been approached a dozen times by the dirty, filthy talking sluts. I hope I never have to go to Munich again. At payday and for the next ten days at least, they're on the street. I guess I shouldn't care, but I can't help but get disgusted at their filthy language and propositions.

About 4 oclock we had all our shopping done honey and went back to the train station but they said the next train to Landsberg was at 4:56 so we went for a walk. After about 10 minutes we went in a G.I. restaurant to get warm hon. Ted sat down at a table and I started playing the pinball machine. The place was full of GIs and their German girls. There was one girl honey that was drunker than anybody in the place. She came over to where I was standing and helped herself to some of my pennies, and started playing the pinball machine beside me. She tilted it and cursed, then came over to where I was. The juke box started playing and she started jitter bugging with herself and rubbing her stomach against me every time she came around. After a few times of that she stopped and stood behind me and just rubbed. She finally went away honey. I didn't touch her Vivian. I didn't say one single word to her nor touch her. I tried to ignore her honey, and I did. And it's hard to ignore a woman when she's rubbing herself against me.

I left then Viv. I wasn't in the place over 15 minutes. Ted and I both left. Maybe it's silly honey, but I wanted you with me then. I wanted you to be there when that happened and I wanted to see you jealous, see you grab her and pull her hair out and call her a filthy slut and pig that she is. I would have given you a million dollars to have had you with me at that time. I didn't feel like I could hit her myself because she was little, and drunk.

Viv honey, you'll never have to worry about me being untrue to you. I can't even get past their language. It makes me sick in the stomach to hear their filthy language and cursing. I could never touch one of them Vivian. I'll be true to you as long as I live. I love you Vivian darling. I'll never love anyone but you. I'll never touch anyone but you.

Goodnight my angel. I'll be thinking of you.

Your husband soon,
Your Johnny

~

February 7, 1954

My Precious Viv,

Viv honey, yesterday in Munich I passed a ladies wear dept, and I saw something I want you to have. It's a nightgown sweetheart, a white silk one. It's a German gown honey, and I don't know if you'll like it or not, but I hope so angel. I thought of you when I saw it and I knew it would look lovely on you, in white, because you're an angel.

Darling, I know you said you don't like nightgowns, but when we're married I want you to wear this one once or twice if you will. I don't think it will work up around your neck sweetheart because it has an elastic waist and should fit you. German measurements are different from ours, but I told the lady that my wife was a little woman, so she said this would fit you.

It isn't expensive darling, but I just know it will be lovely on you. When I was wrapping it last night here in the room and looked at it and felt of it, wishing with all my heart that you were in it. It was wonderful holding it and feeling it, thinking that some day you would be in it. I guess my mind "wandered" a little honey, but then I put it in the box and wrapped it.

You don't mind me giving you a nightgown do you honey, and you will wear it sometime for me when we're married, won't you Viv honey? The reason I'm telling you all about it in advance is so your dad won't know I'm giving you this. On the tag I'm putting "ladies blouse" so honey, don't let your dad know it's a nightgown. You might think he wouldn't mind darling, but then again, he might, so please don't let him know it's a nightgown darling.

And Viv, you sent me a picture of you in a nightgown you made, so I want you to look at this one and try it on, and if you don't think it's too revealing, I want you to send me a picture of you in it. You can have Syl or Jan take the picture hon. That is, if you think you should honey. I sure won't ask you to if you think it would be too bold.

Sweetheart if you will have a picture made for me I'll tell you how I want it. Be standing up straight, close to the camera, just close enough that it gets all of you from head to foot, and don't be smiling. Just have a sweet, solemn expression on your face, and put your hands behind you.

I guess you think I'm crazy Viv. Darling, I feel kind of funny asking you to do this, but I certainly wouldn't ask you to do something like this that you wouldn't want to do. Of course, I wouldn't care how revealing a picture of you was. But then, I'm not the one to say. You are. It's up to you Viv. Please don't get the wrong idea. I'm not asking you to reveal yourself to me, precious. I just want to know how the gown looks on you. That's all darling.

Your husband soon

~

February 9, 1954

My Darling Vivian,

Lately your letters have been heaven. You've answered mine when you get them, and they're as sweet as you've ever written. You've made me the happiest person in the world lately. Everything looks so rosy and wonderful for us now.

And most of the time you do seem as if you're very close to me darling. Only once lately have you seemed distant to me, and you seemed like you were a million miles away then. That was when I got the letter telling me about going to that damned "Kit Kat." That isn't a curse word either Vivian. That place is damned. It and all the other places like it, along with the people that love those places. They're everything that's opposite of goodness.

Friday when I got that letter honey, I tried to forget about that part. You made me so happy with the rest of that letter. But about the middle of the afternoon it hit me like a ton of bricks. I was shaking like a leaf. I couldn't hear anybody when they talked to me. I finally got to shaking so bad that Sgt Richards said, "You better take a break." I went down to the latrine Vivian and locked the door, and I stood there shaking and finally broke down and cried. I started to have someone call an ambulance because I didn't think I could stand it anymore. But after about 20 minutes I finally got control of myself, and went back to work.

For just a minute down there in the latrine Vivian, I could see us a year from now. You getting ready to go out dancing and me begging you to stay at home with me. Then about 2 or 3 AM you'd come in, just a little tight.

It wasn't just that one thing Vivian. It was knowing that all the begging I've done, all the talking has been to no avail. You were out at one of the clubs in town with a drinking crowd, dancing until 12:30 AM with men that were drinking. Then you said, "It was nice honey. I enjoyed it." It wasn't nice Vivian. We could argue about it a million years and you couldn't make me believe it was nice.

Vivian darling, if you love me the way I believe you really do, someday when you really want to make me happy, you'll say, "Darling, I feel so out of place around those filthy people, around their drunkenness, their filthy talk and filthy sex." Right now I can't figure out whether you like to be around that, whether it's something new and fascinating or whether you put up with it because you know you have to.

Vivian darling, you said you love me enough you'd die for me. I don't want that Vivian. I want you to love me enough you'll live for me, and for God.

Oh my precious darling, I love you. I love you so.

Your husband,
Your Johnny

~

February 11, 1954

My Precious Vivian,

Darling, I talked to you last night at 2 AM, and I've been walking on heaven ever since. Oh darling, it was so wonderful talking to you. I couldn't go to sleep till after 4 AM. I lay in bed wanting you so bad I could cry. Darling I love you. I love you so much it hurts. Honey, I lay there trying to remember all our conversation. It was so heavenly hearing your sweet voice again.

You said some wonderful things, Vivian darling . . . things that helped me so much. That phone call did wonders for me. Every time I talk to you I realize that you're not just a heavenly dream but a real woman too. Vivian I love you my darling. I love you so much it hurts. Oh sweetheart I need you.

Viv darling, you said you hadn't heard from me in two days. The last letter from me must have been a very bad one because you kept saying "Darling please don't worry. Please believe me." When I said, "Viv, stay my girl always," I didn't mean that as to be insinuating you hadn't. I meant that as any guy would mean it to his sweetheart, just something to say.

Vivian honey, I know I sounded so silly last night when I said, "Don't tell your dad what I'm sending you." I just ran out of something to say honey, and that's all I could think of. I sure had you puzzled didn't I angel. I felt so silly.

Vivian darling, I'll try my best not to worry about anything. I went to bed last night telling myself what an ass I am. When I talk to you, it wakes me up.

I'm puzzled and I say to myself, "is this the wonderful sweet girl I've scolded and hurt so much?" Vivian, I'm genuinely sorry for every time I've ever scolded you no matter whose fault it was. I'm sorry.

Your husband soon

~

February 11, 1954

My Darling,

Sweetheart, tomorrow I'm taking your picture over to the service club. They're having a "Favorite Sweetheart" contest on Valentines day. All the guys that have a sweetheart can enter her picture in the contest. Two or three officers are doing the judging Valentines day. You'll win it darling. This last picture, the big one that you sent me is perfect for the contest. Your picture will put all the others to shame. You've got the sweetest smile on your face, and you're holding your hands together against your face. It's so sweet darling. When you win 1st place they'll send you a big box of candy angel.

Angel face I've just got to get to bed. It's 1 AM, and my throat is still so sore and I feel so bad.

Goodnight my love. God bless you and keep you for me. I love you my Viv. I love you and need you so. Oh my precious Viv, I need you. I need you in my arms so bad I could cry. I love you so much. Goodnight my love.

~

February 14, 1954

Hello Sweet Valentine,

How's the queen of my heart today? It's 1 PM here angel. I guess you're in bed now. It's six AM there honey. I can see my darling all curled up asleep. Oh how I'd love to slip in and put my arms around you and kiss your sweet lips.

Darling, I hate to tell you, but you didn't win the sweetheart contest. When I got over there this morning they had selected the girl. Honey, she wasn't half as pretty as you are, and I mean it. Two officers did the judging and they selected some crummy blond. In all there were 27 pictures in the contest, and half of them would have beaten the one they picked. You should have been 1st place Viv. I know you should have. Yours was the sweetest picture in the bunch. I was so proud of your picture up there among the other ones honey. I'm sorry they didn't pick yours honey, but they should have because you're the prettiest, sweetest sweetheart in the world.

One of my friends here was stationed in San Antonio two years honey and I figured he knew every hangout in San Antonio. I asked him if he had been in the Kit Kat club, I told him I had a buddy working there. He said, "Yeah,

I've been there. It's a real nice place. Nice upholstery, and everything. A lot of good looking bitches hang out in there. You can really pick up some nice stuff if you can beat the officers time. Mostly officers go there."

That cut like a knife Vivian. Even though I know you're innocent in going there now, I knew what all men think. They think you're in the race. That's the language men use about girls that go there.

Darling, you said we'd go there together when I'm back. I don't know how long ago it was Vivian darling, that I told you I'd never take you to a place where there was drinking and dancing mixed, but it doesn't make any difference honey, because I haven't changed. I don't change Vivian. You're the one that's changed so much. And you can't expect me to change and follow you just because you change. Darling, my life is going to be for God. The clubs in town aren't part of God's plan.

You're unlucky in one way Vivian, maybe in more but this way for sure. Lately you've let dancing be your sole recreation. I don't know why this has happened. But its happened so fast that it's stunned me. I can't figure out where you got your start, or why. But like anything else you want to do, you call it innocent honey, no matter where or who you're dancing with.

I'm not the kind of a person to straddle the fence. I've got to be all on God's side or none at all, and you've got to be with me all the way or your life and mine will be miserable. Stop and think seriously Vivian. Do we want <u>our</u> daughters taught that it's alright to visit the clubs and hangouts, and drink? What kind of people are we going to make out of our children honey? It's up to us.

I'll be with you at prayer my angel. God will surely help us.

Your husband,
Your Johnny

~

February 15, 1954

Oh my precious darling, how I love you and want you and need you.

My darling, last night I was cleaning out the desk drawer and I found one of your old letters that I must have missed when I packed them. It was so sweet and wonderful, and you were so lonesome for me. You loved me and wanted me so that you seemed to be crying all the way through. I've felt the same way ever since I read it. I couldn't sleep last night, and all day today my heart has cried for you, and every minute my arms have reached out for you.

Vivian my darling, <u>nothing</u> will ever make me stop loving you, or think less of you. Do you hear me, my darling? <u>Nothing.</u> Every day my love for you grows. Today my love for you has hurt me <u>deep</u> every second. Do you know what hurts most? You're so sweet and wonderful to me and so perfect and I sit here like a self righteous fool and scold you. Oh my precious Vivian darling. Please don't think hard of me for anything. Oh I love you so.

Honey, I just cried. I guess I've learned how to cry all over again. My love for you has made me a kid again. Can't you see how deep the love is? Can't you see that it's so deep that nothing can ever change my love for you in any way? Oh how I mean that.

Goodnight my precious love. God bless you and keep you for me always. I love you so very very much.

Your husband,
Your Johnny

~

February 22, 1954

Hello My Darling,

This is our last Washington's birthday apart honey. Next year at this time we'll almost have a little baby here. I'll be with my darling wife all the time and have her beside me to love and take care of. I've wanted you in my arms so long Vivian darling.

Darling, last night I was lying in bed thinking of us being together and getting married, and last night I dreamed we were. I dreamed I was in my mom's house, the old house, peeling potatoes, and you were busy running back from the sink to the stove, cooking, etc. My eyes were following every move you made and you'd smile at me every time you looked at me. When you walked by once honey, I caught you around the waist and sat you on my lap. You put your arms around my neck and squeezed and kissed me on the cheek real hard, just like a little girl. It was so wonderful Viv. I felt so close to you and was so disappointed when I woke up.

Someday soon it will be real, Viv. You will be my wife, all curled up in my arms. We'll have each other to love and kiss when we're blue.

Goodnight my love. God bless you and keep you for me always. I love you Vivian.

Your husband,
Your Johnny

~

February 25, 1954

My Precious Darling,

Viv, I got a sweet, precious letter from you today honey. It made me so wonderfully happy Vivian darling.

I'm getting off work tomorrow honey. Since it's my birthday, my Control

Chief said I didn't have to come to work tomorrow. He's going to let one of the boys act as Trick Chief and let me have the day off. Wasn't that nice of them hon?

I believed you Viv honey when you said the Kit Kat was a nice place. I know what you meant honey. The place is expensive looking, clean, and most everybody behaves theirselves. King Herod's palace was a nice place too Viv.

Sugar have you heard the song, "White Azaleas" by Eddy Arnold? It's an old one honey, but it's beautiful. I've got it recorded and I'll send the record to you along with the other ones angel.

Goodnight my love. May God bless you and keep you for me always. I love you my Viv. I love you so.

Your husband soon,
Your Johnny

~

February 26, 1954

My Wonderful Darling,

Honey, I found a guy last night that had some of Hank Snows first songs. They were even older songs than the early album you sent me honey. I don't suppose you've heard them honey. I hadn't either till last night. All of them are Jimmy Rodgers songs. One is "The Engineer's Child," and I don't think I ever heard a song so sad.

I'm so happy you like everything Viv. You make me feel so good darling. I kind of wish I hadn't sang that song on that record. I can beat that. I'm getting a little serious about my singing honey. I think I've improved my voice since I've gotten this recorder. I guess it's only natural. When I'm not working or sleeping, that's about all I do, is listen to music or play it.

I'm so happy you like the gown Vivie. Maybe you can work on it and make it fit on the shoulders honey.

I don't know why I didn't want you to smile Viv. I was just thinking of you in the white gown. I knew you'd look like an angel. I wanted you to have a serene, angelic look on your face, like you were standing there waiting for me to come and put my arms around you and kiss your lips. I wanted your lips raised in the picture, like you were waiting for me to kiss your troubles away. I guess I'm a big dreamer honey. I don't know, maybe I'm a little crazy Viv.

Goodnight my precious love. God bless and keep you for me. I love you my Viv.

Your husband,
Your Johnny

~

Viv, I was going to answer your letters tonight honey, but I feel so bad that I'm going right to bed. I still have a cold and my throat is sore. I've been just miserable at work tonight.

Viv, I'm not griping honey but I'm so fed up I could go crazy. Just sitting here in this crummy lifeless hole, living for mail call, depending on drunken lazy punks to bring in the mail. The same stupid useless life day after day. I sometimes wonder why I'm not a drunkard myself. Maybe I'd be better off if I were. At least I'd have something to look forward to, my 3-day breaks so I could get so drunk every six days that I couldn't think. Instead I look forward to sitting here day dreaming about you and the life I want, like I always do. I can't be untrue to you because I love you so. Sometimes I wish I could Viv. Sometimes I wish I didn't love you so much so I could be untrue to you then lie to you. I know it's good to love you the way I do, but I'm a slave to my own day dreams about my happiness with you.

Your husband soon, I love you

~

March 10, 1954

My Darling Wife,

Last night Viv, I was thinking of you and wishing you were beside me in my arms. I turned over on my side and was making believe you were pregnant, and my arms were around your neck and your stomach was against me. I was thinking how wonderful that's going to be, holding you in my arms, and feeling my own baby against me in the stomach of the most wonderful angel God put on earth. It will be heaven Viv, loving you and taking care of you always. I need you so very much my darling.

Viv, if someone asked me to name the two loveliest women in the world, you'd definitely be first, and Leslie Caron would be second. I saw her in some movie with Gene Kelly soon after I came over here, and I almost went up on the stage she reminded me of you so much. It's your lips and eyes and hair that are almost identical, and your figure is just like hers, wide hips, small waist, large bosom, and your walk. She might be a little heavier than you are but you're "stacked" just like her. She's my only pinup girl, because she's about the only Hollywood woman that doesn't have an illegitimate child, or 3 or 4 divorces.

I love you Vivian darling. I love you so very much.

Your husband,
Your Johnny

March 19, 1954

My Precious Darling,

I don't think I'll ever go anywhere else with Chuck & Alice honey. I'm so miserable with them I could die. At the movie last night and at the ice show, I was alone. There's always an empty chair, and coming back today in that car, they'd kiss and act a fool, and look at me and laugh. They're always doing that, especially Chuck, always whispering. It seems like they'd have sense enough to know how I feel, being without you. Chuck is always telling how he's going to hate to be away from Alice <u>3 whole months</u> when she goes home. Always telling me his troubles.

Hon, I'm going to close now and go to bed. I have to get up early tomorrow and get out of the room because they're having an inspection. Tomorrow is the first day of my furlough honey, that I'm spending in room 62, residence of J. Cash and B. Whitacre.

Take care of yourself Vivian and stay mine always darling. I love you so.

Your husband.

March 20, 1954

Another month is ⅔ gone, precious. The time is so very short till we'll be together isn't it angel. In 2½ months from tonight I won't be sitting in like tonight on Saturday night. I'll be having a date with my darling on all these Saturday nights and all the other nights.

Sweetheart, all the cookies are gone now except some crumbs, and I've certainly enjoyed them. They were so good Viv, every bite of them. Everybody that came in the room ate some too, and loved them. I'm going to have you make those cookies often when we're married angel. I just love them, and I've never eaten any better than these you made. They were perfect darling, just like you.

I'm the luckiest guy in the world to get such a wonderful girl, such a wonderful cook, such a pretty, sexy girl. No, I don't mean "that" word honey. It wasn't meant to be used in reference to you. Your face is beautiful, and your body is lovely and heavenly. That's the way you are. Everything about you has a glow of loveliness, of kindness and decency. You're the most wonderful thing God ever put on earth, and I love you for every bit of it. I do Vivian darling.

Vivie, please try to think about how much I love you, will you hon? Please try to realize that your waiting and your faithfulness won't be in vain. I'm going to make you happy Vivian darling. I'm going to make you the hap-

243

piest girl in the world. Please try to feel my love for you Vivian. I think of you every minute and love you every minute.

Goodnight my precious love.

Your husband soon,
Your Johnny

~

March 22, 1954

My Darling Wife,

Viv honey, I got four wonderful, heavenly letters from you today. Darling, you've made me the happiest person in the world.

Sugar, I'm going to answer all of your letters I can tonight and the rest of them tomorrow. Darling I've got to get up early tomorrow and go on sick call. You know I told you before that this cyst on my jaw is coming back because they didn't get all the roots the other time, well honey, it's just as big as it was before. In the last two or three days it's tripled in size and I'm going to try to get them to cut it out before it gets infected. It's already sore, and sticking out like an egg. They'll probably do like last time though, wait about 2 weeks so it will drive me crazy, then dig it out.

Vivie, did you know you're beautiful? I do, and I sure bet the men around there know it too. I don't see how any man could keep from falling in love with you. I guess I'm a jealous fool, but I love you so much that I hate for any man to look at you. Darling, you really shouldn't wear those tight skirts till I can be with you. You'll have the men clawing at the sidewalk. Honest, honey.

I'd like to see your new black shoes angel. I know I'll love them. I can imagine what they look like. Honey, you shouldn't buy too many more clothes. I'm going to be ashamed to go out with you in the clothes I wear. I know you have a lot of lovely clothes now, so I'll have to buy a lot to look halfway decent with you. You're so beautiful and lovely and smooth looking. Darling I can't take my eyes off this picture.

I'm going to bed Vivian. I'll write a long letter tomorrow night. I'll be thinking of you my angel. God bless you my precious love. I love you so.

Your husband,
Your Johnny

~

March 23, 1954

My Wonderful Viv,

Darling, I went over to that screwed-up dispensary this morning. The doctor looked at my cyst and said it was too hard to cut out, that I'd have to wait about a week till it gets soft. Honey, remember why I had to wait so long last time to get it cut out? It was soft and infected, so they said wait till it gets hard again. This time it's hard but they say wait till it gets soft, in other words, infected. I have sense enough to know they can't cut it out then.

I packed a box to send you this morning honey, and I'll mail it payday. Let me see if I can remember what's in it hon. Three ashtrays, two shirts and a sweater. Darling, if you can think of anything you can make out of it, you can tear up that grey shirt, or give it away or whatever you want. I don't want the thing. I didn't know it was made like it is till I opened it. It's a German shirt.

I'm sending about half of our records too honey. Some of them I wanted to keep to experiment on the recorder. I'm sending a bunch of old pictures, and that little horse and buggy, I bought it in Italy. Those tennis shoes are about 8 sizes too big for me. I don't know what to tell you to do with them, anything you want.

And that tin box of junk darling, it's just stuff I've collected during my 4 years in the service. All of it together probably isn't worth a nickel, but I just hated to throw it away.

And I'm sending back your precious letters darling. There's been so very much happiness for me in them. Keep every precious one of them Viv. Maybe someday when we're old, we can pick some of them out and read them.

Bye precious darling. Stay mine all mine always. I love you so very very much.

Your husband,
Your Johnny

~

March 27, 1954

My Precious Angel,

Honey, my cyst hasn't bothered me so much the last couple of days but it sure is an awful looking thing. I wear a bandage over it. It keeps the cold off of it. I'll be so glad when this thing is cut out again. I hope they can get it all out this time. Your friends are going to be calling me "Scarface John" darling. I'll be so ugly and scarred up honey. No, actually, it will be just a little scar about a half inch long honey.

I've got to go back to work tomorrow at 5 sweetheart. I'm sure going to be lazy after having 12 days off. I guess I'll have to start looking decent again. I haven't shaved in 3 days, but I probably will tomorrow. I'm beginning to look like an ape. Will you be my little monkey darling?

Goodnight precious angel. Please take care of yourself for me. You're my very life Vivian darling. I love you so very very much my love.

Your husband,
Your Johnny

March 26

My Precious Angel,

I love you so. I love you
and miss you and need you so
much Vivian darling. Oh how I
want you my sweetheart. I
love you and need you so.

Vivie, I just got back from
fishing honey. I went with Chuck
& Alice as usual, just us 3. We
left here around noon and went
to a place about 10 miles from
here. I was alone most of the
time honey. Chuck & Alice went
way down the river. I caught
one Rainbow trout honey, but
Chuck or Alice didn't catch a thing
so I threw him back in. I
got so cold and tired sitting

there honey. I built a fire
and sat there by it casting.
I talked to you too Vivie. I
talked to you nearly all afternoon.
I needed you so darling. It would
have been so heavenly if you
were sitting there beside me.
I'm afraid I would have forgotten
all about fishing if you'd been
there with me angel. I need
your precious kisses Vivian darling.
I need you so very much.

Someday we'll be together on
those fishing trips and everything
honey. We'll have so much fun.
It will be wonderful.

Hon, I got two letters from
you when I got back today.
They were short but very sweet.

Hon, I don't know why you weren't getting my mail. I hope you are now angel. I was so happy I got mail today. honey. This is the first Friday in ages that I have. But these were mailed on Saturday and Sunday, so that's why.

Viv, it won't be long till we'll be together sweetheart, then all our worries about everything will be over. Oh how I need you my precious darling. I want you so tonight. I need you for my wife Vivian darling. I need your lips, and your sweet precious little body. I need your love so much, it hurts me.

Sugar, I'll write tomorrow. I'm so tired now that I'm going to take a shower and go to bed.

Goodnight my precious angel. God bless you and take care of you for me. I love you my Vivie. I love you and need you so very much.

Goodnite my love.

Your husband,
Your Johnny

I love you Vivian darling.

~

Hello Sweet Darling,

Darling, in the pictures you sent, is this white coat yours or Grace's? Or maybe you have one almost like hers. It looks so nice sugar. You look good in white. Did you know that darling? It brings out the loveliness of your skin. And hon, is this a turtleneck sweater you have on in the picture in front of the office? I'm going to get one too when I get back darling. We'll both have a turtleneck sweater to wear when we're together. We'll do everything alike and together.

Vivian I want to be with you so bad I can hardly stand it. I want to see you, to talk to you, to hold your hand, to walk with you. Honey, I need you so much it hurts. You're wonderful and so lovely. You would be like a dream walking beside me.

Then you'll be my wife and you'll be all mine. I won't believe it, it will be so wonderful. Coming home to you, kissing you and hearing your voice and sleeping with you and feeling that wonderful body in my hands, and seeing you in your underwear or nightgown. Darling are you sure you're mine? It doesn't seem possible that I'm so lucky. It doesn't seem possible that all that is coming true so soon, but it is, isn't it precious? I'll roll over beside you and say, "Good morning sweetheart." I'll be kissing you and you'll be giving your precious self to me. Oh Viv, I love you so much honey.

Goodnight precious darling. I love you so much.

Your husband.

~

April 5, 1954

My Precious Angel,

Yes sugar, I guess all women are curious. But before long angel, your curiosity will be ended concerning married life. You'll be giving yourself to your husband. I think that's what you're curious about a lot, as any girl is. I thank heaven that you're still curious precious. You're so wonderful, and I love you so. You're the sweetest, heavenliest girl on earth. I love you so Viv.

Honey, I forgot to tell you, but yesterday morning I mashed this cyst and it hasn't bothered me since. Honey, it was all swollen up, and sticking out like an egg. I almost vomited when I mashed it. I got over a spoonful of blood and pus out of it, and something else that I couldn't figure out. It must have been the "body" of the cyst. It popped out and it was about the size of a penny, but round. It was white and fluffy like cotton, and it had a long root on it. Today honey, the cyst is a little thing. It doesn't bother me at all. Day after tomorrow I'll go over there darling and see if they'll cut the roots out so it won't grow back. Maybe I can persuade them to do that. I don't know.

Goodnight my precious angel. God bless you and keep you always for me. Remember that every ounce of you is mine. I love you my Viv.

Your husband,
Your Johnny

~

April 9, 1954

My Precious Angel,

Honey, did you see that cool, crazy "S/Sgt" on the envelope? I made it sweetheart. The orders just came out yesterday, and I made it by George. I sure was proud honey. It's all a person could ask to make in four years.

Darling, I'm at work now. I wanted to write you now because I know I'm going to be so dead tired when I get off. I shouldn't be writing a letter, but actually nobody cares. I had to talk to my little darling. I miss you so.

Before long we'll celebrate this promotion and every thing else together sweetheart. It's so soon too isn't it Vivie. In just a short while all our worries will be over. We'll be together every day and night sweetheart.

Goodnite my Viv. Stay a good girl, and stay my girl always. I love you so very much my precious darling.

Your husband,
Your Johnny

~

April 11, 1954

Precious Baby,

Darling at least there's one good thing about being S/Sgt. I've been eating like a human lately. That 1st 3 graders mess hall is really nice honey. I serve myself on the line, and take whatever I want of anything. I eat out of a plate too honey, and not a tray. When I sit down, a German waitress comes over and pours coffee, and she comes over again and asks if I'd like to have dessert when I finish. Then she takes the dishes away when I finish. It's almost like a restaurant darling. It's really nice. Just getting some decent food for a change is worth making Staff.

Sweetheart, have you heard the religious song by Bill Monroe, "You're Drifting Away"? I have it recorded honey. I just love it.

Take care of yourself my darling and always stay my girl. I love you and need you so.

Your husband,
Your Johnny

April 12, 1954

My Vivian Darling,

Honey, a real woman just walked by outside. She got out of a car and had on heels, and a suit and cool little hat, and she twisted her tail like a worm when she walked. She must be an officer's wife. She looked so phony. I hate phony women. Thank God my woman isn't phony. You have the loveliest body, and the loveliest walk and the prettiest face on earth and you don't even know it. Soon I'll be seeing you too. I'll be so proud of you. You're so beautiful and heavenly, but so down to earth. I love you so my darling.

Your husband.

I love you angel

April 13, 1954

My Darling Vivian,

Honey, I got another precious letter from you today. It made me so happy Viv.

Darling, I don't think I told you I'm taking a 15-day leave the 1st of May. Ted Freeman and I are taking a fishing leave angel. We'll probably stay on the base every night but we'll go fishing and sailing every day that the weather is pretty. It will give me time to get a good suntan angel, and get in shape for marriage. I'm in shape for marriage right now, but what I mean is, I want to look a little better for you. I'll still write every day while I'm on the leave angel. I'll write every day till I leave here to come back to you.

Goodnight my precious Viv. I love you so very much.

Your Johnny

April 14, 1954

My Darling Darling,

Honey, when I was in Zurich Switz. at the museum, I think I did one of the worst things I've done in my life. It was only a thought but I don't think I'll forget it as long as I live. I was walking through the museum with Grady, and we walked up to a large Crucifix. I almost said aloud, "Well, what the hell are you doing up there?" As soon as I said it, I just froze. I was so surprised and dumbfounded that I didn't know what to do or say. The words came to my lips, but still, I don't believe it was me that said it. Always before I'd felt like praying when I saw a Crucifix.

I've prayed for forgiveness for that and I think I have been forgiven, but I still can't understand why I did that.

Darling, one of my friends and I were talking last night about the kind of life we wanted to live after we're married. He's from Detroit, but we both agreed on the same thing. As a "model week" here's what I'd like: Work 5½ days a week, Monday through Saturday at noon. Have Saturday afternoon to work around home, patching things up, building and improving. Go out somewhere, anywhere on Saturday night with my wife (you), and go to a movie or a drive-in a couple of times a week, and to church on Sunday.

Of course there will be lots of other things, but that's the blueprint of the kind of life I'd like. What do you think of it honey?

Stay sweet Viv and remember I love you. Someday darling all our hopes and dreams will come true. We'll be living all the wonderful times we talk about, and it will be heaven. Have faith Viv, and keep on praying. I'll be praying with you.

> Your husband someday.
> Your Johnny

~

April 15, 1954

My Precious Viv,

Honey, I'm going to start a letter, but I don't know how long I'll last. I got 3 precious letters from you today. That made me so wonderfully happy and contented. I want to talk to you so bad Vivie, I wanted to write a long letter and answer them tonight, but I had the cyst cut out today honey, about an hour and a half ago, and I'm feeling kind of awful.

It was just like last time honey. He tied strings around it and cut and sliced and pulled and finally got the body of the cyst out. Then he had the two roots to cut out the same way. It took 40 minutes in all. I was a nervous wreck and wet with sweat when he finished. If this thing grows back I'm going to be ready to die. I just cringe every time I think of how they had to cut that thing out.

Yes hon, take some blue jeans and some shorts too when you go to Dyess. Darling, bring plenty of plain everyday clothes too, and the kind of clothes you used to wear. You know honey, the big skirts that the Italian girls wear and those cute little blouses. You know what I mean sugar. Oh Viv, I can hardly wait to see you. I've wanted to be with you so long. I love you so.

I don't think I'll be able to teach you anything on our wedding night Vivie. I'll be so nervous and will be so weak because you'll be so lovely and I'll need you so. We'll both have butterflies angel. I don't want to teach you anything Viv honey. I want us to learn together. I think it will come natural Viv. We've loved each other so long, that I feel that I know you completely and you belong to me, body and soul. There couldn't possibly be a dirty thought in my mind since

I know you're pure, and the way I love you. Seeing you and having you in my arms naked will only be right. God made us for each other precious.

Darling, you've just got to work it so you can be at Dyess when I come. I want it that way honey, and I'm making so many plans for us.

Little darling, I'm going to bed now. My cheek isn't hurting so much, so maybe I can sleep. I'll write tomorrow little lover. Viv honey, remember you're all mine. Tell everybody to keep them cotton-picking hands off you.

Your husband soon.

~

April 23, 1954

Happy Birthday precious darling. I hope you're happy today. I've thought of you so much Vivie. I've just been miserable for you. I woke up this morning thinking of you and wanting you so bad I could die and I've been that way all day. If our hearts do beat together, you've been thinking of me every minute too.

I went to the movie this afternoon. I would catch myself turning my head to kiss your forehead. I held my hands together making believe it was yours. And to add to my misery, there was a woman in the movie named "Vivian." My heart jumped every time her name was called.

After the movie was over honey, I went out and sat on a concrete block alone in the sun. I talked to you out loud, and I prayed. It was eight oclock where you are. I tried to think of what you would be doing. I felt so close to you and wanted you so.

I've got to go to bed now my darling. On your next birthday, we'll be going to bed together, maybe with a precious little baby between us. Or at least I'll be massaging your swollen little stomach for you. And I'll be holding you in my arms all night long.

Goodnight my love. God bless you and keep you safe for me. I love you so, so very much.

Your husband soon.

~

April 25, 1954

My Precious Love,

Darling, when we're together I'm going to take lots of pictures of you just like I've always wanted. That's going to be one of my hobbies, taking pictures of you, all kinds of pictures, in all kinds of clothes. Will you let me take pinup pictures of you when we're married honey? Pictures of you in shorts, underwear, or nightgown? Of course darling, they'd only be for me to see. I'd put them all in a big album and keep it locked up always. I don't mean dirty pictures Vivie. I mean just pictures like you see in magazines. And with your figure, you could put most of them to shame, believe me.

Darling, I'm getting very very sleepy. I'll write tomorrow precious.

I love you so very very much.

Your husband,
Your Johnny

～

April 28, 1954

Hon, you know what I told you about day dreaming that someday I'd meet an Italian girl and marry her. Honey, I'm proud of that Italian blood in you. I don't know why, but I always feel so proud when I say, "My girl is part Italian." I guess it's because you're my dream come true, and not only that but everyone knows that generally Italian women are exceptionally devoted to their men.

And honey, when I tell you I think you're beautiful and lovely, I'm not just saying it to flatter you. You're right darling, I don't love you just because of your looks. Your looks are extra besides your kindness, sweetness and perfection. I couldn't explain why I love you. I haven't got enough paper in the room to write down all the wonderful things about you.

But I'm not the only one that thinks you're beautiful Viv. I showed Chuck this first picture you sent me and he said "She's one of the most beautiful women I've ever seen." I took my album of you out to let Alice see it, and she said a dozen times, "She's so pretty." And she means it too. She's afraid that you'll be above her class honey. Actually, you are. <u>Way</u> above her class, but forgetting her one big mistake I mean. Chuck says she's asked him a lot of things about you that make me think that. She asked him if you lived in the city all your life, if you smoked or drank, and probably other things. Chuck knows how perfect you are. Every thing he's told her about you has been good. He's always bragging on what a good girl I've got and of course, so have I.

Viv honey, I'll know about the middle of May the exact day I'll leave. Darling I think it's June 2nd, but I can't be sure yet. I'll let you know the day I find out precious.

Darling, can't you just see you and I walking along in the dark, my arm around you, walking real slow, and your head layed over against my face. So soon it will be true my darling. We'll stop and I'll kiss you and hold you close. We'll both be so happy that you'll cry, and I'll have tears in my eyes. Oh how I love you.

Viv honey, it's very late. I'll write tomorrow night my love.

Your husband.

～

April 29, 1954

My Viv, I didn't get a letter today honey, so this won't be very long. There isn't very much to write about. But at least I can try to keep my sweet darling happy.

Vivie, you know I went on leave last night honey? I've got 15 days. I don't have to work again till May 15th. Honey, Ted Freeman, and Orville Rigdon, another friend of mine all took 15 days. We had intended to stay around here and fish all the time, but we've about decided different. Hon, Ted wants to go to Venice, Italy, and I think Rigdon does too, and I think I could afford to go down there a couple of days by pinching my pennies. Train fare round trip is about $20, and by just eating and sleeping, I guess I can go. I can't do anything, but just "see Venice," but I guess it would be worth it.

Goodnight my precious love. God bless you and keep you for me. I love you my Viv, and I'll always love you honey. Always stay my girl. I love you so.

Your husband.

~

April 30, 1954

My Precious Love,

Viv another month is gone honey. Our last one apart will be well on its way to being gone by the time you get this. All our dreams are coming true soon my darling. So very soon we'll be together.

Honey, Ted and I have decided to go to Venice. We're leaving on the train tonight darling. Orville isn't going. He has to work tonight, so just Ted and I are going.

We're supposed to get to Venice sometime tomorrow morning, but we're going to stop over in Verona tomorrow and tomorrow night. You remember that town honey? It's the one I was telling you about where Romeo and Juliet lived. I can imagine how I'm going to feel in the place where I wanted to take you on our honeymoon. Sleeping in the room with Ted instead of with you. I know I'm going to be miserable for you.

I love you and need you so.

Your husband soon.
Your Johnny.

~

May 2, 1954

As I sit here in the warm, peaceful city of Venice, in a humble boarding house, I can look out my window and see the Gondolas gliding down the crazy canals. As I look down on the street below I can see the lovers walking arm in arm beneath the cool moon. It's utterly frantic.

This afternoon we came on to Venice darling. It sure is a nice place Viv. I'd give anything if you could only be here with me. I want you to see everything so bad. You'd love it I know. We walked all over town tonight, up and down the canals and everywhere. It's so nice, and I want you so. I love you Viv.

～

Hello hon, I'm back again. It's 5:30 PM, and Ted and I are sitting on the train in Venice. It pulls out in about 30 minutes.

We went all over this town today sweetheart, taking pictures, sightseeing and buying souvenirs. We sure took in the town hon, and we're really tired, but we've got a 12 hour ride ahead of us back to Landsberg. Viv I miss you so much honey. I wish it were you with me instead of Ted.

Honey, Venice is sure an odd place. It's definitely the most different city I've ever seen. All the streets are canals except a very few. We didn't see over a dozen cars the whole time we were here. Everybody owns a boat. Everybody goes everywhere in boats.

Sugar, it's almost time for the train to pull out so I'm going to close. I'll be thinking of you my darling. I love you Vivie. I love you so much.

Your husband soon,
Your Johnny

～

May 4, 1954

My Precious Darling,

I'm back at the base now, safe and sound and still all yours. We got back at 8:30 this morning honey. After that 12 hour ride we were beat to a frazzle, and we slept all day. I feel fine now angel face.

There sure is a difference between here and Venice honey. It was so nice and warm when we left there. I just had on my corduroy shirt, and a pair of pants as thin as your underdrawers. But when we got back we needed a snowsuit. It's so cold and raining.

Vivie, I had 3 letters waiting on me that made me the happiest person in the world. I took a shower and shaved, then got in bed and read them. As tired as I was, I was so happy, and felt so close to you that I couldn't sleep for an hour. Oh Viv, I love you my precious darling. I love you so much.

Goodnight my love. God bless you and keep you for me. I love you and want you and need you so. Always stay mine darling. I love you so much.

Yours for life.

～

May 12, 1954

My Precious Viv,

Honey, Ted and Reid Cummins, another friend of mine, and I just got back from Obermmergau fishing. We borrowed Chuck's car and went down there this morning. We couldn't stay long because we had to be back by 5 oclock so Chuck could have the car to go home. But we caught 12 trout angel. We cooked some of them down there, and brought the rest back to Chuck.

I was so happy to get away from this place. I drove like a maniac, too fast I guess, but it's so good to feel free once in awhile. I'm on the move every minute, and I'm so tired I could drop now.

I've got a little tan on my face and hands sugar. I want to try to have a good tan when I come home.

You've got a little tan too haven't you angel? You're naturally dark anyhow, and your skin is so lovely. I was thinking of your legs today honey. You don't mind do you? I was thinking how lovely you'd look without a skirt on, those lovely brown legs and a pair of snow white panties on. With lace. It's been so long since I've seen anything like that that it doesn't seem real. But it is real darling. Soon I'll have you, my very own woman. Your lips and your breasts and your lovely legs will be my very own for life won't they honey? No other man but me can ever touch you, right angel? You're all my girl sweetheart, and I love you so very much.

I'm going to close now and go to bed little angel. I'll write tomorrow night.

I love you so very much.
Your husband.

~

May 13, 1954

Precious darling, it's 8:30 AM and I just got up a few minutes ago. I'm waiting on Chuck & Alice honey. We and Ted are going sailing at Lake Ammersee today. It sure is nice and sunny today sweetheart.

I just want to talk to you while I'm waiting Vivie. I miss you so much honey, and I want to talk to you so bad. I love you Vivian. I love you so very much angel. I want you in my arms so bad. Soon you will be love, so very soon. All our dreams are coming true soon my darling.

Hello sugar. Ted and I just got back from Ammersee. It's 6:30 PM. Chuck & Alice stayed out there and got them a hotel room, and Ted and I borrowed Chuck's car and came back. When I got back there was nobody here so I took down your picture and kissed it and told you how much I missed you today and how much I love you.

Hon, no letter today. If I don't get one tomorrow I'm going to cry. I need your sweet letters so much.

Hello Wee-Wee-Ann, I'm back again. I sure get around don't I sugar? I went to the movie. I told you last night that I was going to play Bingo tonight, but it takes a dollar to play Bingo, and I only have 90 cents, so I went to the movie. Now I have 65 cents. Boy, am I loaded. But I don't care. Very soon I'll be with my angel, and I won't need money to be happy.

Oh darling, it will all be so heavenly, every minute of my life with you. I love you Vivian honey. I love you. I feel like I could give you twins now honey. I need that lovely little angel body so much. I need you so. Those lovely lips and breasts, and all of you. You could make me so happy and contented. I love you Vivian.

I love you Viv. I love you. Please always stay mine. I need you so.

Your husband.

~

May 15, 1954

My Precious Viv,

This won't be very long precious darling. I just got off work and I'm very tired. I had to write my sweet darling and tell her I love her though.

Vivian darling, my ship leaves Bremerhaven June 11th. <u>June 11th</u>. Honey it kills me to tell you that. I haven't had the heart so far. I found out 3 days ago. I held off as long as I could but you have to know.

But Viv, I'm even lucky it's that early. They have two shipments in June. One the 11th, and one the 25th. I managed to get on the 11th.

It killed me too Vivian. It seems it's one setback after another, just torture. I wish I could tell you something good once in a while. I just can't help it Vivian honey. Please don't be hurt.

Darling, I want more than anything for you to be happy. When I'm back I know I can make you happy, but I can't fight this crummy service. Darling that job of yours isn't all that important. Us having a few more dollars doesn't make any difference. We'll work and plan together when I'm back. Vivian, if you're tired of that job, if you're tired of any part of the life you're living, will you please quit and go to mom's? Viv, she said she'd be so glad for you to come anytime you wanted to, to stay as long as you want, in this letter the other day.

Darling, I know you must have plenty of clothes. After your next payday, or after Ray's wedding, why don't you go up there and stay till I come Viv? There's plenty to do there now. They've got out a big garden, and Mom sells magazines. You could go around over the country with her. You could take material along and sew, etc. too.

Oh Viv honey, I just want you to be happy and contented. It would be a change for you up there. Don't you think you'd enjoy it precious? That money means nothing. I'll have my discharge bonus to pay our monthly debts till I'm working. Nothing means anything if it makes you unhappy or discontented.

Goodnight my precious love. Oh how I'd love to hold you in my arms tonight to comfort you and kiss you. I love you so much.

I'll always love you my precious Viv.

Your husband.

P.S. Darling, I'm coming back on the U.S.S. Darby. It's the fastest ship they have. It takes 7 days to reach New York. At least that's one good thing.

～

May 22, 1954

My Sweet Viv,

Viv, it doesn't seem possible that in 18 days I'll be on my way back to you. When you get this, it will only be about 12. Happier days are coming for sure. I don't see how I can sweat out these 18 though. When I leave here, if I can stand it, I'll be on my way back. Even the long days on the ship, I'll be moving toward home.

I used to hate to see a bunch of guys leave here because I wanted to be with them so much, but I don't have to watch it anymore. My ship is the next one to leave. Little old me is the next to leave. Your Johnny.

Darling, I've just made up a nice word. I surprise myself, I'm so brilliant. "INHIBERSNAILISPITICS" is the art of spitting on a snail on the right place to make him go in his shell and hibernate. I can't help it if I'm nuts angel. I'm kind of halfway happy, so it doesn't matter if I'm nuts does it? Huh?

Nite precious. I love you so very very much. I'll always love you my Vivie. As long as I live. Always stay mine. I love you Vivian honey.

Your husband

～

May 25, 1954

My Very Own,

Viv, the Germans really suffered a loss today. You know what king of money the Americans use over here honey? I think I sent you some before, but here's a nickel. See, the Germans get this money by black market, and it eventually goes to Russia, when they get it. The Germans probably have hundreds of thousands of dollars stored away. But our money changed today. It changed colors. We get new money for it. If the Germans had known the money was going to change, they could have sold it back to the G.I.s, but that's the funny thing about it, they didn't, and neither did we. At 6 oclock this morning they announced on the radio that all American money would be exchanged for the

May 23rd already

Hello precious,

It's 4 am now, and I'm at work sweetheart. I dont feel like
working, so I'm writing my darling. It wont be long sugar
cause there isn't much to write about, but I wanted to write
you before I get off work, cause I want to go right to bed.
I'm already so tired.

I didn't sleep anymore yesterday honey. I went back to bed
at 6 oclock, and lay there till 7, tossing and turning and
thinking of you and couldn't sleep, so I got up and went to
the movie. I'll be lucky if I make it through the rest of
the night. If I could have just one sweet little hug & kiss
from my Viv, I know I could. I could probably go two more days.

Vivian, I love you honey. I love you so very much. I'd
give anything if I could just be with you now. I want you and
need you so much my darling. We'll be so happy together darling
I've wanted you and needed you so long, and so soon you'll be
all mine. All that precious love.

Sweetheart, I guess this is a record for shortness, but
there isn't anything to write about, so I'm going to ### close.
I'll be with you at prayer to nite honey. So soon we'll be
praying together.

Bye angel. Please keep on loving me and always stay all my
girl. I love you so very much. I love you so much it hurts.
I'll always love you my Viv.

your Johnny
for life.

I love you Viv.

261

new kind by <u>noon</u>. That's every cent in Europe, Africa, England, Ireland, Scotland and everywhere. Millions of dollars have to be changed by noon, or it isn't worth a cent. You can see what a big thing it is hon, and not one word of it leaked out. The Germans were completely caught off guard. They say Munich & Frankfurt is a mad house, every German trying to sell the guys their money back, and for practically nothing.

A lot of guys are really going to lose some money. Bob is on leave and I know he had at least a hundred dollars in this money. I'm sure glad I was already broke sweetheart.

I bet Syl did look pretty honey. From her pictures, she sure looks like a pretty girl. But I still think her little sister is the prettiest. I still love her little sister just as much as I did the day I said, "Will you marry me?" I love her so.

Vivian honey, soon you will be in my arms and hear me say, "I love you." It's all coming true so soon. Darling, please think of that. Think of how wonderfully happy we'll be, and how its going to be, being close in each others arms, kissing. Think of the wonderful way we're going to get along. We will be happy Vivie. We'll be the happiest couple on earth. I love you my Viv. I love you so much precious darling.

Honey, I'm going to close now and go to lunch. I'll be back tomorrow Wee-Wee. Stay my girl and keep on loving me. I'm always thinking of you my darling.

I love you Vivian honey.

Your husband.

~

May 30, 1954

Honey, this won't be very long because it's getting pretty late and I have to get up for work tomorrow.

Honey, we caught a baby crow down on the river last night, or late yesterday afternoon. He was just about half grown, and could hardly fly. He was about the size of a blackbird I guess, only fatter. He was the cutest thing. I brought him back and made a perch for him, and he stayed in the room last night. On the river he swallowed a hook with a worm on it, and this morning he swallowed 2 thumb tacks. But none of it seemed to bother him.

This morning he woke me up crowing. He was sitting in the window. He heard the other birds. He was just barely big enough to caw, but he sure wore himself out. I turned him loose, and another crow took up with him, but some of the boys caught him and brought him back. I got him again this afternoon and turned him loose again, and I haven't seen him since. He was so cute honey. He would get mad and try to peck me, but he was so weak that I would hardly feel it. He'll probably die with that hook and those tacks in him.

Honey, I'm going to bed. I'll write tomorrow sweetheart. I love you Vivian darling. I love you so very much.

Your Johnny

~

My Darling Vivian,

Sweetheart, when we're married I'll buy you a set of panties with the days of the week on them. I'll buy you all kinds of sweet little panties darling. I want you to have some with my name embroidered on them angel.

I lay in bed this morning thinking of you Viv, thinking of how sweet and lovely you are, and how wonderful it would be if you were my wife and were lying beside me with just a pair of panties & bra on. For a while when we're first married honey, that's all I'm going to let you wear in bed. Either that or a nightgown with nothing on under it. I don't think you'll mind precious. The weather will be warm. Besides, you'll be in my arms. You'll never get cold sweetheart. I won't believe it Vivian darling. <u>Me</u> actually having my <u>own</u> woman, putting my hands on silk panties, and have lips and breasts to kiss. Vivian honey you'll make me the happiest person in the world. I'll make you happy too Vivian darling. I know I can make life heaven for you.

Honey, today was my last day of work. I certainly was happy to walk out of that place. Now I want to forget it.

Sweetheart, it's late and I'm so tired. I'm going to bed. I'll be thinking of you my darling. I love you so.

Your husband, I love you.

~

June 3, 1954

My Precious darling,

Honey, it's 5 oclock, and I've worked every minute since I got up this morning at 7:30. I've washed clothes, shined shoes, waxed the floor, worked on my hand bag, went to the PX, and did a dozen other little things.

Vivian honey, it will all be so wonderful. You, my own woman around the house, to love and take care of and keep happy. That will be my life Vivian darling, keeping you happy and giving you lots of little angels to make us more happy. It will be so wonderful seeing you, my wife, feeding our little baby. You'll have lots of healthy milk for them too, cause I'm going to take care of you and make you eat lots. And by the time our first angel arrives you'll have about a size 40 bust. Cause I'm going to caress those soft lovely breasts, and love them and kiss them so much. They fascinate me so much darling.

Vivian honey will you please eat and sleep plenty before you make that trip

263

up there. Please darling. And when you get there, eat all you can hold every meal and get 8 hours sleep every night. Honey you aren't going to get much sleep when I'm back. I'm not going to run you down, but we just won't have much time for sleep, there'll be so much to do.

Darling be careful on that trip up there. Don't take any chances. Find some lady, or old couple to sit with, and be careful of the traveling sex maniacs. I know you could spot them, but don't get friendly with any men honey. Please be careful angel. You're so precious to me.

Vivian honey, the thing that made me so happy in these letters was you said, "You're the only one Johnny darling." I love to be told Vivie. It makes me so happy. You're the only one too Vivian darling.

Honey I was going to play Bingo tonite but I can't afford it. I'm going to make a box to send home our clock and my razor. I'll write tomorrow precious angel.

Goodnite my little lover. God bless and keep you for me. I love you so.

Your husband soon,
Your Johnny

~

June 7, 1954

My Precious Vivian,

Vivian darling, I suppose your little heart has been broken enough that it can stand it once more. I don't leave here till the 19th Vivian. Honey go ahead and cry, if you can still love me enough to cry. I did when I found this out. It killed me. Honey, they called us all down this morning and told us that they couldn't put us on the shipment for the 11th. The Army did it. They shoved us back to the 19th. I've got to stay here 12 more days.

I came back to the room and cried. Not for my sake, but because I knew I had to write you this letter. What can I do. I can't do one damned thing. Nothing but tell you discouraging things, and sit here and sweat and get nervous and walk the floor.

Honey, I'm not asking anything else of you. You've done too much for me. Maybe you've begun to realize it. I want you. Oh how I want you. But I don't deserve you. You're not human, you're an angel. No human being could sacrifice so much as you have. Not one damned girl on earth would do what you've done for me.

Honey, I'm going to hope and pray that you'll be there when I get there. If you go up to mom's, I hope you'll quit that job and go on to mom's the 18th like you planned. Please do, and if you run out of money, use some of ours. Honey we won't be hurting for money. Even if we are broke, it doesn't matter. I can get a job doing something. If you'll still marry me, I'm going to marry you just as quick as you'll marry me when I'm back. Money or no money. It doesn't matter if we have it or not. Please don't keep on working. Please go on up to mom's and stay there Vivian. You'd enjoy it so much and there'd be hardly nothing you'd need money for.

Honey, I'm going to take it for granted that you go up there the 18th. I'm going to mail your letters to you in care of my folks at Dyess after the 18th. If you aren't there, then they can save them till you come.

Just as quick as you'll have me we're going to get married. Still July 18th, if you will. We deserve it. You deserve it. I'm tired of you saving yourself for me, and I'm going to have you just as soon as you will. Nothing else matters.

I'll be looking forward to that last letter my darling. I hate to go so long without one from you, but I'm happy for your sake that you won't have to write any more. You probably won't know what to do with your pretty little self, not having to write a letter. I hope you'll have fun and be happy.

Well precious darling, I'm going to close now and write the folks. I have to tell them the same thing. At least the hardest part is past. All day long, I've said to myself, "How can I tell her." It hurts so.

Vivian honey, I love you so much. I love you so much it hurts. Oh please be mine. I need you so. Honey, you can figure I'll be there 10 days later than was originally planned. I'm still praying that something will happen that we can leave Thursday, but it would be a miracle.

Goodnite my precious love. May God bless you and help you and keep you. Stay sweet. Please don't feel too bad. Oh please don't be hurt honey. I love you so. I love you so very very much.

Your husband,
Your Johnny

~

June 8, 1954

My precious Viv,

I woke up this morning just dying for you. Last night I dreamed that I was writing a letter honey, and you were standing right beside me. You had on a white blouse but from the waist down you just had on a pair of blue panties with a little white bow at the hip. You were standing there beside me so unconcerned darling. I put my arm around your waist and kissed the little bow and you gave me the most puzzled look honey. As if you didn't know that you were the sweetest thing God ever put on earth. You looked so sweet.

Oh darling, every day I want you and love you more. I want you so. Vivian darling please keep on loving me. I love you so much. I need you for my wife. I'll make you so happy honey. I know I will. There could never be anyone but you for me.

Vivian darling, I'm going now. I'll write you tomorrow night when we get back precious. Stay my sweet girl always. God bless you my little darling. I love you so.

Your husband,
Your Johnny

~

June 10, 1954

Viv, I got your last letter today sweetheart. It was so wonderful. It made me so very very happy Vivie. You're so sweet. You said everything you could think of to keep me happy. You almost didn't stop saying, "I love you." Vivian, I love you too honey. If only I could make you see how much. Please always be mine. I love you so.

Today was supposed to be the day. I know you think I'm on my way back. Oh honey if I could only do something. I'm almost going crazy here. And I know how it hurts you for this to happen. Vivian darling please try to be happy. It's just for a little while longer. Bless your heart, you've waited half a lifetime and it's still one disappointment after another. Honey, it honestly won't be long now. I'll be out of this crummy screwed up service and I'll be free. We can do what we please. Darling please keep your chin up and be happy. I want you so much my love.

Viv honey, this is the last letter I'll mail to you at San Antonio. This will go out tomorrow and get there before the 18th. But any more won't. Darling I'll tell Mom to keep them for you in case you aren't there, but I hope you're there honey. I wish you'd quit the 18th and go on up there.

Vivian darling, please don't feel bad about going up there and staying. You know you're welcome honey. Of course you wouldn't be any expense and dad wouldn't take any money, but I told him I'd pay him for any expense. And don't you pay them anything honey. I'm taking over all your expenses when I get back. Go on up there and enjoy yourself. You need a long vacation.

And Viv honey, please be careful traveling. Be sure you and mom have it worked out so she knows exactly when & where to meet you. Be careful precious darling.

Sweetheart, isn't it going to be wonderful? We're going to be out together those warm summer nights. I'm going to kiss you a thousand times every night.

Honey, I'm going to close now and go to bed. I'll write tomorrow lovely Viv. It's raining so I probably won't go anywhere. Goodnight my angel. God bless you honey. I love you so much. So very very much Vivian darling. Always be all mine. I love you so.

Your husband,
Your Johnny

~

Hello Sweetheart,

How's my sweet baby? I miss her so tonite. If I could only be with you I'd be so happy Viv. I want you so very much.

Honey I haven't done a thing today but just sit around. I did clean up the room a little, but outside of that, I've just walked the floor. I want you and miss you so. I don't see how I can live these next 8 days.

Vivie, I hope you're at mom's having a good time and enjoying yourself. Honey take care of yourself and eat and sleep good. I'll be there with you soon precious darling.

Maybe it will be nicer there this time sweetheart, with running water and an indoor toilet. Everything should be more convenient and nicer. I hope you and Joann can find plenty to do to keep you occupied. I'll keep you occupied when I'm back angel. I'll probably never let you go to bed, so you get plenty of sleep hon.

Vivie, I have so many plans for us honey. It's going to be so wonderful when we're together. We're going to be so happy and have so much fun.

Stay sweet Viv, and always stay all mine. I love you and need you so very much my darling.

Your husband, I love you.

~

June 14, 1954

My Darling Viv,

Honey, I didn't write Saturday and Sunday. We did the same thing exactly this weekend that we did the last. We went fishing Saturday and came back and cooked them in the room. We didn't get to bed till about midnite Saturday nite, then got up at 6 oclock yesterday morning and went fishing again. We fished all day and came back and cooked them again.

I'm not going fishing any more honey. I'm so sick of it I could die. I think I've been fishing 5 days out of the last 8. I've eaten so many fish that I can't stand the smell of them anymore. I caught 28 trout yesterday honey. I even got tired of catching them. I've never had such a day fishing in my life. All of us together, 4 of us caught 60. I caught the most. We gave about 4 families a mess, and ate all we could hold last nite.

Honey, I don't know what I'm going to do these last 4 days, but I'm not going fishing. I guess I'll just sit around here. I'll try to write every day honey.

Oh does this room stink. I can hardly stand to stay in here. I never thought fried fish would be so sickening. It almost makes me vomit. I'll probably never like them.

Viv, I love you honey. I miss you so, and I think of you so much. I can hardly live for the day when we'll be together. We've waited so long. I love you so Vivian honey.

There's no news Viv, so I might as well close. I miss your letters so much. I'll write tomorrow honey. I'm going to the movie. I love you my Vivie. I love you so very much.

I love U.

Your husband soon.

~

June 15, 1954

My Darling Viv,

Honey this has been another dead day. I've done practically nothing but sit around. I miss your letters so much Viv. And I miss you so much.

I've got 3 more days to do nothing. If the sun is out tomorrow I guess I can go out and get a little sunshine, but it's been raining all day. So very soon I'll be leaving this cold wet place. I'm so sick of this.

Darling, I'm going to bed. There's nothing to write about. I'll try to write a long letter tomorrow honey.

Goodnite my Viv. I love you so very much.

Your Johnny for life.

~

June 17, 1954

My Darling Vivian,

I'm all ready to go Saturday morning honey. I'm going to be so glad to leave. I'm so sick of this place. I've got to write you once more honey. We thought our letter writing never would come to an end but it has. I'll write you once more here, and once at Bremerhaven just before we leave, if I have time. Then the next time I talk to you, you'll be tight in my arms. We've waited so long for it Vivian honey. At last it's coming true.

Honey it's been cloudy and raining every day. We can't even get out in the sunshine. If I had to stay here much longer I'd go crazy. This waiting kills me.

Darling, I'm going to stop now. I've got to go down and get my partial payment. I suppose I'll go to the movie again tonite. There's nothing else to do.

Goodnite sweetheart. Be sure and take good care of yourself. Stay sweet Viv, and always be all mine. I love you so much. So very much darling. Soon I'll be telling you in person honey.

Your husband soon,
Your Johnny

I love you Vivian.

PART TWO

In my opinion, there was never a day more befitting fireworks and big band celebrations than July 4, 1954. That was the day Johnny finally returned home from Germany.

I woke to the sound of Johnny's mother fixing breakfast in the kitchen of their new home in Dyess. I had spent the last two days with Johnny's family, anxiously waiting for this big day to arrive. I looked at the clock and knew that at that very moment Johnny was boarding a plane headed to the West Memphis, Arkansas, airport where in three hours we would meet him. We would finally be together! I shot out of bed like a gazelle, in a rush to get ready. The entire house was already buzzing with excitement.

The whole bunch of us—me, Louise, Roy, Tommy, and Johnny's folks—all loaded into the Cash family car for the fifty-mile drive to West Memphis. I had never been more nervous in my life. Three years I'd waited for this day.

Not only was I anxious to see Johnny, but I was nervous about his family being there, staring, knitting their brows, anxious to see us finally reunite. Johnny's family was very old-fashioned. Not backward old-fashioned, but very conservative and proper. They frowned upon outward displays of affection. I was worried what they might think if they saw us hug or kiss.

Repeatedly they wondered aloud while we waited in the airport terminal, "What do you think Johnny will do when he finally sees Vivian? What do you think he'll say? Vivian, what are you thinking? What will you say?" I was in a daze, so excited, not knowing what to think or say. The only thing I wanted to know was when Johnny was going to arrive.

After pacing the length of the airline terminal fifty times or more, impatiently counting the minutes as each arriving plane pulled in, I walked up to the airline ticket counter and, with all the composure I could fake, asked the lady, "When does the next train arrive?" Everybody in our group collapsed in laughter.

And then he appeared with no warning. At a distance, through a terminal doorway, there he stood in his khaki uniform, blue tie tucked into his button-down shirt, wearing his air force overseas cap. He was scanning the crowd, just like that first night at the skating rink. He looked amazing—more handsome than I ever remembered.

Johnny first caught sight of his mother ("Grandma Cash," as I've always called her). She was taller than the rest of us, towering above the crowd . . . and then finally he spotted me. He was grinning ear to ear, very excited. The moment we had waited for had finally arrived. I broke away and ran to him.

I've been asked before, "What were your first words to each other?" The truth is, we didn't say a word. I just fell into his arms, he scooped me up, and we kissed. All we could think to do, all we wanted to do, was kiss. It was one of those remember-for-a-lifetime kind of moments when words are unimportant.

Johnny's family looked on, grinning and laughing. I was far too preoccupied to worry now about their reaction to our very un-Cashlike public display. The months of waiting melted away in that one kiss, and it was like he never left. It all felt so right.

"Vivian, you look like you're gonna eat him up, and in nine months you'll look like you did!" his daddy interrupted jokingly. I blushed, hiding my face in Johnny's embrace.

"Let's go home!" Johnny answered, laughing.

All we could think about from that point on was starting our life together as soon as possible. We immediately began planning our wedding to take place the following month. Daddy wanted us to wait thirty days to be certain of our decision. And for now, Johnny insisted on heading to San Antonio to properly ask Daddy for my hand.

Daddy always judged a person by his handshake, said it was a window into a man's character. He hated it when anyone had a weak grip, or would keep his hands folded and not look him in the eyes, or worse yet, not shake at all. But Johnny's handshake was strong and firm and sincere. And Daddy and Mother loved him. They had no fear or anxiety about us getting married anymore. They loved Johnny's faith and his love for me, and how good he was to me, and how good he was to them. He also had a sense of humor that kept them entertained. Even though Daddy took Johnny aside several times in the days leading up to the wedding and talked to him about the seriousness of getting married and taking care of his little girl, Mother and Daddy just loved Johnny. He had secured their complete and wholehearted approval.

Back home in San Antonio, I stayed busy organizing the wedding, planning the reception, designing my wedding dress, and getting ready for my new life with Johnny. My aunt hosted a huge bridal shower for me at her house. All my girlfriends and relatives were there. And the girls at the insurance office hosted a shower as well. We received lots of wonderful gifts, including some rather funny ones too, such as an enormous case of Kraft macaroni and cheese, which Johnny and I both loved.

In the meantime, Johnny headed to Memphis, where he had decided we would settle, to find us a place to live. With the money we had saved, he bought a car from his brother Roy, who worked for the Chrysler Corporation: a shiny, brand-new green 1954 Plymouth four-door sedan. He also secured a job for himself selling appliances for the Home Equipment Store, and he found us a little sixty-five-dollar-a-month apartment on the west side of town.

Almost exactly one month after Johnny got back home, our wedding day arrived. On August 7, 1954, we were married in a beautiful afternoon ceremony presided over by my uncle, Father Vincent Liberto, in St. Anne's Catholic Church in San Antonio. The day was everything we hoped it would be: simple, elegant, family-oriented. And true to Johnny's only demand, the reception was alcohol-free.

People always talk about being nervous and scared on their wedding day. But I was not one bit nervous about marrying Johnny. I never had a single doubt, wasn't nervous at all. I knew it was the right thing to do.

So as Johnny stood tall and proud in his air force dress uniform, handsome as always, we vowed to always love each other and to be faithful until the day we died. Finally I was Mrs. Johnny Cash!

~

"Mom, where do babies come from?"

I remember asking my mother that question one evening while washing dinner dishes in our kitchen. I was a senior in high school at the time, and my sheltered upbringing had left some curious gaps in my education.

"God plants a seed in your heart and you have a baby," Mother answered, clearly uncomfortable with the direction of my questioning. Such topics were not easily discussed in our family.

It's no wonder I was naïve about many things at my age. I later learned on my own that it took a man and a woman to make a baby. I remember calling one of my girlfriends in disbelief: "I don't believe that!"

And so the extent of my knowledge about what was to happen on our wedding night was limited. I knew we would go to bed and make love, but beyond that I didn't know what to expect or how it all would happen. After our wedding ceremony, with $500 in cash and the car loaded down with wedding gifts and suitcases, Johnny pointed the car north toward Memphis and we set out on our new life together.

As we drove, I laid my head down in Johnny's lap, scared to death I was going to touch him in a private place. I had to consciously remind myself,

This is my husband . . . it's okay to touch him. That's how much of a prude I was. But he was too. We both were.

About halfway to Memphis, at a hotel where Johnny had made reservations, we spent our first night together. He carried me across the threshold to our room and I learned about all those things I had never understood before.

I went to sleep that night staring at Johnny as he slept soundly beside me. He looked so peaceful and serene. Never before had I felt so protected and safe. I was right where I was supposed to be. It all felt so natural, like it was meant to be, even the long wait.

We had learned so much about each other through our letters. Probably more than most people do in a lifetime being together, and there was such intimacy. Both of us, daily, pouring out our hearts and telling everything we did and how we felt and who we were. We had revealed everything about ourselves to each other. So I never had a doubt. After three years it was just like we picked up at the day he left.

I guess you could say I'm a believer in fate. How else could we have predicted that our romance would have lasted three long years of separation and that we would marry? And how could the series of events that were about to unfold during our first months of marriage in Memphis be explained? It certainly couldn't all have happened by chance.

When Johnny and I rolled into Memphis later that following morning, Elvis Presley was the biggest thing happening musically in Memphis. "That's All Right Mama," his first single, was playing on every radio station in town. The buzz was this: Elvis was about to become a huge nationwide star. Never in our wildest dreams did we imagine that in less than a year Johnny would be singing on the radio right alongside him. Or that Elvis would become a close friend of ours. Still yet, that Johnny would have his own following of fans.

Being one of those artists like Elvis, making songs you hear on the radio, was something completely out of reach—or so we thought. The closest Johnny felt he could ever hope to get to a music career was as a disc jockey. But instead Johnny was set to start a new career selling appliances door-to-door, just as soon as we settled into our apartment.

When we arrived in Memphis, I still hadn't seen the apartment. So when we pulled up to 1624 East Moreland, I got my first peek at our new home. Johnny carried me from the car, over the threshold, into the apartment, and set me down to explore. I felt like a kid playing house, running room to room. I was thrilled. We had a place of our very own!

It wasn't a palace by any means, but it was absolutely perfect in my eyes: modest and simple, but with big spacious rooms and hardwood floors, and furnished. (Thank goodness, because Johnny and I had nothing in that way.) It was oddly laid out, as most apartments chop-blocked in old houses are. You had to climb a flight of stairs to get to the front door, which led to the bedroom, bathroom, and guest room. Another flight of stairs led to the living room and kitchen, which to my surprise was huge. As I opened and closed the cupboards, looking around, I imagined all the wonderful home-cooked meals I would be preparing for Johnny.

It was in a horrible neighborhood, and we couldn't afford a telephone, but it was home—our home. Honestly, if it had been a tent I would have been happy. Or if Johnny had wanted us to move to tiny Dyess and live with no running water and just a wood stove like where he grew up, I would have done so happily.

I felt like a princess. And Johnny was treating me as every bit the princess I felt. He doted on me constantly, and was tender and romantic every minute of the day. He was all over me every chance he could, "making up for lost time," he said, and I indulged him shamelessly. Everything was "Baby" this and "Honey" that. In fact, from that point on, we never called each other by our actual names. That never changed. Our children would later be surprised to learn that Honey and Baby Cash weren't our real names.

That first night after we unpacked our clothes and dishes and gifts, we laid in bed, covered head to toe in mentholatum to keep from being eaten alive by the mosquitoes coming in through the torn window screens. We didn't know what the future held for us, but we knew we were in God's hands.

I fell asleep thinking that the only thing I wanted to do with my life was marry Johnny and have kids. And I was on my way!

~

It didn't take Johnny long to figure out one thing. People don't much like door-to-door salesmen. His job selling appliances on commission for the Home Equipment Store was one he took pride in, but one he soon hated.

More times than not he would return home at the end of the day despondent. "I didn't sell a thing," he'd say as he came in the door, discouraged. Nine hours of knocking on doors, and nothing to show for it.

But Johnny had a wonderful sense of humor about it. He made light of his frustration, imitating the people he'd call on in his best high-pitched old-lady voice. "No, Sir, Mr. Cash, I shore can't afford no refrigerator," or, "Sure, come on in, Mr. Cash, I need a new refrigerator!" And they'd try to buy one but they couldn't.

They didn't have any money, any more than we did. As soon as their credit was checked, their applications were promptly denied. Only problem was, we never found that out until after Johnny had been paid for the sale. So we had to return a lot of the money that he earned on occasional good days. My heart ached seeing Johnny working so hard and coming home empty-handed for his efforts. Financially speaking, we were quickly moving backward, not forward.

Mr. Bates, who owned the Home Equipment Store, was a good-hearted man. He loaned us money to get by. And Daddy did too. If it weren't for the both of them and that case of Kraft mac and cheese, I don't know how we would have eaten. We were rich in love, but dirt poor. We woke up every day never knowing where our next dollar would come from. We just struggled together, blissfully unconcerned about the future.

It was about that time that Johnny's brother Roy introduced Johnny to two mechanics who worked with him at Chrysler, Marshall Grant and Luther Perkins. Johnny, Marshall, and Luther hit it off from the start, and realized they shared a common passion for hillbilly music. They liked each other's company and liked what they heard when they played music together. Although none of them were skilled musicians by any stretch, they vowed to meet regularly and rehearse. They practiced in Marshall's garage while we wives played cards in the kitchen. After a while the three of them began to sound really good. At least I thought so.

With Johnny on guitar and lead vocals, Marshall on bass, and Luther on guitar, they had a sound of their very own. One night Luther was trying to get a lick right and stumbled upon a unique sound. "That's it!" Johnny yelled. And that was the birth of their signature "boom chicka-boom" sound. Johnny loved that sound, and so they kept it.

When the three of them weren't working at their respective day jobs— Johnny selling appliances and Marshall and Luther up to their elbows in oil and grease—the three of them spent every spare minute rehearsing their music, and became increasingly serious about it.

Johnny was in heaven when he was practicing. He began writing lyrics incessantly. Driving around in the car, Johnny would think up lines and lyrics and have me jot them down on pieces of scratch paper, or on paper napkins in coffee shops, or anything that was available. He would accumulate piles of scraps of paper, with lines written on them, and then put them together in a song. He knew nothing about musical notation, so he simply wrote out the lyrics and then put a tune to them by strumming around on the guitar. Sometimes you couldn't reach him because he was off in his own world dreaming up songs and melodies. If the lyrics didn't fit the tune, he would keep working at it until the two finally came together. It was a very unorthodox way of writing songs, but it always worked.

Johnny's ambitions to become a disc jockey quickly faded. Instead he now wanted a shot at making his own music on the radio and writing his own songs. Pounding on doors selling washing machines was not his life, and we both knew it. As unlikely as it may have seemed, we knew Johnny had to give music a shot.

"You can do anything you want to do, baby," I kept telling him. "You can do it." I was excited for him. Where a music career would take us, if anywhere, I didn't know. But I believed in him. And he did too.

Sam Phillips was the owner and producer at Sun Records, where Elvis had recorded his hit songs. So Johnny set out to get his foot in the door there. He became determined to meet Sam. Johnny was bold enough to think he might be able to get a record deal if only Sam would just listen to him.

I don't know how many people Sam Phillips had pounding on his door. I am sure it ran in the hundreds, but Johnny was relentless. Maybe the hundreds of doors Johnny had pounded on selling appliances were God's little way of preparing him for what it would take to get Sam's attention.

~

Two months after our wedding, I woke up with sore breasts and was petrified, scared to death about what horrible ailment had befallen me. I made a beeline for the doctor's office.

Of course nothing was wrong. I was pregnant. And Johnny and I were thrilled! We had no idea how we would ever pay the hospital bill to get the baby home, but we were overjoyed. Again, blissfully unconcerned, knowing God would provide and answer our prayers as He always did.

Unlike Johnny's mother, though, who was tough as nails when it came to having babies (I swear she would go work in the cotton fields, come in, have a baby, and go right back out again), I wasn't made of tough country farm stock. I was soon struck down with morning sickness—in my case, morning, noon, night, anytime sickness. All I could do was lie in bed and throw up. I lost nearly fifteen pounds within a few weeks, couldn't keep a thing down, and I was growing weaker by the day. I was a pitiful sight.

Johnny was the perfect loving husband, though. He didn't want me out of his sight. He moved us to an apartment closer to his work, on Tutwiler Avenue, so he could check on me throughout the day. Ever the optimist, he would come home after work and take me for rides in the car, hoping that a dose of fresh air would do me good. I think I threw up on every street corner in Memphis.

As I think back to that time, it occurs to me how many people talk of the ups and downs of a newlywed couple's first year. But we never had any downs except for money, and even that never caused any friction between us. We just toughed it out together.

Sometimes I'd hide a dollar here and a dollar there in the vase on the mantel, trying to save up a little money. He'd find my hiding spot and buy himself a pack of cigarettes. I didn't even get mad at him. And he never got mad at me. We were just two perfect lovebirds. We saw eye-to-eye on everything, agreed on everything—or I should say, *I* agreed on everything.

Our fortunes changed the day that Johnny auditioned with Sam Phillips. That one hour would change everything. Johnny was excited and nervous as he, Marshall, and Luther left for Sun Records. I stayed home, five months pregnant, pacing the floor, wringing my hands, and hoping for the best but preparing to console Johnny if the worst came to pass.

I'll never forget Johnny's excitement when he got home. I had been pacing nervously on the front porch, waiting, when I saw him running down the street toward our house. I was puzzled as to why he was running, but as he got closer, he had a huge smile on his face. "Baby, we're cuttin' a record!" he said as he hugged me and kissed me all over my face. I screamed in disbelief. He couldn't be serious. We both started laughing hysterically. I'm sure the neighbors thought we'd lost it.

"As soon as I write another song, we're cuttin' a record!" Johnny explained. With that his attention shifted, and he walked straight into the living room, sat down on the couch, and began writing as I watched. In just fifteen minutes, he wrote "Cry, Cry, Cry." He just scratched it out on a piece of paper in no time flat.

A few days later Johnny played the new song for Sam, and Sam loved it, as I knew he would. It had simple lyrics but was very catchy. They recorded it on the spot. And at that moment Johnny Cash and the Tennessee Two became Sun Records' newest artists.

Johnny rushed straight home with the good news. He leaped onto the front porch, picked me up, hugged my big pregnant tummy, and screamed at the top of his lungs, "We did it! We cut a record!"

"Lordy, lordy, what a feeling . . . honey, send me to the ceiling!" My mother used to say that whenever there was really fantastic news. Johnny had done it! I don't want to say I didn't believe it, because Johnny sounded really good, but I was so surprised. Things like that just didn't happen to regular people like me and Johnny. What started out as an optimistic pinkie swear and kiss to blindly follow a dream was becoming a dream come true.

We wanted to celebrate but we didn't have a dime. We didn't even have a phone to call anyone with the good news. Instead, Johnny went out later that afternoon and tried to make a couple of sales to bring in a few dollars. After all, we had a baby coming.

Before he left, I remember Johnny asking me, "Honey, you know if this hits, I'm gonna be traveling. How do you feel about that?"

"That's okay, baby," I answered. I imagined him going to Arkansas, Mississippi, here and there, maybe within a hundred-mile radius. Never in my wildest dreams did I think he'd be touring all over the world. Neither did he, actually. It was inconceivable to both of us.

Certainly neither of us realized the magnitude of changes that were about to come into our lives. Or imagined that in fifty years, Johnny would go down in history books as one of the most influential performers of all time. But it didn't take long for things to play out differently from what we expected.

~

A few weeks before my due date, Johnny and I learned from my doctor that we were having twins. Then later we learned we weren't having twins. The additional heartbeat detected earlier was simply mine. All the same, on May 24, 1955, at my final checkup, one day before my due date, when the doctor examined me and said, "Pack your clothes, get to the hospital, this baby's coming now," Johnny and I were thrilled to meet however many little babies we had to greet.

Our first baby girl, Rosanne, was born four hours after we arrived at the hospital, and she was the most beautiful baby girl Johnny and I had ever seen. She had no middle name. Johnny never wanted to give people the option of calling our children by their middle names. Our baby would be called simply Rosanne—a combination of Rose and Ann, the two names Johnny had playfully given my breasts.

Rosanne was the cutest little thing. She had a big curl right in the middle of her forehead, and layers of dark beautiful hair. Johnny and I were thrilled to death. Johnny was the father he longed to be, and I was finally a mother. We were one child closer to the eight that we wanted.

On the music front, it was only weeks after Rosanne was born that "Cry, Cry, Cry" was released. Miraculously, it was an instant hit. In the car, you could hardly turn the radio on and not hear it within ten minutes:

Here's a new artist from Sun Records. He hails from the cotton fields of Arkansas, but calls Memphis home now. And from the looks of it, he's giving Elvis a run for his money. Here's Johnny Cash and the Tennessee Two with "Cry, Cry, Cry."

The single shot to number one on the charts in Memphis in a matter of days. It was such an exciting time, let me tell you. To hear somebody you knew on the radio—let alone your husband—was a thrill. And Johnny could hardly believe his ears. That first taste of success fueled his desire to practice and rehearse constantly with Marshall and Luther. His confidence soared. Every other night we gathered at Marshall's house so they could rehearse in the garage while we wives gathered in the kitchen.

Meanwhile, Marshall's wife, Etta, became my best friend. She was funny and sweet. She had long, black, naturally curly hair, and I admired how perfect she looked at all times. I also marveled at what a meticulous housekeeper she was. She ironed Marshall's socks, his undershirts, his shorts, everything he put on his body. She ironed the towels, everything. Her house, her family, the way she dressed, her hair—everything was absolutely perfect all the time. On the other hand, I was trying to master making the domestic appear perfect and ordered like her. Johnny and I tried, but we had our own style.

Johnny changed diapers. That never bothered him, but he wasn't gentle at it. He'd just lay Rosanne down, throw her little legs up, and brute-force change her diaper. Our family still refers to it as "Johnnying it" when you're rough-like with anything or doing something haphazardly. (He never knew we said that, but he'd probably have gotten a kick out it.)

Another time, when Rosanne was just a month old—just a tiny little thing—Johnny and I went to eat at a restaurant and were sitting in a booth. I had Rosanne lying beside me, holding her with my hand, but she rolled right off the seat onto the restaurant floor—right onto the dirty floor.

Johnny absolutely freaked. I can still see him, arms flailing, trying to get out of the booth fast to get under the table to save her. Those long legs of his thrashing about in all directions as he tried to crawl under the table. Johnny just went bananas, and I was there in the middle of the booth and couldn't get out. I'm certain everybody around us thought, "This poor little brand-new baby, and just look at those parents." We were not the calm, collected Cash family. Take it from me, Johnny was not good in a crisis.

Onstage, however, he was always calm and collected. Even at his first public appearance opening for Elvis, when the worst thing I could ever imagine happened. The night was August 5, 1955, at the Overton Park Shell in Memphis, an outdoor amphitheater just minutes from our house. I was nervously sitting stage left. I wanted Johnny to do great. He saw me from the stage and winked.

Then, just as Johnny was about to sing, the stage spotlight went dark and the sound system went dead. He just stood there in the dark, and my heart sank. I thought, "My God, what is he going to do?" What *can* you do in that situation? There was an uncomfortable hush in the amphitheater.

"Does anybody have a deck of cards?" Johnny asked the audience, joking. That was just the icebreaker needed. Everybody laughed and relaxed, and he did too. He was always a quick thinker like that. Despite his inexperience, he handled the situation like a pro. The microphone was fixed within a few minutes and the show went on. But I still admire that way he handled that. If it had been me up there, I would have frozen.

Two days after that first performance, we celebrated our first wedding anniversary. Within a year's time, we had been blessed with a beautiful baby girl, and Johnny was having musical success beyond our wildest dreams. Even better, we had just found out we were expecting again.

~

"Baby, are you ever tempted by those women at your shows?" I asked. It was breakfast and Johnny was reading a newspaper. It wasn't a question that stemmed from jealousy so much as my curiosity.

Ever since "Cry, Cry, Cry" was released, Johnny had a growing schedule of outdoor flatbed truck performances in the area with other Sun artists—Elvis and Carl Perkins mostly. I had never seen such wild women in my life. Everywhere Johnny went, it was the same: girls screaming, clamoring, carrying on, and hugging him.

"What women, honey?" he answered, continuing to read the paper.

"You know, the ones that scream . . . and proposition you."

Johnny was quickly developing a huge following of fans, including women of the throw-themselves-all-over-my-husband-with-me-standing-right-there ilk. I was intimidated by their boldness, and they were bold, let me tell you. I was never that outgoing and confident.

"No, baby," he answered tenderly, putting his paper down. "Honey, I am never tempted . . . and do you know why?"

He went on to explain. "When those women come up to me, I think of them as mannequins. I look at 'em like they're mannequins. Just phony, plastic mannequins," he said. "You don't ever need to worry, baby. You're on my mind every minute, day and night. I walk the line for you." He turned those words into the biggest song of his entire career.

I remember him writing "I Walk the Line," asking me to scribble down lyrics while driving in the car. Every time I heard Johnny sing that song—no matter how many thousands of times I heard it, no matter how many hundreds of people were next to me—I always knew he sang every word for me. They were the exact words he told me often.

> I keep a close watch on this heart of mine
> I keep my eyes wide open all the time
> I keep the ends out for the tie that binds
> Because you're mine, I walk the line

That deep, incredible voice of his was so sexy. And every time I'd watch him perform it or hear it on the radio, I felt so proud. I listened to each and every word carefully each time, and I believed them.

> I find it very, very easy to be true
> I find myself alone when each day is through
> Yes, I'll admit that I'm a fool for you
> Because you're mine, I walk the line

As sure as night is dark and day is light
I keep you on my mind both day and night
And happiness I've known proves that it's right
Because you're mine, I walk the line

I found it very easy to love Johnny. He was a wonderful man. He was my gentle, loving, protective husband, and I knew he loved me.

And so even though I felt compelled to periodically ask about those crazy women who threw themselves at him, I knew I didn't need to worry. Johnny was true.

~

Elvis was leading the pack of Sun artists, I guess you could say. He was the first to get his career going and was having the biggest success. Johnny followed closely behind him. And Carl Perkins, Jerry Lee Lewis, and Roy Orbison all came within a short time too. Johnny and I knew all of them well because they all worked together often. We came to know Carl Perkins and Elvis the best. Johnny and I especially liked Elvis. He was an all-around great guy and became a very close friend.

Jerry Lee was the wild one of the bunch. He drank a lot and tore up pianos when he played. He'd bang on pianos like he had every intention of tearing them up. He'd stand on them, bang on them, play them with his feet. It's a wonder any piano he played ever survived. He was crazy, but a lot of fun.

So those were the original Sun Records artists in the beginning: Elvis, Johnny, Carl, Jerry Lee, and Roy. We were a close-knit family. As time went on and success came to each, everybody went his own direction and headlined his own tours. That time came quickly for Johnny.

We were fortunate that Johnny's brother Roy and his wife, Dean, lived close by in Memphis. They offered to help watch Rosanne often, so I could accompany Johnny on the road. In those days I went everywhere with Johnny. We traveled through the night from town to town—with Marshall and Luther in tow, of course—and Johnny performed for audiences across the country.

I sewed all of Johnny's stage clothes back then. Luther and Marshall wore black shirts and pants, and Johnny wore a white suit, not black. It was a cross between a tuxedo and a suit. I bought silver trim and sewed it by hand down the lapels, down the sleeves, and down the sides of his pants. He looked great.

As we passed through each city, Johnny did interviews at every radio station along the way. I would wait and listen in the car when he went in. I found it fascinating to sit in the car outside, knowing that Johnny was right inside, his voice beamed live to tens of thousands of radio listeners.

One night Johnny came back out to the car after an interview and told me the disc jockey offered him a cup of coffee inside. There was a cup on the disc jockey's desk that had been used, and Johnny picked it up. The DJ said, "Wait, man, let me get you a clean cup! I don't know who drank out of that."

"He was a human, wasn't he?" Johnny answered, and he used the cup.

Apparently that made quite an impression on that disc jockey. Word spread that Johnny was an everyman's man. And it did say a lot about Johnny's character. He never felt above anybody else. He didn't have an ego. People everywhere just couldn't help but like him.

I was never able to enjoy the kind of instant intimacy with people that Johnny did. I was timid and shy and always felt a little out of place. I felt awkward meeting famous people. I don't know why, because I met a lot of famous magicians with Daddy growing up.

At shows I would sit in the back of the stage by myself, in a little corner, and hardly speak to anybody. I know some people thought I was snobbish, but I wasn't snobbish. That's the last thing I would ever be. I was too afraid to even speak with anyone. And Johnny understood that. He knew I was shy and would never walk up to people and start talking to them, calling attention to myself. He said he loved that about me, and he never tried to change me. I was the shy daughter of an insurance salesman from San Antonio, and my life's ambition was to be a wife and mother. I was never comfortable in the spotlight.

Sometimes, though, Johnny would insist on bringing me onstage and introducing me to the audience. He'd drag me out, let everyone take a good look at me, and have me take a bow. Every time I would tremble head to toe. Once, while I was standing onstage, I dropped a program I had in my hand. I was wearing a skirt—nothing revealing, just proper and conservative. When I bent over to pick it up, everybody in the audience started whistling and clapping. I wanted to die. Johnny egged them on with a wink and a smile—"She's cute, isn't she?"—knowing full well I was embarrassed beyond words. He was very proud of me and loved to show me off, but I never grew comfortable with the attention.

Within our little group that toured together, though, I did feel right at home. There was always fun and silliness on the road, and I was right in there with them having a great time, throwing water balloons out of hotel windows, running up and down the halls, visiting all the other rooms, what have you. Once, someone in our group put a bobcat in a bag and handed it to somebody to open. It was dangerous but very funny. Another time, Johnny had five hundred baby chicks delivered to an associate "just for the hell of it." His imagination for having fun on the road was immature, but good for lots of laughs.

With each passing week, Johnny was succeeding in carving out a place for himself in the music world. He was gaining fans by the thousands, radio was playing his music, and his records were selling briskly. That's when the royalty checks started to come in.

The first one was about two thousand dollars—a fortune when you're borrowing just to survive. I can't tell you how exciting it was to finally have money. Never again would we have to rely on the kindness of Daddy or Mr. Bates or friends and family to feed us, we thought. Just to have money to pay the rent and bills was wonderful. "Does this mean we can't shop at Sears anymore?" Johnny joked. We couldn't believe our good fortune.

The first thing we did was drive to San Antonio and pay Daddy back for every check he had ever written to us—close to eight hundred dollars. We also gave Mother and Daddy our green '54 Plymouth and bought a brand-new Cadillac. Then we returned to Memphis, repaid Mr. Bates all the money we had borrowed, and Johnny quit his job to go on the road. We trusted there was no turning back.

To this day I remember Johnny leaving on that first long tour without me. I had to stay behind to take care of Rosanne. It was one o'clock in the morning, and Luther and Marshall had loaded all of their instruments into our car. Johnny checked all the windows and doors around the house, then hung at the door saying good-bye.

"I gotta go, baby," he said. "I love you. I'll check in on you." He didn't want to leave. And I didn't want him to go. We had just moved into a new house, and I didn't know anyone in the new neighborhood. He was taking our only car, and I had a brand-new little baby and was pregnant with another. He left with me crying at the door holding Rosanne, and I know it just killed him.

This would be the one downside to our new life. Gradually the tours got longer and I had to stay behind. Foreshadowing a pattern that I should have begun to see at that point, I simply waited.

~

In the spring of 1956, "I Walk the Line"—my favorite of all of Johnny's songs—was released and quickly rose to number one on the charts, selling over a million copies. We felt like we'd struck gold.

At twenty-four years old, Johnny was providing for us beyond our wildest expectations. His royalty checks were several thousand dollars now, and we made our first big purchase, a house of our own at 4492 Sandy Cove Circle in Memphis. Also, on April 16, we welcomed our second beautiful baby girl, Kathy, into our growing family.

A homemade sign in the front yard as we arrived home from the hospital read: INSTRUCTIONS HERE ON HOW TO HAVE A BOY—a little Cash humor courtesy of Johnny's brother Roy. Johnny had boys' names picked out for every one of our children, but he never admitted to hoping for anything other than a healthy, bouncing baby girl. Meanwhile I was too busy juggling two babies— a ten-month-old and a newborn—and Johnny's increasing tour schedule to take much notice either way.

Johnny signed with Bob Neal, Elvis's manager at the time, who promised to kick Johnny's career into high gear, and he did just that. The coming months were a blur of special appearances and career milestones: Johnny's first appearance on the *Grand Ole Opry*, *The Ed Sullivan Show*, *The Jackie Gleason Show*, the *Louisiana Hayride*, and Carnegie Hall. And Johnny wanted me with him everywhere, and I wanted to be with him too, so as much as possible I juggled babies and suitcases and did whatever it took.

In no time Johnny was the third-best-selling country music artist in the country, and we moved up again, to a bigger, more beautiful new home at 5676 Walnut Grove. I was thrilled with the new house and took pride in my role of supporting Johnny from the wings, making a happy home for him to return to. By the end of '57 we were expecting our third child. The rate of change was dizzying at times.

Johnny moved up in managers too. He met Stu Carnall, a manager in Los Angeles who had booked a few of his shows. The day they met, they immediately hit it off, and Stu became Johnny's new full-time manager. Stu was a tenacious, never-take-no-for-an-answer kind of guy, and he had one simple goal: Make Johnny a household name. And within a few short weeks, Stu convinced Johnny to move us out to California, closer to where he lived.

At the time, I simply agreed with whatever Johnny wanted to do. I can't say I had much of a mind of my own. When we married, he said, "We're moving to Memphis." I said, "Okay." Now he said "We're moving to California," I said, "Okay, honey," and we moved. I was the perfect anything-you-want-dear kind of wife and knew my place.

So four weeks after our third daughter, Cindy, was born on July 29, 1958, we packed our belongings and boarded a plane for sunny California. Columbia Records, a major record label in California, had aggressively pursued Johnny and offered him a fifty-thousand-dollar signing bonus—a whale of a deal back then. So Johnny took the deal and we left tiny Sun Records and Memphis behind.

Just a few years earlier, we had been pinching pennies back on Tutwiler Avenue, not knowing where our next meal would come from. Now we were flush with more cash than we knew what to do with, shopping for a home in the same neighborhood as stars like Clark Gable and John Wayne. And we found the perfect home, a house on Havenhurst Avenue in Encino that we bought from Johnny Carson.

The house was beautiful and spacious. It had a large pool in the backyard, four bedrooms, a huge kitchen, a fantastic living room, separate maid's quarters, and an office.

I still smile when I think of the girls' reaction upon seeing one of the back bedrooms that they would share. It was a huge room that Johnny Carson's three boys had used, and it had a mural on one wall with a large monster, his teeth exposed. Rosanne and Kathy were scared to death at first. They swore he was growling at us, not smiling as their dad and I insisted. But after a while they grew used to him.

We loved our new surroundings and the new lifestyle that Johnny's success afforded us. Johnny took me on lavish shopping trips in Los Angeles and New York City, where I was now buying $350 dresses with spun gold thread—astronomically expensive, I thought. But Johnny loved to pick out extravagant clothes and jewelry for me. We'd go into a store and he would never once ask for a price. He'd just say, "I want this, this, and this for her. How much do I owe you?" That's how we shopped. Price was never an issue.

But Johnny still remained a simple Arkansas farm boy at heart. There in the front yard of our fancy new house, he planted rows of cotton from cottonseed he brought home from Dyess. We'd watch his little plants struggle to grow, and he would nurse them along. It was really quite pitiful, but very sweet. Johnny hated picking cotton and working in the fields when he was growing up, but he didn't want to let go of those roots for anything.

We also acquired a houseful of animals while living on Havenhurst. Stu gave us an Irish setter named Penny. And someone else gave us a parrot named Jethro and a monkey named Homer (both named after Homer and Jethro from the *Grand Ole Opry*). I loved that monkey best. He was so much fun. We would walk down the street with him, holding his hand just like a little person. And we'd pull him around in a wagon. He played with the girls and entertained friends who visited. He ran around the house and sat in the kitchen while I worked. And I swear, Homer had Johnny's personality. He was funny and smart, but that little monkey had a mind of his own.

Jethro, the parrot, sang songs and had a huge vocabulary of words and phrases he'd hear us use. When the phone rang, he'd scream, "Answer the phone!" He'd cry just like Cindy, cough just like Johnny, and when there was a knock on the door, he'd yell, "Shit—come in!"

So ours was a busy, bustling household. And with the powerhouse of Columbia Records marketing Johnny's music now, Johnny was increasingly away on tour. He was playing bigger venues now, for larger audiences, and playing internationally as well. From all corners of the globe he would send letters and postcards while on tour. And he would call every day.

The girls and I were always excited when Johnny came home off the road. We'd count down the days on the calendar until he returned: "Daddy will be home in four days," then three days, then two days. When he'd burst through the door, the girls would pile into his arms.

And he never came home empty-handed. He always brought surprises home for the girls that he picked up along the way. From every country he visited overseas, he'd bring them a doll. Soon they had a wonderful collection of dolls from every part of the world.

For me, Johnny would bring beautiful clothes and jewelry. Or he would arrange for surprise gifts to arrive while he was away. Like the time on my birthday he bought me a pink—"titty pink," as he called it—El Dorado Cadillac. The doorbell rang, I opened the door, and there stood a man from the dealership, smiling and holding the keys out to me. Johnny was so good at picking out gifts. Everything he bought I absolutely loved.

Johnny also became a featured performer on *Town Hall Party*, a popular weekly television show that was broadcast from Los Angeles. And he made musical appearances on various television shows and had a few small roles on western shows like *Wagon Train*.

It was also about this time that Johnny gave his first free performance at a prison, something he later became well known for. Stu arranged a performance at Folsom Prison that was to be recorded for a record, and Johnny insisted I go with him. He thought it would be a new and interesting experience for both of us, and it was.

I remember walking in through the entrance, nervous and full of anticipation. And Johnny was nervous too. We didn't know what to expect. Guards walked us down a long hallway into the compound, where we were frisked and patted down before entering another building. Some of the inmates we passed were really scary-looking, and Johnny was very protective. He kept his arm tight around my shoulders, and when it was time to take the stage, he made sure that the guards looked after me while he performed.

"Hello, I'm Johnny Cash," he said, as he took the microphone.

It was the first time Johnny had used that introduction, and it worked in firing up the crowd of inmates. They all went absolutely wild and loved the show and loved Johnny. I'm sure they didn't get much live entertainment like that often.

One thing that struck me most about that Folsom Prison performance was how everyone—inmates and guards alike—was very respectful and appreciative of the show. So it was quite an experience for all of us. After that, San Quentin and other prisons became regular performance stops.

And Johnny also started acting in movies. He hadn't planned to do films, nor did he really want to, but movie producers approached him and extended the invitation. Again, it was another new adventure for the both of us. We found the world of moviemaking fascinating.

When we arrived to the set of his first movie, *Five Minutes to Live,* a woman producer or director of sorts stopped us at the door. "I'm sorry, she can't come," she said to Johnny, motioning to me. "Guests aren't welcome."

Johnny just stopped and looked her straight in the eye and said, "Well, I'm sorry. If she doesn't go, I don't go." And he meant it. He wasn't going on set without me. So they let me stay. He was adamant about us staying together at all times.

Johnny really did make me feel like a princess—like the most important woman in the entire world. He always wanted me to be with him, to go with him everywhere. And I didn't want to be anywhere else but by his side. We were several years into our marriage, and we still felt and acted like newlyweds.

In 1959, Johnny insisted we get away together and take a long romantic trip to Europe—the honeymoon we never had. We visited seven countries in all, including Ireland and Spain (which we loved!) and Germany too.

In Landsberg, several of Johnny's old friends welcomed him back with open arms, and they seemed so excited to see me too. "Vivian! *This* is the Vivian we heard so much about!" they all said. It was exciting and fun to finally meet them and see where Johnny had spent so much time during our courtship.

It was also thrilling to hear Johnny's music playing on the radio all the way over in Europe, where just a few years earlier Johnny and I had been so frustrated, wondering if God had anything good and promising in store for us. We trusted God back then, not knowing what was to come. It was fun to look back and see how things had played out.

Johnny showed me the barracks where he had lived and the office where he had worked. This time, though, he was a VIP of sorts, walking through the place, signing autographs as we went. We also saw what was to have been our apartment if Daddy had only allowed me to go there, and laughed at our disappointment back then. We also went fishing at Johnny's favorite fishing spots, and he showed me the store where he bought his guitar, as well as other stores he frequented, and we went back to the jewelry store in Munich where Johnny had picked out my engagement ring.

Johnny insisted on buying me another diamond on that trip, and, with his encouragement, I smuggled it into the U.S. tucked inside my bra. I'd never done anything like that in my life. I was a nervous wreck. I wrapped it up in a little piece of fabric, tucked it under my breast, and got on the plane, sweating the whole time. Johnny was tickled silly, but I would have died if anybody had stopped me.

Looking back at those early years in California brings back so many happy memories. But the move to Los Angeles did mark a subtle, almost imperceptible, change in Johnny. He began spending more and more time with Stu Carnall, who, while a fantastic manager and a nice enough guy in most every respect, loved the fast California lifestyle. Stu enjoyed late-night partying, playing the horses, and drinking. And Johnny slowly began to enjoy those very same things.

All of the things that Johnny had called "filthy and dirty" and had insisted would destroy our lives were things he began to embrace. That's when I began to sense a dangerous current running just beneath the exciting new life we were living.

I longed for the simpler days we enjoyed back in Memphis, before all the trappings of money and fame, when we promised to never compromise. Away from Los Angeles, away from the lifestyle I began to fear might pull Johnny under.

~

It was five o'clock in the morning on November 5, 1960, when the phone rang in our hotel room and I answered.

"Johnny Horton was just killed head-on by a drunk driver. He's dead," said the voice on the other end.

Johnny and I were in Nashville for the annual radio convention and were sleeping off the parties of the night before. Johnny woke briefly when the phone rang, then fell back asleep. I sat there and received the horrible news while I watched him sleep peacefully. When I hung up the phone, I contemplated how in the world I was going to break this news to him. He would be devastated.

Horton had been Johnny's best friend since his earliest days on the *Louisiana Hayride*. He and his wife, Billie, were the closest of friends to us both. The four of us took trips together, we met up on the road while touring, we visited them at their home in Shreveport, Louisiana, and they visited ours in California. We saw them often and everywhere. We always knew, God willing, we'd see each other again in a few short weeks.

But now I was faced with telling Johnny that his best friend was dead. Just then there was a loud knock on our room door. Dewey Phillips, a disc jockey, burst in.

"Hey man, did you hear Johnny Horton died?" he yelled, waking Johnny out of his sound sleep. "He got killed by a drunk driver, man! He's dead!"

I hung my head, stunned by Dewey's lack of sensitivity.

Johnny sat up in bed, put his head in his hands, and let out the most agonizing moan I've ever heard: *"Noooooooooo!... Nooooo!"*

My heart just broke—for Johnny's pain, for Horton, and for Billie too. She had already been widowed once when her first husband, Hank Williams, died. And now again.

"He died with a smile on his face, Johnny, it's the truth. If you want me to prove it, let me call my wife," Dewey said as he reached for the phone. He would not let up. It was a crushing moment made worse.

Without a doubt, Johnny Horton's death had a profound impact on Johnny, and on me too. It hit us both hard. For the first time as adults, we realized how fragile this life is and how much we took for granted. It could have been one of us in that car accident.

Up until then we had always been so carefree and foolish, never afraid of anything. We used to take little two-seater and four-seater flights from show to show. You couldn't pay me to get on one today. One time the pilot said to us, "Okay, guys, my radio's dead. Look out the windows and make sure no planes are coming." Even that didn't worry us. There we were, looking out the window, making sure another plane didn't run into us, oblivious to the danger.

Johnny Horton's accident was a sobering dose of reality. And his death brought back all the horror for Johnny of losing his brother Jack, all those years ago when Johnny was only twelve. After Jack fell on top of the table saw, it was his last words that affected Johnny more than anything else.

"Mama, do you hear the angels?" Jack whispered. "The beautiful angels singing?" Then Jack looked straight at Johnny's dad and said, "Daddy, God's taking me so you'll quit drinking."

Can you imagine a more powerful thing to say to your father on your deathbed? After Jack died, Johnny's dad quit drinking forever, became deeply religious, and that's when Johnny grew really close to God. Those final words affected both of them deeply.

Just a week before Johnny Horton's accident, I had answered the phone at home in the kitchen, and it was Horton. "Tell Johnny to call me, will you?" he said. We chatted for a minute more and then hung up.

I gave Johnny the message, but at the time he was busy with this or that, and never called Horton back. And now it was too late. For a long time Johnny anguished, wondering what Horton had needed, or what reason he had for calling. He tortured himself for not returning that call.

One week after the accident, Johnny and I went to Shreveport to be with Billie. She and I visited the hospital where Horton's bandmates—the ones who had been in the car the night of the accident—were recovering. One by one we visited each room, and with unbelievable composure and grace, Billie talked and visited with each one of them, comforting them, saying, "You're gonna be just fine. . . . I'm praying for you. . . . You get well real quick, okay?" She was strong and composed.

But as we left the last room and walked to the end of the hall, she collapsed in a heap on the floor. The reality of losing Horton finally hit her. She just lost it, crying uncontrollably.

"It's so final," she cried. "It's just so final!" I never forgot those words.

It's true, and so haunting, that death is so final. There's no way to say what you didn't have a chance to say, or to ask any question you left unasked.

Over the years and lately, I've thought about Billie a lot. I don't know why, but she's been in my thoughts and on my heart, and I've wondered often how she's doing. I have a little ashtray that one of their daughters made and gave us. I think of her every time I look at it. I lost track of her over the years, but I think of her and pray for her often. She was a good friend back then.

That trip to Nashville, when we learned of Horton's death, was life-changing indeed. Since then I've often thought about the mystery of God's plan for our lives.

Unfortunately, it wouldn't be the last time Johnny and I would lose someone dear to us. Two and a half years later we would lose another close friend, Patsy Cline. Johnny and I were standing in the kitchen cooking together when we heard the awful news about the plane crash on the radio. We were stunned. Just a few days earlier, Patsy had been at our house for a barbecue, laughing and carrying on in our kitchen, entertaining us all with jokes as only she could tell them. Why did God have to take her?

The day after we received the horrible news about Johnny Horton's accident, I was scheduled to fly home to Los Angeles. Johnny, meanwhile, was scheduled to push out early to some northern booking dates, and wouldn't be able to see me off at the airport. While still reeling from the news about the crash, Johnny asked a disc jockey friend from KFOX radio in L.A. to wake me up early to catch my flight.

The next morning, that disc jockey was hung over from partying the night before, and never did wake me up. I missed my flight.

That very flight crashed in the Gulf of Mexico, killing everyone on board. Had I been awakened on time and gotten on that plane, I'd be at the bottom of the Gulf of Mexico right now, somewhere on the Nashville side of New Orleans. It humbles me still today to know that, for whatever reason, my life was spared.

When I returned home to California, I prayed that night before going to bed. I thanked God for sparing me from that flight and not taking me away from the girls. I prayed for the people who lost loved ones in that crash. I begged God to protect Johnny on the road, and the same for Marshall and Luther and everyone else. And I asked for a peace and calmness to replace the sense of foreboding that was starting to haunt me. Just as it had for Johnny and Billie Horton, I sensed that life as I knew it could change at any moment.

～

The first time I met June Carter was in 1958 at a music industry party in Nashville. Within minutes of being introduced, she thrust out her arm and showed me the ring on her left hand. She had just married her second husband.

"Look, with every husband, my diamond gets bigger!" she exclaimed.

For some reason, that first encounter haunted me for years. On my hand, tucked inside my pocket, I wore the simple quarter-carat diamond Johnny had given me as an engagement ring, and which I now wore as my wedding band. By her standards it was small, but I loved it.

Call it what you will—female intuition or a discerning spirit—but I do believe women know when they have to worry and when they don't. And all I know is, from the first day that I met her, and with each subsequent encounter, my intuition told me to worry. This woman was dangerous to my family. I sensed an unspoken agenda. If she were the type of woman to judge a marriage by the size of a diamond, I thought, she would judge a man by the measure of his success. And Johnny was ripe for picking.

So in 1961 when I learned that she was jockeying for a spot on Johnny's tour—and rumor had it she was working her way to the end of her second marriage—I didn't like the idea at all.

At the time I was growing more and more concerned with Johnny's increased and sporadic drinking. More frequently now, he wasn't the same clear-thinking man I was accustomed to. And repeatedly I witnessed on the road just how alcohol could make a person do and say things he normally wouldn't. Our dear friend George Jones provided no better proof of that.

Once, driving home late one night after a show, heading to our home on Havenhurst, Johnny was at the wheel driving, I was in the passenger seat, and George, Marshall, and Luther were in the back. I don't know what instigated it—nothing really had to—but George was drunk, and out of the blue screamed at the top of his lungs, "I'm gonna beat the *shit* out of you, Johnny . . . stop this damn car!"

I was scared to death. I honestly thought George was going to kill Johnny if he got his hands on him. Johnny just kept driving, calmly telling him, "Sit down, George," as Marshall and Luther restrained him.

I absolutely loved George. When he wasn't drinking, he was a wonderful person, one of my favorite people of all time. He was the nicest man you could ever meet. But alcohol changed him totally.

With Johnny, I noticed a drastic change soon after June joined the tour. His drinking escalated uncontrollably and he began taking all sorts of pills. He told me he needed them to help with the rigors of his schedule. Everyone on the road took them, he said, and I knew that to be partly true. There were pills to stay awake, pills to go to sleep, pills to get up, pills to take the edge off. I began to find them hidden all over the house, stashed away in socks and in corners of drawers, and I witnessed all the side effects. Johnny's behavior and mood suddenly changed.

I would go to bed at night and wake up the next morning to find Johnny still up, restless and agitated. He wouldn't look me in the eyes. And as much as I repeatedly asked, he refused to tell me what was bothering him. He was distant and detached. He wasn't Johnny anymore.

To this day I have no idea exactly what kinds of pills Johnny was taking. They were all colors, tiny and—to me—awful-looking. Every time I found them, I threw them down the toilet and flushed before he could stop me. I hated all those pills. I still do. Almost overnight they took control of Johnny, and nothing was the same after that.

Having been a show business wife for several years by this time, I was aware of another reality of road life: performers covering for each other's dalliances while on tour. For years, Luther Perkins carried on an extramarital affair that he kept secret from his wife, Birdie. I hate to admit it, but I knew about the affair along with everyone else and did nothing. I remember Johnny telling Luther one time, "Don't worry, Vivian won't say anything." At the time I thought, "Why do you assume that, Johnny?" That was such a bold assumption, but he was right. I didn't think it was my place, so I stayed quiet and kept the secret. Birdie and Luther eventually divorced and he married the other woman. Birdie was left devastated. She was madly in love with Luther and had three kids at home.

Occasionally I would hear rumors about Johnny and other women. They were troubling, of course, but I always trusted him. I honestly didn't believe he would ever, in a million years, be untrue to me.

However, my original instincts about June would prove right on the money. Not only would she become the source of a lifetime of pain for me, but she would forever affect the lives of our children and Johnny too. She would eventually contribute to Johnny's addiction, pursue him relentlessly, and destroy our marriage. But I didn't know all that back then. All I knew was that I felt the bottom begin to slowly drop out from under our marriage when she came into the picture.

So as often as possible, I loved it when Johnny, the girls, and I were able to get away from everything and spend time in the country with Johnny's parents. We had moved them out to California to be closer to us, and Johnny had bought them a trailer park to run near Casitas Springs, a small town about seventy-five miles northwest of Los Angeles. It was about an hour's drive from our home on Havenhurst.

It was there that we enjoyed camping, and fishing, and hunting, and the freedom that the country mountains offered. It was also where we met Curly and Carol Lewis, who became good friends. We bought their house, which was near the trailer park, so we would have a place to stay. Carol was a quiet housewife and mother like me. We became fast friends. Curly was a short, mouthy smart-ass—a building contractor who built custom homes—and he and Johnny hit it off famously.

One day, at the edge of a spread of tobacco fields, perched high on the side of a hill, Johnny found a piece of land—perfect, he thought, for us to build our dream home. "Here at the end of Tobacco Road, you get to heaven," Curly said. And with his help, we began designing the house.

Johnny detailed everything he wanted in our new home. At the building site, he lay down in the dirt and told Curly, "I want the master bathtub this big, and right *here.*" Curly built the house to every one of Johnny's detailed specifications. We were very excited.

I'm sure some people wondered why in the world we wanted to move from our comfortable neighborhood on Havenhurst to no-man's-land. But that's what Johnny wanted, and Johnny always got whatever Johnny wanted. Besides, I was hopeful that getting him away from the city and into the country would settle him down. No more late-night partying. No more drinking. No more pills. No more whispered rumors of other women. I thought the change would do us good. I was more than ready for my little slice of heaven at the end of Tobacco Road.

~

The house in Casitas was fabulous when it was finished. It was a sprawling, five-thousand-square-foot, ranch-style home with maid's quarters and a huge fifteen-by-thirty-foot kitchen that I loved. Our bedroom was incredible too. It was huge and had a dressing room with swinging doors and black bathroom fixtures. The ceiling was black. It was stunning. All the carpet was white and the walls were white, and it was decorated with black ebony furniture—a triple dresser and a big king bed—that we bought and had shipped from Dallas. It was absolutely beautiful. Two weeks after our fourth daughter, Tara, was born on August 24, 1961, we moved in.

What I had hoped to be my little bit of heaven at the end of Tobacco Road, unfortunately, ended up more of a horror. It wasn't long after we moved that everything, I mean everything, started to fall apart. There were a lot of happy times before Casitas, but after the move the happy times came fewer and farther between. Johnny was on the road 250 days of the year now, with June Carter and her family in tow. His use of pills continued to worsen. And I was home alone with four small children in a new house in the middle of nowhere.

You would think the location of the house itself, high up on the side of a mountain, would lend to privacy. But as it was, everyone in the area knew we had moved in. Our arrival was big news in the tiny town of Casitas. From the day we arrived, strangers who had heard about "Johnny Cash's new house on the hill" came driving up our long driveway, peeking in our windows, and knocking on our front door.

A local preacher by the name of Floyd Gressett also came marching up the driveway the day we moved in. He came bearing a bouquet of flowers and wasn't shy about his desire to meet and become friends with Johnny. Indeed, they did become friends.

Johnny started attending Floyd's church when he was off tour. And Floyd was over at our house constantly. Then they started taking trips together up to Pine Mountain, where Floyd had a ranch. They would stay the weekend, hunting and fishing and drinking and partying, and then come carousing back down out of the mountains to continue the fun. The last time Floyd called at the house drunk and looking for Johnny, I explained to him just what I thought about his style of small-town ministry.

"Floyd, where I come from," I explained, "they call folks like you 'two-faced hypocrites.' You preach from the pulpit every Sunday, and then slop around drunk with Johnny the rest of the week." I had always been timid and meek when it came to confronting people or voicing my own opinion, but my patience for Floyd's brand of dishonesty, and for Johnny's continued drinking and pills, had run thin.

I know I owe a debt of thanks to my Aunt Mamie for teaching me how to finally speak up. She was very wise in an ordinary way, and used to tell me, "Honey, you can call somebody a son of a bitch as long as you have a smile on your face." She knew just how to deal with elements like Floyd. He came to me later and apologized, by the way, but my questioning did nothing to stop his and Johnny's regular trips to Pine Mountain.

Johnny's behavior was becoming more and more troubling. His use of pills was increasing still, and he nervously paced around the house when off tour, smoking cigarettes, drinking endless cups of coffee, and downing pills behind the closed bathroom door. He was always on edge. He couldn't sleep. Sometimes he would go over to Carol and Curly's house in the middle of the night and let himself in while everyone was in bed. He'd turn their radio on to Morse code, volume blaring, and sit at their kitchen table, tapping his foot nervously to the clicks and reading it like he did back in the air force. Then he would wander off to somewhere else, or disappear for days on end.

We took a family vacation to a ranch in Palm Springs, where Johnny left the room for what he said would be a few minutes and then disappeared. The next call I got was from the local jail, telling me he had been arrested. I never knew what was to come next.

Johnny was constantly in trouble with the law, crashing "Ole Jessie" (his car and camper), starting fires at our house, carelessly rolling his tractor, and taking more and more pills as each day passed. I was constantly on guard, hunting down the pills to throw away and having to watch Johnny so he wouldn't hurt himself, or hurt the girls, or leave. And worse yet, some of Johnny's band members began dropping not-so-subtle hints to me that June was after Johnny on the road, and I should really do something about it.

When I confronted Johnny with the reports, he insisted June had done none of those things I had been told. He said I was letting my imagination get the better of me, and not to listen to gossip. I chose to believe Johnny, but I couldn't shake the uncomfortable feelings I had about her. She was a regular on Johnny's show now, and I knew they were together a lot at meals and traveling, and he seemed to talk about her more than anyone else. Again, that female intuition. And why would these band members say those things to me if they weren't true?

One time I drove to Bakersfield with a couple of girlfriends to watch Johnny perform, knowing I would run into June. Despite that fact, it was still an exciting trip for all of us. That was one of the fun parts of being Johnny's wife—great shows, backstage passes, rubbing elbows with celebrities, hearing the hushed whispers of fans, *"That's Johnny Cash's wife!"* We all dressed up in our finest—I remember wearing a white leather coat that I loved. Backstage we bumped into her.

"Vivian, what is that on your coat that looks like . . . *dirt?*" June asked loudly, pointing to the shoulder of my jacket.

I felt a roomful of eyes looking at me . . . *dirty* me. June laughed as she waited for my answer.

I couldn't speak. Even though I wanted to confront her and set her straight about going after Johnny, I was embarrassed and hurt. Looking back now, I can see how it seems like such an insignificant comment, really. But I knew her intent was to bring me down a notch, and it worked. It would be a trend that would continue for several years.

One day in early 1963, while gardening in the yard, Johnny told me about a song he had just written with Merle Kilgore and Curly while out fishing on Lake Casitas. "I'm gonna give June half credit on a song I just wrote," Johnny said. "It's called 'Ring of Fire.' "

"Why?" I asked, wiping dirt from my hands. The mere mention of her name annoyed me. I was sick of hearing about her.

"She needs the money," he said, avoiding my stare. "And I feel sorry for her."

I was so naïve and trusting. The idea made me uncomfortable, but I didn't argue about it. I still believed everything Johnny told me.

To this day, it confounds me to hear the elaborate details June told of writing that song for Johnny. She didn't write that song any more than I did. The truth is, Johnny wrote that song, while pilled up and drunk, about a certain private female body part. All those years of her claiming she wrote it herself, and she probably never knew what the song was really about. But I was the bigger fool.

I began stumbling upon receipts for other gifts Johnny gave to her and her daughters and family. Purchases of things like tape recorders and other items, which at the time were quite expensive gifts. Johnny clearly didn't want me to know about these things. The receipts were hidden away in places where I was unlikely to find them. And there were more telltale signs.

One evening Johnny phoned me from Nashville while on the road. As we ended our conversation, I signed off as I always did, telling him, "I love you, honey."

"Me too," he answered this time, softly—not the usual "I love you" that I was accustomed to hearing.

It was all too painfully obvious. I knew in my heart that she was standing there within earshot of our conversation and was the reason for his hesitation. Johnny had never hung up the phone without telling me he loved me, ever. But after she came into the picture, that changed too.

"You're not going to tell me you love me?" I pressed.

After skirting the issue, he finally said it. "I love you too, Viv."

Later I learned that June indeed had been with Johnny, just as I had suspected. They were in a kitchen, probably at her home. After hearing Johnny tell me "I love you," she broke every dish in the kitchen. Ole Preacher Gressett told me that. Johnny confided many things to him.

The epiphany for me—if you want to call it that—happened one afternoon in our bedroom in Casitas. Johnny was sitting on the edge of the bed, having another one of his hallucinations. By this time I was used to such episodes brought on by the pills. Sometimes they happened several times a day. While the hallucinations were always upsetting, they no longer alarmed me. But this time was different. This time Johnny was talking to June. He was having a conversation with her and her youngest daughter. Then he drifted off to sleep.

While Johnny slept, I started piecing everything together—"Ring of Fire," the receipts, everything that Floyd Gressett had told me, Johnny not wanting to say "I love you," the rumors, everything. I don't know why it took me so long to admit it to myself, but I finally had clarity. I could no longer pretend to not see it. I was slowly but surely losing my husband to June Carter.

Day by day I watched as Johnny began dividing his affection and time and money between June's family and our family. I felt him slipping away. Let me tell you, it is a degrading, horrible experience when you realize you're losing your husband to another woman. I felt completely helpless, not knowing how to bring him back. I longed for the days when Johnny told me he'd always walk the line for me. He didn't tell me that anymore.

To this day I don't even know exactly when their relationship started, but after it did, confirmations of the rumors and my suspicions came from every corner. Grandma Cash courageously came to me and told me of things she witnessed on the road, of June's behavior toward Johnny, and of seeing June follow Johnny into his hotel room wearing only a nightgown. She told me of her appeals to Johnny to end the affair. And Johnny's bandmates confirmed to me that Johnny and June were sleeping together openly.

With the realization of what was happening crashing down on me, I confronted Johnny about the affair. I hadn't eaten for three days straight when I cornered him in the bedroom.

"Johnny, I can't take care of the children until we get something settled," I began. He could see my stress level and looked concerned. I think I finally had his attention.

"Johnny, I *know* there's something going on between you and June."

I went on to tell him what I had been told, who had told me what, that I loved him more than anything else in the world, and please let's fix our marriage. Johnny's response was swift and simple: "She's off the tour," he said. He promised that June would be out of our lives.

The matter was settled as far as Johnny was concerned; nothing more needed to be said. He hugged me and kissed me and told me not to worry, that everything would be fine. But I still had a gnawing feeling that the issue wasn't resolved. She didn't strike me as a woman who would go easily.

And sure enough, no sooner than Johnny said she was off the tour, she was right back on again. I was no match for what I was up against.

As Princess Diana once said of her marriage to Prince Charles, "There were three people in our marriage . . . it was a bit crowded."

～

Our kitchen table in Casitas was custom-built by Johnny's design. It was thick and solid and heavy with notches around the edges. It had a rustic appearance that he liked. And there was a little notch, a dip in the tabletop, exactly in the place where my cup went. Johnny always thought that was so funny. He had a weird sense of humor.

Most mornings I would sit at the breakfast table with the girls, contemplating the notch while they ate. I was seldom hungry. During the roughest of times, I lived on cigarettes and coffee.

"Daddy didn't come home last night?" Kathy asked. The girls had a keen ability to bring up uncomfortable subjects when I was least prepared. My mind was numb from lack of sleep and pacing the floor, waiting for Johnny to come home. Only an hour earlier, I had gone to bed to try to get some sleep before getting up to ready them for school. My daily morning routine consisted of fixing breakfast, combing their hair, brushing their teeth, putting out their uniforms, and taking them to the bus for the ride to St. Katherine's Catholic School in Ventura.

Johnny's tour had ended on the fourteenth and the girls and I had antici-
pated his arrival that evening. Today was the twentieth. Still no sign of
Johnny. I might hear from him today, I might not.

"When *is* Daddy coming home?" asked Rosanne. I had no answer and I was
running out of stories to make up. I was eager for the girls to go to school so I
could stop pretending everything was normal. I felt awful. I felt frustrated and
hurt and helpless all at the same time. What could I do to make Johnny come
home? How could he make promises to me and the kids, then break them?

The girls would frequently ask, "What's wrong? Why isn't Daddy home?"
My answer was always, "Daddy's not feeling well." Or I would make up some
cockamamy story. I hid everything from them. In hindsight, that wasn't
always the right thing to do. I should have been more honest, but they were
so little. I just couldn't.

Years later the girls have told me they knew much more than I thought.
They knew Daddy was acting "weird," and said they hated to see him come
home because of his strange behavior and because of all the arguments. Kathy
told me she would hide her head under her pillow to muffle the sounds of us
arguing. I thought we were careful to not let them hear. But evidently they saw
and heard more than I want to admit.

Unfortunately, during one or two of our more heated arguments, I know
the girls witnessed Johnny pushing me around. It just kills me to know that
they saw those things. But Johnny never hit me hard enough to cause any
bruises. By far the biggest blow I ever sustained was losing him to June. She
was still on tour with him despite my continued protests. She had more influence in my life than I did.

There were fewer and fewer occasions when Johnny would allow me to
come on the road with him. Every time I'd ask, "Can I go on this trip?" he
would say no and offer some kind of half-hearted explanation. Eventually he
offered no explanation. Finally I wasn't allowed to go on any tours at all. I
didn't want to believe it, but in the back of my mind I knew I was powerless
to stop Johnny from drifting away. Helpless to do much else, I waited.

I still remember the first time I called June to confront her directly about
the affair. I was tired of Johnny thwarting my every attempt to go on tour. My
hand was trembling as I dialed her phone number.

What would I say to her? How would she respond? What would Johnny
say when I told him I spoke to her? I knew he would be furious, but I didn't
care. I wasn't afraid of him or intimidated by him like everyone else was. I was
in a fight to save our marriage.

"June, the only problem Johnny and I have in our marriage is you." I
thought that said it nicely and to the point, even if it wasn't entirely true.
Actually, two things were causing trouble: her and drugs. But why confuse the

issue? She was the more relentless of the two threats, according to Grandma Cash and other observers.

"Yes, well, I just stay on my knees praying," she answered.

I wondered to myself, What are you praying for? And what kind of answer was that anyway—"Yes, I stay on my knees praying"? She claimed to be a God-fearing Christian woman, but I didn't believe it. I believed I'd finally met a bigger hypocrite than Johnny's preacher friend, Floyd Gressett.

She never did give me a straight response to my appeals that she please leave Johnny alone. I don't think she cared much about what I wanted. To her I was merely a nuisance, the only thing standing between her and what she wanted. In recent years she's admitted in interviews that she was relentless and "never would let go" of Johnny. Let me tell you, it was horrible to be on the receiving end of her determination.

I would confront her again, the next time in person backstage at a show. It was an ugly, tense five minutes of angry words, posturing, and June punctuating her position with five devastating words that rendered me speechless: "Vivian, he *will* be mine." With that, she turned and walked away.

~

Christmas. That magic word. The mere mention of Christmas sent us scrambling, decorating, baking, wrapping, and celebrating to exhaustion. Christmas was always a big deal at our house. It was Johnny's favorite time of the year. And mine too.

Every year, Johnny put up Christmas decorations all over the hillside at our house, including a giant star on the highest mountaintop. He also installed loudspeakers that blared Christmas carols for all to hear. We thought it was a very special thing to do for the neighbors, but someone complained about the noise. So that put an end to our hillside Christmas concert, but not to our joy of the season.

But as Johnny's drug use escalated and worsened, Christmases weren't always the happy occasion they once had been. Christmas morning 1964 was one I'd rather forget, but can't.

"Look, babies, Santa was here last night!" Johnny said excitedly, pointing to a trail of sooty black footprints leading from the fireplace to the front door. Under the tree, there were four heaping piles of new toys set out in a row for each of the girls according to age: Rosanne, Kathy, Cindy, Tara. Johnny waited for their reaction and looked at me as if to say, "Come on, let's be happy!"

I couldn't pretend to be happy. I wasn't. I could tell Johnny was high. He had made those footprints himself on the floor with ashes from the fireplace, and I was annoyed with the mess and with him. The kids, though, thought the whole presentation was just fabulous. But I couldn't look past the fact that

Johnny had that all-too-familiar edge about him. He had been up all night, doing drugs and writing, and now he wanted me to act happy-go-lucky.

In fact, Johnny had become almost a stranger in the house. He was seldom home, and when he was home, he acted "strange" and "weird," as the girls would say. His behavior and appearance frightened them. He shook and trembled. He was pale and gaunt, and his eyes had a harrowing, hollow look about them. This Christmas morning, the gifts and toys and sooty foot-prints were successfully distracting the girls from his condition, but not me.

I was weary from dealing with Johnny's behavior. He continued to disap-pear for days and weeks on end, leaving the house saying, "I'll be home by midnight" or such. Then he wouldn't return at all. And no calls to let me know his whereabouts, or if he was all right. I never knew when, or if, he was going to come home, or the state he would be in when he did.

Night after night, for hours, I paced in front of the picture window in the living room, watching for his car heading up the hill. From the spot where I usually stood, I could see the property line of our land through the trees where our driveway turned off Nye Road. Any second I hoped to see those familiar headlights of his camper bumping up the driveway to the house. Sometimes I waited for hours. Sometimes days. It was awful not knowing if I would ever see him again, not knowing if he was going to be arrested, or wreck the car. And at one time or another, all those things did happen.

That's how I spent most of my nights. Pacing and crying, hoping and wait-ing. After rolling the girls' hair and polishing their shoes and putting them to bed, my pathetic routine was to pace and pray out loud, whispering, "God, please send Johnny home safely. Make him come home." Begging was my last resort. "Please remove June from our lives, and I will do anything in return." I bargained endlessly with God.

Once I thought, "I'll show him!" I collected up the kids and went to a motel for the night. I wanted Johnny to come home and be worried to death when we weren't there, and learn just how it felt to worry. I never counted on him never coming home at all. He never even knew we had gone. It was a complete waste of time and money.

Johnny's arrivals home were more frequently strained, not the happy occa-sions they had been in the past. I would pace in front of the picture window until I would finally see his headlights coming up the side of the mountain. I was always so relieved to see those headlights and finally know where he was, that he was alive and okay. But the excitement was always quickly tempered by worry over what condition he would be in when he walked through the door. His arrivals were never pleasant. His entrance usually followed the same general script each time.

"You're home . . . finally," I'd say.

"Yep, here I am. What's *your* problem?"

"Johnny, I've been worried sick. For three days, could you not pick up a telephone and call me? I didn't know if you were dead or alive."

Johnny's response: silence.

"Where were you?" I begged.

"Out." And with that, Johnny would have nothing more to say on the subject. He was in no mood to deal with a questioning wife. I may as well have been talking to a wall. He was not coherent. Not communicating. Belligerent.

Without another word, Johnny would head to the bedroom and go to bed, and that's where he would stay for two or three days. That was his usual pattern: be gone for two to three days, then come home and sleep for two to three days.

Exhausted and coming off the drugs, Johnny would lie in bed with a lit cigarette dangling out of his mouth, winding down. And as a matter of routine, I sat on the floor and leaned up against the bed to stay awake until he fell asleep so I could take the cigarette out of his mouth. I was desperately afraid of falling asleep before he did. No matter how late it was, I'd fight my own sleepiness and wait for him to fall asleep first. We all could have burned to death if I hadn't. Oh, but I loved it when he was asleep. It was peaceful then, and I knew he was safe.

A friend once told me she couldn't understand how or why I stayed in that insane situation for as long as I did. I must be either a saint or just plain crazy. Crazy in love, I definitely was. I never stopped praying for a miracle.

~

Johnny Western toured extensively with Johnny beginning in the late fifties, and became a dear friend of ours. I always liked him a lot. Unlike many musicians, Johnny Western didn't drink, didn't chase women, and was dependable and honest. He could also tell a story better than anyone I've ever met. For years he's told one about me that brings a smile to my face every time I hear it.

Back while we were living on Havenhurst, I was the bookkeeper for Johnny's tours. When I wasn't managing our busy household, hosting get-togethers, taking care of three little girls (and birthing a fourth), I managed the money that Johnny was bringing in. I did it all on our kitchen table—unsophisticated, I know, for one of country's biggest touring acts, but that's how we did it.

My system was this: Johnny would collect money and expense receipts while out on the road and place everything in a metallic insulated ice cream bag for safekeeping. At the end of the tour he'd bring the ice cream bag back to me, with all the money and receipts, and I would do the bookkeeping, make deposits, and so forth.

At the time, I used to do my weekly grocery shopping at a little store called

Gelson's supermarket on Ventura Boulevard, just around the corner from our house. One day, I had loaded up the shopping cart as usual when I made my way to the checkout aisle to pay. The girl at the checkout stand was new, someone I had never seen before. I proceeded to write a check for the groceries, but she stopped me short. She wouldn't take my check.

"I'm Mrs. Johnny Cash," I explained, pointing to my name on the check, next to Johnny's name. But this young girl didn't have a clue who I was, or who Johnny Cash was for that matter. She just wanted cash for the groceries, and that was that. After a few minutes of back and forth, and the line behind me growing longer with impatient customers, I motioned for her to wait.

"Leave everything right here. Don't put any of this stuff away. I'll be right back," I said.

I grabbed my purse and headed to the car to return to the house to get some cash. At the house I grabbed one of the ice cream bags from the kitchen table.

When I returned to the supermarket, I threw over $25,000 in cash onto the checkout counter in front of the checker. Then I looked her in the eye and demanded, "*Now* do you think my check will clear?"

Apparently Johnny Western and Johnny told and retold that story countless times, and always admired me for doing that.

I would admire myself too, if the story were true. It never happened. I have no idea how or why Johnny (my Johnny, that is) made up that story, but he was never one to let facts get in the way of a good story.

I can't tell you how many times Johnny gave interviews and simply made up stories as he went along. For years the girls and I have laughed about that. Johnny would leave people scratching their heads trying to figure out the truth. It's no wonder journalists and media people claim Johnny was a complex man, a "walking contradiction/Partly truth and partly fiction." Fifty years of fibs will do that.

~

From as far back as the day we married, Johnny and I always had a strong intuitive bond between us. Whenever we were separated, we routinely had premonitions about each other's actions and safety.

Back in Memphis, I remember once when Johnny was away in Nashville recording. I got a call from him a little after ten o'clock at night. He had stopped in the middle of a recording session and said he had a strange, sudden urge to call me—that he felt something was wrong. "Is anything wrong?" he asked.

I explained to Johnny that everything was fine and not to worry. The girls were tucked in bed asleep and the doors were all locked. Johnny's nephew, Roy Jr., who was staying at the house with me so I wouldn't be alone at night, would be home from work soon. But Johnny insisted that he stay on the phone until Roy Jr. got home. He said he had a gnawing, uneasy feeling.

Just then, while I was talking to Johnny on the phone, I heard a strange noise outside the house. It came from the direction of the bathroom. I stepped into the bathroom to see what it was, and there stood a stranger in the dark just outside the window. I was terrified. I ran to check on Rosanne and Kathy to make sure they were safe.

Thankfully, within minutes Roy Jr. arrived home and went outside to investigate. He found the screen to the window torn off and footprints in the soil. Had I not been on the phone with Johnny, the person likely would have broken in.

I remember many incidents like that. Johnny said something was wrong and sure enough it was. And other times I would sense trouble about to happen to him. Like the time Johnny became the first private individual to be sued by our federal government for causing a forest fire.

I was literally on my knees in the driveway, begging Johnny, screaming and crying for him not to leave.

"Johnny, I have a horrible feeling something bad is going to happen if you leave. Please don't leave!" He was high on pills and hell-bent on heading up into the mountains by himself.

"Viv, get out of the way," he demanded, waving me off. His tone was arrogant and cocky and scared me to death. I thought if I could just get his keys away from him, he wouldn't be able to leave. He might try to ride Kathy's bike down the hill, like he'd done many times before, but wouldn't get far.

I reminded Johnny about our premonitions and how they never failed us before. "Please don't go," I cried. I tried to tell him he was in no shape to be driving. But I couldn't stop him. He was the judge of his own sobriety and he felt just fine, so off he went. Two days later, I got a phone call that he had been arrested for starting a massive forest fire. The police were questioning him.

By that time I was so tired of Johnny's antics, always one thing after another. I was disgusted and embarrassed. I wanted to crawl into a hole because everybody knew about the things he did. Once again he made front-page news. "Did Johnny Cash's careless actions cause the forest fire?" "Was the fire an accident, caused by sparks from Johnny's truck, as Johnny claims?" "Or did he set it on purpose?"

The following week, while I was in line at the grocery store, a little checker boy looked at me and asked, "How *did* Johnny Cash start that fire up in the mountain?"—right there in front of everybody. Our family problems were now the hot topic of local gossip. I wanted to hide and never leave the house again. In the end, Johnny was fined $82,000 and given five years to pay it. As bad as that whole episode was, though, the worst was yet to come.

Johnny was arrested yet again, this time at an airport in El Paso after crossing the border into Mexico and smuggling back hundreds of pills. I immediately flew down to be by his side for the court appearance. This time, though, the headlines weren't limited to our area of Casitas Springs. The story and a photo of Johnny and me leaving the courthouse were published in papers coast to coast, and worldwide.

Everyone in the world saw the photo, including the Ku Klux Klan, who decided, after looking at my picture, "Johnny Cash is married to a Negro woman." Johnny and I received death threats, and an already shameful situation was made infinitely worse. The stress was almost unbearable; I wanted to die. And it didn't help that Johnny issued a statement to the KKK informing them I wasn't black. To this day I hate when accusations and threats from people like that are dignified with any response at all.

As much as I prayed and hoped for things to get better, they only continued to get worse. Every time I thought we had reached bottom, we sank deeper. Every time I had reason to hope for a turnaround, something else happened. And the repeated rumors that Johnny and June were sleeping together were still there.

Johnny refused to talk to me anymore. He didn't like confrontation of any kind. I'd say, "Can we please talk?" and he'd say, "I don't want to argue," and he'd leave. I'd say, "I don't want to argue either, but we really need to talk." He would just leave. That was our big problem in the end: He didn't want to be confronted or questioned.

Marshall phoned me one day from the road. "Vivian, we need to put Johnny in a hospital right away, he's in really bad shape," he said. "He needs to be placed in a treatment center right away." I immediately began making inquiries to find a place where we could get Johnny some help, hopeful that this might be the solution Johnny needed. However, what happened next left me confused and betrayed.

Inexplicably, Marshall had a change of heart. "Don't go home," he told Johnny. "Vivian's going to have you committed." And the alienation grew. Before long, Johnny stopped coming home at all.

~

I remember the moment I signed the divorce papers as clear as yesterday. It was the worst day of my life—in a way, worse than all the pills, worse than all the nights pacing and waiting, worse than any other woman, worse than all of it put together. Signing those papers was the most horrible moment of my life. I felt as if I couldn't swim hard enough to keep from going over the falls, and I was finally swept over.

Emotionally and physically I was a wreck. I was skin and bones, nervous and distant, just a ghost of the woman I used to be. I hardly recognized myself when I passed by a mirror. And the few friends I had were gravely concerned that I might harm myself.

I alternated between moments of self-pity and fits of anger—one minute believing I somehow deserved all the misery I was experiencing, and the next furious at Johnny, furious at June, and disgusted with myself for hanging on to foolish hope that everything would somehow be all right.

I kept telling myself that there *was* hope for a fresh start, that Johnny would want to come home and things would get better. Like the afternoon he called me from Whizzin's Corner, a truck stop about fifty miles south of Casitas Springs on Highway 101.

"Honey, would you come get me?" he asked. There was a sound of resignation in his voice. How he got there, I have no idea, but I dropped everything and rushed to pick him up.

When Johnny saw me, he grabbed me and hugged me and gave me the most wonderful, passionate kiss, as if to say, "I'm so sorry." I didn't know what to think; it was so unexpected. I hoped that it meant he had finally come to his senses. Maybe he was ready to give up the pills, maybe he had broken up with June. To this day I don't understand what brought on the sudden display of tenderness. Whatever the reason, it was short-lived.

Let me tell you, it is hard to walk away from a marriage when you hold a shred of hope. And I always held out hope. My heart kept reminding me that every time I'd waited for Johnny before, he'd always come back. I had waited three years for him to return from Germany, and he came back. I had waited I don't how many times late at night for him, and he always returned—sometimes days later, but eventually. And I still loved him. I absolutely, to the core of my being, loved him. And our girls needed him desperately.

I couldn't picture a life without Johnny. I always believed we would be together and married forever. But now as I sat at the conference table in my attorney's office, I came to the realization that "forever" wasn't nearly as long as I thought it would be. A private investigator stood ready in Denver, where Johnny was winding down a tour, to serve him with the divorce papers. What happened next hinged on me signing those papers.

Just a few months earlier I had reached a crossroads and I knew there was no turning back. During a routine doctor visit, my doctor came into the exam room and sat down across from me. I know I looked pathetic. I was down to weighing ninety-five pounds, and I was weak and sickly and crying (my permanent state behind closed doors). I knew I needed help but didn't know how to ask. I was rapidly deteriorating. My doctor's face grew serious as he leveled his stare and looked me straight in the eyes.

"Vivian, you need to do *something*," he said. "If you don't, somebody *else* will be raising your girls."

His words got my full attention. The first thing that popped into my mind was June. And that was the moment I knew something would have to change. Nobody else was going to raise my daughters, especially not her. I cried for what seemed like an hour upon the realization of what would come next.

I knew I could continue on with the dysfunction of the current situation indefinitely—no matter how deeply rooted in love the dysfunction was, no matter how wrong, no matter how hopeless. But Johnny wasn't coming home most of the time now, and things were only getting worse. I couldn't just stand by and continue to simply hope that things would get better. For almost five years now I was still in the same horrible place. It was the most difficult decision of my life, but I had just made it. I would need to file for divorce to save myself and the girls.

Reflecting back to that day is still difficult for me. It was the point in my life when I began to box up my emotions, run from my past, and refuse support from anyone. I would learn that if you "stuff" your feelings, push them aside, and ignore them, you don't have to deal with them until, well . . . forever, if you choose. But the cost would be high. A piece of me died on that day.

So on a Friday afternoon in June of '66, I uncapped the pen and signed the divorce papers, sealing my fate. The next thing I needed to do was tell our families and the girls before the inevitable media onslaught that would come when the news leaked out.

Luckily the girls were on summer break, so they wouldn't have to face questions and comments at school. I took them all into one bedroom and sat them down.

"Babies, I have something I need to tell you," I said. "I have something I need to talk to you about." I was sad and frightened, all at the same time, to tell them what I needed to say.

"Daddy and I aren't going to live together anymore," I explained. To this day, I can still see their innocent faces staring at me as they listened. "We're not going to be married anymore."

To my complete surprise, their reaction was simply, "Okay, what's next?" No outpouring of "Why? What do you mean, Mommy?" None of them cried or showed any sadness or even surprise. They simply wanted to go on with their business of playing. They all ran off, leaving me alone on the bed.

I had expected them to be upset. They should have been upset, but they weren't. Looking back, I know Tara didn't understand what a divorce was at her age. Cindy and Kathy probably didn't understand either. Rosanne, who was eleven at the time, told me years later that she was relieved. She hated to hear the arguments and Johnny was gone most of the time anyway, she said. I remember thinking to myself that it was a good thing that the girls weren't upset, but I wondered whether they were stuffing their emotions like me. In retrospect, I believe they did.

Next I called Grandma and Grandpa Cash and told them the news. They were not at all surprised, having witnessed what they had seen on the road. They vowed their support and anything I needed.

Then I called my parents, who were surprised and sad but supportive nonetheless. They never knew the extent of our troubles, only what they read in the papers about the arrest in El Paso, the fire, and miscellaneous other arrests (too many to think of at the moment). They were just very disappointed. My sister, who had already read about the divorce in a newspaper over the weekend, was very upset, as were my friends as I told each of them one by one.

I recently ran across a short story that Cindy wrote as a child about that period of our lives. It breaks my heart to read her words of those final months of us all as a family.

December 20th a cold, foggy day. Mama was standing in the kitchen cooking breakfast for her four impatient daughters. Only five more days until Christmas and Santa would be there. Rosanne and Kathy were hoping and praying Santa wouldn't forget about the bicycles they wanted so much. Cindy was thinking about the bright, shiny, red wagon she had asked Santa for in every store she'd seen him in. Tara really didn't care what he brought her. She'd be happy with any toy. And that was the truth.

Cindy sat at the window listening to every sound she heard hoping that one of them would be the sound of her Daddy's car coming up the long driveway. He just had to get home for Christmas day. It wouldn't be the same without Daddy leading his family into the front room Christmas morning where Santa had been the night before. It was the most exciting day of the year.

Daddy was away from home often. He worked on the road traveling from town to town. Whenever he returned home he always seemed so tired and restless. The girls had often heard their mother talking on the phone to her sister, Aunt Sylvia, saying that Johnny wasn't trying very hard to break his pill habit, whatever that meant. She had said that he was taking up to 100 pills a day, taking uppers and downers and that was ruining their marriage. The girls didn't really understand what that meant. To them everything seemed fine.

The days went by and Christmas Eve finally arrived. What a beautiful morning. It was too bad it never snowed in Casitas Springs, but the foggy day still gave the small town the Christmas spirit. Hours went by and still no Daddy. The four girls sat by their Christmas tree in the front room rattling their already wrapped gifts. "I wonder what this is?" "I don't know. Mama bought it for Daddy." "I wish Daddy would hurry. He has to be in bed before Santa Claus comes." Mama walked in and sat down by her children. She didn't look too happy. It was probably because Daddy wasn't home yet. She worried about him when he was late arriving, if he did come home. For years, Daddy was following the same routine. Home for a week or so, then gone for two weeks or so at a time.

Then the back door slammed. The girls jumped up and ran to the door. It was Daddy. He hugged his four happy daughters. He really missed them. But where was Mama? Daddy walked back to his bedroom after being smothered with hugs and kisses by his children. Mama and Daddy were in the bedroom for a long time. Finally, Mama came out and told her children to hurry and get in bed because Santa would be there soon. Daddy came out and kissed them goodnight. Mama wasn't smiling like she should have been. It was a restless night for everyone.

The kids couldn't sleep because of the excitement that would surround them the next morning. They could hear their mama and daddy talking most of the night. There were some words in their conversation that were kind of difficult to understand for the girls. Morning finally arrived, but only Mama led her children to the front room. "Oh, look at all the presents!"

"Where's Daddy, Mama?" "He's very tired. He doesn't feel too well. He's going to sleep now, but he'll be out later." Rosanne and Kathy got their wish and were outside riding their new bicycles. Cindy was sitting in her new red wagon opening her first present. Tara couldn't pull herself away from all her goodies. Cindy had heard her Mama and Daddy talking the night before and she was confused. She went outside to talk to her older sister. "Rosanne, I heard Mama say last night that everything was final. What's a divorce?"

Even today, it's impossible for me not to get emotional reading that. I know it would kill Johnny to read it too. I so badly miss the happy Christmases we spent together as a family.

Naïve and foolish as I was at the time that I signed the divorce papers, I still held out hope that somehow such a drastic move might be just the thing to shake some sense into Johnny and bring him home. I called Johnny on the road after the filing.

"Honey," I asked, "is there any chance, one last chance of us making a go of it, or trying again?"

When he answered the phone, I could tell he was high. My stomach sank as I heard him struggling to make a sentence. In the background I could hear her hushed insistences that he hang up the phone.

I waited for his answer, which came after a long pause.

"No," Johnny said. "It's too late."

~

"Mrs. Cash, please return to children's clothing . . . Mrs. Johnny Cash, please return to the children's clothing department."

The voice over the JCPenney loudspeaker stopped me just as I was leaving the store. I assumed I had left my charge card, or my wallet, or worse yet my purse. I wasn't myself lately. A store manager greeted me when I arrived back at the checkout counter.

"Mrs. Cash, I'm so sorry, but can you please tell me how you're going to pay for these clothes?" he said. "You're getting divorced aren't you? . . . So just how do you plan to pay for these?"

I was stunned. Johnny and I had always paid our bills on time and in full. And to be publicly questioned in such a way was humiliating. Overnight it seemed I went from celebrity wife to throwaway spouse, tossed out like something with no value.

And along with the humiliation came more anger as I began uncovering more receipts, dating back several years, for tens of thousands of dollars in gifts Johnny had purchased for June and her family behind my back. I deduced that they had been together a lot longer than I originally suspected. Unbelievably, there was even a receipt for a house that he had bought for June's mother, Mother Maybelle. When I questioned our accountant about the receipts, he told me that Johnny had specifically instructed him not to tell me. I felt such the fool.

I do have to stop and say, though, that unlike millions of other women who have faced similar circumstances as mine, Johnny did financially support me and the girls. We agreed that I would get the house and some other property, as well as alimony of one thousand dollars per month, child support of sixteen hundred dollars per month, and 50 percent of royalties on all songs Johnny had written and recorded up to that time. In return, Johnny got the trailer park, one antique love seat and corner chair, and a crystal silver set. Those were the only things he wanted. I know he wanted to do as much for me as he could.

The only thing I never got was closure, and that was perhaps the thing I needed most. Everything ended abruptly, and Johnny was just gone. We never said good-bye. Once he moved to Nashville, June never allowed us to talk alone. And that made it more difficult for me and the girls because nothing was ever resolved. I just had to close the door and try to move on with my life.

It would have been so much easier, I would have maybe understood a lot more, accepted a lot more, if we had talked. I wish so much that had happened. I probably would have been more at peace about the situation, and been able to put it behind me, if we had talked.

Johnny later apologized to the girls for having been what he called a terrible father. But he never apologized to me. It would have helped if he had. Even if he had come to me before he remarried or before I remarried and said, "Look, let me tell you the situation. I really regret what I did to you. I'm sorry." Anything. I think the guilt kept him from doing it. It was easier to set it aside and pretend as if it didn't happen.

Instead, in January of 1968, after a one-year waiting period, the divorce was finalized with nothing said.

~

Once, back in the summer of 1964, during one of the many times I hadn't been able to keep him from driving while under the influence, Johnny was pulled over in Casitas and caught with a stash of pills. Instead of arresting him, though, the cop let him go, and Johnny offered to repay the kind gesture by performing for free at the local police fund-raiser. That's when Johnny and I first met Dick Distin, a Ventura police officer charged with organizing the concert where Johnny performed.

During the course of planning the concert, Dick and his wife became casual friends of ours, coming over to the house and playing cards while our children played together. Years later, during my most difficult time after filing for divorce from Johnny, Dick—who by that time had suffered through the breakup of his own marriage—became a loyal friend to me. He provided a much-needed shoulder to lean on and became my companion, my confidant. For the first time in a long time, I felt protected. So, soon after my divorce was finalized, when Dick asked me to marry him, I said yes. In hindsight, it was much too soon to get married again, but I worried at the time that no man would want to marry me with four children, and Dick was very persistent in asking for my hand.

So I sold the house on the hill in Casitas, knowing it held far too many haunting memories to begin a new life there. And Dick and I flew to Vegas to get married, then moved into a house in Ventura, California, high atop a mountain overlooking the Pacific Ocean. Two months later, Johnny and June married as well.

I was ready for a new start and desperately wanted to give Dick my whole heart, but I couldn't. I was tortured with thousands of thoughts about Johnny: *What could I have done differently to save our marriage? What did I do so wrong to make it possible for another woman to come into the picture?* Admittedly, these were all the same thoughts and feelings that other women feel after losing their husbands to other women. But unlike other women, my ex was Johnny Cash.

Complete strangers would walk up and ask the most insensitive questions. "So who's better in bed, Johnny or your new husband?" "What do you think of Johnny's wife, June Carter?"

And they'd ask Dick, "So, what's it like being married to Johnny Cash's ex-wife?" There was no limit to their rudeness. Overnight Dick became "Mr. Vivian Cash," and he hated that. I can't blame him. For years my identity had been defined by someone else, first as my mother and father's daughter, then as Johnny Cash's wife. Then years later as Rosanne Cash's mother, when she established herself in the music business. I'd never been just Vivian. It's suffocating not to have your own identity.

And Dick resented all of Johnny's photos and gold records displayed around the house—"a shrine to Johnny," he called them. And he hated the TV programs that the girls and I watched when Johnny appeared. "Do the kids want to see it, or do *you* want to see it?" he'd ask me angrily. Not so unexpectedly, he accused me of still being in love with Johnny. I pretended that the accusations were ridiculous, but he was right. I *was* still in love with Johnny.

In his frustration, Dick started drinking and taking pills, mimicking all of Johnny's bad behavior. And he became downright mean (not in a physical way, but verbally and emotionally on a near-daily basis). I felt like I went from one nightmare right into another. I longed for Johnny, and was married to someone else who was increasingly abusive.

Meanwhile Johnny's career underwent a strong resurgence. *Johnny Cash at Folsom Prison* shot to number one on the charts. And with the start of his very own *The Johnny Cash Show* on the ABC network, Johnny now had superstar status—just my luck. He was bigger than ever, and everywhere to be seen, with June always smiling by his side.

Let me tell you, it would have been much easier if Johnny's celebrity had not been so enormous and thrown in my face via every form of media. I not only had to deal with my life, but my life exposed to the entire world. It was not easy. It was wrong of me, I know, but most of my frustration was directed toward June, not Johnny. He was as much to blame for everything, but I was angrier with her because of those words that still echoed in my head, "Vivian, he *will* be mine."

Over the coming years, there she was, on every variety show, every talk show, the Billy Graham Crusades, everywhere where Johnny was asked to appear. And every appearance was the same—the both of them sitting in the guest seats, glowing and happy, as June gushed on about how gloriously happy they were and the rigors of raising a family.

"Raising all these kids makes me plumb tired! Plumb tired!" she'd say, heaving a big sigh.

With every interview she announced how utterly exhausted she was from the effort of raising seven children—Rosanne, Kathy, Cindy, and Tara, her two daughters from two previous marriages, and John Carter (the son she and Johnny had). I wished a big hook would come down and drag her off the stage each time she started in. She was in no way caring for or raising the girls. Anyone listening would have thought I had abandoned them, when in fact they were living with me. They had always lived with me.

Nevertheless, June successfully convinced enough people otherwise and was named Mother of the Year by some organization in California. I was furious. My only recourse was to tell myself, *It doesn't matter . . . the people that do matter, my friends and our family, know the truth . . . let it go.*

Family members, in the meantime, explained to me that June never allowed Johnny to do interviews alone. She insisted that she always be present. For that reason, I know that if he had been alone, he would have been more honest and fair to me and the kids. I know he must have been very uncomfortable when she made those statements about raising the girls. But because he hated confrontation, and because of the repercussions he would suffer if he stepped forward to correct her, he kept quiet. It was just easier that way.

Honest to God, I hate to say this, but I couldn't understand how anybody could have control over another person like she did unless it was devil-driven. It certainly wasn't God-given power. And you should have heard all the things that people said about her—starting with the girls, to the office workers, to Johnny's parents, to people in the business. The only reason anybody put up with her was because of Johnny.

And the girls had frustrations of their own to deal with after the divorce. When they visited Johnny and June in Nashville over summer vacations, they saw June's two daughters living it up back in Nashville—expensive sports cars, closets full of fancy clothes, fancy makeup. Meanwhile back in California, Rosanne, Kathy, Cindy, and Tara's wardrobes consisted of their school uniforms and maybe two or three other outfits. No extras. No luxury items. I didn't believe in spoiling them. So compared to June's daughters and John Carter, I know the girls felt second-rate.

Cindy once told me of shopping with June and finding a pair of shoes that she wanted. She asked June to buy them for her, but June's terse response was, "Tell your mother to buy you your shoes."

Things like that would just set me off. It was beyond me how she could refuse to buy a pair of shoes for Cindy while Johnny was buying her kids all sorts of ridiculous stuff. If it wasn't for Johnny, I thought, she wouldn't have any money at all.

On top of that, while the world was singing June's praises for having "saved Johnny from drugs," the girls came home from visits describing June's own drug use. By this time they were expert in identifying abuse, I suppose.

311

They described her arriving at the breakfast table, incoherent and confused, eyebrow pencil scrawled over her forehead, clearly not "right." And as the years went on they would tell me of June passing out or fainting from taking too many pills. Or passing out cold in the middle of them having a conversation with her. Or her saying things that didn't make sense—like the time she was certain she had zebras in her head. The girls would come home and laugh about it. But it wasn't funny to me.

The breathless assertions that June saved Johnny from drugs are simply not true. Our family knows it's not true. And it takes the credit away from Johnny, who got himself off the drugs. It was a story that made her look good, and it made them both look good to the world to say that, but like a lot of stories floated out there, it wasn't accurate. I know, and others do too, that she had a drug problem of her own for the duration of their marriage. In fact, I was surprised to learn that her drug habit hasn't long been public knowledge.

Here's what I believe to be true. When Johnny and I were married and June entered the picture, Johnny succumbed to her advances. As a result, he was riddled with guilt. On the one hand, he was convicted by his conscience and wanted to do the right thing. On the other hand, she was relentless toward him. She would not let go. Once I remarried, he felt relieved of the guilt that had plagued him and was able to come to terms with his addiction.

I'm not saying that Johnny never wanted to be with June. They shared the drugs and they shared the music business. They had a lot in common. But whether he did or didn't want to be with her initially, she wasn't going to let go. And once I remarried, he felt vindicated and felt he had permission to be with her without his conscience bothering him. He no longer needed the drugs to smother his guilt. But I know for a fact that she was supplying his drugs, had a drug problem of her own, and always did.

In any event, just about the time that Johnny's career began to cool, I found a new peace about everything. The watershed moment for me occurred after watching June and Johnny on *The Mike Douglas Show* one day. I finally came to my senses and realized that my anger and frustration were only destroying me. Nobody else knew how I felt. Johnny and June didn't have a clue how I felt. Our girls didn't know; I never shared anything with them. The only person suffering was me. I was the one hurting. Nobody else.

I recently stumbled across a letter I wrote that day to Johnny after watching him and June on that Mike Douglas show. I never mailed it. At the time, it was enough to get my angst down on paper.

Johnny,

I just finished watching the Michael Douglas Show and can hardly control my blood pressure. I know you respect me as a mother, if nothing else. I only wish you would let the world know I am still alive. I raised the girls alone for the most part. Then with much help and support from Dick. I resent so much her claiming my four girls. No disrespect, but I don't feel she deserves that credit. Neither of you know the hell and heartache that I've been through. But with my faith, which gave me the strength, we made it. Anyone can look at any of the four girls and know that God and I did a pretty good job. I'm not patting myself on the back, because without God I would never have made it. I ask nothing of you. I always stay quietly locked away and never cause any problems or make any public waves . . . Can you please ask her to separate the girls. They resent it almost as much as I do, but would never tell you about the reason they feel that way. I hope you will give me that little respect and credit. I never put you down. I always give credit where credit is due and I have no way at this point of defending myself. I do hope someday to write a book and let the world know my side of our life. I am waiting until I know all the kids are secure in their lives. Until then give me a little credit for all that I've had to put up with over the years.

On the day that I wrote that letter, I made the decision to never again watch Johnny and June on shows anymore, and I didn't. I gave myself permission to not read or watch anything that didn't serve a purpose other than to elevate my blood pressure. I finally let it all go instead of frustrating myself.

So for my own sanity I turned off the TV and stopped following Johnny's career and watching his television appearances. The less I knew, the better I felt. Too bad it took me a couple of years to figure that out. I'm a slow learner, I guess.

Around this time, Dick simply and deliberately made the decision to put the past behind him too. He quit drinking and taking pills, and never once looked back. To this day, he's never touched a drop or pill, nor wanted to. And so we both moved on together, finally with a newfound peace. And I found love again in the arms of a man—my sweet, precious husband, Dick—who truly understood.

In 1975 Johnny published his autobiography, *Man in Black,* and sent me a copy with a note.

> To Vivian, I hope this will make people know and understand what a good wife and mother you always were.

I put it away on a shelf and never read it.

~

"Mom, she went into cardiac arrest . . ." Kathy said. It was May 2003 and June had just undergone heart surgery in a Nashville hospital. I was expecting a routine update, but this update was anything but routine. I could tell through the sound of her voice that she was shaken. "It's not good . . . not good at all," she said, crying.

Kathy went on to explain that the doctors feared June went without oxygen for over twenty minutes before they could resuscitate her. I could hear the strain in her voice, and then silence. "The doctor says she's gone . . . there's no brain activity."

For all intents and purposes, June was gone. All of her organs failed, and the only thing keeping her alive was a pacemaker. Every time her heart stopped, it kicked in. It was a horrible situation for everyone involved, most especially poor June.

Just a week earlier she had come through the surgery fine and had impressed the doctors with how well she was doing. Never once did any of us dream that things would go this drastically wrong.

"And Dad's in terrible shape," Kathy went on to explain in a follow-up call. "This is killing him. It's killing all of us to see him like this," she said. She went into detail about Johnny's behavior, how June looked, how they'd never forget the horror, how sad and upsetting it was. All four girls were at the hospital along with John Carter. My heart ached for him.

Another four days passed, then five, and June's condition remained the same. She was "gone," but her body was inexplicably hanging on. All anyone could do was sit, wait, and pray for a miracle.

My mind was on June's condition and the prayer vigil we were keeping when the phone rang again. It was my dear friend Carol Daly.

"Vivian, I have a confession to make," she said. I couldn't imagine what it could be. She proceeded to tell me about an announcement she heard about Johnny from the KHAY disc jockey at the local country music station:

As many of you know, Johnny Cash's wife remains in critical condition this morning in a Nashville hospital after complications from heart surgery. Johnny is calling for a nationwide prayer vigil, asking everyone to please pray for his wife at eight a.m. tomorrow morning.

Carol recounted the announcement almost verbatim. It didn't surprise me that Johnny would make this appeal.

"Get this," Carol continued, eager to get to the payoff. "The disc jockey

314

went on to say, 'I'm sure Rosanne Cash joins her dad in asking for your prayers for her mommy too.'"

"I couldn't help myself, Vivian. I phoned the radio station and told them they had their facts wrong. I told them June is *not* Rosanne's mother, and that you live right here in Ventura." She was breathless by the time she finished.

Over thirty-five years later, and many people still believe that June is our girls' mother. As news of June's medical condition spread, I was continually reminded of that fact.

Through the daily reports I received from the girls, June's prognosis was increasingly grim, and it was a sad scene at the hospital. Johnny remained at her bedside from seven a.m. to seven p.m., every minute allowed for visitation. He wasn't eating. He wasn't resting. The doctors were concerned about his condition. I was worried about him too.

I was reminded of years earlier, when Grandma Cash was in a coma. The situation was the same: She was just hanging on, with no hope of recovery. Johnny went to her bedside and told her, "Mama, you can go. We're all going to be fine." He gave her permission to go. And shortly after, she did.

I told one of the girls to pass along the suggestion to Johnny to do the same. "Tell him she might be waiting for him to say it's okay for her to leave," I said. Later I learned Johnny had done just that. She died two days later.

It's hard to describe the emotions that came over me when I heard the news. I felt so many emotions. One was sympathy for Johnny. I knew this would be a terrible blow for him. No matter what I thought of their marriage, they had been together for a very long time. And I thought about our girls. June had been in their lives ever since they were very young. This would be tough on them too.

To be honest, Johnny's health had been weakened for so many years, I had assumed he would go first. I was surprised that God took her instead. Yet if it had to be one or the other, I was so relieved that Johnny was still alive. I was happy that God spared his life.

I hoped this could be an opportunity for him to get closer to the girls, to make up for lost time and have more years with them. The girls have always told me they have never been able to feel close to Johnny. Through the years, they struggled to have a relationship—a close relationship—with him. For whatever reason at the time—drugs, travel, schedule, June—they'd always felt at arm's length. Now maybe they could grow closer to him before it was too late. I knew they desperately wanted that.

I also felt pity for June. I know she more than paid for anything she ever did wrong in God's eyes, suffering through the years with various troubles. I think that's why she tried to drown it all with drugs herself. I'm no psychiatrist, but I believe with all my heart that's why she was the way she was. She

315

lived for those pats on the back that she got from the audience. That's why she acted so foolish onstage, to get laughs and put it in her life. She lived in a fantasy world. She felt the audience loved her, and that fed her.

Then on the other side of the coin, I thought about God being in charge. For whatever reason, her death was part of God's greater plan, one that we can't understand. We can only wonder.

But perhaps most notably for me, when she died, I felt an inexplicable, overwhelming sense of relief. In that single moment, all the years of hurt and resentment were replaced with compassion for Johnny, for the girls—and for her too.

~

It's so funny to me. When Johnny and I were newlyweds, the road that lay ahead of us seemed so endless and full of possibilities. And now, as I near the end of my life and can reflect back on the journey we took, it all seems to have passed in the blink of an eye. It's been over fifty years since that night at the skating rink when Johnny first smiled at me and asked me to skate.

Rosanne, Kathy, Cindy, and Tara are all grown and settled now with busy lives and children of their own. My life has settled into a comfortable routine with my husband, Dick. And I stay busy with garden club meetings, church activities, tending to my house and garden, and spending time with friends and family. Sadly, it's been over a year since Johnny died.

In one of Johnny's last interviews, Larry King asked him, "Do you have any regrets in your life?" Johnny answered, "No." That seems so strange to me. Everybody has regrets. I certainly have many.

There are things I wish I had done differently, things I wish I hadn't done, and things that if I had done, I know Johnny and I would still be married today. I could have affected the outcome of our lives differently, but I didn't. Those things have tortured me. Not that I'm unhappy with the way my life has turned out now, but there are some things I would do differently if I had been given a second chance. I have many regrets.

First of all, I regret that drugs ever came into our lives. I regret not being astute enough to have recognized early on, during our correspondence even, that Johnny might be susceptible to addiction. I will go to my grave knowing that if it hadn't been for drugs, things would be different today. Johnny would have remained the real Johnny, first of all. He would still be alive today, second. He would have been a much better father, third. And he would have had a much happier life. Instead he was tortured. We were all tortured, especially the girls. They know their lives would have been much different if Johnny had never been on drugs. They didn't have a Daddy because of them. I remember Tara telling me her thoughts on the subject just a few months ago.

"Mom," she said with anger in her voice. "You look at every photograph taken after I was born, and Dad was on drugs . . . he was on something ever since I was born."

I hate to admit it, but she's right. There were occasions when Johnny was straight in Casitas after she was born, when he was loving and attentive to her, but she was so young that she evidently doesn't remember the good, only the bad.

"And being the youngest, with Dad on drugs, I was never heard. I never had a voice. I was invisible," she went on to say. It breaks my heart for her to feel that way.

"Tara, with me you've always been heard," I told her. And that's the truth. I know how horrible it feels to be overlooked and not have a voice of your own. I know, because that's part of the reason I'm writing this book.

I also regret that I didn't get counseling. I wish I had trusted others, and leaned more on my friends for help and guidance. I wish I had gone to support groups and attended Al-Anon meetings, to learn more about addiction and how to help Johnny. I might have been too shy to share my own story, but I would have listened and I would have learned. As it was, I was too scared and too private to let anyone help me. I should have formed a close circle of women friends and leaned on their support. Instead I chose to go it alone, and that was foolish.

I also regret not having revisited the letters with Johnny. I wish we had read them together in our first several years of marriage. I wish we had reminded ourselves what our love was based on: honesty, decency, and a deep and true love for each other. And I wish we had had a chance to revisit the letters before he died as well.

I also regret not fighting harder to save our marriage. I should have been relentless at saving it, as relentless at saving it as June was at destroying it. I gave up when I shouldn't have. I should have tried harder for the girls. Instead I crawled into a hole. I will regret that for the rest of my life.

But most of all, I regret all the anger that I have carried around all these years. I spent some of my best years angry, dwelling on every injustice. I let that anger fester into bitterness, and I held onto that bitterness for far too long. It paralyzed me emotionally and spiritually. And more importantly, it hurt my children.

And it wasn't just anger and bitterness toward June. When Johnny and I were first married, I used to be so close with his sister Reba. She was my best friend for a very long time. But when Johnny left California and moved to Nashville, she followed him and I was devastated. She left without saying good-bye. And further, she made statements during an interview with *TV Guide* that I was the cause of our divorce. I was devastated and never got over that. Through the years we continued to see each other on various occasions, and it always bothered me.

Recently I wrote to Reba. I wanted to let her know that I've been thinking about her. Her health isn't good lately, and I've been praying for her. Along with the note, I included a scarf that I knitted just for her. I wanted to reach out to her. I miss my friend. And I wanted to let go of the hurt and anger.

Reba wrote me back the most beautiful note. She thanked me for the scarf and thanked me for all of the wonderful memories we shared. She told me she loved me, and she added, "Vivian, I want to ask for your forgiveness, for ever having hurt you . . . I want to set myself free."

That touched me so much. I had no idea that she struggled with what happened for all these years ago too. She and I began exchanging letters after that and, through our correspondence, we have found our way back to each other. Nearly thirty-seven years later, we're back as best of friends, and it feels wonderful to be free of that burden on my heart.

Those simple words—"I'm sorry"—have such a curious, healing quality about them. I'd have given anything to hear Johnny say the same. All those times in therapy and rehab, that's one of the steps he was encouraged to make, but he never could. He apologized to the girls but never to me. But anyway, there's no need.

The last time I was in Nashville, I visited Johnny's grave. I stood there in front of his headstone, staring at the inscription carved in the granite that reads, WALK THE LINE, thinking back over the last fifty years. How I wish he and I had taken the opportunity to talk more before he died. There are so many things I would have told him, and so many things I'd have asked.

Before I left, I looked around the area immediately surrounding Johnny's grave for Grandma and Grandpa Cash's graves, not wanting to leave without seeing them. I still miss the both of them so much. But only the graves of June and her family members are around and beside Johnny. Grandma and Grandpa Cash, I would discover with the help of a cemetery worker, are buried far away down at the bottom of the hill. For a second there was that familiar flash of anger, and then sadness. Some days I still have to remind myself to let it go.

Just the other day I asked my brother, "Ray, how are you?" He answered simply, "I'm grateful."

That struck me as such a humble, simple, and beautiful state of mind. I'm grateful too. I'm grateful for a lot of things. No doubt I have complained too much about the injustices that life brought me, and haven't spent nearly enough time thanking God for all my blessings. For one thing, I'm grateful for my husband, Dick. Some people go a lifetime and don't find love even once. I found it twice.

I'm also grateful for my faith. It's the reason I'm here today. It kept me going when I absolutely didn't think I would make it. Sometimes the road I traveled was so narrow that I felt I was getting nowhere at all. I see now that God was leading me during those times, guiding me to where I am today.

I'm also grateful that God protected Johnny long enough for him to enjoy a long, full life, and I celebrate the fact that he accomplished so much in his lifetime. His success in life was in a small way *our* dream fulfilled—that dream we blindly followed back on Tutwiler Avenue in Memphis all those years ago. For all the happiness that gave him, I will *never* regret that.

I'm so grateful for my children. Rosanne, Kathy, Cindy, and Tara are four talented, exceptional women. They are great mothers and I'm happy in the fact that they all know God. And I'm grateful for my grandchildren, my great-grandchildren, my stepchildren, my sister, Sylvia, my brother, Ray, and my friends. I love them all. I feel very blessed.

And I'm grateful that June has peace now too. I simply ask God to bless her. I forgive her for everything she ever did, and I ask God to please forgive me for holding her accountable. That wasn't my job.

And I'm equally grateful for the journey that I have just completed in the writing of this book, and for my partner on this remarkable journey, Annie. Only she and I will ever know the mysterious and beautiful journey it was. I hope it blessed her in some small way. For me, I'm prepared to live the rest of my life now with new appreciation and freedom. I have finally found reconciliation. The experience allowed my pain to fully settle in my bones, I felt its full effect, and it has dissipated.

For the rest of my life I will be grateful that God brought Annie into my life. She is uncomfortable with me saying this, but in my lifetime I experienced the very worst that women are capable of inflicting on each other, and I also experienced the strongest of loyalties and bonds possible between two women. The latter describes our friendship. I love you, Annie. I could not have made this journey with anyone else.

I'm reminded of a favorite hymn of Johnny's during the early years of our marriage, one from which he pulled strength during hard times. When Elvis's mother died, I remember Johnny attempting to comfort Elvis, who at the time was inconsolable, crying on the front porch at his house. Johnny tenderly put his arm around Elvis's shoulder and asked him if he'd ever heard the lyrics to Stuart Hamblen's "These Things Shall Pass." He began to softly recite them to Elvis, who was instantly calmed.

> These things shall pass, and life be sweeter
> When love and faith are strong, they cannot long endure.

I began the writing of this book emotionally weak and broken, afraid of examining my past. I was afraid to face my true feelings, afraid to admit that my husband could ever love another woman. For the first time in my life, instead of stuffing my emotions and hiding, I feel emotionally exposed, and yet I've never felt more safe. I've looked at my life, dealt with it, and I'm ready to go on. I'm excited about what the future holds. There were no shortcuts to the place I am now. I had to go through the thick of the worst myself to get here. But I did it, and I'm proud. I'm happy. I'm through it. I'm thrilled to see what life has in store for me now.

I do still miss Johnny, and I know I always will. I miss the man I married so many years ago. I look at photos of him as a young man and my heart still hurts. I know my heart will never stop loving him.

The girls believe they're going to see Johnny again someday, and I hope I do. I've been having dreams about him lately. He's always standing by a dark car and motioning for me to come over. Sometimes I walk over to him and he tells me anxiously, "I want to speak with you." Other times he's just standing by the car, motioning with his hand for me to come toward him. It disappoints me that I never get to hear what he wants to tell me. I hope someday we get to finally speak.

I realized something today that hasn't occurred to me before. I miss Johnny, of course, but I have him with me here every day in the presence of the girls. He's still right here, every time I speak with them, see them, love them. He's here. And he will always be here.

Johnny's most wonderful qualities, in their purest form, are right here. In Cindy's passion and uncompromising sense of right and wrong. In Kathy's sense of humor and quick wit. In Rosanne's bold creativity. In Tara's compassion and gentle spirit. And in June and Johnny's son, John Carter, too. In the time I have left, I hope to discover for myself the best of Johnny's qualities in him. I can say without hesitation to each of them that one of the best things I ever did was marry their daddy.

And until I see Johnny again, I will celebrate the fact that Rosanne, Kathy, Cindy, Tara, and John Carter remind me of the very best things I experienced in life. I hope they are proud of me for telling our story. I want them to be proud of me. And I hope they know now, more than ever, just how much I loved their daddy. I did, more than I can say.

AFTERWORD

In the weeks before Vivian died, I asked her one afternoon, "What do you think your legacy will be? What do you *want* it to be?" She was at first visibly startled by the question, and then became contemplative as she considered the importance of her answer. She and I both sensed her time was growing short.

After first commenting on the obvious enormity and reach of Johnny's legacy, she wondered aloud if anyone would remember her after she was gone (aside, of course, from Rosanne, Kathy, Cindy, and Tara, her husband, grandchildren, and some friends). Then she answered simply, "I hope my legacy is one of being a devoted mother and a devoted wife."

Vivian also went on to add, "I also hope I'm remembered as a faithful Christian, and a good friend to the friends I was blessed with." And she explained that for the first time in her life, she finally liked the woman she was. She finally liked who she was after years of being at odds with herself. She told me she hoped this book would help other women do the same, and she looked forward to talking with and helping even one single woman who needed help. Vivian said she felt led to write this book for that purpose.

Our discussion of legacy turned into a conversation of lessons learned, and her conclusions spilled out: love generously, forgive, trust in God, pray, be grateful for everything you've been blessed with. Fight passionately for the ones you love. Consider your job as parent your most important contribution in this world. And don't complain.

I cannot explain how or why Vivian and I both knew that her time would be cut short. The last time I visited her at her home in California, the week was full of "last times." It was the last time we would visit the Ventura Garden Club meeting together. The last time we would go shopping together. The last time we went to our favorite restaurant together. The last time we did so many things together.

"If it's your time, are you ready to go?" I asked her during one of our last conversations. Without any hesitation, she answered.

"Yes . . . yes, I am," she said. "Not that I *want* to go, but yes, I'm ready."

I knew that spiritually, her bags were packed. That worried me. I had promised to her that I would go on and tell her story in her absence if anything should "happen." But it was a promise I didn't want to believe I might be called upon to make good.

Vivian died on May 24, 2005, after surgery to remove cancer on her lower right lung. After making it through the surgery fine and being transferred to intensive care, inexplicably her condition turned worse, and she died, just as she and I had feared would happen.

Two nights later she appeared in my dream, sitting quietly in a chair in the corner of her kitchen. She looked at me and smiled, not saying a word. She just spoke to me through those beautiful eyes of hers.

It wasn't the first time she had spoken to me this way. Several times before, she and I had experienced moments together where in silence, with just a look, she communicated volumes. Like the time we made yet another painful discovery—another betrayal by someone she thought was a friend—and her eyes told me her grief all over again. Or like the day after she and Johnny discussed her decision to write this book, and she couldn't wait for me to sit down beside her and hear the details of their meeting. The tears of joy and her struggle to find words to speak told me everything she wanted to say.

And now in my dream, those beautiful eyes again told me what I wanted to know. She told me she's safe. She told me she's in a wonderful place, that there's no other place she'd rather be. She told me she's happy and not to worry. Then I felt the cool touch of her hand holding mine, and a gentle squeeze. To this day I still feel the minutest detail and softness of her skin as her hand held mine. It gave me such comfort to be able to touch her one last time.

To this day I am grateful for that dream, and for being afforded that mysterious glimpse into the world where Vivian is now. It reminds me of another dream that Vivian's daughter Kathy shared with me on the very day that we learned of Vivian's cancer diagnosis. Still reeling from the news, she and I were speaking on the telephone when as an aside she added, "I had a dream about Dad last night."

Kathy went on to describe her dream, in which Johnny came walking down a flight of stairs and she was overjoyed at seeing him. They enjoyed a long conversation together, and then suddenly he turned to go back up the stairs.

"Dad, wait, where are you going?" she called out.

Johnny turned around. "It's okay, Kathy," he said. "I'll be back . . . I'll be back in a month." And he turned and left.

The next time I saw Kathy in person was the day before Vivian's funeral in

Ventura, California. She was on the patio of Vivian and Dick's home when I arrived from the airport. "Annie, do you remember the dream I told you about?" were the first words out of her mouth. To be honest, I had nearly forgotten. But her question brought back the details fresh in my mind.

"I had that dream *exactly* one month to the day before Mom died," Kathy said as she stared at me, waiting for my reaction. It was at that moment that I was stunned by the realization: Johnny had been there to greet Vivian on the other side.

There are not too many things in this life that I can say that I am absolutely certain of, but I am certain of one thing. I do know Vivian's heart. It was pure, and trusting, and hopeful. And if she were faced with the choice of choosing Johnny's outstretched hand or coming back to this world, I know what she would choose. And she did just that. She and Johnny are having those conversations right now that she longed to have.

I'm not sure that I will ever be able to fully explain or understand all the mysterious things that happened during the journey that Vivian and I took together . . . or my dream . . . or Kathy's dream. Or the inexplicable fact that at the very moment Vivian died, my little boy—in another room on the other side of our house, unaware of her passing—felt compelled to make a crayon drawing of what he explained was the exact moment she died. "Mommy, look . . . it's Aunt Vivian going to heaven. Look at the lights and the special things around her," he explained, pointing to the detail in his drawing.

Every day I continue to be astonished as I find connections and meaning in old notes and events. They serve as constant reminders to me of the mystery of this life, and the fact that Vivian's journey didn't end on May 24, 2005. That day was simply a horizon to something more beautiful and more sacred. Only that makes me miss her even more, knowing she's more alive and vibrant than ever before but outside my reach.

We're supposed to live by faith, I know that. We are not supposed to have "proof" of God. Yet I've seen it. My walk with Vivian gave that to me. I'll never know why I was chosen for such a gift, but I will be forever humbled and grateful. To have done that for even one person—to me there can be no greater legacy than that.

I miss my precious friend. In her absence, I share her story with you and pray it will be the light she wished it to be.

Love, Annie

ACKNOWLEDGMENTS

Thank you to the following people who made this book possible:

Dick Distin—Thank you for your loving determination in seeing Vivian's wishes carried out.

Dan Strone—A terrific agent, thank you for believing in the importance of Vivian's story being told and for your tireless efforts to that end.

Susan Moldow—Thank you for giving Vivian a voice.

Brant Rumble—Thank you for your unrelenting attention to every detail of this book, as well as your friendship, editorial guidance, suggestions, gentle humor, and spot-on advice every step of the way.

Steve Feder and Phil Anderson—Thank you for your expert legal guidance and friendship.

Ben—This journey was just as much yours as it was mine. Thank you for being by my side each step of the way. I love you.

Mom/"Girl" and Dad—Thank you for so generously giving of your time, attention, and support in so many ways. Your loving contributions touched every aspect of this book. I love you.

Thank you to the following people who have blessed this project along the way:

Sylvia Flye, Jessica and Chris Hess, Sister Joy Ann, Katrina Plate, Cynthia and James Burrell, the ladies of the Ventura Garden Club, Lincoln St. George, Johnny Western, Alice Smith, Alan Stoker, Paul Hastaba, Kelli Bodenheimer, Murfy Alexander, Jenny Crawford, Betty Sells, Peggy Sells, Kim Mercier, Vicki Dietz, Susan Davis, Tamara Boe, Sharon Austin, Lindella Johnson, Krista Berg, Kelley Tansil, Earl Smith, Kelly Greene, Chris Woodhull, Steven Goldmann, John Sawyer, Jamie Ing, Ron Box, Dawne Davis, Shelly Belvin, Lisa Moore, Jan Williams, Ben and Beverly Sharpsteen, the staff at the Brentwood Library in Brentwood, Tennessee, Liz Chapman, Drew Jackson, Tom Hotchkiss, Walter and Charlotte Baumgartner, Marlaine and Derek Belanger, Greg Smith, John Ambrose, Kaye Davis, Jason Douglas-Harris, Eva Kotylak,

David Reid, Aida Garcia-Cole, Shawn McCrohan, John and Patti Speer, Al Buch, Melissa Masitto, Martha Stewart Hunter, and Allen Bernstein.

Also, a special thanks to:

Kate Bittman, Anna deVries, Dan Cuddy, Will Georgantas, Jason Heuer, and the rest of the team at Scribner—Your hard work is evident in every detail of this book.

Rosanne, Kathy, Cindy, and Tara—Thank you for sharing your precious mother with me.

Stacey—Thank you for encouraging me, crying with me, praying for me, and always understanding.

Matt—Being your Mommy is my favorite thing in this whole world. I love you, sweetheart.